THE POSTCARD PRICE GUIDE

Third Edition

A Comprehensive Reference

J. L. Mashburn

Thousands of Prices, Representing Millions of Cards

COLONIAL HOUSE
ENKA, NORTH CAROLINA USA

Publisher: J. L. Mashburn
Editor: Emma Mashburn

Cover and Interior Design: Picture Perfect Publishing, Inc
Electronic Page Assembly: Picture Perfect Publishing, Inc.

A Colonial House Production

Printed in the United States of America

Third Edition

10 9 8 7 6 5 4 3 2 1

Library of Congress Cataloging-in-Publication Data

Mashburn, J. L. (Joseph Lee)
    The Postcard Price Guide: a comprehensive reference / J. L. Mashburn. -- 3rd ed.
      p.   cm.
    "Thousands of prices, representing millions of cards."
    Includes index.
    ISBN 1-885940-03-3
    1. Postcards--Collectors and collecting--United States--Catalogs.
    2. Postcards--History--20th century--Catalogs.   I. Title.
    NC1872.M37   1997
    741.6'83'075--dc21   96-38126
                                                           CIP

AN IMPORTANT NOTICE TO THE READERS OF THIS PRICE GUIDE:

The comprehensive nature of compiling data and prices on the thousands of cards, sets and series in this publication gives many probabilities for error. Although all information has been compiled from reliable sources, experienced collectors and dealers, some data may still be questionable. The author and publisher will not be held responsible for any losses that might occur in the purchase or sale of cards because of the information contained herein.

The author will be most pleased to receive notice of errors so that they may be corrected in future editions. Contact: J. L. Mashburn, Colonial House, Box 609, Enka NC 28728 USA.

This book and other Mashburn price guides are available worldwide on the Internet at Colonial House Website: http://www.postcard-books.com

Contents

ACKNOWLEDGMENTS

It takes many willing hands and minds to make a book of this size and very comprehensive nature. Without the tremendous input and support from knowledgeable collectors and dealers it would have been an impossible task. Appreciation is extended to the following contributors who have given their time and effort by creating, revising or verifying listings and checklists, lending cards for scanning, and for help in valuing countless entries.

Special thanks are given to **John and Sandy Millns and Shirley and Dale Hendricks** for their continued support in supplying beautiful cards from their collections for scanning and for additions to checklists. The numerous images they have supplied have helped decorate these pages and have provided a broad insight to collectors as to what is actually available in the wonderful world of postcards.

Special thanks also to collectors **Jane Morrison and Naomi Welch** for important additions to the Harrison Fisher checklists; to **Sixto Campano and Russell Hughes** for many additions to the Afro-Americana listing and also to **Peter Weiss** of Hamburg, Germany for additional listings of European blacks; to **George Parola** for additions and editing of the Bessie Pease Gutmann and Meta Grimball listings; to Martin Shapiro for his outstanding contributions concerning cards and checklists of *Wiener Werkstaette, Mucha, Bauhaus,* and other quality cards; to **Fred Kahn** for his tremendous help in providing reports on U. S. market conditions and values, as well as cards for scanning.

A very special thanks also to **Dr. Antonio and Pia Dell'Aquila** of Bari, Italy for allowing us to update our checklist of Raphael Kirchner using various listings and values from their wonderful new book, *Raphael Kirchner and His Postcards.*

To **Alyce Thorson, Marilyn Brust, Elaine Taylor, Vernon Ham, Dr. Dennis Hart,** and **Kosti Kallio** of Finland who continue to supply very valuable information on new additions and cards for scanning; to the hundreds of collectors and dealers who have called or written to express their approval and acceptance of our labors; and most of all to Emma.

"The "Kewpie Cook"
No. 103

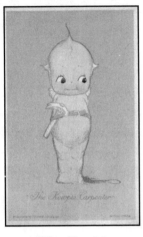

"The Kewpie
Carpenter" -- No. 101

"The Kewpie's careful
of his Voice"
No. 104

"The Kewpie
Gardener" -- No. 105

"The Kewpie Army"
No. 100

"The Kewpie wears
Overshoes" -- No. 102

Rose O'Neill's Lovable "Large Image Kewpies"

Series of Six by Edward Gross, New York

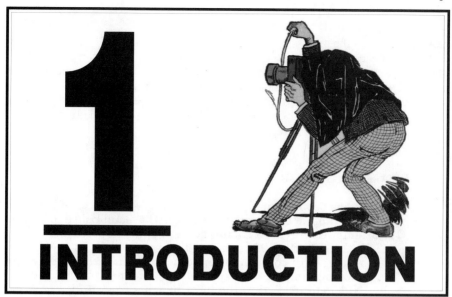

INTRODUCTION

A THRIVING HOBBY!

It has been two and one-half years since the second edition of *The Postcard Price Guide* was released. During that time, interest in the postcard hobby has grown tremendously. Many new and very avid collectors, both young and old, have entered it with much enthusiasm to pursue their favorite motifs. We would like to think that the information in our various books, the two great books by Susan Nicholson and Diane Allmen, and the selected quality writings of Roy Nuhn and other postcard historians have made a very beneficial impact. Our major reason for writing books and articles is to provide information and to show the collector the wonderful realm of material that is available.

As more collectors enter the market and the demand grows for varied motifs, new and important material is finding its way into dealer stocks and auctions. Having been a very avid collector of Harrison Fisher's beautiful ladies over the last 35 years I have been amazed at the number of his new cards that have now been discovered and have been added to his checklists. From the results of my European travels and the efforts of collectors Jane Morrison and Naomi Welch, there are now well over 100 confirmed additions to the list. This is just one example and there are many more. These new findings breathe new life into dormant collectors and give them the inspiration to search for more.

It must be noted and acknowledged that there have been increases in values in most all types of cards, especially in the high quality material and those in superior condition. However, some groups have not increased and are lying dormant until their demand cycle reappears. Junk cards, no matter the type or motif, are not wanted by collectors, and we fear that there is no future demand cycle for them.

Reports abound of the impossibility of finding good material for U.S. collectors on the foreign scene. Having been on four trips to Europe this year I can attest to this. Dealers there now carry large stocks of damaged, dirty, written or cancelled on face cards that no one will buy. To make matters worse the dealers there say that there is no new material available to replinish their stocks. It seems that all the quality cards are now already in the U.S.or they are being placed in high-priced auctions that will eventually find buyers here.

—J. L. Mashburn

HOW TO USE THIS PRICE GUIDE

This price guide has been uniquely designed to serve the needs of both the beginning and advanced collector, as well as the established postcard dealer. Our attempt to provide a comprehensive guide to postcards dating from the 1890's through the 1960's makes it possible for even the novice collector to consult it with confidence and ease in finding each particular listing. The following important explanations summarize the general practices that will help in getting the most benefits from its use.

CATEGORICAL ARRANGEMENT

Cards are arranged by category, and each category is listed in the Table of Contents. All Artist-Signed cards are listed under a particular type or theme. Artists are always listed alphabetically, as are the publishers if the cards are unsigned.

Topical cards are listed alphabetically with individual listings of some of the most prominent cards and their values. Otherwise, the prices listed are for generalized cards in the particular topic or theme.

LISTINGS

Listings may be identified as follows:

1. **SECTION** (Artist-Signed, Fantasy, etc.).
2. **TOPIC** (Beautiful Women, Cats, Dogs, etc.).
3. **ARTIST** (Listed in Bold Capital Letters) when available.
4. **PUBLISHER** (Listed in Bold, Lower Case Letters).
5. **NAME OF SERIES; OR SERIES NUMBER.**
6. **NUMBER OF CARDS IN SET OR SERIES**(Enclosed in Parentheses) when available.
7. **CAPTION OR TITLE OF CARD** (Enclosed in Quotation Marks).
8. **PRICE RANGE OF 1 CARD IN VERY GOOD CONDITION**
9. **PRICE RANGE OF 1 CARD IN EXCELLENT CONDITION**

Example of above:

1. **ARTIST-SIGNED**
2. **BEAUTIFUL WOMEN**
3. **HARRISON FISHER**

4. **Reinthal & Newman**
5. 101 Series
6. (12)
7. "American Beauties"
8. $12 - 15
9. $15 - 20

CONDITION AND GRADING OF POSTCARDS

The condition of a postcard, as with old coins, stamps, books, etc., is an extremely important factor in pricing it for the collector, the dealer, and for those having found cards to sell. Damaged, worn, creased, or dirty cards —cards in less than Very Good condition—are almost uncollectible unless they are to be used as a space filler until a better one is found. **Collectors should never buy a damaged card if they expect to sell it later on.**

It is necessary that some sort of card grading standard be used so that buyer and seller may come to an informed agreement on the value of a card. Two different collectible conditions, **Very Good** and **Excellent,** are used in **THE POST CARD PRICE GUIDE**. There are, of course, higher and lower grades, but these two will be most normally seen and most normally quoted for postcards sold throughout the hobby.

The standard grading system adapted by most dealers and by the leading postcard hobby publications in the field, *Barr's Post Card News* and *Post Card Collector*, is listed below with their permission:

M—MINT. A perfect card just as it comes from the printing press. No marks, bends, or creases. No writing or postmarks. A clean and fresh card. Seldom seen.

NM—NEAR MINT. Like Mint but very light aging or very slight discoloration from being in an album for many years. Not as sharp or crisp.

EX—EXCELLENT. Like mint in appearance with no bends or creases, or rounded or blunt corners. May be postally used or unused and with writing and postmark only on the address side. A clean, fresh card on the picture side.

VG—VERY GOOD. Corners may be just a bit blunt or rounded. Almost undetectable crease or bend that does not detract from overall appearance of the picture side. May have writing or postally used on address side. A very collectible card.

G—GOOD. Corners may be noticeably blunt or rounded with noticeably slight bends or creases. May be postally used or have writing on address side. Less than VG.

FR—FAIR. Card is intact. Excess soil, stains, creases, writing, or cancellation may affect picture. Could be a scarce card that is difficult to find in any condition.

Postcard dealers always want better condition cards that have no defects. Collectors should keep this in mind if they have cards to sell. Therefore, anyone building a collection should maintain a standard for condition and stick to it. Even if the asking price is a little higher when a card is purchased, it will be worth the cost when it is resold.

VALUATIONS

The postcard values quoted in this publication represent the current retail market. They were compiled with assistance from five of the leading dealers in the U.S., dealer pricing at shows, personal dealer communications, from the author's personal purchasing world-wide, from his approval sales, and from his active day-to-day involvement in the postcard field.

Some values were also compiled from observations of listings in auctions, auction catalogs (U.S., Europe, and Great Britain), prices realized and fixed price sales in the fine hobby publications, *Barr's Post Card News* and *Postcard Collector*, and other related publications. **In most instances, listings of high and low values were taken for each observation, and these were averaged to obtain the "Very Good" and "Excellent" prices quoted. It must be stressed that this price guide and reference work is intended to serve only as an aid in evaluating postcards. It should not be used otherwise. As we all know, actual market conditions change constantly, and prices may fluctuate.** The trend for postcards seems to always be to the upside.

Publication of this price guide is not intended to be a solicitation to buy or sell any of the cards listed.

Price ranges for cards in both **Very Good** and **Excellent** conditions are found at the end of each listing. Prices for cards in less than Very Good condition would be much lower, while those grading above Excellent might command relatively higher prices.

Without exception, prices quoted are for **one** card, whether it be a single entity or one card in a complete set or series. Note that after many entries a number is enclosed in parentheses; e.g., (6). This number indicates the total number of cards in a set or in a series. The price listed is for one card in the set and must be multiplied by this number to determine the value of a complete set.

WHY PRICE RANGES ARE QUOTED

For cards graded both **Very Good** and **Excellent**, price ranges are quoted for four major reasons. Any one, or more, of the following can determine the difference in the high or low prices in each of the listing ranges.

1. Prices vary in different geographical areas across the United States. At this time, they are somewhat higher on the Pacific coast and other western states. They tend to be a little lower in the East and somewhere in-between

in the central and midwestern states. For instance, a card with a price range of $6.00-8.00 might sell for $6.00 in the East, $7.00 in the Mid-West and $8.00 in the Far West.

2. Dealer price valuations also vary. Those who continually set up at postcard shows seem to have a better feel for prices and know which cards are selling well and, therefore, can adjust their prices accordingly. Dealers who sell only by mail, or by mail auction, tend to price their cards (or list estimated values in their auctions) just a bit higher. They usually are able to get these prices because of a wider collector market base obtained by the large number of subscribers served by the nationally distributed postcard auction publications. The publications also reach collectors who are unable to attend shows.

Cards that have been sent on approvals quite often are higher than postcard shows, etc., prices because the dealer has spent more time in selecting and handling.   Quite often he is working from a customer "want list."

3. Cards that are in great demand, or "hot" topics, also have wider price ranges; as collector interests rise there is a greater disparity in values because of supply and demand. If a dealer has only a small number of big demand cards he will almost automatically elevate his prices. Those who have a large supply will probably not go as high.

4. Card appearance and the subject in a set or series can also cause a variance in the price range. Printing quality, more beautiful and varied colors, and sharpness of the image may make a particular card much more desirable and, therefore, it will command a higher price.

Cards that have a wide price range usually are those that are presently the "most wanted" and best sellers. Dealers, most often, will only offer a small discount when selling these because they know there is a good market for them. Cards listed with a narrow price range are usually those that have been "hot" but have settled down and established a more competitive trading range. Dealer discounting on these slow-movers tends to be much more prevalent than those in the wide price ranges.

GUIDELINES FOR BUYING AND SELLING CARDS

As noted above, the prices listed in this price guide are retail prices—prices that a collector can expect to pay when buying a card from a dealer. It is up to the collectors to bargain for any available discount from the dealer.

The wholesale price is the price which a collector can expect from a dealer when selling cards. This price will be significantly lower than the retail price. Most dealers try to operate on a 100% mark-up and will normally pay around 50% of a card's low retail value. On some high-demand cards, he might pay up to 60% or 75% if he wants them badly enough.

Dealers are always interested in purchasing collections and accumulations of cards. They are primarily interested in those that were issued before

1915, but may be induced to take those issued afterwards if they are clean and in good condition.

Collections: Normally, collections are a specialized group or groups of cards that a person has built over the years. They will be in nice condition, without any damage, and may contain some rarities or high-demand cards. If the collection is a group of views from your home town or state it would be to your advantage to sell them to a collector or dealer near you. You might place an ad in your daily paper; you will be surprised at the interest it creates. Set your price a little high; you can always come down.

You might also dispose of your collection by writing to the dealers who advertise in *Barr's Post Card News*, 70 South 6th St., Lansing, IA 52151 or *Postcard Collector*, P.O. Box 5000, Iola, WI 54945. Other publications that have postcard sections are *Collectors News*, P. O. Box 156, Grundy Center, IA 50638-0156, *Paper Collectors' Market Place*, P. O. Box 128, Scandinavia, WI 54977, and *The Antique Trader*, P. O. Box 1050, Dubuque, IA 52004. Write to any of these publications and ask for information on subscriptions or sample copies.

Accumulations: Accumulations are usually groups of many different kinds, many different eras, and many different topics ... with the good usually mixed in with the bad. If you have a large accumulation that you wish to sell, your best bet is to contact a dealer as noted above. You may expect only 20% to 30% of value on a group such as this. Many low demand cards are non-sellers and are worthless to a dealer, but he may take them if there are some good cards in the accumulation.

Buying: Without doubt, the best way to buy postcards is to attend a show where there is a large group of dealers. Compare prices among dealers on cards that are of interest to you, and return to those who have the best cards at the lowest price for your purchases.

Buy from a dealer in your area if there is one. A good dealer will help you with your collection by searching for cards you need or want. If none are available, many dealers listed in *Barr's Post Card News* and *Postcard Collector* run auctions or will send cards on approval. Also, you might try joining a postcard club. It is possible to find an excellent choice of cards at these meetings because attendees bring material that they know is of interest to their fellow members.

It is also possible to find cards at Antique Shows, Flea Markets and Antique Shops. You can, however, waste a lot of time and never find suitable cards. It is best to go direct to the source and that would be a postcard dealer or auctioneer. Here you can almost always find cards that interest you.

IDENTIFYING THE AGE OF POSTCARDS

The dating of postcards for years or eras of issue can be accurately determined if the card is studied for identity points. Research has already been done by earlier historians and guidelines have been put into place.

There were seven eras for the postcard industry and each one has distinguishing points to help establish its respective identity. The following helps determine the era of the card in question:

PIONEER ERA (1893-1898)

The Pioneer Era began when picture postcards were placed on sale by vendors and exhibitors at the Columbian Exposition in Chicago, May, 1893. These were very popular and proved to be a great success. The profitable and lasting future of the postcard was greatly enhanced. These cards are relatively scarce. They can be identified by combinations of the following:

- All have undivided backs.
- None show the "Authorized by Act of Congress" byline.
- Postal cards will have the Grant or Jefferson head stamp.
- Most, but not all, will be multiple view cards.
- The words "Souvenir of ..." or "Greetings from ..." will appear on many.
- Postage rate, if listed, is 2 cents.
- The most common titles will be "Souvenir Card" or "Mail Card."
- Appeared mostly in the big Eastern cities.

PRIVATE MAILING CARD ERA (1898-1901)

The government, on May 19, 1898, gave private printers permission to print and sell postcards. The cards were all issued with the inscription "Private Mailing Card," and today they are referred to as PMC's. It is very easy to identify these because of the inscription. It may be noted that many of the early Pioneer views were reprinted as Private Mailing Cards.

UNDIVIDED BACK ERA (1901-1907)

On December 24, 1901, permission was given for use of the wording "Post Card" to be imprinted on the backs of privately printed cards. All cards during this era had undivided backs and only the address was to appear on the back. The message, therefore, had to be written on the front (picture side) of the card. For this reason, there is writing on the face of many cards; this is becoming more acceptable on cards of this era.

DIVIDED BACK ERA (1907-1915)

This era came into being on March 1, 1907. The divided back made it possible for both the address and the message to be on the back of the card. This prevented the face of the card from being written on and proved to be a great boon for collectors. Normally the view colors or images filled the entire card with no white border.

WHITE BORDER ERA (1915-1930)

The White Border Era brought an end to the postcard craze era. The golden age ended as imports from Germany ceased and publishers in the U.S.

began printing postcards to try to fill the void. The cards were very poor quality and many were reprints of earlier Divided Back Era cards. These are easily distinguished by the white border around the pictured area.

LINEN ERA (1930-1945)

Improvements in American printing technology brought improved card quality. Publishers began using a linen-like paper containing a high rag content but used very cheap inks in most instances. Until recently, these cards were considered very cheap by collectors. Now they are very popular with collectors of Roadside America, Blacks, Comics, and Advertising.

PHOTOCHROME ERA (1939 to present day)

"Modern Chromes," as they are now called by the postcard fraternity, were first introduced in 1939. Publishers, such as **Mike Roberts**, **Dexter Press**, **Curt Teich**, and **Plastichrome**, began producing cards that had very beautiful chrome colors and were very appealing to collectors. The growth of this group has been spectacular in recent years, so much so that there are now many postcard dealers who specialize only in chromes.

REAL PHOTO POSTCARDS (1900 to present day)

Real Photo cards were in use as early as 1900. It is sometimes difficult to date them unless postally used or dated by a photographer. The stamp box will usually show the process by which it was printed; e.g., AZO, EKC, KODAK, VELOX, and KRUXO. Careful study of photo cards is essential to make sure they have not been reproduced.

ART DECO ERA (1910 to early 1930's)

Beautiful **Colors!** Beautiful strong, deep, vibrant **Colors!** This wording only partially describes the new Art Deco movement that began around 1910—just as the Art Nouveau era was ebbing—and continued into the early 1930's. Due to the great influx of Art Deco postcards to the U.S., there has been a great demand for them in recent years as more and more American collectors discover their beauty.

ART NOUVEAU (1898-1910)

Art Nouveau postcards had their beginning at the turn of the century in Europe. Primarily, the movement began in Paris--where the great poster artists congregated--and in Vienna. This new expression of decorative art was the rage of the era, and the posters and magazines such as "*Jugend,*" "*Simplicissimus,*" "*Le Rire,*" "*Le Plume,*" and "*The Poster,*" were used as a means to transmit this expression to the art lovers of the world.

The values of some of these cards have reached unbelievable heights as can be witnessed by the prices revealed in this book. As values of the better known artists such as Mucha, Kirchner and Toulouse-Lautrec spiral ever upward, they also bring values of the lesser publicized artist up with them.

ARTIST-SIGNED

What is an Artist-Signed postcard? It is the original work of an artist, bearing his initials or signature, photographed, colored to represent the original, and then printed into postcard form. The Artist-Signed postcard is overwhelmingly the favorite single type to collect in the entire postcard field. Some may collect views of their home town, transportation or real photos, but almost all collectors search for those of the painted form. Whether they be the beautiful ladies of Fisher or Boileau, or the lovely children of Brundage and Clapsaddle, the artist-signed postcard is the shining star. The beauty and elegance of several cards, or a group or set of cards by a great artist, provide the collector with the desire to eventually possess them.

Since Artist-Signed issues continue to be so extremely popular we have made every attempt to list as many of the major and minor artists in the U.S. in all fields. Also, listing of major and minor foreign artists and their works in the important topics of Art Deco, Art Nouveau, Fantasy, Fantasy Nudes, Color Nudes, Nursery Rhymes, Fairy Tales, Animals, French Fashion, and others is a must. Since the great influx of foreign cards to the U.S. market, today's collectors and dealers desire information and values of this highly collectible material.

BEAUTIFUL LADIES

	VG	EX
B.G. (Art Nouveau and Glamour)	$45 - 50	$50 - 55
ABIELLE, JACK (France)		
Lady/Flower Series	40 - 45	45 - 50
Art Nouveau	50 - 55	55 - 60

T. Axentowicz
Anczyc 301, No Caption

Karl Anderson, Armour & Co.,
1906, American Girl Series

ALBERTARELLI, R. (Italy) Art Deco	12 - 15	15 - 20
ALEXANDRE (France) Erotic		
ALFRED, JAMES D. (U.S.)		
Gray Lithograph Co.		
P.C. 1 through P.C. 9	6 - 8	8 - 10
ANICHINI, EZIO (Italy) Art Deco and Glamour		
"Fairies" Series	18 - 22	22 - 25
Dancer Series	22 - 25	25 - 28
Silhouette Series 458	15 - 18	18 - 22
Exotic Bird Series		
ANLURNY (Art Deco and Glamour)		
Series 2590	12 - 15	15 - 20
ARMSTRONG, ROLF (U.S.)		
K. Co. Inc., N.Y.		
Water Color Series 101 - 112		
102 Blonde hair, blue collar	15 - 18	18 - 22
108 Reddish-brown hair, white collar		
109 Dark brown hair, with locket		
ASTI, ANGELO (Italy)		
Braun & Co., Paris (Sepia) (6) Semi-nudes		
179 "Volupte"	18 - 22	22 - 25
International Art (Uns.) (6) Small images	8 - 10	10 - 12
Raphael Tuck		
Connoisseur Series 2731		
"Beatrice," "Gladys," "Irene"	12 - 15	15 - 20
"Juliet," "Marguerite," "Rosalind"		

Angelo Asti
Anonymous, No Caption

Angelo Asti
H&S, No Caption

Connoisseur Series 2743		
"Helena," "Madeline," "Muriel"	12 - 15	15 - 20
"Phyllis," "Portia," "Sylvia"		
Series 6295 (6)		
Rotograph Co., N.Y.		
Series T. 5268	8 - 10	10 - 15
"Beatrice," "Gladys," "Irene"		
"Juliet," "Marguerite," "Rosalind"		
Salon 1897 (Nudes)		
"Songeuse"	20 - 25	25 - 30
T.S.N. (Theo. Stroefer, Nürnberg)		
Series 505 (6)	10 - 12	12 - 15
Series 508 (8) No Captions		
Semi-Nude Real Photo Series	15 - 20	20 - 25
"Epanouissment"		
"Fantasie"		
"Solitude"		
"Une Favorite"		
"Volupte"		
Valentine's Series (Uns.)	10 - 12	12 - 15
Russian Real Photo Nudes		
826 Same as "Volupte"	15 - 20	20 - 28
Job - Advertising Calendar, 1899	80 - 90	90 - 100
AVELINE, F.		
Lindberg'in Kirjap. Oy, Helsinki Series	8 - 10	10 - 12
Others	6 - 8	8 - 10

AXENTOWICZ, T. (Poland)

Heads and full-length	8 - 10	10 - 15
Fantasy	12 - 15	15 - 18
Nudes	15 - 18	18 - 22

AZZONI, N. (Italy) Art Deco and Glamour

Series 517 (6)	15 - 20	20 - 25
Others	12 - 15	15 - 18

BACHRICH, M. (Art Deco and Glamour)

Ladies/Fashion	12 - 15	15 - 18
Ladies/Sports	15 - 20	20 - 25
Dance Series 102	12 - 15	15 - 18

BAILEY, S. C.

Carlton Pub. Co.

Series 674	6 - 8	8 - 10
Series 689	8 - 10	10 - 12

BAKST, LEON (Russia)

St. Eugenie Red Cross

Secession Exhibition	150 - 175	175 - 200
Girls of the Ballet Puppets, Ladies (10)	75 - 80	80 - 90
Others	40 - 50	50 - 60

BALESTERIERI, L. (Italy) Art Deco	7 - 8	8 - 10
BALL, H. LaPRIAK (U.S.)	3 - 4	4 - 5

BALLETTI, P. (Italy) Art Deco and Glamour

Ladies/Fashion	12 - 15	15 - 20

BALOTINI (Italy)

Ladies & Dogs Series 312	12 - 15	15 - 20
Art Deco	10 - 12	12 - 15

BANERAS, A. (Spain)

154 Tennis	15 - 18	18 - 22
BARBARA, S. Art Nouveau	22 - 25	25 - 30

BARBER, COURT (U.S.)

B.K.W.I.

Series 861 (12)	8 - 10	10 - 12
Series 686 (6)	10 - 12	12 - 15
Series 1200	8 - 10	10 - 12
Others	6 - 8	8 - 10

Minerva

Series 683 (Head Studies)	8 - 10	10 - 15
R.B.H. Series 688 (Head Studies)	10 - 12	12 - 15

J. St. Co., Germany

113 "Good Natured"	8 - 10	10 - 12
116 "Tempting Eyes"		
118 "Lissie"		
140 "Are you offended?"		
J.W. & Co. Series	6 - 8	8 - 9

S.W.S.B.

Series 616, 1236	10 - 12	12 - 15
Others	6 - 8	8 - 10
Ladies & Dogs	10 - 12	12 - 15

S.W.S.B.

"Beauties"	8 - 10	10 - 12
1228 "Following the Race"		

L. Bakst, St. Eugenie Red Cross
La Fee de Poupee Dolls, 10

L. Bakst, St. Eugenie Red Cross
Carnival de Schoumann, "Estrella"

C. W. Barber, Carlton Pub. Co.
688-5, "Promenading"

C. W. Barber, Carlton Pub. Co.
716-3, "A Sun Bather"

Anonymous
    Series 2023, 2024   8 - 10   10 - 12
    Ladies & Horses
      "Miss Knickerbocker"   8 - 10   10 - 15
      "In Summer Days"
      "Thoroughbreds"   10 - 12   12 - 16
      2022 "Ready to Ride"   8 - 10   10 - 15

BARBER, C.W. (U.S.)
    B.K.W.I., Vienna
      Series 861 (12)   12 - 15   15 - 18
      Series 2128 (8)
    Carlton Publishing Co. (6 cards per set)
      Series 549, 660, 661   10 - 12   12 - 15
      Series 676, 677, 678, 687, 688
      Series 709, 716
      Series 735, 861   8 - 10   10 - 14
    S.W.S.B., Berlin
      Series 1236
      "Motor Lady"   10 - 12   12 - 15
      Others

BARRIBAL, L. (G.B.)
    B.K.W.I.
      Series XIX (Fashion)   12 - 15   15 - 18
      Series 860 (Fashion)
    James Henderson & Sons
      Series C6 (6)   10 - 12   12 - 15
    Inter-Art Pub. Co.
      Series 3292   15 - 18   18 - 22
      Artisque Series   10 - 12   12 - 15
    Ladies & Horses
      Artisque
      Series 2234 (6) **and Series 2236** (6)   12 - 15   15 - 20
      Series 15644 (Heads)
    M.K.B.
      Series 2205 (6)   12 - 15   15 - 18
    M. Munk, Vienna (Heads) **Series 882**
    Novitas, Germany
      Series 15464 (6)
      "Mystic Beauty"   15 - 18   18 - 22
      "True Blue"
      "Wearin' of the Green"
      "Yours Darling"
      Series 15644, 15645 (6)
    Valentine Co.
      "Flags of Nation" Series   12 - 15   15 - 20
      "Great Britain"
      "Japan"
      "Scotland"
      "Ireland"
      "Germany"
      "Russia"
    Lindberg's Tryokeria Series (8)   10 - 12   12 - 15
    Lindberg'in Kirjap. O.Y., Helsinki (6)

L. Barribal, M. Munk 882
No Caption

Court Barber, S.W.S.B. 1236
"The Motor Lady"

G. Baneras, N. Coll Salieti 154
No Caption

R. Bennett (Unsigned)
M. Munk, Sporting Girls Series

Ladies & Dogs	15 - 18	18 - 22
H.N. & N.		
15645 Girl in Furs	10 - 12	12 - 15
BARRICK		
Paul Hecksher		
Series 1039 (6)	10 - 12	12 - 15
BASCH, ARPAD (Hungary)		
Art Nouveau and Glamour		
Series 761 (6)	120 - 130	130 - 150
Series 769 (6)	200 - 225	225 - 250
Series 785 (6)	80 - 90	90 - 100
National Ladies (10)	120 - 130	130 - 140
"1900 Grand Femme" (6)	150 - 175	200 - 250
BENDA, WLADYSLAW T. (W.T.)		
"Rosamond"	8 - 10	10 - 12
"Reverie"	8 - 10	10 - 12
BENNETT, R. (U.S.) (Listed as Pennell in 2nd Edition)		
M. Munk, Vienna		
Series 578 Love-Marriage Series (6)	8 - 10	10 - 12
A "Im Restaurant"		
Series 913 Sporting Girls (6)	10 - 12	12 - 15
Series 1114 Same as Series 913 (6)		
Novitas (N in Star)		
Series 15324 Beautiful Ladies (6)	10 - 12	12 - 15
FINLAND		
30/25 Series Same as **Series 913** above	12 - 15	15 - 18
BERTHON, P. (Art Nouveau)	120 - 130	130 - 150
BENTIVOGLIO (Art Deco and Glamour) (Italy)		
Lady & Greyhound	40 - 50	50 - 60
Other Deco with ladies	25 - 30	30 - 35
Pierrots		
BERTIGLIA, AURELIO (Italy)		
Art Deco and Glamour		
Rev. Stampa; Dell, Anna & Gasparini		
Ladies/Heads	12 - 15	15 - 18
Ladies/Fashion		
Ladies/Animals	15 - 18	18 - 22
Golf	25 - 30	30 - 35
Tennis	22 - 25	25 - 30
Perriots (Harlequins)		
Ladies/Pierrots		
Ethnic/Blacks		
Series 163 Big Hats	15 - 18	18 - 20
Series 241 Semi-Nudes	20 - 22	22 - 26
Series 224 Lovers Kissing	10 - 12	12 - 15
Series 2062 Couples		
Ladies & Dogs		
Series 163 (6)	12 - 15	15 - 20
Ladies & Horses		
Series 227 (6)	10 - 15	15 - 18
Series 2132 (6)		
Series 2151 (6)		

BETTINELLI, MARIO (Italy)
Art Deco and Glamour

Series 884	12 - 15	15 - 20
Others	8 - 10	10 - 12

BIANCHI, ALBERTO (Italy)
Art Deco and Glamour
Rev. Stampa and P.A.R.

Series 2024, 2041 Walking (6)	10 - 12	12 - 15
Series 2154 High Fashion, playing cards (6)	12 - 15	15 - 20
Ladies/Heads	10 - 12	12 - 15
Ladies/Fashion		
Ladies/Animals		
Series 183 (6)	12 - 15	15 - 20
Ladies/Golf	20 - 25	25 - 30
Ladies/Tennis	15 - 18	18 - 22
Ladies/Dogs/Horses		
Series 483 (6)	10 - 12	12 - 15
Series 2020 (6)		

BIELETTO, T. (Italy)	5 - 8	8 - 10
BILIBIN, IVAN (Russia) Art Nouveau	60 - 75	75 - 125
BIRGER (Art Deco)	15 - 18	18 - 20

BIRI, S. (Italy)   Art Deco and Glamour

Ladies/Pierrots	18 - 22	22 - 25
Others	12 - 15	15 - 18
BLUMENTHAL, M. L.	4 - 5	5 - 6
BOCCASILE, GINO (Art Deco)	50 - 75	75 - 100
BODAREVSKY, N.K. (Russia)	12 - 15	15 - 20

BOILEAU, PHILIP (Canada-U.S.)

Many say that Philip Boileau ladies are the most beautiful of early great painters and illustrators. His works, as with Harrison Fisher, are popular not only in the U.S. but throughout the world. Boileau was born in Canada but finally settled in New York where he became one of the most prolific painters of the beauties of the era.

Most of his images on postcards, painted during the "postcard craze" years of 1905-1918, were published in the U.S. by the New York firm of Reinthal & Newman. Other principal publishers were Osborne Calendar Co., who did the very rare Boileau calendar cards...National Art Co. with their advertising cards, and The Taylor, Platt Co. who did the Valentine head issues and the scarce flower-decorated cards of the heads in different form.

Other issues were advertising cards by Flood & Conklin, Soapine Mfg. Co., S.E. Perlberg Tailors, and others. These, as well as his other advertising cards, are in extremely short supply and are very high priced when they do surface.

British, European, Finnish, and Russian publishers issued Boileau cards which are very elusive and also command high prices.   The Tuck Connoisseur Series 2819 and German K N G Schöne Frauen, along with the KOY Finnish Series, are among those sought after by collectors worldwide. Several new Russian cards have also surfaced and this has caused added interest in works of this premier artist.

Boileau cards have been very active during the past two years and prices have risen at an average of 10 to 20 percent. This is especially true of higher valued issues such as the Osborne Calendar cards and the Finnish and Russian issues.

PHILIP BOILEAU

AMERICAN PUBLISHERS
  Reinthal & Newman
    Series 94*

"At the Opera"	20 - 25	25 - 28
"Peggy"		
"Schooldays"		
"Sweethearts"		
"Thinking of You"		
"Twins"		

  * Card with Series No. on back, add $5.
    Series 95 *

"A Mischiefmaker"	20 - 25	25 - 28
"Anticipation"		
"Forever"		
"Little Lady Demure"		
"My Chauffeur"		
"Nocturne"		
"Passing Shadow"	20 - 22	22 - 26
"Spring Song"**		
"Today"	18 - 22	22 - 25
"Tomorrow"	20 - 22	22 - 26
"Winter Whispers"	15 - 18	18 - 22
"Yesterday"	15 - 20	20 - 25

  * Cards with Series No. on back, add $5.
  ** Cards distr. by Chas. H. Hauff, add $5.
    Series 109*

"Evening and You"	20 - 25	25 - 30
"Girl in Black"		
"Her Soul With Purity Possessed"	22 - 27	27 - 32
"In Maiden Meditation"		
"June, Blessed June"	20 - 25	25 - 30
"My Moonbeam"		
"My One Rose"		
"Ready for Mischief"		
"The Secret of the Flowers"	25 - 30	30 - 35
"True as the Blue Above"		
"Twixt Doubt and Hope"		
"Waiting for You"		
"With Care for None"		

  * Cards with Series No. on back, add $5.
    200 Series

204 "Rings on Her Fingers"	18 - 22	22 - 25
205 "Question"		

*Philip Boileau, Russian Real
Photo 2683, Russian Caption*

*Philip Boileau, Russian Back
N:O 3 (Pebbles on the Beach)*

*Philip Boileau, Taylor, Platt Co.
"Violets"*

*Philip Boileau, Anon. Ser. 682-2
"True as the Blue Above"*

205 "Chrysanthemums"		
206 "The Enchantress"		
207 "A Hundred Years Ago"		
208 "Miss America"		
209 "Youth"	10 - 15	15 - 20
210 "Joyful Calm"		
211 "Chums"		
212 "Sweet Lips of Coral Hue"		
213 "His First Love"		
214 "For Him"		
215 "I Wonder"		
282 "Ready for the Meeting"	18 - 22	22 - 25
283 "Miss Pat"		
284 "Old Home Farewell"		
285 "A Serious Thought"		
286 "I Don't Care"		
287 "The Eyes Say No, The Lips Say Yes"		
294 "Blue Ribbons"	20 - 25	25 - 30
295 "A Little Devil" ("Good Little Rogue")	15 - 20	20 - 25
296 "Once Upon A Time"	10 - 15	15 - 20
297 "My Big Brother"		
298 "My Boy"		
299 "Baby Mine"	20 - 25	25 - 28
Water Color Series 369-380*		
369 "Vanity"	25 - 30	30 - 40
370 "Haughtiness"		
371 "Purity"		
372 "Loneliness"	30 - 35	35 - 45
373 "Happiness"	25 - 30	30 - 40
374 "Queenliness"		
375 "Whisperings of Love" (Annunciation)		
376 "Fairy Tales" (Girlhood)		
377 "Parting of the Ways" (Maidenhood)		
378 "Here Comes Daddy"		
379 "Lullabye" (Motherhood)		
With blue blanket		
With pink blanket		
380 "Don't Wake the Baby"		
* Cards without Sub-title, add $5.		
445 Series* (Dist. by Charles Hauff)		
1 "Spring Song"	25 - 30	30 - 35
2 "Today"		
3 "Tomorrow"		
4 "Forever"		
5 "My Chauffeur"		
6 "Nocturne"		
* With German caption, add $5.		
474 Series * * (Dist. by Charles Hauff)	25 - 30	30 - 35
1 "Spring Song"		
2 "A Passing Shadow"		
3 "Mischiefmaker" (also "A Mischief Maker")		
4 "Anticipating"		
5 "Yesterday"		

Philip Boileau, R&N 751
"Absence Cannot Hearts Divide"

Philip Boileau, R&N 820
"Devotion"

    6 "Little Lady Demure"
*   With German caption, add $5.
** Cards are more rare than Series 95.
    700 Series*

750 "Be Prepared"	20 - 25	25 - 28
751 "Absence Cannot Hearts Divide"		
752 "A Neutral"		
753 "The Chrysalis"		
754 "Pensive"		
755 "The Girl of the Golden West"		
756 "Pebbles on the Beach"		
757 "Snowbirds"		
758 "One Kind Act a Day"		
759 "The Flirt"		
760 "In Confidence"		
761 "The Coming Storm"		

* With German caption, add $5.
    800 Series

820 "Devotion"	35 - 40	40 - 45
821 "Golden Dreams"		
822 "Every Breeze Carries My Thoughts..."		
823 "Priscilla"		
824 "Fruit of the Vine"	30 - 35	35 - 40
825 "Butterfly"		
826 "When Dreams Come True" *	20 - 25	25 -30
827 "Sister's First Love" *		
828 "The Little Neighbors" *		

829 "Peach Blossoms" *
830 "When His Ship Comes In" *
831 "Need a Lassie Cry" *
* With German caption, add $5.
Water Color Series 936-941
936 "A Bit of Heaven"   30 - 35   35 - 40
937 "Chic"
938 "Have a Care"
    also "Hav a Care"
939 "Just a Wearying for You"
940 "Sunshine"
941 "Sincerely Yours"
2000 Series
2052 "Thinking of You"   25 - 30   30 - 35
2063 "Chums"
2064 "His First Love"
2065 "Question"
2066 "From Him"
2067 "The Enchantress"
2068 "Joyful Calm"
Others in Series
Unnumbered Series
"The Dreamy Hour"   25 - 30   30 - 38
"Out for Fun"
Reinthal & Newman Copyright
Distributed by **Novitas**. No Numbers.
"A Mischiefmaker"   40 - 45   45 - 48
"A Passing Shadow" (Also by **Wildt & Kray**)
"Anticipating"
"Forever"
"Little Lady Demure"
"My Chauffeur"
"Nocturne"
"Spring Song"
"To-Day?"
"Tomorrow"
"Winter Whispers"
"Yesterday!"
Reinthal & Newman, N.Y.
Distributed by **J. Beagles & Co.**, London   25 - 30   30 - 35
No No. "Little Lady Demure"
No No. "Nocturne"
No No. "Winter Whispers"
A. P. Co.
"His First Love" (1911)   150 - 175   175 - 200
"Miss America" (1911)
ADVERTISING
First Nat. Bank, Cripple Creek, CO
"Virginia"   125 - 150   150 - 175
Flood & Conklin (Calendar Card Ad)   100 - 125   125 - 150
"Girl in Blue"
"The Girl in Brown"
"His First Love"

Others
Holland Magazine (Ad on Back)   100 - 110   110 - 125
   "Miss Pat"
   "Ready for the Meeting"
Metropolitan Life   Advertising
   American Lithographic Co.   35 - 40   50 - 60
National Art Company
   17 "Spring"   70 - 80   80 - 100
   18 "Summer"
   19 "Autumn"
   20 "Winter"
   150 "The Debutantes"   75 - 85   85 - 105
   160 "Summer"   80 - 90   90 - 100
   161 "Autumn"
   162 "Spring"
   163 "Winter"
   230 "Spring"   90 - 100   100 - 110
   231 "Summer"
   232 "Autumn"
   233 "Winter"
National Cloak & Suit
   Catalog Card, 1910   140 - 150   150 - 160
Osborne Calendar Co.*
   459 "Winifred"   250 - 275   275 - 325
   940 "A Fair Debutante"
   941 "The Blonde"
   942 "Phyllis"
   943 "Pansies"
   944 "True Blue"
   945 "Army Girl"
   946 "Day Dreams"
   947 "Passing Shadow"
   948 "The Girl in Brown"
   949 "Goodbye"
   950 "Passing Glance"
   951 "A Winter Girl"
   1436 "Violets"   275 - 300   300 - 350
   1459 "Rhododendrons"
   1489 "At Play"
   1738 "Virginia"
   2076 "Suzanne"
   3525 "Autumn"
   3625 "Chrysanthemums"
      "Carnations"
   Others
   * The Osborne Calendar Cards are the
   rarest U.S. series.
S. E. Perlberg Co., Tailors (Ad on Back)   100 - 125   125 - 140
   "My Moonbeam"
   "My One Rose"
   "Secret of the Flowers"
   "True as the Blue Above"
   "Twixt Doubt and Hope"

C. N. Snyder Art
"Spring Song"   90 - 110   110 - 130
Soapine   Advertising
Sparks Tailoring (Ad on Back) by **R&N**
"Tomorrow"   90 - 110   110 - 130
Taylor, Platt*
"Chrysanthemums"   80 - 90   90 - 110
"Poppies"
"Violets"
"Wild Roses"
* 12 cards issued; only 4 have surfaced.
Will's Embassy Pipe Tobacco Mixtures
"Nocturne"   100 - 125   125 - 150
Worthmore Tay Tailors, Chicago
"Ready for Mischief"   100 - 125   125 - 150
Unsigned, Unknown U.S. Publisher *
"Au Revoir"   30 - 35   35 - 45
"Chrysanthemums" **
(To My Sweetheart)
"Day Dreams"
"Debutantes"
"Devotion"
"Poppies"
(A Greeting from St. Valentine)
(A Token of Love) 2 types exist.
"Violets"
(A Gift of Love)
"Wild Roses"
(To My Valentine)
* Others may exist.
** Embossed and un-embossed varieties exist;
possibly in all four cards.
Wolf & Co.
"Fancy Free" (Silk) Very Rare!   400 - 450   450 - 500

FOREIGN PUBLISHERS
A.V.N. Jones & Co., London
"Quite Ready"   150 - 175   175 - 200
Distributed by **B.K.W.I.**, Vienna
Series 500   150 - 175   175 - 200
"Spring"
"Summer"
"Fall"
"Winter"
Apollon Sophia, Bulgaria
"My Big Brother" (No. 21)   50 - 60   60 - 75
B.K.W.I., German*
"Ready for Mischief"   150 - 175   175 - 200
"June, Blessed June"
* Die-cuts on headbands, necklaces, foil inside.
Others that exist without die-cut holes.   100 - 125   125 - 150
Diefenthal, Amsterdam (Sepia)
"A Hundred Years Ago"   110 - 120   120 - 130

"C'est Moi"
"The Enchantress"
"His First Love"
"Question"
H & S, Germany
"Au Revoir"   100 - 125   125 - 150
"At Home" (White border)
"Fancy Free" (White border)
"Paying a Call" (White Border)
"Paying a Call" (No border; rev. image)
"I am Late" (Unsigned; blue rev. image)
FINLAND
A.P. Co.
"His First Love"   125 - 135   135 - 150
K. K. OY, 1/20 Series
"Baby Mine"   150 - 175   175 - 200
"Sister's First Love"
"Snowbirds"
"Here Comes Daddy" (Light Pastels)
K.K. Oy - KFP-K. Oy
"Snowbirds"   175 - 200   200 - 225
N:O Numbered Series
N:O 14 Same as "Purity"   175 - 200   200 - 225
Untitled Series, No Publisher
(With "Stamp Here" in Stamp Box)
"From Him"   125 - 150   150 - 175
"His First Love"
"Question"
"Sweet Lips of Coral Hue"

EUROPE
AWE Real Photo   125 - 150   150 - 175
#38 No Caption
H & S, Germany (Untitled)
"Au Revoir"   120 - 140   140 - 160
"At Home" (White Border)
"Fancy Free" (White Border)
"Paying a Call" (White Border)
"Paying a Call" (No border, rev. image)
"I am Late" (Unsigned; blue rev. image)
KNG, Germany (Untitled)
Schöne Frauen Series 8010
"I am Late" (No border)   125 - 150   150 - 170
"Paying a Call" (No border)
"Summer Breezes" (No border)
"Fancy Free"
"Au Revoir"
"At Home"
Schöne Frauen Series 8011
"I am Late" (White border)   100 - 110   110 - 130
"Fancy Free"   110 - 130   130 - 150
"Paying a Call" (White border)   100 - 110   110 - 130
"Summer Breezes" (White border)

Philip Boileau, Finnish N:O 14
(Purity)

Philip Boileau, Rishar 114
"Warum"

Schöne Frauen Series 8012		
"I am Late" (rev. image, uns., untitled)	100 - 110	110 - 130
"Fancy Free"		
Schöne Frauen Series 8013		
"I am Late" (reversed image, uns.)	100 - 110	110 - 130
"Paying a Call" (reversed image, uns.)		
"Summer Breezes" (blue rev. image)	100 - 125	125 - 150
MEU Publisher Logo on Back		
Untitled, Woman/Dark Hat, Dated 1905	90 - 100	100 - 110
Albert Schweitzer, Germany	80 - 90	90 - 100
H. S. Speelman, Netherlands		
"Eva" (Same as "Peggy")	100 - 110	110 - 125
"Peggy"		
Raphael Tuck, London		
Connoisseur Series 2819		
"At Home"	175 - 200	200 - 225
"Au Revoir"		
"Fancy Free"		
"I am Late"		
"Paying a Call"		
"Summer Breezes"		
Uitg de Muinck & Co., Amsterdam		
"His First Love"	90 - 100	100 - 110
Weinthal Co., Rotterdam		
Friedrich O. Woehler, Berlin		
1058 - "Studie"	75 - 85	85 - 100

Philip Boileau, AWE Real Photo
Russian/Polish Back

Philip Boileau, "Orohek" No. 13
"Sweet Lips of Coral Hue"

RUSSIAN PUBLISHERS
  AWE - Russian/Polish Back
    Real Photo Series No Captions
      "Joyful Calm"   200 - 225   225 - 250
      "Miss America"
  "OROHEK" - Russian/English Back *
    Series 71293 - 3000 (Total Run)
      1 "From Him"   175 - 200   200 - 225
      4 "Question"
     13 "Sweet Lips of Coral Hue"
     ? "His First Love"
  * This appears to be same series as Finnish
     with "Stamp Here" in stamp box but with-
     out captions. Card stock is also heavier.
  "Richard" (Rishar, Petrograde)   150 - 175   175 - 200
     104 "Winter"
     105 "Spring"
     106 "Autumn"
     107 "Summer"
     108 "Poppies" (Unsigned)
     109 "Wild Roses"
     110 "Violets"
     111 "Chrysanthemums"
     112
     113
     114 "Warum" (Why)
     116

Unknown Russian Publisher
Real-Photo Type, Russian-Polish back
"The Enchantress"　　　　　　　　　125 - 150　　150 - 175
"I Don't Care"
Unknown Russian Publisher
"Autumn"　　　　　　　　　　　　125 - 150　　150 - 175
Unknown Russian Publisher
5　"Rings on Her Fingers" (Unsigned)　125 - 150　　150 - 175
18　"A Brotherly Kiss" (Peb. grain paper)
Unknown Russian Publisher
N:O 3　　　　　　　　　　　　　125 - 150　　150 - 175

UNKNOWN PUBLISHERS
　　Series **682**　(6)
　　682-1 "Anticipation"　　　　　　　50 - 60　　　60 - 80
　　682-2 "True as the Blue Above"
　　682-3 "In Maiden Meditation"
　　682-4 Unknown　　　　　　　　175 - 200　　200 - 225
　　682-5 "Twins"　　　　　　　　　50 - 60　　　60 - 80
　　682-6 "The Girl in Black"
　　Unsigned
　　"Miss America"　　　　　　　　　50 - 75　　　75 - 100
　　"Miss America" (signed, 1910, blue ink)
　　"Rings on Her Fingers"
　　Unknown Publisher　(Probably Dutch)
　　Series R
　　R.236 "Miss America"　　　　　　50 - 75　　　75 - 100
　　R.238 "His First Love"
　　R.239 "Chums"
BOLETTA　　　　　　　　　　　　6 - 8　　　　8 - 10
BOMPARD, LUIGI　(Italy)　Glamour　12 - 15　　　15 - 20
BOMPARD, SERGIO　(Italy)
　　Art Deco and Glamour
　　Artistica Riservata,
　　Series 472, 513　(6)　　　　　15 - 18　　　18 - 22
　　Degami
　　　Series **434**　(6)　　　　　　12 - 15　　　15 - 18
　　　Series **639**　With Animals
　　Rev. Stampa;　Dell, Anna & Gasparini
　　　Series **208, 431, 508, 931**　Fashion　(6)　10 - 12　　12 - 15
　　　Series **461**　Doing Nails, Fashion　(6)
　　　Series **464, 467, 439**　Heads (6)
　　　Series **474**　Semi-Nudes (6)　　18 - 20　　　20 - 25
　　　Series **534, 914, 955, 476**　Heads　(6)　10 - 12　　12 - 15
　　　Series **407, 472, 496**　High Fashion　(6)　12 - 15　　15 - 18
　　　Series **506, 985**　High Fashion　(6)
　　　Series **401, 449, 555**　High Fashion　(6)　15 - 18　　18 - 22
　　　Series **971, 972, 987**　High Fashion　(6)
　　　Series **321, 940, 951**　High Fashion　(6)
　　　Series **907, 950, 956**　Fashion　(6)
　　　Series **948**　Sitting, Fashion　(6)　15 - 18　　　18 - 20
　　　Series **986**　With Doll　(6)　　20 - 22　　　22 - 25
　　　Series **456**　With Hats　(6)　　15 - 18　　　18 - 22
　　　Series **994**　Woman/Child, Snowing　(6)　12 - 14　　14 - 16

Series 458, 498 Lovers Hugging	10 - 12	12 - 15
Series 498, 609 Lovers Talking		
Series 448, 988 Lovers Hugging	12 - 14	14 - 16
Series 433 Small Image-Kissing	8 - 10	10 - 12
Series 462 Taking His Pulse (6)	12 - 15	15 - 18
Series 960 Fixing His Tie (6)		
Golf	22 - 25	25 - 30
Tennis	15 - 20	20 - 22
Erotic and Semi-Nude	20 - 22	22 - 25
Ladies & Dogs		
Rev. Stampa; Dell, Anna & Gasparini		
Series 11, 17 (6)	15 - 18	18 - 22
Series 343 (6)	12 - 15	15 - 18
Series 457 (6)	15 - 18	18 - 22
Series 461 (6)	12 - 14	14 - 16
Series 637 (6) With Puppies	12 - 15	15 - 18
Ladies & Horses		
Series 343 (6)	12 - 15	15 - 18
Series 457 (6)		
Series 641, 931, 556 (6)	12 - 14	14 - 16
Harlequins (Pierrot)	22 - 25	25 - 28
BONNATTA, L. (Italy)		
BONORA (Italy) Art Deco and Glamour		
Ladies	15 - 18	18 - 22
Harlequins (Pierrot)	20 - 25	25 - 30
BORRMEISTER, R. (Germany)		
Ladies & Horses	10 - 12	12 - 15
BOTTARO, E. (Italy) Art Deco and Glamour		
Series 135, Ladies 1900's	20 - 25	25 - 30
Series 123, Bathers 1900's	25 - 30	30 - 35
Others 1920's	12 - 15	15 - 18
BOTTOMLEY, G.	8 - 10	10 - 12
BOUTET, HENRI (France) (Art Nouveau)	25 - 30	30 - 35
Charming Ladies	15 - 20	20 - 25
Collection des Cent. No 8	300 - 325	325 - 350
BRADLEY, W. H. (U.S.) (Art Nouveau)	150 - 200	200 - 250
BRAUN, W. H. (Austria)	10 - 12	12 - 15
BREDT, F. M. (Germany)	5 - 6	6 - 8
BREHM, GEORGE (U.S.)	5 - 6	6 - 8
BRILL, GEORGE (U.S.) Sporting Girl Series	6 - 8	8 - 10
BRISLEY, E. C. (G.B.)	6 - 8	8 - 10
BROCK, A. (Germany)	5 - 6	6 - 8
BROWN, J. FRANCIS (U.S.)	4 - 5	5 - 6
BROWN, MAYNARD (U.S.)	3 - 4	4 -6
BRUNELLESCHI, UMBERTO (Italy)		
Art Deco & Glamour		
Silhouettes	150 - 175	175 - 200
Advertising, La Tradotta Series (6)	90 - 100	100 - 110
R et Cie, France		
"Femmes 1920" Series 31 (6)	150 - 175	175 - 200
Art Nouveau	70 - 80	80 - 100
BRUNING, MAX (Germany)	8 - 10	10 - 15
Erotic	12 - 15	15 - 20

L. Bonnatta
Aquarella, 139, No Caption

Sergio Bompard
Artistica Riservata, 513-1

A. Busi, Degami, 1017
No Caption

BRYSON (U.S.)
  S.S. Porter, Chicago

143 "Secrets"	5 - 6	6 - 8

BUHNE, BUNTE

Deco Silhouette Series 225-228	15 - 20	20 - 25

BULKELEY   5 - 6   6 - 8

BUKOVAC, PROF. V. (Poland)   4 - 5   5 - 6

BULAS, J. (Poland)   8 - 10   10 - 12

BUSI, ADOLFO (Italy)   Art Deco and Glamour
  Degami

Series 1017 Pierrots (Harlequins)	28 - 32	32 - 35
Series 2074 Pierrots		
Series 2107 Deco	22 - 25	25 - 28

  Dell, Anna & Gasparini

Series 112 Diabolo (6)	20 - 25	25 - 30
Series 100 Fantasy (6)	25 - 30	30 - 35
Series 153 Pajamas (6)	22 - 25	25 - 28
Series 126 Girls/Fruit (6)	15 - 18	18 - 22
Series 110, 193, 1020 Fashion (6)	18 - 20	20 - 25
Series 628 Scarves/Heads	20 - 25	25 - 28
Series 437 Gypsy Type (6)	15 - 18	18 - 22
Series 558 Couples on Sled (6)	15 - 20	20 - 25
Series 575 Lovers in Moonlight (6)		
Series 615 Couples/Autos (6)	22 - 25	25 - 28
Series 651 At the Beach (6)	18 - 20	20 - 22
Series 3038, 3540, 3555 (6)	15 - 20	20 - 25
Golf	25 - 30	30 - 35

Tennis	22 - 25	25 - 28
Ricordi, Milan Ladies Series	25 - 28	28 - 32
Ross-Monopol		
Pierrots (Harlequins)	20 - 25	25 - 30
Ladies & Dogs	18 - 22	22 - 25
C.E.I.C. **Series 159**	15 - 20	20 - 25
Dell, Anna & Gasparini		
Series 170, 533 (6)	15 - 18	18 - 22
Ladies & Horses		
C.E.I.C. **Series 157** (6)	15 - 20	20 - 25
Degami		
Series 687 (6)	12 - 15	15 - 20
Series 1087 (6)	22 - 25	25 - 28
BUSSIERE, G. (Art Nouveau)	35 - 40	40 - 50
BUTCHER, ARTHUR (G.B.)		
Inter-Art Company		
Series 956 "Red Cross Angel"	15 - 18	18 - 22
Series 1098	8 - 10	10 - 12
Series 1234 Song Series		
Series 2510	6 - 8	8 - 10
Comique Series - "Leap Year"	15 - 18	18 - 22
United Six Girls Series	10 - 12	12 - 15
"Belgium" "Japan"		
"Britain" "Russia"		
"France" "Serbia"		
"Artisque" Series 1509 (6)	8 - 10	10 - 12
A.R.i.B. Series 1963 (6)	8 - 10	10 - 12
CADORIN, G. (Italy)		
Ladies/Fashion	10 - 12	12 - 15
CALDONA (Italy) Art Deco	10 - 12	12 - 15
CAPIELLO, L. Art Nouveau	200 - 250	250 - 300
CARSON, T. Art Nouveau	25 - 30	30 - 35
CASWELL, E. C. (U.S.)	6 - 8	8 - 10
CAUVY, L. Art Nouveau	40 - 50	50 - 60
CASTELLI, V. (Italy) Art Deco	12 - 15	15 - 18
CELEBRI (Italy) Art Deco	10 - 12	12 - 15
CENNI, E. (Italy) Art Deco		
CHAMBERS, C.E. (U.S.)	6 - 8	8 - 10
CHARLET, J.A. (Belgium)		
Delta Series 4	15 - 18	18 - 22
CHERET, JULES Art Nouveau	200 - 300	300 - 500
CHERUBINI, M. (Italy) Art Deco		
Rev. Stampa		
Series 790 National Ladies	15 - 20	20 - 25
Series 423, 977 Off-Shoulder Fash. (6)	12 - 15	15 - 20
Series 997 With Cupids (6)	12 - 15	15 - 18
Series 408 In Bubbles (6)	12 - 15	15 - 18
Series 887, 959 Beauties (6)	12 - 15	15 - 20
French Glamour	15 - 20	20 - 25
CHIOSTRI, S. (Also SOFIA) (Italy)		
Art Deco and Glamour		
Ballerini & Fratini		
All Series contain 4 cards		

S. Chiostri, B&F 309

S. Chiostri, B&F 295

S. Chiostri, B&F 197

S. Chiostri, B&F 359

S. Chiostri, B&F 388

S. Chiostri, B&F 240

S. Chiostri, B&F 257

S. Chiostri, B&F 252

S. Chiostri, B&F 320

Series 166	Deco Fashion	32 - 35	35 - 40
Series 167	Pierrot	45 - 48	48 - 52
Series 178	Easter Pierrot	30 - 35	35 - 40
Series 181	Bathers	25 - 30	30 - 40
Series 197, 212	Pierrot	40 - 45	45 - 50
Series 200, 201	Easter Ladies	25 - 30	30 - 35
Series 202	White Haired Ladies	30 - 35	35 - 38
Series 211	Harem Girls	35 - 40	40 - 45
Series 220	Santas/Father New Year	35 - 40	40 - 50
	Black Robed Santas?	50 - 60	60 - 75
Series 224, 228	Pierrot-Ladies	35 - 40	40 - 45
Series 225	Man and Lady Pierrots		
Series 237, 252	Ladies with Cupid		
Series 238	Mermaids	50 - 60	60 - 75
Series 240	Fantasy Flower Ladies	40 - 45	45 - 50
Series 241	"Il Destino" Series	45 - 50	50 - 55
Series 243	Fortune Teller	30 - 40	40 - 45
Series 244	Very Colorful Pierrots	45 - 50	50 - 55
Series 257	Pierrot	35 - 40	40 - 45
Series 259	Gem Series	45 - 50	50 - 55
Series 248, 268, 294, 301	Christmas Ladies	30 - 35	35 - 38
Series 290	Japanese Ladies	35 - 38	38 - 42
Series 295	Colorful Christmas Ladies	40 - 45	45 - 50
Series 302	Winter Sports Lovers-Cupid	30 - 35	35 - 38
Series 304	Fairy-Pierrot Series	40 - 45	45 - 50
Series 305	Pierrot-Mask Series	35 - 40	40 - 45
Series 308	Easter Lovers	18 - 22	22 - 25
Series 309	High Class Easter Ladies	35 - 40	40 - 45
Series 316	With Animals	35 - 40	40 - 50
Series 317	Mermaids	50 - 60	60 - 70
Series 320	Lady with Wild Animals	40 - 45	45 - 55
Series 354	Russian Harem Girls	35 - 40	40 - 45
Series 357	Pierrot-Ladies	30 - 35	35 - 40
Series 358	Girls with Umbrella	40 - 45	45 - 40
Series 359	Ladies-Bird of Paradise	45 - 50	50 - 55
Series 363	Pierrot Children	25 - 30	30 - 35
Series 388	Classical Japanese Ladies	40 - 45	45 - 50
Series 426	Russian Lovers	30 - 35	35 - 38
Other **Pierrots**	(Harlequins)	35 - 40	40 - 50
Others, Colored Background		25 - 30	30 - 40
Others, Seasons Greetings		12 - 15	15 - 20
Comics, Flowers & Fruits in Deco Style		15 - 18	18 - 22
Signed FOFI			
Series 164			
French Dressed Couples		20 - 25	25 - 28
W.O.			
Series 663	Russian Lovers (Uns.)	25 - 30	30 - 35
CHRISTIANSEN, HANS (Art Nouveau)			
"Pari" Series, High Fashion Ladies		175 - 200	200 - 225
"Twentieth Century Women"		140 - 150	150 - 160
Darmstadt Expo, 1902			
Lady Vignettes (6)		175 - 200	200 - 225

CHRISTY, F. EARL (U.S.)

F. Earl Christy was one of the leading artists who depicted the total beauty of the American girl, especially of the college and university varieties. Most of his early works were in this category, as he helped start the tradition of glorifying the beauties of the era. He pictured them as high classed, always beautifully dressed, and seemingly in complete command of the situation. These were the girls who attended football games, played golf and tennis, rode in new automobiles and were gifted with musical talent. His was the *All-American Girl*.

His first College Girl series was published by the U.S.S. Postcard Co. in 1905. This series revealed an artist with promising talents, and he went on to design many of the "College Girl" series for numerous publishers. Among his most popular works were Tuck's College Queens and Kings.

After the college/university girl fad had run its course, Christy used his many talents to paint beautiful ladies and man/woman lover types. The Reinthal & Newman Co. of New York was his major publisher; however, he did many fine sets for the Knapp Co., Edward Gross, and others. His images were also published and distributed in Europe and Scandinavia.

Earl Christy's cards, with the exception of high-flying College Queens and Kings series, have elevated only slightly (an average of only 10%) since our second edition. The works of this talented artist should be a favorite of those who collect American artist-signed beautiful ladies.

F. EARL CHRISTY

    Reinthal & Newman, N.Y.

No Number Series		
"Love"	15 - 18	18 - 22
"A Sandwitch"		
"Be With You in a Minute"	10 - 12	12 - 15
"Always Winning"	15 - 18	18 - 22
"Love Dreams"	12 - 15	15 - 18
"Lovingly Yours"		
"Swimming"		
"A Sweet Surrender" Series		
168 "A Sweet Surrender"	12 - 15	15 - 18
169 "The Pilot"		
170 "My Love is Like a Red, Red Rose"		
171 "Come Sit Beside Me"		
172 "Come With Me"		
173 "Love All"	22 - 25	25 - 30
"The Siren" Series		
228 "Masks Off!"	12 - 15	15 - 20
229 "Lovingly Yours"		
230 "Be With You in a Minute"		
231 "The Rose Maid"		
232 "The Siren"		
233 "Roses are Always in Season"		

"The Path of Love" Series

276	"The Love Song"	12 - 15	15 -20
277	"Love Dreams"		
278	"The Love Story"		
279	"The Love Match"		
280	"The Love Waltz"		
281	"Love"		

Water Color Series

363	"A Bit of Tea & Gossip"	15 - 18	18 - 22
364	"The Sweetest of All"		
365	"For the Wedding Chest"		
366	"The Message of Love"		
367	"The Day's Work"	20 - 25	25 - 28
368	"A Finishing Touch"	15 - 18	18 - 22

Series 428-433

428	"What Shall I Answer?"	10 - 12	12 - 15
429	"I'm Waiting for You"	10 - 12	12 - 15
430	"Tender Memories"	10 - 12	12 - 15
431	"A Message of Love"	10 - 12	12 - 15
432	"On the Bridal Path"	10 - 12	12 - 15
433	"Always Winning"	15 - 18	18 - 22

Series 618-623

618	"The Girl I Like"	12 - 15	15 - 18
619	"The Girl I Like to Chat With"		
620	"The Girl I Like to Walk With"		
621	"The Girl I Like to Flirt With"		
622	"The Girl I Like to Play With"	18 - 22	22 - 25
623	"The Girl I Like to Sing With"	10 - 12	12 - 15

Series 624-629

624	"By Appointment"	12 - 15	15 - 18
625	"As Promised"		
626	"What Shall I Say?"		
627	"A Sandwitch"		
628	"With Fond Love"		
629	"Nearest Her Heart"		

Water Color Series 942-947

		15 - 18	18 - 22
942	"Protected"		
943	"Someone is Thinking of You"		
944	"Are You There?"		
945	"Love, Here is My Heart"		
946	"Worth Waiting For"		
947	"Not Forgotten"		

ENGLISH REPRINTS

2106	"On the Bridal Path"	15 - 20	20 - 25
2107	"Tender Memories"		
2109	"Nearest Her Heart"		

FAS (F.A. Schneider)

197	Horseback Riding	15 - 20	20 - 25
198	Skates	15 - 18	18 - 25
199	Tennis	20 - 25	25 - 30
200	Golf	30 - 35	35 - 38
201	In an Auto	15 - 18	18 - 25
202	"What the Waves are Saying"		

F. Earl Christy, R&N No No.
"Lovingly Yours"

F. Earl Christy, R&N 169
"The Pilot"

203 Daisies		
Edward Gross		
Series 3		
"Black Eyed Susan"	12 - 15	15 - 20
"Gold is not All"		
"Her Pilot"		
"In Deep Water"		
"Oldest Trust Co."		
"World Before Them"		
Knapp Co., N.Y. W. M. Sanford		
Paul Heckscher Import		
Series 304		
1 "Annie Laurie"	15 - 18	18 - 22
2 "The Lost Chord"		
3 "Louisiana Lou"		
4 "The Rosary"		
5 "The Largo"		
6 "Love's Old Sweet Song"		
7 "Daughter of the Regiment"		
8 "Good Night, Beloved"		
9 "The Gypsy Maid"		
10 "Maryland, My Maryland"		
11 "Home, Sweet Home"		
12 "Wish I Was in Dixie"		
Paul Heckscher Import W. M. Sanford		
Miniature Image Series 304	12 - 15	15 - 18
(Same as above but with different Nos.)		

371 "Annie Laurie"	15 - 18	18 - 22
381 "The Lost Chord"		
391 "Louisiana Lou"		
401 "The Rosary"		
411 "The Largo"		
421 "Love's Old Sweet Song"		
431 "Daughters of the Regiment"		
441 "Good Night, Beloved"		
451 "The Gypsy Maid"		
461 "Maryland, My Maryland"		
471 "Home, Sweet Home"		
481 "Wish I was in Dixie"		

Paul Hecksher Import
   Series 1025
   1025-3 "I'm Ready"   12 - 15   15 - 20

Knapp Co. (Cont.)
   103 Girl in Sailor Blouse and Hat   12 - 15   15 - 20
   105 Girl with Lace Collar
   114 Girl in Sailor Blouse
   115 Beauty, with Pearl Necklace
   116 Sweet Girl with Long Curl
   119 Blonde Girl with Black Pearls
   124 "Prudence"
   169 "Let's Go"
   176 "Skipper's Mate"

F. Earl Christy, R&N 363
"A Bit of Tea and Gossip"

F. Earl Christy, R&N 2105
"Always Winning"

F. Earl Christy, FAS
No Caption

F. Earl Christy, K. Co. 169
"Let's Go"

215 "Beauty"
219 "Anna Belle"
Note: There may be cards missing from
103 through 219.

Knapp Co.
   H. Import Series 318

"The Best of Chums"	12 - 15	15 - 20
"Blossoming Affection"		
"Goodbye Summer"		
"The Springtime of Friendship"		

Knapp Co.   H. Import
   Series 319

"Embracing the Opportunity"	12 - 15	15 - 20
"In Sweet Accord"		
"The Message of the Rose"		
"Tempting Fate"		

Knapp Co. by Sanford
   Calendar Card, 1916

"I Wish I Was in Dixie"	18 - 22	22 - 25
Others		

Julius Bien, 1907

College Series 95	18 - 22	22 - 25

Girl and Boy on Football
950   "Yale"
951   "Harvard"
952   "Columbia"

953 "Penn"
954 "Princeton"
955 "Cornell"
Atkinson News Agency
"Tilton Seminary" ⸴ 30 - 35 ⸴ 35 - 40
Chapman, N.Y., 1910
1032 "A Brisk Walk" ⸴ 10 - 12 ⸴ 12 - 15
1034 "Waiting Their Turn"
1039 "At the Horse Show"
William B. Christy (His Father)
Unnumbered Series
"Harvard," "Michigan," "Penn," ⸴ 12 - 15 ⸴ 15 - 20
"Princeton," "Yale"
EAS (Ea. Schwerd Teger)
Girl on Brick Wall Series
"Columbia," "Cornell," "Harvard" ⸴ 15 - 18 ⸴ 18 - 22
"Penn," "Princeton," "Yale"
H. Henninger Co.
40 Driving ⸴ 8 - 10 ⸴ 10 - 12
44 In an Auto (Same as **FAS** 201) ⸴ 10 - 12 ⸴ 12 - 15
45 Daisies
Illustrated Postal Card & Novelty Co.
Series 133*
1 "Cornell" ⸴ 12 - 15 ⸴ 15 - 20
2 "Harvard"
3 "Yale"
4 "Penn"
5 "Princeton"
6 "Columbia"
* With Silk Applique Dress, add $10-15.
Series 150* ⸴ 10 - 12 ⸴ 12 - 15
1 "Cornell"
2 "Harvard"
3 "Yale"
4 "Penn"
5 "Princeton"
6 "Columbia"
* With Silk Applique Dress, add $10-15.
Note: Nos. are on backs of some cards.
Series 160, 1907
160-1 "A Drama" ⸴ 12 - 15 ⸴ 15 - 18
160-2 "A Critical Moment"
160-3 "The World was Made ..."
160-4 "An Attractive Parasol"
160-5 "Getting Acquainted"
160-6
"Sports" Series
552D Swinging ⸴ 8 - 10 ⸴ 10 - 12
554 Bowling
557 Rowing
562 Swimming
567 Driving Old Car
569 Four Princeton Girls in Auto
572 Golf ⸴ 15 - 18 ⸴ 18 - 22

574	Princeton Belles in Old Car	8 - 10	10 - 12
577	Buggy		
582	Three Yale Girls in Auto		
584	Tennis	15 - 18	18 - 22

Ill. P.C. & Novelty Co.

Series 5006   6 - 8   8 - 10

3	"Swinging"		
7	Golf Girl	15 - 18	18 - 22
8	Horse & Buggy	6 - 8	8 - 10
9	Old Car-Harvard		
10	Old Car-Yale		
11	Old Car-Princeton		
12	Old Car-Penn		

Platinachrome, 1907
Girl/Pennant form Letter, College Yell
"Chicago," "Columbia," "Cornell," "Harvard"   22 - 25   25 - 30
"Michigan," "Penn," "Princeton," "Yale"

Platinachrome, © 1905 F. Earl Christy
No Numbers or Captions

Two Women in a Car	10 - 12	12 - 15
Woman Golfing	15 - 18	18 - 22
Woman Bowling	10 - 12	12 - 15
Woman-Ice Hockey		

P. Sander, N.Y., 1907 (Ill. P.C. Co.)

Series 198

1	"Is a Caddie always necessary"	20 - 25	25 - 30
2	"Is horseback riding ..."	10 - 12	12 - 15
3	"Trying to make a hit"		
4	"A Good Racquet for Two"	15 - 18	18 - 22
5	"Out for a catch"	10 - 12	12 - 15
6	"Hockey is not the only game"	12 - 15	15 - 18

P. Sander, N.Y., 1908

Series 246   Large Hats*   (6)

1	Full Photo	6 - 8	8 - 12
2	1910 Calendar	10 - 12	12 - 15
3	Christmas, Silver	6 - 8	8 - 10
4	Christmas, Gold		
5	Woman in Easter Egg		
6	Valentine		

* Full card is signed; others cropped & uns.
Note: There are 6 diff. cards of each image!

Series 304-A   (6) Signed, 1908

1	Full Card	8 - 10	10 - 12
2	Birthday, White	6 - 8	8 - 10
3	Birthday, Gold	6 - 8	8 - 10
4	Birthday, Silver		
5	Woman in Egg		
6	Valentine, Checkered		
7	Valentine, Gold		
8	Horse Shoe, Birthday, White		
9	Horse Shoe, Birthday, Gold		
10	Horse Shoe, Birthday, Silver		

F. Earl Christy, P. Sander, Series 198-1
"Is a Caddie Always Necessary"

Note: 10 different cards of each image!

W. H. Sanford   Series 371
   "Goodbye Summer"   12 - 15   15 - 18
   "Tempting Fate"

Stecher Litho Co., N.Y.
   Series 618, Valentines   8 - 10   10 - 12
   A   "To My Sweetheart"
   B   "Valentine Thoughts" (Unsigned)
   C   "To My Valentine" (Unsigned)
   D   "A Valentine Greeting"
   F   "A Valentine Greeting"

Souvenir Postcard Co., © 1907 E. Christy
   Girl and Football Player with Banner   15 - 18   18 - 22
   1   "Michigan"
   2   "Chicago"
   3   "Princeton"
   4   "Penn"
   5   "Cornell"
   6   "Yale"
   7   "Harvard"
   8   "Columbia"
   University Girl Series 2453
   "Georgetown," "Oberlin College"   18 - 22   22 - 25
   "Syracuse," "West Point"
   "Tennessee," "U.S. Naval Academy"
   Series 2590
   "Ames," "U. of Arkansas," "Iowa,"   18 - 22   22 - 25
   "Kentucky, "Penn State," "Valparaiso U."
   "Penn State"

Series 2593
"Bucknell," "Colby"   18 - 22   22 - 25
"U. of Maine," "U. of Notre Dame"
Series 2717
"Mary Baldwin Seminary"   22 - 25   25 - 30
University Girl Series 2625
"Columbia," "Cornell," "Harvard"   15 - 18   18 - 22
"Penn," "Princeton," "Yale"
Series 2626
"U. of Chicago," "U. of Illinois"   15 - 18   18 - 22
"Indiana U.," "U. of Michigan"
"U. of Minnesota," "U. of Wisconsin"
Series 2627
"Brown U.," "McGill College"   18 - 22   22 - 25
"Tulane of La." "Vanderbilt U."
"U. of Virginia," "Williston Seminary"
Series 2766 College Kings
"Columbia," "Cornell"   70 - 80   80 - 90
"Chicago," "Michigan"
Series 2767 College Queens
"Yale," "Penn," "Harvard," "Princeton"   70 - 80   80 - 90
"Good Luck" Series 2769
"Not only for today ..."   10 - 12   12 - 15
"Good luck attend you ..."
"Good wishes greet you ..."
"May Fortune spin ..."
Series 2794, "Williston"   100 - 125   125 - 150
Ullman Mfg. Co.
College Girls, Series 24, © 1905 (Uns.)
   1498   "Penn"   12 - 15   15 - 18
   1499   "Columbia"
   1512   "Yale"
   1513   "Harvard"
   1514   "Leland Stanford"
   1515   "Cornell"
   1516   "Princeton"
   1517   "Chicago"
College Football Players
Series 24, © 1905 (Unsigned)
   1464   "Harvard"   12 - 15   15 - 18
   1465   "Princeton"
   1466   "Penn"
   1467   "Yale"   12 - 15   15 - 18
   1518   "Columbia"
   1519   "Leland Stanford"
   1520   "Chicago"
   1521   "Cornell"
Ullman 1907
Girl in Big College Letter Series
   1990   "Chicago"   15 - 18   18 - 22
   1991   "Cornell"
   1992   "Michigan"
   1993   "Columbia"

1994	"Penn"		
1995	"Yale"		
1996	"Princeton"		
1997	"Harvard"		

Other Ullman College Girls

569	"Princeton"	10 - 12	12 - 15
574	"Penn"		
575	"Harvard"		
582	"Yale"		

Ullman Co., 1905, N.Y.

501	"Golf"	10 - 12	12 - 15
506	"A Pleasant Ride"	4 - 6	6 - 8
507	"In Fair Japan"	4 - 6	6 - 8
1583	"The Graduate"	8 - 10	10 - 12
1583	Var. of "The Graduate" (with verse)	12 - 15	15 - 18
Series 93		8 - 10	10 - 12

U.S.S.P.C. Co. 1905 College Seal Series

1	"Penn"	10 - 12	12 - 15
2	"Princeton"		
3	"Harvard" (also leather) *		
4	"Yale"		
5	"Michigan"		
6	"Chicago"		
7	"Columbia"		
8	"Cornell"		

* Add $5-10 for leather cards.

Valentine & Sons

"Artotype" Series, No Numbers	15 - 18	18 - 22
"Columbia"		
"Penn"		

Friedman-Shelby Shoe Co.

Big Hat Series

Shoe Style 3324	25 - 30	30 - 35
Shoe Style 3332		
The Style 3151		
Red Goose School Shoes		
Shoe Style 3339		

Greenfield's Delatour Chocolates, 1911

Girl W/Big Hat, Walks Right	25 - 30	30 - 40

Bulls-Eye Overalls
UNKNOWN
© **1910 F. Earl Christy**

Bust of woman w/nosegay & big hat	8 - 10	10 - 12
Blue dress and pink flowers		
Blue hat and red flowers		
Orange hat and yellow flowers		

Water Colors

650-5	"Embracing the Opportunity"	12 - 15	15 - 18
656-5	"In Sweet Accord"		
657-5	"Vacation Days"		

FINNISH ISSUES
Pain. Karjalan Kirjap. Oy, Viipuri

N:0 12 Unsigned, no caption.		
Same as R&N 173, "Love All" Tennis	30 - 35	35 - 40

N:0 6   Signed, no caption.
Girl in white, w/big red umbrella .... 30 - 35 ... 35 - 40
No Identification Series
Unsigned, no caption. Same as
R&N 365, "For the Wedding Chest" .... 25 - 30 ... 30 - 35
W. & G. American Series N:o 7001/1-35
Girl with long stemmed roses. .... 30 - 35 ... 35 - 40
CHRISTY, HOWARD CHANDLER
Moffat, Yard, & Co., N.Y., 1905
"The Christy Post Card"

1	"Arbutus" (B&W)	8 - 10	10 - 12
2	"At the Opera"	10 - 12	12 - 15
3	"A City Girl" (B&W)	8 - 10	10 - 12
	Also in partial color.	10 - 12	12 - 15
4	"The Dance"		
5	"The Debutante"		
6	"Encore"		
7	"Mistletoe" (B&W)	8 - 10	10 - 12
	Also in partial color.	10 - 12	12 - 15
8	"A Moment of Reflection"		
9	"Reverie" (B&W)	8 - 10	10 - 12
10	"A Suburban Girl" (B&W)		
11	"The Summer Girl" (B&W)		
12	"Violets" (B&W)		
	Also in partial color.	10 - 12	12 - 15
13	"Waiting"		
14	"Water Lilies" (B&W)	8 - 10	10 - 12
15	"The Winter Girl" (B&W)		

Unnumbered Series, 1908

"The American Queen"	10 - 12	12 - 15
"American Beauties"		
"At the Theater"		
"Canoe Mates"		
"Drifting"		
"Excess Baggage"		
"A Fisherman's Luck"		
"The Golf Girl"	20 - 25	25 - 28
"Lilies"	10 - 12	12 - 15
"On the Beach"	10 - 12	12 - 14
"Sailing Close"	8 - 10	10 - 12
"A Summer Girl"	10 - 12	12 - 14
"Teasing"	8 - 10	10 - 12
"A Winning Hand"	10 - 12	12 - 14

Edward Gross
Series 3, 1909

"Black-Eyed Susan"	8 - 10	10 - 12
"Gold is Not All"		
"Her Pilot"		
"In Deep Water"	10 - 12	12 - 14
"Miss Demure"		
"The Oldest Trust Company"	8 - 10	10 - 12
"A Plea For Arbitration"		
"The Sweet Girl Graduate"	10 - 12	12 - 14
"The Teasing Girl"		

H. C. Christy, Moffat, Yard
"A Suburban Girl"

H. C. Christy, E. Gross, Ser. 3
"Miss Demure"

Series 4, 1909
  "Au Revoir," "Congratulations"   10 - 12   12 - 15
  "The Heart of America," "Her Gift"
  "Honeymoon," "Into the Future"
  "Life's Beginning," "Love Spats"
  "Mistletoe," "Overpowering Beauty"
  "A Rose on the Lips"
Series of 6
  "A Fisherman's Luck," "The American Queen" 10 - 12   12 - 15
  "Teasing," "The World Before Them"
Scribner's   **Series of 8**   10 - 12   12 - 15
Armour & Co, Chicago, 1901 Ad Card
  "The Howard Chandler Christy Girl" (B&W)   15 - 20   20 - 25
  Same, by German Publisher (B&W)   20 - 25   25 - 30
A & V, Jamestown Expo., 1907
  "The Army Girl" and "The Navy Girl"   225 - 250   250 - 275
H. Choate & Co.
  Djer-Kiss Rouge & Face Power Compacts
  "American Brunette"   25 - 30   30 - 35
Curt Teich & Co.
  "Boy Scout Jamboree" (Linen, 1937)   10 - 12   12 - 15
T.P. & Co.
Judge Co., N.Y., Series 751
  "You Have a Wonderful Future!"   12 - 15   15 - 18
  "Going Away" (Unsigned)

FOREIGN
Novitas   Series 21655

"City Girl," "Drifting"	12 - 15	15 - 20
"Reverie," "A Summer Girl"	14 - 16	16 - 20
"Violets" "The World Before Them"	12 - 14	14 - 18
Series 21657 (6)	12 - 14	14 - 18

Pain. Karjalan Kirjap. Oy, Viipuri

N:O 2 Three Bathing Girls	22 - 25	25 - 30

CLAY, JOHN C. (U.S.)
Detroit Pub. Co.

	10 - 12	12 - 15

Rotograph Co.
Water Color Series 160-172

"Garden of Love" Ser. (12) Head in Flowers	30 - 35	35 - 40

Armour & Co., Advertising Card

"The John C. Clay Girl" (B&W)	10 - 12	12 - 15
Same, by German Publisher (B&W)	12 - 15	15 - 18

CLIRIO, L. (Italy) Art Deco
Degami

Series 29	15 - 18	18 - 22

Series 30 Couples
COFFIN, HASKELL (U.S.)
R. C. Co., N.Y.
Series 205

"A Modern Eve"	20 - 25	25 - 28
"An American Queen"		
"The Glory of Autumn"		
"The Lure of the Poppies"		
"Miss Jack Frost"	20 - 22	22 - 25
"Motherhood"		
"Queen of the Court"		
"The Spring Maid"		
"Vanity Fair"		
"Winter's Charm"		

K. Co. Inc., N.Y.
Water Color Series

Water Color Series	18 - 22	22 - 25

152 "Motherhood"
215 "Beauty"
216 "Sally"
217 "Ruth"
218 "Billy"
Photo Color Graph Co. (PCG Co.)
Ser. 205 "Art Studies" (10)

1 "Bohemia"	15 - 18	18 - 22

2   "Senorita"
3   "Sweet Sixteen"
4   "The Final Touch"
5   "Her First Love Letter"
6   "Girl From the Golden West"
7   "June Roses"
8   "Pride of the Orient"
9   "News from the Sunny South"
"Flower & Figure Subjects"

Series 280, with verse (12)

1	Iris	15 - 18	18 - 22
2	Violet		
3	Poppies		
4	Narcissus		
5	Goldenrod		
6	Daffodils		
7	Hollyhock		
8	Water Lily		
9	Nasturtium		
10	Rose		
11	Sweet Pea		
12	Morning Glory		

Fantasy Women Series, Semi-Nude   18 - 22   22 - 25
"Celia"
Others

A. R. & C.i.B. Co. (R.C. Co.)
417 "An American Queen"   12 - 15   15 - 20
"A Modern Eve," "The Glory of Autumn"
"The Joy of the Hunt," "Miss Jack Frost"
"Ruth," "Winter's Charm," "Vanity Fair"
536 "The Heyday of Youth"

H & S Co.
1551 D3 "A New York Belle"   15 - 18   18 - 22
1551 D6 "Thoughtful"
Others with Captions
Others, No Captions   8 - 10   10 - 12

Novitas
   Series 15670
   1. Girl in white, yellow bow, big straw hat   15 - 18   18 - 22

Advertising Cards
Blue Bell Brand Candies (2)   22 - 25   25 - 30
ESK Co.
   02 Girl with Big Slouch Hat, No Caption   12 - 15   15 - 20
Hires Root Beer Girl   30 - 35   35 - 45

COLIN, PAUL   50 - 75   75 - 100
COLLINS, G.T. (G.B.)   10 - 12   12 - 15
COLOMBO, E. (Italy) Art Deco and Glamour
   Dell, Anna & Gasparini; Rev. Stampa

416 Couples, with Umbrella (6)	12 - 15	15 - 18
436, 451, 453 Hats (6)	15 - 18	18 - 22
228, 445, 560 High Fashion (6)	20 - 22	22 - 25
443, 522 High Fashion (6)	15 - 18	18 - 22
360, 419, 981 High Fashion	18 - 22	22 - 25
Series 178, 539, 925 High Fashion		
Series 948 "Egyptian" (6)	15 - 18	18 - 20
Series 459 Heads (6)	14 - 16	16 - 18
Series 478 Dancers (6)	18 - 20	20 - 22
Series 936 (6)	12 - 15	15 - 18
Golf	25 - 28	28 - 32
Tennis	18 - 22	22 - 25
Harlequins (Pierrot)	22 - 25	25 - 28
Colonial-Style Deco Ladies, Lovers	12 - 15	15 - 18

Ladies & Dogs		
Series 330 (6)	12 - 14	14 - 18
Series 530, 894, 1165, 1763 (6)	15 - 16	16 - 20
Series 1494 (6)	10 - 12	12 - 16
Ladies & Horses		
Series 202 (6)	12 - 15	15 - 18
Series 488, 813, 1676, 1869 (6)	15 - 18	18 - 22
COMBAZ, GISBERT (Belgium) Art Nouveau		
Dietrich, Brussels		
"Elements" Series (12)	140 - 150	150 - 175
"Proverbs" Series (12)		
"The Fishermen" Series (12)	150 - 175	175 - 200
"Sins" Series (12)		
COPPING, H.	4 - 6	6 - 8
CORBELLA, TITO (Italy) Art Deco & Glamour		
Dell, Anna & Gasparini; Rev. Stampa		
Miss Edith Cavell Death-Head Series	20 - 25	25 - 30
Series 127-M Small Images (6)	10 - 12	12 - 15
Series 162-M Small Image, Lovers (6)	8 - 10	10 - 12
Series 162, 355 (6)	14 - 16	16 - 20
Series 160, 203 High Fashion (6)	18 - 22	22 - 25
Series 408 Fans (6)	12 - 15	15 - 20
Series Chair and Fans (6)	15 - 18	18 - 22
Series 233, 356, 546, 718 Heads (6)		
Series 130, 203, 763 High Fashion (6)		
Series 282, 316, 317 Fashion (6)	12 - 15	15 - 20
Series 118, 324 Hats (6)	12 - 15	15 - 20
Series 357 Bear-Cupids (6)	14 - 16	16 - 20
Series 344, 467 High Fashion (6)	15 - 18	18 - 22
Series 102, 232, 267, 236, 516 (6)		
Series 162, 234, 269 Lovers-Kissing (6)	8 - 10	10 - 12
Series 225, 367, 531 Lovers-Kissing (6)		
Harlequins (Pierrot)	20 - 25	25 - 28
Degami		
Series 319, 868, 1011, 1049 (6)	16 - 18	18 - 22
Series 790, 1019 (4) Pierrot	20 - 25	25 - 30
Series 2087, 3026 (4) Pierrot	25 - 30	30 - 35
Series 2249 "Gypsy" (6)	10 - 12	12 - 15
Series 2250 In Oval (6)	8 - 10	10 - 12
Series 2071 Pierrot and lady (4) (Uns.)	20 - 22	22 - 25
Series 2072, 2160, 2287, 3033 (6)	12 - 14	14 - 16
Series 2214, 2224, 2228 (6)	15 - 18	18 - 22
Series 3016, 3027, 3055, 3056, 3123, 3560 (6)		
Series 617, 832 Lovers-Kissing (6)	8 - 10	10 - 12
Series 2283 (6) Not Deco		
Colonial-Style Deco Ladies, Lovers	12 - 15	15 - 18
Golf	25 - 30	30 - 35
Tennis	20 - 25	25 - 28
Erotic/Semi-Nudes		
Harlequins (Pierrot)		
Ladies/Dogs/Horses		
Rev. Stampa; Dell, Anna		
& Gasparini, Degami		
Series 117, 230 (6)	12 - 15	15 - 20

T. Corbella
Dell, Anna & Gasparini 237-6

E. Colombo
Proprieta Artistica 451-1

Series 233, 237, 316, 330 (6)	15 - 18	18 - 22
Series 335, 464, 624 (6)	12 - 15	15 - 18
Series 516, 532, 578 (6)	15 - 18	18 - 22
Series 530, 1085 (6)	12 - 15	15 - 18
Degami		
Series 636, 2224, 2258 (6)	22 - 25	25 - 30
Series 4646 (6)	15 - 18	18 - 22
COSTANZA, G. (Italy)		
Ladies	12 - 15	15 - 18
Comics/Erotic		
CRAMER, RIE	12 - 15	15 - 18
CRANDALL, JOHN BRADSHAW (U.S.)		
K. Co. Inc., N.Y.		
Watercolor Series		
113 "Tad"	15 - 18	18 - 22
Also with no caption		
118 Girl in white sunbonnet		
121 "Toots"		
137 "The Bohemian Girl"		
170 "The Pace Maker"		
No No. "A Romany Lass" (Uns.)		
CREMIEUX, ED. (France) French Glamour		
Delta Series 44	15 - 18	18 - 22
Series 27	15 - 18	18 - 20
CROTTA		
Rev. Stampa		
Series 3029 Lovers Kissing (6)	8 - 10	10 - 12

CYRANICUS (Italy)

Series 204 (6)	12 - 15	15 - 18
Ladies/Heads		
Ladies/Fashion		
Ladies/Animals	15 - 18	18 - 22
Golf	22 - 25	25 - 28
Tennis	15 - 18	18 - 22

Ladies & Horses

Series 150 (6)	10 - 12	12 - 15
Series 430 (6)	12 - 14	14 - 16

DANIELL, EVA (G.B.) Art Nouveau

Raphael Tuck (Uns.)

"Art" Series 2524 (6)	90 - 100	100 - 110
"Art" Series 2525 (6)	80 - 90	90 - 100
DAVIS, STANLEY (U.S.)	8 - 10	10 - 12
DAY, FRANCES (U.S.)	4 - 5	5 - 8
DEDINA, JAN (Poland)	10 - 12	12 - 15
DE FEURE, GEORGES Art Nouveau	25 - 35	35 - 40
DE MARZO (Art Deco)	22 - 25	25 - 35
DENNISON (U.S.)	3 - 4	4 - 5

DERNINI, D. (Italy) Art Deco

Ladies	15 - 20	20 - 25

DERRANTI, D. (Italy) Art Deco

"Elite" Series 2568	25 - 30	30 - 35

DESCH, FRANK (U.S.)

Knapp Co. (K Co., N.Y.) *

H. Import Series 300

"Laura"	18 - 22	22 - 25

Series 303 Watercolors

2 "Stella"	18 - 22	22 - 25
3 "Violet"		
4 "Elouise"		
5 "Grace"		
6 "Ida"		
7 "Isabel"		
8 "Eleanor"		
9 "Lillian"		
10 "Laura"		

* H. Import and Paul Heckscher distributed
Series 303 with same images but with
different numbers. H. Import and Heckscher
are the same company.

Series 308 (8) Watercolors

2 "Phoebe"	18 - 22	22 - 25
Others		

Series 309 (**H. Import**) Watercolors

1 "Katharine"	18 - 22	22 - 25
2 "Virginia"		
3 "Olivia"		
4 "Diana"		
6 "Florence"		
Others		

Series 336 (**H. Import**) No Captions

Same as "There He Goes"	15 - 18	18 - 22

Series 337 (H. Import)
Same as "Diana"
Series 1025 (Paul Heckscher) Watercolors

1 "There He Goes"	15 - 18	18 - 22
2 "Here They Come"		
Others		

Series 1027 (Paul Hecksher) Watercolors

1 "Katharine"	18 - 22	22 - 25
5 "Annette"		
Others		
Series 50	10 - 12	12 - 15
Others	12 - 15	15 - 18

Knapp Co., Calendars *   **
Some are calendars, others calendar types

515-4 "Annette" May, 1913	18 - 22	22 - 25

Series 6 (12)

502-3 "Stella"	18 - 20	20 - 25
50N-3 "Laura"		
9403 "Flora"		
9423 "Violet"		
9443 "Grace"		
9453 "Rosina"		
9473 "Isabel"		
9483 "Eleanor"		
9493 "Lillian"		
9503 "Laura"		
9513 "Felicia"		
69453 "Rosina"		
69513 "Felicia"		
No No. "Stella" Ad for Montgomery Ward	25 - 30	30 - 40

* Add $5-8 for Calendars
** Add $1-15 for Advertising Calendars
McGowan-Silsbee Litho

No caption (Grace)	10 - 12	12 - 15

Novitas (N in Star)

No captian Girl wearing Green Dress	15 - 18	18 - 22

Advertisement
Djer-Kiss Rouge (non p.c. back)

"Titan Type"	20 - 25	25 - 30
Others		

DEWEY, ALFRED (U.S.)
Boston Sunday Post

Romantic Baseball Series 22	10 - 12	12 - 15
"Caught Stealing," "A Costly Error"		
"A Double Play," "A Sacrifice"		
"A Single," "A Shut-Out"		

Reinthal & Newman

"Weather Forecast" Series 221 (12)	7 - 8	8 - 10
"Eventful Hours" Series 270-275	8 - 10	10 - 12
"Mother & Child" Series 450-455	7 - 8	8 - 10
"Love Signal" Series 456-461		
"Moon" Series 462-467	8 - 10	10 - 12
"Smoke" Series 668-673		
"Love & Nature" Series 807-812	7 - 8	8 - 10

Jean Domergue, Salon de Paris
6473, "Josephine Baker"

Jean Domergue, Salon de Paris
6465, "Josephine Baker"

DeYONCH, JOHN (U.S.)	5 - 6	6 - 8
DIEFENBACH, K.	8 - 10	10 - 15
DIETZE (Ladies & Dogs)		
Series 6026	10 - 12	12 - 15
DIHLEN, CHARLES WEBER (U.S.)	5 - 6	6 - 8
DILLON, C. B. (U.S.)	6 - 8	8 - 10
DITZLER, H. (U.S.)		
Gibson Art - Water Color Series	6 - 8	8 - 10
DOBROWOLSKI, A. (Poland)		
MJK Seasons Series 282 (4)	10 - 12	12 - 15
DOCKER, E. (Austria) Art Nouveau		
Raphael Neuber, Vienna, Head Series 26	50 - 60	60 - 75
Others	10 - 12	12 - 15
DOMERGE, JEAN-GABRIEL (France)		
A.N., Paris Nude Paintings on Real Photos		
6465 "Josephine Baker"	100 - 125	125 - 150
6466 "The Parasol"	40 - 50	50 - 60
6473 "Josephine Baker"	100 - 125	125 - 150
Others		
DONADINI, JR. (Italy)		
Series 1471 (6) Lovers-Cupid Series	8 - 10	10 - 12
Alfred Schweizer		
Military Heads	18 - 22	22 - 25
DOUBEK, F.		
Ackerman Co.		
"Historic Ladies" Series	12 - 15	15 - 18

Douky, Anonymous
"Joyeuses Paques"

G. Ellka, M. Munk 443
No Caption

EMM		
585 "Schmetterling"	10 - 12	12 - 15
DOUKY (France)		
Fantasy Fashions	12 - 15	15 - 18
E.D.F., Paris		
Series 505 Big Skirt (6)	12 - 14	14 - 16
Others	12 - 14	14 - 16
DRESSLER, A. E. (U.S.)	6 - 8	8 - 10
DUDOVICH, M. (Italy) Art Deco		
"Eureka" Series IV (6)	12 - 15	15 - 20
Early Deco Series	75 - 100	100 - 150
Lovers Series (in car; picnic)	30 - 35	35 - 38
Others		
DuFRESNE, PAUL	4 - 6	6 - 8
DUNCAN, FREDERICK (U.S.)		
K. Co. Inc., N.Y. Watercolors		
125 "Dorothy"	15 - 18	18 - 22
126 "Meditating"		
128 "Reflecting"		
129 "Gloria"		
130 "Posing"		
131 "Beautifying"		
132 "Dreaming"		
134 "Helene"		
135 "Patricia"		
136 "Florella"		

137 "The Bohemian Girl"		
138 "Florence"		
139 "Pleading"		
140 "Muriel"		
141 "Shopping"		
142 "Marjorie"		
143 "Kathleen"		
144 "Watching"		
173 "Motoring"		
174 "Riding"		
175 "Phoebe"		
178 "Swimming"		

M. & B. (Meissner & Buch)
Series 1415 (6)

On Train - His Hat	10 - 12	12 - 15
Others		

Reinthal & Newman
930-935 Series   Watercolors

930 "She's My Daisy"	12 - 15	15 - 20
931 "A Reserved Seat"	15 - 18	18 - 22
932 "For You a Rose"	12 - 15	15 - 20
933 "So Near, Yet so Far"		
934 "The Call of the Country"	15 - 18	18 - 22
935 "Won't You Come Back"	12 - 15	15 - 18

EB (Italy)

Rev. Stampa **Series 61** (Art Nouveau Ladies)	20 - 25	25 - 30

ELLETTI (Italy) Art Deco

Celesque Series National Ladies	15 - 20	20 - 25

ELLIOTT, KATHRYN (U.S.)

Gartner & Bender Issues	6 - 8	8 - 10
G.O.M. **1985-1990 Deco Birthday Series**	12 - 15	15 - 20

ELLKA, G. (Austria)
M. Munk, Vienna (Chromolithographs)

Series 443 Head Studies (6)	15 - 20	20 - 25

ERTE (France) Modern

"Stolen Kiss" (Serigraph)	4 - 5	5 - 8
"Foiles Bergeres"		

FABIANO (France) Art Deco and Glamour

Delta Series 5	12 - 15	15 - 20
Series 7, 11, 15	18 - 22	22 - 30
Series 32, 59, 63	15 - 18	18 - 22

M.L.E., Paris Series 63 At the Beach

FAINI (Italy)	10 - 12	12 - 14

FARINI, MAY L.

Black & White Issues	5 - 6	6 - 8
With "Feliz Dia" Caption - Lady/Dog	6 - 8	8 - 10
Color Issues	10 - 12	12 - 16
FERRARIS, A.V.	8 - 10	10 - 12
FIDLER, ALICE LUELLA (U.S.)	12 - 15	15 - 18
(Also Alice Fidler Person)		
FIDLER, PEARLE EUGENIA	12 - 15	15 - 18
(Also Pearle Fidler LeMunyan)		
FIDLER, ELSIE CATHERINE	12 - 15	15 - 18

The Fidler Works by **E. Gross & Ullman Mfg.**

Alice Louella Fidler	*Pearl Fidler LeMunyan*	*Alice Fidler Person*
E. Gross, 72	*E. Gross, 119*	*E. Gross, 132*

FINNEMORE, J.	5 - 6	6 - 7
FISCHER, C. (U.S.)	6 - 8	8 - 10
FISCHER, PAUL (Denmark)		
Arthur Schurer	10 - 12	12 - 15
Tennis	12 - 15	15 - 18
FISHER, BILL		
John Neury-Geneva		
Romantic Couples, ladies	6 - 8	8 - 10

FISHER, HARRISON (U.S.)

Harrison Fisher was one of the most prolific of all American illustrators and his beautiful ladies postcards are collected by more people than any other artist. His works of glamorous women of the era are desired by collectors throughout the world. The values of his postcards tend to rise yearly as new image findings tend to inspire all who collect them.

The New York firm of Reinthal & Newman was the principal publisher and distributor of Fisher postcards. They produced many of his cards in various series ranging from the No-Numbered, the 100's, and on through the rare and final 900 series, and then did the American and English reprints in the 1000 and 2000 series.

The Detroit Publishing Company, beginning around 1905, published a small group of Fisher cards from what were originally illustrations for stories in the old *LIFE* magazine. The cards were numbered in the 14,000 series and were printed mainly in sepia with a few in black and white.

American book publishers who used Fisher's illustrations in their novels issued postcards to advertise their books. These advertising postcards usually showed a beautiful Fisher lady on one-half of the double cards and an order form on the other half. These cards are among the most sought after and most expensive of his American-published cards.

Foreign publishers also did several series which are very much in demand. Among the most elusive, and those commanding the highest prices, are the cards produced in Finland and Russia. The flow of beautiful cards from Russia since the wall was removed has been very dramatic and has given Fisher collectors more wonderful cards to add to their collections. Over 100 new Fisher cards have surfaced since the release of the 2nd edition of "The Postcard Price Guide," and these are included in this 3rd edition.

Albertype Co.
    Indian Maid - Painted on Sandstone Rock

Tassajarla Hot Springs, California	80 - 90	90 - 100
Daley-Soeger Co.		
Indian Maid, as above	90 - 100	100 - 110
Detroit Publishing Co.*	15 - 18	18 - 22
14028 "I don't see ..."		
14036 "An Important ..."		
14037 "So you don't Kiss ..."		
14038 "Between Themselves ..."		
14039 "Can you give your Answer?"		
14040 "I suppose you Lost ..."		
14041 "It's just Horrid ..."		
14042 "Wasn't There ..."		
14043 "And shall we Never ..."		
14044 "I fear there is no Hope"		

* 2 Different Varieties: 1 -- Information at Top and 1 -- Information at Bottom

Book Adv. Cards (G&D, Dodd-Mead, etc.)

Double-folded Cards, Entire Card	200 - 250	250 - 300
With Reply Section Missing		
"The Bill Toppers"	150 - 175	175 - 200
"Half A Rogue"		
"The Hungry Heart"		
"Jane Cable"	100 - 125	125 - 150
"Jewel Weed"	150 - 175	175 - 200
"The Man From Brodney's"		
"My Lady of Cleeve"		
"Nedra"	100 - 125	125 - 150
"The One Way Out"	150 - 175	175 - 200
"The Stooping Lady"		
"The Violet Book" by Bettina von Hutten	250 - 300	300 - 325
"A Taste of Paradise"	150 - 175	175 - 200
"The Title Market"		
"To My Valentine"		
"The Goose Girl"	250 - 300	300 - 325
"Francezka"	150 - 175	175 - 200
"My Commencement"		
Armour & Co., U.S. (B&W), Narrow Size	50 - 60	60 - 70
Armour & Co., German (B&W), Narrow	70 - 75	75 - 80
Warren's Featherbone Corsets		
"The Featherbone Girl"	90 - 100	100 - 120
Frank V. Draper Co., Des Moines		
Illustration from *"Jane Cable"*		
"His feeble glance took in her face..."	125 - 150	150 - 175

Klaus Mfg. Co., NY
   K. 405 Advertising Play *"Beverly of*
     Graustark" "Beverly Calhoun" 150 - 175 175 - 200
Metropolitan P.C. Co. (M in Bean Pot)
   "Illustration from *"Jane Cable"*
   No Caption. Old man and sitting girl 125 - 150 150 - 175
Curt Teich (C.T. American Art)
   Illustration from *"Nedra"*
     No Caption. Sailor Girl on ship deck
   Illustration from *"Jane Cable"*
     No Caption. Girl and man at table.
Tichnor Bros., Boston
   Illustration from *"Truxton King"*
   126984 No Caption. Man, boy and dog
Zim (H.G. Zimmerman, Chicago)
   Illustration from *"Jane Cable"*
   No Caption. Girl's backview sits in chair
Anonymous
   Illustration from *"Nedra"* by Dodd-Mead
   "Grace Vernon"
Reinthal & Newman
   Unnumbered Series (some by Chas. Hauff)
     "A Fair Driver" 12 - 15 15 - 20
     "All Mine"
     "After the Dance"
     "The Critical Moment"
     "The Motor Girl" 18 - 22 22 - 25
     "Over the Teacup" 12 - 18 18 - 22
     "Ready for the Run" 12 - 15 15 - 20
     "Ruth"
     "A Tennis Champion" 22 - 25 25 - 30
     "The Winter Girl" 15 - 18 18 - 22
       With overprinting 18 - 22 22 - 25
     "Those Bewitching Eyes" 15 - 18 18 - 22
   101 Series (12)
     "American Beauties" With cat 12 - 15 15 - 20
     "American Beauties" With dog
     "Anticipation" 12 - 15 15 - 18
     "Beauties"
     "Danger" 10 - 12 12 - 15
     "A Fair Driver" 15 - 18 18 - 22
     "Odd Moments" 12 - 15 15 - 20
     "The Old Miniature"
     "Over the Tea Cup" 15 - 18 18 - 22
     "Reflections" 15 - 18 18 - 22
     "The Study Hour" 12 - 15 15 - 18
     "A Thoroughbred" 18 - 22 22 - 25
     "Those Bewitching Eyes" 12 - 15 15 - 18
   102 Series (6)
     "American Girl in England" 15 - 20 20 - 25
     "American Girl in France"
     "American Girl in Ireland"
     "American Girl in Italy"
     "American Girl in Japan"

(1) H. G. Zimmerman
From "Jane Cable"

(2) Metropolitan PC Co.
From "Jane Cable"

(3) C. T. American Art
From "Jane Cable"

(4) C. T. American Art
From "Nedra"

(5) Tichnor Bros.
From "Truxton King"

"HIS FEEBLE GLANCE TOOK IN HER FACE WITH LIFELESS INTEREST"

(6) Frank V. Draper Co.
From "Jane Cable"

GRACE VERNON

(7) Anonymous
From "Nedra"

New U.S. Publisher Images from Book Illustrations by Harrison Fisher

No Captions Listed Other than ...

(6) "His Feeble Glance Took In Her Face ..."
(7) "Grace Vernon"
(8) "Beverly Calhoun" The Play

BEVERLY CALHOUN
George Barr McCutcheon's
"Beverly of Graustark."

(8) Kraus Mfg. Co., K.405
"Beverly of Graustark"

"American Girl in Netherlands"

103 Series (6)

"An Hour with Art"	15 - 18	18 - 22
"The Canoe"	12 - 15	15 -20
"Engagement Days"		
"Fisherman's Luck"		
"Fore"	22 - 26	26 - 30
"Wanted, an Answer"	12 - 15	15 - 18

108 Series (12)

"An Old Song"	12 - 15	15 - 20
"The Ambush"		
"The Artist"		
"The Bride"	20 - 22	22 - 26
"The Debutante"	15 - 18	18 - 22
"Dumb Luck"		
"He's Only Joking"		
"His Gift"		
"The Kiss"	12 - 15	15 - 20
"Lost?"	15 - 18	18 - 22
"Oh! Promise Me"		
"Song of the Soul"		
"Two Up"	18 - 22	22 - 25

123 Series (6)

"Making Hay"	12 - 15	15 - 20
"A Modern Eve"	15 - 18	18 - 22
"Taking Toll"	12 - 15	15 - 20
"You Will Marry a Dark Man"		
"The Fudge Party"	15 - 18	18 - 22
"The Canoe"		
"In Clover"		

180-185 Series

180 "Well Protected"	18 - 22	22 - 25
181 "The Rose"	15 - 18	18 - 22
182 "Miss Santa Claus"	25 - 28	28 - 32
183 "Miss Knickerbocker"	15 - 18	18 - 22
184 "Following the Race"		
185 "Naughty, Naughty!"	20 - 22	22 - 25

186-191 Series "The Greatest Period in a Girl's Life"

186 "The Proposal"	15 - 18	18 - 22
187 "The Trousseau"		
188 "The Wedding"		
189 "The Honeymoon"		
190 "The First Evening ..."		
191 "Their New Love"		

192-203 Series

192 "Cherry Ripe"	18 - 22	22 - 25
193 "Undue Haste"		
194 "Sweetheart"		
195 "Vanity"		
196 "Beauties"		
197 "Lips for Kisses"		
198 "Bewitching Maiden"		
199 "Leisure Moments"		

200 "And Yet Her Eyes..."		
201 "Roses"		
202 "In the Toils"		
203 "Maid to Worship"	22 - 25	25 - 28
252-263 Series		
252 "Dreaming of You"	15 - 18	18 - 22
253 "Luxury"		
254 "Pals"		
255 "Homeward Bound"	12 - 15	15 - 18
256 "Preparing to Conquer"	15 - 18	18 - 22
257 "Love Lyrics"		
258 "Tempting Lips"		
259 "Good Night"	12 - 15	15 - 18
260 "Bows Attract Beaus"	15 - 18	18 - 22
261 "Girlie"		
262 "Beauty and Value"		
263 "A Prairie Belle"		
300 Series		
300 "Auto Kiss"	18 - 20	20 - 25
301 "Sweethearts Asleep"	22 - 25	25 - 30
302 "Behave!"	15 - 18	18 - 22
303 "All Mine!"	12 - 15	15 - 18
304 "Thoroughbreds"	20 - 22	22 - 25
305 "The Laugh is on You"	15 - 18	18 - 22
Water Color Series 381-392		
381 "All's Well"	18 - 22	22 - 25
382 "Two Roses"		
383 "Contentment"		
384 "Not Yet - But Soon"	15 - 18	18 - 22
385 "Smile Even if it Hurts"		
386 "Speak!"	15 - 20	20 - 25
387 "Welcome Home"	12 - 15	15 - 18
388 "A Helping Hand"		
389 "Undecided"	15 - 20	20 - 25
390 "Well Guarded"		
391 "My Lady Waits"		
392 "Gathering Honey"	15 - 18	18 - 22
400-423 Series		
400 "Looking Backward"	25 - 30	30 - 35
401 "Art and Beauty"		
402 "The Chief Interest"		
403 "Passing Fancies"		
404 "The Pink of Perfection"		
405 "He Won't Bite"		
406 "Refreshments"		
407 "Princess Pat"		
408 "Fine Feathers"		
409 "Isn't He Sweet?"		
410 "Maid at Arms"		
411 "He Cometh Not"		
412 "Can't You Speak?"		
413 "What Will She Say?"		
414 "Music Hath Charm"		
415 "Do I Intrude"		

416 "My Queen"
417 "My Lady Drives"
418 "Ready and Waiting"
419 "The Parasol"
420 "Tempting Lips"
421 "Mary"
422 "Courting Attention"
423 "My Pretty Neighbor"
600-617 Series

600 "A Winter Sport"	25 - 30	30 - 35
601 "Winter Whispers"		
602 "A Christmas Him"		
603 "A Sprig of Holly"		
604 "Snow Birds"		
605 "A Christmas Belle"		
606 "The Serenade"		
607 "The Secret"		
608 "Good Morning, Mama"		
609 "A Passing Glance"		
610 "A Fair Exhibitor"		
611 "Paddling Their Own Canoe"		
612 "Tea Time"		
613 "The Favorite Pillow"		
614 "Don't Worry"		
615 "June"		
616 "Sketching"		
617 "Chocolate"		

700-705 Water Color Series
"The Senses"

700 "The First Meeting" Sight	25 - 30	30 - 35
701 "Falling in Love" Smell		
702 "Making Progress" Taste		
703 "Anxious Moments" Hearing		
704 "To Love and Cherish" Touch		
705 "The Greatest Joy" Common Sense		

762-773 Series

762 "Alone at Last"	12 - 15	15 - 20
763 "Alert"	15 - 18	18 - 22
764 "Close to Shore"		
765 "Looks Good to Me"	12 - 15	15 - 20
766 "Passers By"		
767 "At the Toilet"	15 - 18	18 - 22
768 "Drifting" *	12 - 15	15 - 20
768 Untitled, Oversize "Her Favorite Him" *	22 - 25	25 - 30
769 "Her Favorite Him" *	12 - 15	15 - 20
770 "The Third Party" *		
771 "Inspiration" *	15 - 18	18 - 22
772 "Dangers of the Deep" *	12 - 15	15 - 20
773 "Farewell" *		

*Add $5 to prices if German caption.
Cards usually are slightly oversized
and have Universal copyright.
800 Series

819 "Here's Happiness"	20 - 22	22 - 25

800 Series
Cosmopolitan or Star bylines, etc.

832 "Wireless"	32 - 35	35 - 38
833 "Neptune's Daughter"		
834 "Her Game"	35 - 38	38 - 42
835 "All Mine"	32 - 35	35 - 38
836 "On Summer Seas"		
837 "Autumn's Beauty"		
838 "The Only Pebble"		
839 "A Love Score"	30 - 35	35 - 40
840 "Spring Business"	32 - 35	35 - 38
841 "The King of Hearts"		
842 "Fair and Warmer"		
843 "Baby Mine"		
844 "Compensation"		
845 "Sparring for Time"		
846 "Confidences"		
847 "Her Future"		
848 "Day Dreams"		
849 "Muriel"		
856 "Song of the Soul"	25 - 28	28 - 32
860 "By right of Conquest" *	28 - 32	32 - 35
861 "The Evening Hour" *		
862 "Caught Napping" *		
863 "A Novice" *	25 - 28	28 - 32
864 "Winners" *	30 - 35	35 - 38
865 "A Midsummer Reverie" *		
866 "When the Leaves Turn" *	25 - 30	30 - 35
867 "Over the Teacup"		
868 "A Ripening Bud" *		
869 "I'm Ready" *		
870 "Reflections" *		
871 "Peggy" *		
872 "Penseroso" *		
873 "The Girl He Left Behind" *		
874 "A Spring Blossom" *		
875 "A Study in Contentment" *	25 - 28	28 - 32
876 "A Lucky Beggar" *		
877 "Roses" *		

*With Cosmopolitan Print Dept. byline, add $5.

900-979 Series

970 "Chums"	100 - 125	125 - 150
971 "Cynthia"		
972 "A Forest Flower"		
973 "The Dancing Girl"		
974 "Each Stitch a Prayer"	125 - 150	150 - 175
975 "The Sailor Maid"		
976 "My Man"		
977 "My Hero"		
978 "Her Heart's in Service"		
979 "Somewhere in France"	150 - 175	175 - 200

1000 -1005 Series - American Reprints

1000 "Drifting"	30 - 35	35 - 40

R&N 974
"Each Stitch a Prayer"

R&N 975
"The Sailor Maid"

R&N 976
"My Man"

R&N 977
"My Hero"

R&N 978, "Her Heart's
in the Service"

R&N 979
"Somewhere in France"

The Harrison Fisher cards shown above are the World War I service-related issues and are the rarest and most desired of the 900 Series.

2046 "Princess Pat"
2047 "Good Little Indian"
2048 "Chocolate"
2049 "Beauty and Value"
2050 "Contentment"
2051 "Preparing to Conquer"
2053 "The Kiss"
2054 "What to See in America"
2069 "Paddling their own Canoe"
2076 "Good Morning, Mama"
2086 "The Pink of Perfection"
2087 "He Won't Bite"
2088 "Following the Race"
2089 "The Rose"
2090 "Well Protected"
2091 "Sketching"
2092 "Ready and Waiting"
2093 "The Parasol"
2094 "Courting Attention"
2095 "Mary"
2096 "Refreshments"
2097 "Isn't He Sweet?"
2098 "The Old Miniature"
2099 "Beauties"
2100 "Odd Moments"
2101 "Tea Time"
2102 "Good Night!"
2103 "A Prairie Belle"

FOREIGN ISSUES

FINNISH

The numbering system for all series of Finnish cards was taken from "The Super Rare Postcards of Harrison Fisher."

All Finnish cards are very rare and extremely elusive. None have the R&N Copyright and all are untitled with the exception of **The Real Photo Series**. Cards are titled using names from similar R&N images. Several have not appeared as postcards and are named if a title is known. Three have been entitled by the author until the true title surfaces. (Titles have now been found for **"Merry Christmas"** in the **30/25 Series** and for **"Eavesdropping"** in the **W. & G. American Series 7031/1-7** and **Publisher at Polyphot Series.**

30/25 Series -- The unsigned cards in this series have been found to be much rarer than first anticipated by the author. For that reason, values for all unsigned cards are now listed.

S=Signed; US=Unsigned

3025-1-S "Snowbird" *	225 - 250	250 - 275
3025-1-US "Snowbird"	250 - 275	275 - 325
3025-1-S Variation "Snowbird"	275 - 300	300 - 350

3025-2-S "Merry Christmas" by author *	225 - 250	250 - 275
True title is "The Debutante"		
3025-2-US "The Debutante"	250 - 275	275 - 325
3025-3-S "Welcome Home," variety *	200 - 225	225 - 250
3025-4-S "A Midsummer Reverie"	200 - 225	225 - 250
3025-4-US "A Midsummer Reverie"	250 - 275	275 - 325
3025-5-S "Close to Shore"	150 - 175	175 - 225
3025-5-US "Close to Shore"	175 - 200	200 - 250
3025-6-S "Winners"	150 - 175	175 - 225
3025-6-US "Winners"	175 - 200	200 - 250
3025-7-US "My Hero"	150 - 175	175 - 225
3025-8-S "Winifred" *	150 - 175	175 - 225
3025-8-US "Winifred"	175 - 200	200 - 250
3025-9-S "When the Leaves Turn"	125 - 150	150 - 175
3025-9-US "When the Leaves Turn"	175 - 200	200 - 250
3025-10-S "My Man"	125 - 150	150 - 175
3025-10-US "My Man"	175 - 200	200 - 275
3025-11-S "King of Hearts"	125 - 150	150 - 175
3025-11-US "King of Hearts"	150 - 175	175 - 200
3025-12-S "Not Yet, But Soon"	125 - 150	150 - 175
3025-12-US "Not Yet, But Soon"	150 - 175	175 - 200
3025-13-S "Autumn's Beauty"	125 - 150	150 - 175
3025-13-US "Autumn's Beauty"	175 - 200	200 - 225
3025-14-S "On Summer Seas"	150 - 175	175 - 200
3025-14-US "On Summer Seas"	175 - 200	200 - 225
3025-15-S "Baby Mine"	125 - 150	150 - 175
3025-15-US "Baby Mine"	150 - 175	175 - 200
3025-16-US "Muriel"		
3025-17-S "Caught Napping"		
3025-18-S "Beauty and Value"		
3025-19-S "Day Dreams"		
3025-19-S "Stringing Them" * **	175 - 200	200 - 225
3025-19-US "Stringing Them"	200 - 225	225 - 250
3025-21-S "All Mine"	150 - 175	175 - 200
3025-21-US "All Mine"	175 - 200	200 - 225
3025-22-S "Two Roses"	150 - 175	175 - 200
3025-23-S "Reflections"		
3025-23-US "Reflections"	175 - 200	200 - 250
3025-24-S "Love Lyrics"	125 - 150	150 - 175
3025-24-US "Love Lyrics"	150 - 175	175 - 200
3025-25-S "An Idle Hour"	125 - 150	150 - 175
3025-25-US "An Idle Hour"	150 - 175	175 - 200

* Has not appeared on any R&N postcard.
** Name from Bowers-Budd-Budd Book,
    "Harrison Fisher"

The N:O Numbered Series

N:O-4-S "Close to Shore" (764)	175 - 200	200 - 250
N:O-5-S "Playing the Game," (Uns.) *	275 - 300	300 - 325
N:O-7-S "A Novice" (863)	175 - 200	200 - 250
N:O-10-S "Midsummer Reverie," Untitled	200 - 250	250 - 300
N:O-11-US "At the Toilet" (767) (Uns.)	175 - 200	200 - 250
N:O-13-S "Welcome Home" (387)	175 - 200	200 - 250

* Appears only on Finnish cards.

W.&G. American Series No. 7001/1-35
Unsigned, no Numbers, no Captions

WG35-1-US "Following the Race," (184)	175 - 200	200 - 250
WG35-2-US "American Beauties" (101)		
WG35-3-US "Alert" (763)		
WG35-4-US "Yet Some Prefer Mountains"	200 - 250	250 - 275
WG35-5-US "At the Toilet" (767)	175 - 200	200 - 250

W.&G. American Series No. 7001/36-50
Unsigned, no Numbers, no Captions

WG50-1-US "A Sprig of Holly" (603)	175 - 200	200 - 250
WG50-2-S "The Favorite Pillow" (613)		
WG50-3-US "Girlie" (261)		

W.&G. American Series No. 7031/1-7
Unsigned, no Numbers, no Captions

WG7-1-US "Eavesdropping" *	225 - 250	250 - 275

New title is "Their Honeymoon Trip"
* Has not appeared on an R&N postcard.

Pain. Karjalan Kirjap. Oy., Viipuri Series
Numbered, Unsigned, no Captions

PKK N:O-5-S "Playing the Game" *	250 - 275	275 - 300
PKK N:O-10-S "A Midsummer Reverie"	200 - 250	250 - 275
PKK N:O-4-S "Close to Shore" (764)	160 - 190	190 - 235
PKK N:O-7-S "A Novice" (863)	160 - 190	190 - 235

* Has not appeared on an R&N postcard.

K.K. Oy N:O 1-20 Series
Signed, no Numbers, no Captions

K.K. 20-1-S "Mistletoe" * **	250 - 275	275 - 300
K.K. 20-2-S "Thoroughbreds" *** (304)	200 - 225	225 - 250

* Has not appeared on an R&N postcard.
** Titled by Author.
*** Also by KYK-KFP

The Publisher at Polyphot Series
Unsigned, no Numbers, no Captions

PP-5-US "At the Toilet" (767)	150 - 175	175 - 225
PP-1-US "Eavesdropping" *	250 - 275	275 - 300

Real title is "Their Honeymoon Trip"

PP-2-US "A Sprig of Holly" (603)	150 - 175	175 - 225
PP-3-US "Don't Worry" (614)	200 - 225	225 - 250
PP-4-US "Following the Race" (184)	150 - 175	175 - 225

* Has not appeared on an R&N postcard.
** Titled by the Author.

The "No Identification" Series
Unsigned, no Numbers, no Captions

NOP-1-US "Autumn's Beauty" (837)	175 - 200	200 - 250
NOP-2-US "Following the Race" (184)	175 - 200	200 - 250
NOP-3-US "Contentment" (383)	175 - 200	200 - 250
NOP-4-US "The Only Pebble" (838)	175 - 200	200 - 250

The S & K Kouvola Reversed Image Series
Unsigned, no Numbers, no Captions

SKK-1-US "Snowbird" *	275 - 300	300 - 350
SKK-2-US "Winners" (864)		
SKK-3-US "Study in Contentment" (875)		

* Appears only on Finnish cards.

The Real Photo Card Series
    5 Additional images have been found.
    S=signed; US=Uns.,   *   ** Captions
    RP-4-S "A Novice" (863)   125 - 150   150 - 175
    RP-5-S "All's Well" 505 ** (381)
    RP-6-S "Alone at Last" C-68 ** (762)
    RP-1-S "American Beauties," Series 101
    RP-2-US "Daydreams" * (848)
    RP-3-US "Drifting" ** (768)
    RP-7-S "Fair and Warmer" (842)
    RP-8-S "June" ** (615)
    RP-9-US "My Hero" (977)
* Some cards numbered, but not R&N numbers.
The Otto Andersin, Pori Series
    Unsigned, no Numbers, no Captions
    OA-1-US "All's Well" (381)   300 - 350   350 - 400
    OA-1-US-MB * "Close To Shore" (764)
    OA-2-US "Drifting" (768)
 * With Multilingual Back.
Untitled Series, No Publisher
    (With "Stamp Here" in Stamp Box)
    There are possibly 25 unnumbered cards
    in this series and at least 4 are known to
    be by Philip Boileau and 20 by Fisher. The
    remaining card is yet to be identified.
    There is also a **Russian Set** which we have
    titled **"Orohek"** (publisher). The cards
    have the same captions written on back and
    are numbered up to 25. See Russian section.
    Captions for **"Stamp Here"** are as follows:
    "A Beauty"   150 - 175   175 - 200
    "A Dane"
    "A Prairie Belle"
    "A Rose"
    "Bubbles"
    "Dolly"
    "Friends"
    "Good Night"
    "Homeward Bound"
    "June"
    "Love Lyrics"
    "Preparing to Conqueor"
    "Princess Pat"
    "Ready and Waiting"
    "Sport"
    "To Ball"
    "To Walk" White hat, dog in arms
    "To Walk" Black hat, brown dog
    "Vanity"
    "Yet Some Men Prefer Mountains"
ADVERTISING
Maailma Magazine, 1919, of cover
    "The Evening Hour"   250 - 300   300 - 350

RUSSIAN
  D. Chromov & M. Bachrach, Moskau
    Black & White on pebbled paper
    No caption - Same as "Miss Santa Claus"   200 - 250   250 - 300
    No caption - Same as "The Rose"   125 - 150   150 - 175
  Frolov and Shourek, Moscow
    Unknown title   125 - 150   150 - 175
    E.K. No. 19 "Maid at Arms" *   150 - 175   175 - 200
  * Same back as Frolov and Shourek
  Leningrad Region Literature (Linen)
    Total Number in 4 series unknown
    Series 5350, 15,000 (Total Run)
    Signed - No Captions
    No. 1 "And Yet Her Eyes..."   150 - 175   175 - 200
    No. 6 "Those Bewitching Eyes"
    No. 54 "Vanity"
    Series 5351, 20,000 (Total Run)
    No. 60 "Cherry Ripe"
    Series 52836, 10,000 (Total Run)
    No. 2 "Leisure Moments"
    No. 54 "Vanity"
    No. 71 "Bewitching Maiden"
    No. 72 "Lips for Kisses"
    No. 1 "And Yet Her Eyes Can Look Wise"
    Series 9402, 20,000 (Total Run)
    No. 60 "Cherry Ripe"   150 - 175   175 - 200
  Rishar ("Richard" or "Phillips")
    St. Petersburg or Petrograde) Backs * **125 - 150   150 - 200
    No. 54 "Vanity"
    No. 117 "Hexenaugen"
    No. 824 "Made to Worship"
    No. 827 "The American Beauty"
    No. 828 "Teacup Time"
    No. 830 "A Faste (Taste) of Paradise"
    No. 831 "Spring Time"
    No. 832 "Food for Thought"
    No. 833 "Lips for Kisses"
    No. 834 "Vanity"
    No. 835 "Cherry Ripe" Signed
    No. 836 "Bewitching Maiden"
    "May-Time"
    "Food for Thought"
    Others
  * Some cards have captions on front while
    others are on the back.
  ** Fisher's name is spelled "Fischer."
  Russian-Polish Real Photo Types
  AWE With Russian/Polish Back
    "Beauties" (196)   150 - 175   175 - 200
    "Miss Knickerbocker" (183)
    "Miss Santa Clause" (182)
    "Vanity" (195)
    Others

5351-20,000 "Cherry Ripe"

52836-10,000 "Vanity"

52836-10,000 "Leisure Moments"

5350-15,000 "And Yet Her Eyes ..."

Harrison Fisher's Russian "Leningrad Region Literature " Series (Linens)

Harrison Fisher, Rishar 827 "The
American Beauty"

Harrison Fisher (Russian)
D. Chromow & M. Bachrach

Russian-English Backs by "Orohek" (25)
   Published 1927 in Soviet Russia
   Series 71293 - 3000 (total run)
   Paper stock is thicker than normal.
     2 "To Walk" (409) "Isn't He Sweet?"   150 - 200   200 - 250
     3 "Dolly"
     7 "Friends"
     9 "Bubbles"
   12 "A Dane"
   14 "Preparing to Conquer"
   15 "To Ball"
   17 "A Rose"
   20 "Princess Pat"
   21 "Homeward Bound"
   22 "Ready and Waiting"
   23 "To Walk" (180) "Well Protected"
   24 "Sport" (Following the Race)
   25 "A Prairie Belle"
      "A Beauty"
      "Good Night!"
      "June"
      "Love Lyrics"
      "Yet Some Men Prefer Mountains"
      "Vanity"
Note: #1, 4, 13 & one other are Boileau's.
The remaining image is unknown.

"*Dolly*"

"*A Dane*"

"*A Beauty*"

"*Princess Pat*"

"*Good Night*" (*Uns.*)

"*A Rose*"

"*To Walk*"

Card Back

Harrison Fisher
Finnish "Stamp
Here" in Stamp
Box Series

"*To Walk*"

Eight Images from the 21-card "Stamp Box" Series; same as "Orohek" Series.

7 *"Friends"*

9 *"Bubbles"*

14 *"Preparing to Conquer"*

15 *"To Ball"*

22 *"Ready & Waiting"*

25 *"A Prairie Belle"*

13 *"Homeward Bound"*

Russian "Orohek" Back

24 *"Sport"*

Eight Images from the 21-card "Orohek" Series; same as "Stamp Box" Series.

Series 66391 - 5000 (Total Run)
Same images as Series 71293 but
only the following images have surfaced.

12 "A Dane"	150 - 200	200 - 250
20 "Princess Pat"		
Others		

Russian Backs, Sepia, Signed
  Untitled

"Fine Feathers"	125 - 150	150 - 200
"Homeward Bound"		
"Isn't He Sweet"		
"Well Protected"		

Russian-French Backs

E.R. No. 12 (B&W) "Beauties"	125 - 150	150 - 175
Flying bird T.M. "The Rose" cheap paper		

EASTERN EUROPE
Appolon Sophia (Bulgaria)

No. 21 "La Musique" (The Artist)	75 - 90	90 - 125
21 "Title" Same as "A Kiss"		
Others		

Modern Art, Sofia (Same as above)

No. 024 "A Kiss"	75 - 90	90 - 100
Other Russian	75 - 100	100 - 125
No. 024 "Kuss" (Kiss)	75 - 80	85 - 90
Linen, No. 192 "Cherry Ripe"	125 - 150	150 - 175

O.K. & Co. P. Error card, artist listed "Cermak"

See Finnish Series WG7-1-US (Variation)		
2057 "Voyage de Noce" (Honeymoon Trip)	150 - 200	200 - 250

Polish & Ukranian Backs

"A Sprig of Holly"	100 - 125	125 - 150

WAE   Probably Polish (Real Photo)
  "Well Protected"
Real Photo #3270, (Anon.) "Thoroughbreds"

EUROPE & GREAT BRITAIN
B.K.W.I., Austria

No No., No Caption ("Naughty, Naughty")	125 - 140	140 - 160

J. Beagles & Co. (Charles H. Hauff)
  (R&N backs)

No No. "The Winter Girl"	70 - 80	80 - 90
No No. "A Fair Driver"		
No No. "Those Bewitching Eyes"		

MEU No Captions

Same as "A Critical Moment" (R&N No #)	100 - 110	110 - 135
Same as "Beatrice" (Vienne Series 806)		
Same as "In the Country" (R&N 131)		
Same as "Marcia" (R&N 111)		
Same as "On the Avenue" (R&N 121)		
Beauty in large polkadot hat; no caption	100 - 150	150 - 175

MEU/Alfred Schweizer, Hamburg
  Series 4380

Either or Both, No Captions	75 - 100	100 - 125

Alfred Schweizer
"Santa Claus' First Visit"
    (J. Henderson Co.)   150 - 175   175 - 200
  Gibson Karte No. 1013 (J. Henderson Co.)
"A Critical Moment"   90 - 100   100 - 110
"Vienne" Series 806
  "Beatrice"   80 - 90   90 - 100
JTK "Kron-Trier" Series
  "A Portrait Sketch"   80 - 90   90 - 100
M.J.S.
  "The Kiss" (No Caption) (108 Series)   40 - 50   50 - 60
Muinck & Co., Amsterdam
  Water Color Series (English Captions)
  R.185 "The Kiss"   100 - 125   125 - 150
  R.188 "Dumb Luck"
  R.192 "A Study Hour"
  R.217 "The Artist"
  R.223 "The Proposal"
  R.224 "The Honeymoon"
  R.225 "The First Evening in Their..."
  R.226 "Their New Love"
  R.232 "Lost?"
  "His First Love"
  "The Dollar Princess, in Holland"
Utigave Louis Diefenthal, Amsterdam
  "A Thoroughbred"   100- 120   120 - 135
Friedrich O. Wolter
  "Peggy" (871)   60 - 75   75 - 90

FRENCH
  Affiches De La Grande Guerre, No. 11   450 - 500   550 - 600

FLAGG, JAMES MONTGOMERY (U.S.)
Detroit Publishing Co.
  B&W 14000 Series   8 - 10   10 - 15
  14011 "The Sweet Magic of Smoke"
  14149 "Sir Charles"
  14150 "It Certainly Wasn't"
  14151 "For Heaven's Sake"
  14152 "So Sensible"
  14153 "Not Bad to Take"
  14154 "Beyond More Conjecture"
  14155 "A Cold Proposition"
  14156 "If You Get Gay"
  14157 "If You're a Perfect Gent"
  14158 "Make it Pleasant for Him"
Henderson Litho
  501 "Engaged - His Attitude"   8 - 10   10 - 12
  2503 "Something on Account"
  Golf   18 - 22   22 - 25
Novitas
  20696 "Etwas a Conto!"   10 - 12   12 - 15
Reinthal & Newman
  "Miss Behaving" Series   12 - 14   14 - 16

288 "A Club Sandwich"		
289 "Putting Out the Flames"		
290 "Miss Behaving!"		
291 "The Most Exciting Moment"		
292 "The Real Love Game"		
293 "Dry Goods"		
TP & Co., N.Y.		
Series 738 Sepia		
"Trouble Somewhere"	8 - 9	9 - 10
Series 751		
"The Hypnotist"	10 - 12	12 - 15
"The Only Way to Eat an Orange"		
"Say When"		
Series 818		
8 "Holding Hands"	10 - 12	12 - 14
10 "In The Hands of the Receiver"		
FONTAN, LEO (France) French Glamour		
Series 17, 80	25 - 28	28 - 32
Series 23, 5016	15 - 18	18 - 22
Series 95 Dance Series (Semi-nudes)	20 - 25	25 - 35
FOSTER, F.D. (U.S.)	4 - 5	5 - 6
FRANZONI, ROBERTO (Italy) Art Deco		
Dell, Anna & Gasparini; Uff. Rev. Stampa		
Series 44 Heads (6)	15 - 18	18 - 22
Series 78 Hands/Head	12 - 15	15 - 18
Series 4358 Fashion - Windy Day (6)	15 - 18	18 - 20
Ladies/Fashion	12 - 15	15 - 18
Erotic/Semi-Nudes	18 - 20	20 - 22
Golf	22 - 25	25 - 30
Tennis	18 - 20	20 - 22
Ladies & Dogs		
B.K.W.I.		
Series 369 (6)	10 - 12	12 - 15
Series 6309 (6)	12 - 15	15 - 20
P.R.S.		
Series 50 (6) High Fashion		
FREDILLO (France) Art Nouveau	25 - 30	30 - 38
FREIXAS, J. (U.S.)		
Winsch, Copyright	20 - 25	30 - 40
FREYSCHLAG, G.	4 - 6	6 - 8
FRÜNDT, H. (Art Nouveau)	25 - 30	30 - 35
GALLAIS, P. (France) French Glamour		
Semi-Nude Series	20 - 22	22 - 26
GAYAC (France) French Glamour		
P.J. Gallais		
Series 210-?	20 - 25	25 - 28
Series 290-310 Dancing Semi-nudes	18 - 22	22 - 25
GERBAULT, H. (France) French Glamour		
Series 36	15 - 18	18 - 22
GIBSON, CHARLES DANA (U.S.)		
Detroit Publishing Co.		
B &W 14000 Series		
14000 "Has She a Heart?"	8 - 10	10 - 12
14003 "Their Presence of Mind"		

Gayac, P. J. Gallais 308
"Dancing Girl"

Gayac, P. J. Gallais 307
"Dancing Girl"

14004	"Melting"		
14005	"When Hunting ..."		
14006	"Last Days of Summer"		
14008	"The Dog"		
14009	"Who Cares"		
14017	"Good Game for Two" (Golf)	20 - 22	22 - 25
14019	"Here it is Christmas"	8 - 10	10 - 12
14027	"Is a caddy always necessary?" (Golf)	20 - 22	22 - 25
14029	"The Half Orphan"	8 - 10	10 - 12
14046	"Bathing Suits"		
14048	"The Half Orphan"		
14050	"America Picturesque"		
14051	"The Stout Gentleman"		
14052	"No Wonder the Sea Serpent ..."		
14054	"Stepped On"		
14055	"Mr. A Merger Hogg ..."		
14057	"Ill Blows the Wind ..."		
14059	"Rival Beauties"		
14065	"The Gibson Girl"	12 - 15	15 - 18
14066	"Jane"	10 - 12	12 - 15
14067	"Mabel"		
14068	"Amy"		
14069	"Eleanor"		
14070	"Margaret"		
14071	"Molly"		
14072	"Helen"		

C. D. Gibson, Henderson & Sons
No. 15, "One Difficulty of the ..."

C. D. Gibson, Henderson & Sons	*C. D. Gibson, Detroit Pub. Co.*	
No No., "Eileen"	*No. 14,027, "Is a Caddie ..."*	

14074 "The Sporting Girl"	12 - 15	15 - 18
14185 "The Eternal Question"	10 - 12	12 - 15
James Henderson & Sons		
Sepia Heads		
"Amy," "Annie," "Clorinda," "Gladys"	10 - 12	12 - 15
"Maude," "Nina," "Peggy," "Beatrice"		
"Bertha," "Eileen" "Violet"		
James Henderson & Sons		
Life's Comedy Series (36)	6 - 8	8 - 10
Golf	18 - 22	22 - 25
Schweizer & Co.		
Embossed, Sepia Series	10 - 15	15 - 18
Pictorial Comedy Series	10 - 12	12 - 15
Snap-Shots	6 - 8	8 - 10
Golf	18 - 22	22 - 25
GIGLIO	4 - 6	6 - 8
GILBERT, C. ALLEN (U.S.)	8 - 10	10 - 12
Calendar, 1911	10 - 12	12 - 15
Taylor-Platt Issues		
Schweiser "Pictorial Comedy" (Sepia)		
GILLEY (Art Deco)		
Paris Gravure		
Series 1961, 1971 Semi-Nudes	12 - 15	15 - 20
GILLIS, RENE	12 - 15	15 - 18
GINI, M.		
T.A.M. Series 7618	10 - 12	12 - 15

C. Allan Gilbert
Henderson & Sons 99, "Dorothy"

Will Grefé, Moffat, Yard
"Queen of Hearts"

GIRIS, C. (France)		
Uff. Rev. Stampa		
Deco Bathing Beauties Series	22 - 25	25 - 28
GNISCHAF, RUAB (Germany) Romantic couples	6 - 8	8 - 10
GOBBI, D. (Italy) Art Deco		
Majestic		
Series 2546, Chinese Dragon	15 - 18	18 - 22
Ladies	22 - 25	25 - 28
Gondola/Lovers	18 - 20	20 - 25
Series 1216	12 - 15	15 - 20
Series 2474 Pierrots/Harlequins	20 - 25	25 - 30
Series 2477, 2494	15 - 18	18 - 22
Series 2479	12 - 15	15 - 18
Series 2530, 2556, 2560	20 - 25	25 - 28
Elite		
Series 2631	12 - 15	15 - 18
Series 2550	18 - 20	20 - 22
GODELA, D. (Italy)		
Series 272, 296 Head Studies	12 - 15	15 - 20
D.A.G. Series 409 In Oval - Sitting (6)	8 - 10	10 - 12
GRAF, MARTE or MG		
Art Deco & Silhouettes		
Series 733-758	10 - 12	12 - 15
Other Deco Silhouettes		
GRANDE (Italy) Art Deco and Glamour		
Series 437 (6)	12 - 15	15 - 20

GRASSET, EUGENE (Swiss) Art Nouveau	100 - 120	120 - 130
Collection Cinos	125 - 135	135 - 150
Collection des Cent	500 - 550	550 - 600
GREENE, FREDERICK (U.S.)	6 - 8	8 - 10
GREFE, WILL (U.S.)		
Moffat, Yard Co.		
Playing Card Queens		
"Club," "Diamond," "Heart," "Spade"	15 - 20	20 - 25
Moffat, Yard Co. Series 3	10 - 12	12 - 15
Brown & Bigelow		
Advertising Calendars Romantic Couples	12 - 15	15 - 20
GREINER, MAGNUS (U.S.)		
Auburn Publishing Co., Pennant Series	6 - 8	8 - 10
Anonymous German Series 1500	8 - 10	10 - 12
GRIMBALL, M. M. (U.S.)		
Gutmann & Gutmann Series 106		
"Verdict...Love for life"	18 - 22	22 - 26
See Children Section		
GROSS, BELLA	5 - 6	6 - 8
GROSZE, MANNI (Italy)		
Art Deco Silhouettes		
Deco Series 2041 Nudes	18 - 22	22 - 25
Others	12 - 15	15 - 20
PFB (In Diamond)		
Series 2042, Nudes	15 - 20	20 - 25
Series 3339, Nudes		
Series 2052, Dancing	12 - 15	15 - 18
Others		
GROTT Bathing Girls	8 - 10	10 - 12
GUARINO, ANTHONY	5 - 6	6 - 8
GUARNERI (Italy) Art Deco		
Ladies	15 - 18	18 - 22
GUERZONI, G. (Italy)		
Art Deco and Glamour		
Ladies/Heads/Fashion	8 - 10	10 - 12
Ladies/Animals	10 - 12	12 - 15
Erotic/Semi-Nudes	12 - 15	15 - 20
Ladies & Dogs	12 - 15	15 - 20
Ladies & Horses		
B.K.W.I.		
Series 702 (10)	12 - 15	15 - 20
Series 710 (6)	8 - 10	10 - 12
Series 729 (6)	10 - 12	12 - 15
Rev. Stampa		
Series 1010 (6)	15 - 18	18 - 22
Series 1017 (6) Mother-Daughter	8 - 10	10 - 12
Series 1023, 1025, 1029, 1046 (6)	10 - 12	12 - 15
Series 1030, 1919 (6) Semi-nudes	18 - 22	22 - 25
GUIDO (Italy) Art Deco	10 - 12	12 - 15
GUILLAUME, ALBERT (France) Art Nouveau	75 - 100	100 - 125
Collection des Cent No. 22	200 - 225	225 - 250
GUNN, ARCHIE (U.S.)		
J. Bergman		
Black & White Series (6)	5 - 6	6 - 8

National Art Co.

13	"Bowling Girl"	10 - 12	12 - 15
14	"Tennis Girl"	12 - 15	15 - 20
15	"Skating Girl"	10 - 12	12 - 15
16	"College Mascot"	7 - 10	10 - 12

"City Belles" Series

33	"Miss New York"	10 - 12	12 - 15
34	"Miss Philadelphia"		
35	"Miss Boston"		
36	"Miss Chicago"		
37	"Miss Pittsburg"		
38	"Miss Cincinnati"		
39	"Miss Toronto"		
40	"Miss Washington"		
41	"Miss Seashore"		
69	"Bride of Niarara"		
71	"Miss Milwaukee"	10 - 12	12 - 15
72	"Miss Detroit"		
77	"Miss Cleveland"		
87	"Miss San Francisco"		
90	Untitled	6 - 8	8 - 9

"Clans"

249	"McDougal Plaid"	7 - 8	8 - 10
251	"McPherson Plaid"		

"College Belle" Series

147	"College Mascot"	10 - 12	12 - 15
148	Girl in red, pennant and Collie dog		

Miscellaneous

175	"In the Good Old Summertime"	10 - 12	12 - 15
190	"Forget Me Not"		
216	"Jack O' Lantern"		
218	"Commencement"		

"National Belle" Series

214	"Lady & the Bear"		
217	"Devotion"	8 - 10	10 - 15
219	"Yuletide"		
220	"Sables"		
221	"Ermine"		
222	"Driving"		
223	"Automobiling"		
276	"The Fencer"		
277	"On Guard"		
	Full-Length Santa	12 - 15	15 - 20

Illustrated Postal Card & Novelty Co.

WWI Army Series 1368   (12)

"The American Spirit"	6 - 8	8 - 10
"Army, Navy, and Reserves"		
"Don't Worry About Me"		
"If Wishes Came True"		
"Lest We Forget"		
"None but the Brave Deserve ..."		
"Pals"		
"Parting is Such Sweet Sorrow"		

"Repairing a Man of War"
"Rosemary! That's for Remembrance"
"Shoulder Arms"
"When the Last Goodbyes are Whispered"

WWI Army Series 1371 (12)	6 - 8	8 - 10

"A Parting Message"
"Hello! I Haven't Heard from You"
"Don't Worry, We're Alright"
"Guardian Spirits"
"Letters are Always Welcome"
"Liberty and Union Now and Forever"
"Pleasant Memories"
"The Rose for Remembrance"
"Sentry Moon"
"Warmth in the Camp and ..."
"We Won't Come Back Till it's Over ..."
"Worthwhile Fighting For ..."

Taylor-Platt

American Beauty Series (6)	10 - 12	12 - 15
Statler Calendar Cards, 1912 (12)	12 - 15	15 - 20

Anonymous

Girl Holding Basketball	12 - 15	15 - 18
Girl Wading in Water	6 - 8	8 - 10
Girl at Wheel of Sail Boat	6 - 8	8 - 10
Girl Holding Golf Club	15 - 18	18 - 22
Girl Holding Golf Club, but in Color	20 - 25	25 - 28
Beautiful Lady, Red Bow, Red Dress	6 - 8	8 - 10
Beautiful Lady, Pink Bow, Pink Dress		
Beautiful Lady, Bust, Holding 3 Roses		

Series 67

Beautiful ladies, flowers at breast, w/verse	10 - 12	12 - 15
B&W/Sepia, Women, No Captions (3)	5 - 6	6 - 8

Lowney's Chocolates

Golf Girls Series (6)	20 - 25	25 - 28
GUYMA "The Amours of Pierrot" (4)	20 - 22	22 - 25
HAGER, NINI (Austria) Art Nouveau	100 - 125	125 - 150

HAHN (Germany)

A.R. & C. Deco Series 1197 (6)	15 - 18	18 - 22
H.G.R. (Art Nouveau) **Series 316** (6)	25 - 30	30 - 35

HAMMICK, J.W. (GB)
Photocom "Celesque" Series

531 "The Motor Girl"	12 - 15	15 - 20
532 "The Society Girl"	12 - 15	15 - 18
533 "The Ball Room Girl"		
534 "The Sporting Girl"		
535 "The Sea Side Girl"		
HAMPEL, WALTER (Austria) Art Nouveau	75 - 100	100 - 150
HARBOUR, JENNIE (G.B.)	12 - 15	15 - 20

HARDY, DUDLEY (G.B.)
Raphael Tuck Series 1502
Celebrated Posters

"Egyptian Mail Steamship"	25 - 30	30 - 40
"Liebig Meat Extract"		
"The Pearl Girl"		

"The Ball-Room Girl"   *"The Sporting Girl"*   *"The Society Girl*

J. W. Hammick, Photochrom Company -- Celesque Series

"Royal Naval Tournament"		
Hartman Ladies Sports Series	10 - 12	12 - 15
HARDY, HAYWARD (G.B.) Art Deco		
Ladies	8 - 10	10 - 12
Ladies/Animals	10 - 12	12 - 15
Pierrots/Harlequins	15 - 18	18 - 22
Erotic/Semi-Nudes		
HARE, J. KNOWLES (U.S.)		
Empire Art **Series 112**	6 - 8	8 - 10
K Co., Inc., N.Y.		
Mother-Child Series Watercolors		
154 "A little bit of heaven"	10 - 12	12 - 15
157 "Happiness"		
Paul Heckscher		
Series 1009 (6) Watercolors	12 - 15	15 - 18
1 "Eugenie"		
2 "Rosamond"		
3 "Beryl"		
4 "Clarice"		
5 "Madeline"		
6 "Charmion"		
Series 1026 (6)	10 - 12	12 - 15
M&H Fine Woolens	10 - 12	12 - 15
Statler Advertising Cards, 1912 (13)	12 - 14	14 - 16
HARPER, R. FORD (U.S.)		
Reinthal & Newman Water color Series		
350 "Peg O' My Heart"	12 - 15	15 - 20
351 "My Summer Girl"		
352 "Love's Locket"		
353 "True Blue"	15 - 20	20 - 25
354 "The Favorite Flower"		
355 "Miss Innocence"	12 - 15	15 - 18
Gibson Art Co. Issues	10 - 12	12 - 15

Helli (Icart), G.H., Paris
Series 53 (French Caption)

Helli (Icart), G.H., Paris
Series 53 (French Caption)

P. Herkscher
    Series 1010

2 "Constance"	18 - 22	22 - 25
Series 1013		
Series 1025		
P. Sander Lady Santa Claus (4)	30 - 35	35 - 45
K.K. OY 1/20 (Finland)		
Girl wearing straw hat, sailor blouse	20 - 25	25 - 30
HART, JOSEF (Germany) Art Nouveau	25 - 30	30 - 35
HARRISON (U.S.)	6 - 7	7 - 8
HARTLEIN, W.	4 - 5	5 - 6
HAVILAND, F.	4 - 6	6 - 8
HAYDEN, A.E.	3 - 4	4 - 5
HEINZE, A.	6 - 8	8 - 10
HELLEU, PAUL (France)		
Ladies of Paris	20 - 25	25 - 35
HELLI (ICART Pen name) (France)		
Series 53 (6) Ladies	60 - 70	70 - 80
HEROUARD (France) French Glamour		
Series 55, 300	20 - 25	25 - 35
HERSCHEL, OTTO (Austria)	6 - 8	8 - 10
HERVE, G. (France)		
Lapina **Series 5064** "Smoker"	10 - 12	12 - 15
HILDER, G. HOWARD		
Platinachrome **National Girl Series**	10 - 12	12 - 15
HILLSON, D.		

P. C. 10

P. C. 11

P. C. 12

P. C. 13

P. C. 14

P. C. 15

P. C. 36

P. C. 134

P. C. 136

Beautiful Ladies of Maud Humphrey (Unsigned) by Gray Litho Co. of New York.

Girl Series in Red & Black (23)	6 - 8	8 - 10
HOCK, F. (Art Nouveau)	30 - 35	35 - 40
HOFER, A.	6 - 8	8 - 10
HOFFMAN, JOSEF (Art Nouveau)	150 - 200	200 - 300
"Ver Sacrum"	1000 - 1500	1500 - 2500
HOHENSTEIN, A. (Russia) Art Nouveau		
1901 Milano Int. Expo Series	30 - 35	35 - 40
HOLZMAN, A.	6 - 8	8 - 10
HOROWITZ, H.		
Raphael Tuck		
Series 1 "A Dream of Fair Women" (6)	10 - 12	12 - 15
HORRELL, CHARLES	4 - 6	6 - 8
HORSFALL, MARY (G.B.)	8 - 10	10 - 12
Ladies & Horses	12 - 15	15 - 18
HUMPHREY, MAUD (U.S.)		
Gray Litho. Co., N.Y. (G. in Diamond)		
(All her lady postcards are unsigned.)		
P.C. 10 through P.C. 16		
Large Hat and bust images	20 - 25	25 - 30
P.C. 18, P. C. 20, P.C. 25, P.C. 26	18 - 22	22 - 25
* **P.C. 36, P.C. 37, P.C. 37A, P.C. 38**		
P.C. 113, P.C. 133, P.C. 134,		
P.C. 135, P.C. 136, P.C. 139, P.C. 141		
* Same images as 130 series except larger		
Peroxident Toothpaste		
Ads of Beautiful ladies (Uns.)	25 - 30	30 - 35
HUNT, ESTHER		
National Art Co.		
9-12 Little Chinese Girls	5 - 6	6 - 7
HUNTER, LILLIAN W. (U.S.)	6 - 8	8 - 10
National Art Co.		
107 Girl sits in Wreath (Yellow Dress)	6 - 8	8 - 10
109 Wreath Series (Purple Dress)		
HUTT, HENRY (U.S.)		
Detroit Publishing Co.		
B&W 14000 Series		
14202 "Sincerity"	10 - 12	12 - 15
14203 "Curiosity"		
14204 "Tired of Life"		
14205 "Expectancy"		
14207 "Frivolity"		
14208 "Courageous"		
14209 "Shy"		
14211 "Pleasure"		
14212 "Joy"		
14213 "Whimsical"		
H & S, Germany	12 - 15	15 - 20
ICART, LOUIS (France) French Glamour		
Lady & Black Dog	60 - 80	80 - 100
Series 48 (6)	60 - 70	70 - 80
"L'Eternal Feminin" (6)	125 - 150	150 - 175
ICHNOWSKI, M. (Poland)	10 - 12	12 - 15
IRIBE, PAUL	150 - 175	175 - 200
JANK, ANGELO (Germany) Art Nouveau	25 - 30	30 - 35

JANKE, URBAN See Wiener Werkstätte		
JANTSY-HORVATH, C.	5 - 6	6 - 8
JAPHET (Alex Jean Louis Jazet) (France)		
Costume Series	25 - 30	30 - 35
JARACH, A. (France) French Glamour		
Delta Series 18, 156, 158	18 - 20	20 - 25
JAY, CECIL	5 - 8	8 - 10
JIRASEK, A.J. (Austria)	4 - 5	5 - 8
JIRAS, A. (Czech)	8 - 10	10 - 12
JODOLFI (Germany)	6 - 8	8 - 10
JONES, J. (U.S.)		
P. Gordon, 1908		
"Opera Girl"	6 - 7	7 - 8
"Vacation Girl" (Unsigned)	4 - 5	5 - 6
College Girl Series	6 - 7	7 - 8
JOSSOT, HENRI (France) Art Nouveau	100 - 200	200 - 300
JOZSA, KARL (Austria) Art Nouveau		
A. Sockl, Wien		
"Femme au Coeur"	70 - 80	80 - 90
"Sirens and Circeans" Series (6)	200 - 250	250 - 300
E.S.D.B., Austria		
"Coeur Dame" Series (6)	60 - 70	70 - 85
Simon Steffans		
"Smoke Rings" Series (6)	110 - 115	115 - 125
JUNG, MORITZ (Czechoslavakia) Art Nouveau		
See Wiener Werkstätte		
KABY	6 - 8	8 - 10
KAINRADL, L. (Germany) Art Nouveau	75 - 100	100 - 250
KALHAMMER, G. (Austria) See Wiener Werkstätte		
KALOUS, GRET	6 - 8	8 - 10
KALVACH, RUDOLPH (Austria)		
See Wiener Werkstaette		
KANDISKY, W. (Russia)		
Bauhaus Series, 1923 See Bauhaus Section		
KASKELINE, F.		
Deco/Silhouettes	12 - 15	15 - 18
Nudes-Semi-nudes	15 - 18	18 - 22
S.W.S.B.		
Ladies and Horses Series 1119	10 - 12	12 - 15
KATINKA (Sweden) Art Deco		
KAVAL, M. (France) Art Deco		
Lapina, Paris		
Series 5027, 5029, 5030 Hats (6)	12 - 15	15 - 18
Series 5031, 5032 Hats (6)		
Series 5034, 5036 Hats (6)		
KELLER, A. I. (U.S.)		
Historical Sweethearts Series		
"The Introduction"	4 - 6	6 - 8
"The Wooing of Anne Hathaway"		
"The Proposal"		
"The Wedding"		
KEMPF, TH. (Austria) Art Nouveau		
Series 165 (10)	50 - 60	60 - 70
Series 166 (10)	55 - 60	60 - 65

Hamilton King, F. A. Schneider
455, "Secure"

Hamilton King, Henry Heininger
41, "After the Ball"

KENYON, ZULA (U.S.)	6 - 8	8 - 12
Gerlach-Barklow		
Advertising Calendars - 1910-1914		
Beautiful ladies with flowers	10 - 12	12 - 15
KIEFER, E.H. (G.B.)		
Bamforth & Co.		
"Could You Be True," "Dear Heart"	8 - 10	10 - 12
"Good Bye," "I'm Growing Fond of You"		
"Love a Lassie," "My Chum"		
"There's Nobody Like You"		
"You Know You're Not Forgotten"		
"Waiting For You," "When Dreams Come True"		
"When You Feel Dreamy"		
"When You Feel Naughty ..."		
"When You're Traveling ..."		
"When Your Heart Aches ...," "Would You Care"		
"Would You Learn to Love Me"		
Gray Litho, 1909		
"When you feel drowsey..."		
KIENERK, G. (Italy) (Art Nouveau)		
"Cocorico"	450 - 500	500 - 600
KIEZKOW (Poland) (Art Nouveau)	80 - 90	90 - 100
KIMBALL, ALONZO (U.S.)		
Reinthal & Newman Series 122, Lovers (6)	6 - 8	8 - 10
KING, HAMILTON (U.S.)		
Coca Cola Girl (Advertising Card)	1000 - 1100	1100 - 1200
Coca Cola Motor Girl	1200 - 1400	1400 - 1600

E. Gross
    American Girls Series   8 - 10   10 - 12
    Bathing Beauties (12)
    "Asbury Park Girl," "Atlantic City Girl"   15 - 20   20 - 25
    "Bar Harbor Girl," "Cape May Girl"
    "Coney Island Girl," "Long Branch Girl"
    "Larchmont Girl," "Manhattan Beach Girl"
    "Narragansett Girl" "Newport Girl"
    "Palm Beach Girl," "Ocean Grove Girl"
Henry Heininger Co.
    Sports Series (6) Watercolors
    "After the Ball," "Beneath the Sun Shade" 12 - 15   15 - 20
    "The Fencer" (Uns.), "In the Swim"
    "Lady in Blue," "On a Skate"
F.A. Schneider
    454-459 Series (6) Watercolors
    454 "Contented"   12 - 15   15 - 18
    455 "Secure"
    456 "Graceful"
    459 "Stunning"
Raphael Tuck
    Series 1605 Gem Glosso
    "My Lady Fair"   12 - 15   15 - 20
Brown & Bigelow
    Advertising Calendars, 1907 (12)
    Beautiful ladies   15 - 18   18 - 22
Armour & Co. See Advertising
KING, JESSIE M. (G.B.) Art Nouveau 70 - 80   80 - 90
    Miller & Lang
    Series 122 "The National Series"
KINNEYS, THE (U.S.)   8 - 10   10 - 12

KIRCHNER, RAPHAEL (Austria)

The Check list below has been greatly enhanced from the previous edition with additional listings and publisher information available in the wonderful new book, *RAPHAEL KIRCHNER AND HIS POSTCARDS,* by Antonio and Pia Dell'Aquila of Bari, Italy. According to the authors there were three distinct periods for classifying his works - **The Early Period**, from 1897 through 1899; **The Golden Age**, from 1900 through 1907; and **The Glamour Age,** from 1910 through 1916. Raphael Kirchner died in New York in 1917 at the early age of 42 from complications of appendicitis.

Kirchner's works were extremely popular during his lifetime and many of his sets and series were published by more than one publisher making it almost impossible to catalog each and every one. Therefore, our listing is incomplete and readers should obtain a copy of the above book for a more complete checklist and other vital publisher information.

RAPHAEL KIRCHNER
    Art Nouveau & Art Deco

Raphael Kirchner (Unsigned), M. Munk
Girls with Purple Surrounds

EARLY PERIOD

Back & Schmitt, Vienna
"**A Quatre Feuilles**" (Clovers) (6)   175 - 200   200 - 250
"**Aus Arkadien**" (From Arkadia) (6)
"**Fleur de Chemin**" (Street Flowers) (10)
"**Myths and Legends**" (6)
"**Music Postcards**" (1)   500 - 600   600 - 700
"**Radlerei**" (Girl Cyclists) (6)   275 - 300   300 - 350
"**Wiener Blut**" (Viennese Blood) (6)   175 - 200   200 - 250
"**Um die Liebe**" (To the Love) (7)
J. Gerson, Paris
"**Happy New Year**" (10)   150 - 175   175 - 200
Philipp and Kramer
"**Auf Sommerfrische**" (On Holiday) (10) 175 - 200   200 - 250
KK, Munich
"**Eisblumen**" (Ice Flowers) (10) (Uns.)
Theo. Stroefer, Nürnberg
"**Coeur Dame**" (Heart Lady) (10) (Uns.) 100 - 125   125 - 150
Anonymous (Signed R.)
"**Wiener Typen**" (Viennese types)   (12) 175 - 200   200 - 250

THE GOLDEN AGE

Anonymous
"**All Heil**" (Cyclists) (10)   175 - 200   200 - 250
"**Au Serail**" (In the Harem) (6)
"**Christmas**" **signed w/Paris Ser. 184** (6) 75 - 100   100 - 125
    Santa Claus   300 - 350   350 - 400
"**Delighted Girls**" (4)   400 - 450   450 - 500
"**Erika**" Heads on Flowers background (6) 100 - 125   125 - 150

"Fruits Douces" (Sweet Fruits) (6)
 Also by ESW (Emil Storch, Wien)

"Girls and Eggs" Horizontal (1)	250 - 300	300 - 350
"Girls' Head in Circle, white b.g." (6)	100 - 125	125 - 150
"Hinter den Coulissen"		
(Behind Scenes) (10)	150 - 175	175 - 200
"Portraits of Girls" Gray Border (6)		
"Portraits of Viennese Ladies" (6)	100 - 125	125 - 150

E. Arenz, Wien

"Leda & the Swan" (10)	100 - 125	125 - 150
"Santoy" (Japanese Life) (6)	75 - 100	100 - 125

B.K.W.I. (Bruder Kohn, Wien)

"Bijoux" (Jewels) Emb. Heads **538** (6)	75 - 100	100 - 125
"Christmas Pictures" Ser. 2049 (10)	150 - 175	175 - 200

J. Beagles & Co.

"Girls Holding Bunnies" (3)	300 - 325	325 - 350

"COCK" in small shield

"Girls in Car on White b.g." 4325 (1)	275 - 300	300 - 350
"The Christmas Girls" Ser. 4329 (5)	200 - 225	225 - 250

B. Dondorf, Frankfurt (BD)

Series 109 "Girls and Eggs, Vertical" (6)	150 - 175	175 - 200

H.M. & Co.

"Christmas, signed w/Paris" 184 (6)	80 - 100	100 - 125

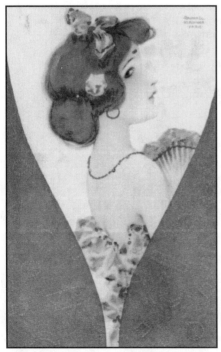

Raphael Kirchner, B.K.W.I. 538
"Bijoux" (Jewels)

Raphael Kirchner, ESW
Mikado Series

Raphael Kirchner
Theo. Stroefer, 99

Raphael Kirchner, A. Sochl
"Demi Vierge"

Santa Claus	300 - 350	350 - 400
K. & B. D.		
"Rauchende Damen" (Women Smoking) **Series 4501** (6)	150 - 175	175 - 200
MMP in circle		
Die-cut Hold-to-Light (5)	800 - 900	900 - 1000
"Vitraux d'Art" (Stained Gl. Windows) (5)	400 - 450	450 - 500
Also R. Tuck Series 3051		
Meissner & Buch, Leipsig		
"Modern Madchen" Series 1129 (Modern girls) (6)	100 - 125	125 - 150
M. Munk, Vienna		
"Bronzes d 'Art (Emb.) (10)	100 - 125	125 - 150
"Fleur Au Pied" (10)	125 - 150	150 - 175
"Geisha" Series (10)	65 - 75	75 - 100
"Girls and Eggs" (5) (Uns.)		
"Girls with flowers at feet" (10)	150 - 175	175 - 200
"Girls' faces in circle, violet b.g." (10)		
Girls with turquoise surrounds (10)		
Girls with beige border, Ser. 113 (10)	100 - 125	125 - 150
Girls w/olive green surrounds (10)	150 - 175	175 - 200
Girls with purple surrounds (10)		
"Girls' faces, red border" Ser. 115 (10)	200 - 225	225 - 250
"Love Thoughts" (10)		
"Maid of Athens" Series 73 (9)	50 - 75	75 - 100
"Mikado" Series (6)	65 - 75	75 - 100

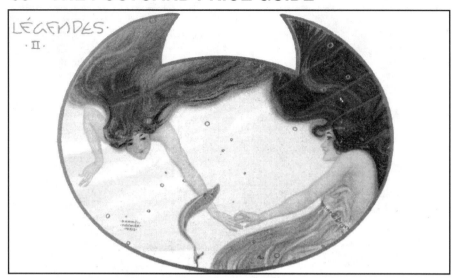

Raphael Kirchner, Theo. Stroefer Series 311
"Legendes II"

"Les Cigarettes Du Monde" (6)	125 - 150	150 - 175
"La Favorite" (6)	125 - 150	150 - 175
Pascalis, Moss & Co.		
"Girls and Eggs" Yellow signature (6)	100 - 125	125 - 150
"Marionette" Series 4140 (6)	75 - 100	100 - 125
Also by E. Storch & H.M. & Co.		
"Leda & the Swan" (10) Unsigned	150 - 175	175 - 200
Also by E. Arnenz, Wien		
Edgar Schmidt, Dresden		
"Girls Between Green & Brown Borders"		
Series 350 (6)	100 - 125	125 - 150
Raphael Tuck		
"Flashing Motorists" Series 2709 (6)	100 - 125	125 - 150
"Girls Heads-Christmas Foilage b.g."		
Christmas C.316	400 - 450	450 - 500
"Girls & Pig Heads" Ser. 1902 (3) B&W	50 - 75	75 - 100
"Girls Surrounded by Hearts, Stars, Etc.,		
Series 1190 (B&W) (3)	100 - 125	125 - 150
"Salome" (6) **Series 2555** (6)	75 - 100	100 - 125
"Les Sylphides" Series 285 (6)	100 - 125	125 - 150
Raphael Tuck, Paris		
"Les Ephemeres" (Mayflies) **375** (6)	200 - 225	225 - 250
Also by **R. Tuck Series 2642**		
"Farfadets" (Elves) **286** (6) Sculptures	100 - 125	125 - 150
"Osterautomobil" (Easter autos) **777** (6)	100 - 125	125 - 150
"Reveries" (Dreams) (2)	400 - 450	450 - 500
"Salome" Series 241 (6)	75 - 100	100 - 125
"Sylphides" Series 285 (6)	100 - 125	125 - 150
A. Sockl, Wien		
"All Heil" (Bicycle Girls) (10)	200 - 225	225 - 250
"Demi Vierge" (6)	100 - 125	125 - 150

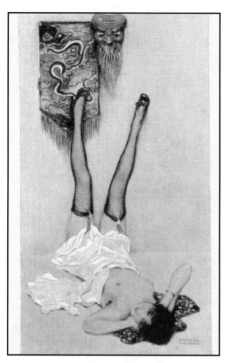

Raphael Kirchner, L-E 15
"Le masque impassible"

Raphael Kirchner, L-E 21
"La Mer fleurie"

Christoph Reisser's Söhne, Wien

"Couples Between Red Borders" (6)	150 - 175	175 - 200
"Enfants de la Mer" (10)	100 - 125	125 - 150
"Erika" Series 1123 (6)	150 - 175	175 - 200

E. Storch, Wien

"Les Cigarettes du Monde" (Cigarettes from the world) (6)	100 - 125	125 - 150
"La Favorite" (The Favorite) (6)	100 - 125	125 - 150
"Fables" (6)	75 - 100	100 - 125
"Femmes Soleil" (Women in the Sun) (6)	100 - 125	125 - 150
"Fruits Doux" (Sweet Fruits) (6)		
"Geisha" Series (10)	50 - 75	75 - 100
"Les Parfumes" (Perfumes) (6)	100 - 125	125 - 150
"Marionettes" (Girls with puppets) (6)		
"Mikado" (Japanese Girls) (6)	75 - 100	100 - 125
"Red & White Figures," Small Shields (6)	250 - 300	300 - 350
"Vieux Temps" (Old Times) (6)	150 - 175	175 - 200

Theo. Stroefer, Nürnberg (T.S.N.)

"Fleurs d'Amour" (Love Flowers) 332 (6)	150 - 175	175 - 200
"Froliche Ostern" (Happy Easter) 222 (6)	100 - 125	125 - 150
"Girls, Good Luck Charms" 235 (10)		
"Girls dominating landscape" 427 (6)	200 - 225	225 - 250
"Greek Girls" Series 71 (16)	50 - 75	75 - 100
"Greek Vierges" Series 99 (12)	100 - 125	125 - 150
"Legendes" Series 311 (6)	150 - 175	175 - 200
"Moderne Madchen" Series 1129 (6)	125 - 150	150 - 175

Mela Köhler
Wiener Werkstaette, 581

Mela Köhler
Wiener Werkstaette, 555

"Noel!" Series **184** (Christmas) (6)	75 - 100	100 - 125
"Noel!" Series **197** (Christmas) (6)	150 - 175	175 - 200
"Roma" Series **220** (10)	100 - 125	125 - 150
Santa	300 - 350	350 - 400

GLAMOUR AGE

Photographic Postcards
"Kirchner's Erotic Pictures" (B&W + Brown)

Signed & Unsigned (20) Some P/LP	150 - 175	175 - 200

Lustigen Blatter

"In den Karten steht's geschrieben" (1)	275 - 300	300 - 350
Novitas, Berlin "Vain Girls" (3)	100 - 125	125 - 150

Marque L-E
"Pour le Droit et la Libertie"

"For Rights & Freedom" (1)	75 - 100	100 - 125

Puzzle **"Pour le Droit et la Libertie"** (8)

"Les Peches Capitaux" (7 Deadly Sins) (7)	50 - 60	60 - 75

L-E Glamour Series (32)
    Various 9 - 311

Bruton Galleries
    Delta **"Kirchner Girls"** (24)
    Alphasia Pub. Co. (12)
Reinthal & Newman, N.Y.

"The Pierrot's Loves" **990-999** (10)	75 - 100	100 - 125

ADVERTISING, ETC.

"Bellage des "Sect" (2)	150 - 175	175 - 200
"Byrrh" Tonic (1)	500 - 600	600 - 700
"Gruss von der Hochzeit" (Wedding Wish) (2)	275 - 300	300 - 350
"Int. Exhibition of Paris, 1900" (1)	800 - 900	900 - 1000
"Les Graces" (The Graces) (1)	100 - 125	125 - 150
"Robert Schlesinger, Wien" Viennese footwear emporium (1)		
S.P. (English Silver Ad) (B&W) (Uns.)	100 - 125	125 - 150
"Sirene" Real Photo		
Salon 1904 (1)	100 - 125	125 - 150
"Streeter"		
Streeter & Co. Jewellers (1)	200 - 225	225 - 250
"Union Cartophile Universelle"	350 - 400	400 - 500

KLEE, PAUL   See Bauhaus Listing

KNOEFEL

Novitas Illumination Series

Series 668 Nudes (4)	20 - 25	25 - 28
Series 20888 Mother/Baby	10 - 12	12 - 15
Series 15662 With Japanese Lantern	15 - 20	20 - 25
Other Illuminated	12 - 15	15 - 18

M. Munk Illumination

Series 1992 Japanese Lanterns	15 - 20	20 - 25

KÖHLER, MELA (Austria)

Art Nouveau/Art Deco

M. Munk, Vienne

Series 1118 (6)	60 - 70	70 - 80
Series 1188 (6) Ladies at leisure		
After 1915	30 - 40	40 - 50

B.K.W.I. (Bruder Kohn, Wien)

Series 131 (6) Ladies Fashion	80 - 100	100 - 125
Series 143 (6) Ladies Fashion		
Tennis	100 - 125	125 - 150
Series 187 (6) Women Sports		
Series 178, 187, 188 (6)	80 - 100	100 - 120
Series 201 (6) Fashionable ladies & children		
Series 271 (6) Women's Winter Sports	100 - 125	125 - 140
Series 481, 641 (6) Fashionable Hats	80 - 100	100 - 120
Series 620, 843 (6)	80 - 100	100 - 110
Series 641 (6) Ladies with flower bouquets		
Series 3089 (6) Christmas Ladies		
Series 3090 (6) Xmas, wallpaper b.g.	100 - 125	125 - 150
Series 3121, 3142 (6) Christmas Ladies	75 - 85	85 - 100
After 1915	40 - 45	45 - 50

See Wiener Werkstaette Section

KOISTER (France) French Glamour

Delta Series 71	15 - 18	18 - 22

KOKOSCHKA, OSCAR (Austria)

See Wiener Werkstatte

KONOPA, RUDOLF (Austria) Art Nouveau

Philipp & Kramer	50 - 70	70 - 90
KOPAL Art Nouveau	30 - 35	35 - 40

KOSA (Austria) Art Nouveau	150 - 165	165 - 175
KOSEL, H.C. **B.K.W.I. Series 181**	10 - 12	12 - 15
KOTAS, V.	6 - 8	8 - 10
KOVIES, K. Art Deco		
D.A.G. Series 474-1, 474-3, 474-4 (Skating)	12 - 15	15 - 20
KRATKI, F.	5 - 6	6 - 8
KRAUSZ, J.V. (Austria)	8 - 10	10 - 12
KRENEK, CARL (Austria) See Wiener Werkstaette		
KRENNES, H. (Poland)	8 - 10	10 - 15
KUANI, C. COLAN Art Deco		
Ultra - Series 2166 Shoulders (6)	10 - 12	12 - 15
KUCHINKA, JAN (Czech.)		
Praha-Podol 150 Erotic Series	25 - 30	30 - 35
H. Co. Semi-Nudes	30 - 35	35 - 40
KUDERNY, F. (Austria)		
M. Munk, Vienna		
Series 606, 634 (6)	12 - 15	15 - 20
Series 841 Semi-Nudes	15 - 18	18 - 22
Series 835 Tiny Men	12 - 15	15 - 20
KULAS, J.V. (Germany) Art Nouveau	35 - 40	40 - 45
KUNZLI, MAX	6 - 8	8 - 10
KURT, E. MAISON Art Deco		
P.F.B. (in Diamond)		
Fantasy Doll Series	15 - 20	20 - 25
Fantasy Dance Series (Lesbian Types)	30 - 35	35 - 40
Japanese Series	12 - 15	15 - 18
KUTUW, CHRISTO (Poland)	8 - 10	10 - 12
LAFUGIE Series 45	15 - 18	18 - 22
LARCOMBE, ETHEL Art Nouveau	25 - 30	30 - 35
LARRONI (Italy) Art Deco		
S.W.S.B. Series 6733 Lovers Kissing (6)	8 - 10	10 - 12
LASKOFF, F. (Poland) Art Nouveau		
Ricordi Ladies Series	75 - 85	85 - 100
LASALLE, JEAN	5 - 8	8 - 10
LAURENS, P.A. (Czech.)	8 - 10	10 - 12
LAUDA, RICHARD (Denmark) Art Nouveau	60 - 65	65 - 70
LE ANDRE, CHARLES (France)		
"Cocorico" Series	400 - 450	450 - 500
"Collection des Cent" No.7	200 - 225	225 - 250
"Collection Job" No.3	60 - 70	70 - 80
LEARNED	5 - 6	8 - 10
LEBISCH, FRANZ (Austria) See Wiener Werkstaette		
LE DUCIS, A.		
Rev. Stampa		
Series 2039 High Fashion (6)	10 - 12	12 - 15
LeDUEI	10 - 12	12 - 15
LEINWEBER, R.	6 - 8	8 - 10
LELEE, L. (France) Art Nouveau		
Collection des Cent.	70 - 80	80 - 100
Other Ladies	15 - 20	20 - 25
LENDECKE, OTTO (Poland) See Wiener Werkstaette		
LENG, MAX Art Nouveau	20 - 30	30 - 40
LENOLEM (France) French Glamour		
Meissner & Buch Series 219	18 - 20	20 - 25

Ludolfs Liberts, Em.Benjamin
Kostims "Blondai"

Ludolfs Liberts, Em. Benjamin
Kostims "Judite"

LENZ, M. (Austria) Art Nouveau	40 - 50	50 - 60
LEONNEC, G. (France)	15 - 20	20 - 30
LESKER, H. Art Deco	8 - 10	10 - 12
LESSIEUX, LOUIS (France) Art Nouveau	35 - 40	40 - 45
Diamonds, Emeralds, etc. Series	25 - 30	30 - 35
LHUER, VICTOR	15 - 18	18 - 22
LIBERTS, LUDOLFS (Latvia)		
Graphic Arts of Ladies & Costumes		
"Pas des Deux" Series	20 - 25	25 - 30
"Pas des fleures" Series		
"Samsons un Dalila" Series		
Kostims "Blondai"Opera "Begsan no Seraja"	25 - 30	30 - 35
Kostims baletam "Judite"		
Kostims Opera "Salinieki"		
LIKARZ-STRAUSS, MARIA (Austria)		
See Wiener Werkstätte		
LINDSELL, L.	8 - 10	10 - 12
LIST, WILHELM (Austria) Art Nouveau		
B.K.W.I Series 130 (6)	70 - 80	80 - 100
LIVEMONT, P. (Belgium) Art Nouveau	200 - 250	250 - 350
LLOYD, T.	4 - 6	6 - 8
LOFFLER, B. (Austria) Art Nouveau		
Wiener Werkstatte	200 - 250	250 - 300
LONGLEY, CHILTON (U.S.) Art Deco		
A.G. & Co. Ltd.		
Series 422 (6	25 - 30	30 - 35

Series **845** (6)	40 - 50	50 - 75
Series **90** Hats (6)	10 - 12	12 - 14
LORELEY Art Deco	12 - 15	15 - 18
LORENZI, FACIO (Italy)	15 - 18	18 - 22
LÖW, FRITZI (Austria)		
See Wiener Werkstätte		
LUDOVICI, ANTHONY (Italy)	12 - 15	15 - 20
LUDSON Series 90 Hats (6)	10 - 12	12 - 14
M.M.S.	5 - 6	6 - 8
MSM Meissner & Buch	15 - 18	18 - 22
MACDONALD, A. K. (G.B.) Art Nouveau	40 - 50	50 - 60
MAGRITTE, RENE (Belgium)		
Surrealistic Real Photo-types (Cont. size)		
15 "La Solution de Rebus" (1937)	80 - 90	90 -100
3531 "Der Sommer" (1938)		
MAILICK, A.	10 - 12	12 - 15
MALUGANI, G. (Italy)	10 - 12	12 - 15
MANASSE, A. (Austria)	5 - 6	6 - 8
MANNING, FREDERICK S. (U.S.)		
Series 117 Portraits	8 - 10	10 - 12
Others	6 - 8	8 - 10
MANNING, G.		
P.A.R. - Series 144 Coat-Hat (6)	10 - 14	14 - 16
MANNING, REG (U.S.)	8 - 10	10 - 12
MG or MANNI GROSZE (Silhouettes)	12 - 15	15 - 20
Nudes	15 - 20	20 - 25
MANUEL, HENRI (France) French Glamour		
Series 51, 55	18 - 20	20 - 25
MANSELL, VIVIAN (G.B.)		
"National Ladies" Series	10 - 12	12 - 15
Others	8 - 10	10 - 12
MARBACH, MITZI (Austria) (Deco)		
B.K.W.I.		
Series 3091 "Frohliche Weihnachten!" (6)	25 - 30	30 - 35
MARCOS. J. (Italy)		
Lady/Bubbles Fantasy	15 - 18	18 - 22
Others	12 - 15	15 - 20
MARCO, M.		
Raphael Tuck, **Series 2763** (Asti-type)	10 - 12	12 - 15
MARECHAUK, C.	6 - 8	8 - 10
MARSHEL, HARRY		
Djer-Kiss Rouge	12 - 15	15 - 18
MARTIN-KAVEL		
Lapina Series 5027-5036	10 - 12	12 - 15
Lapina Nudes	12 - 15	15 - 18
MARTINEAU, ALICE	6 - 8	8 - 10
MASTROAINI, D. (Italy)		
Ladies	8 - 10	10 - 12
MATALONI, G. (Italy) Art Nouveau (Japanese)	25 - 30	30 - 35
MAUZAN, L. A. (Italy) Art Deco & Glamour		
Dell, Anna & Gasparini; Rev. Stampa		
Series 386, 394 Lovers - Kissing (6)	10 - 12	12 - 15
Series 462, 498 Lovers-by--the-Sea (6)		

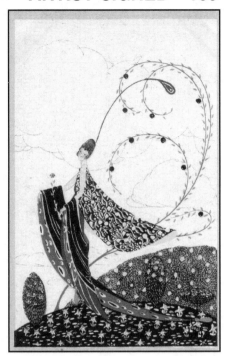

Chilton Longley, A. G. & Co.
Series 845-1

Chilton Longley, A. G. & Co.
Series 420

Series 343, 424 Couples (6)		
Series 248 Roman "Lovers" (6)	12 - 14	14 - 16
Series 42 Sport (6)	15 - 18	18 - 22
Series 301, 438 (6)		
Series 279, 297 Heads - Green Ring (6)	20 - 22	22 - 25
Series 145, 252 Hat & Scarf (6)		
Series 46, 230 Fashion (6)	15 - 18	18 - 22
Series 83 Little Men		
Series 250, 174 Walk, Traveling (6)	20 - 22	22 - 25
Series 247, 298 Beauties (6)		
Series 53 Man Sits on Giant Shoes (6)	10 - 12	12 - 15
Series 43, 235 Shoulders Up (6)	12 - 15	15 - 18
Series 321, 343, 414 Fashion (6)	15 - 18	18 - 22
Series 8, 14, 80 High Fashion (6)		
Series 201, 202, 2050 Walking (6)	10 - 12	12 - 15
Series 126 Waist-Up, in Chair (6)	18 - 22	22 - 25
Series 2, 10 With Cupid (6)	12 - 15	15 - 18
Tennis/Golf	20 - 25	25 - 30
Erotic/Semi-Nudes	22 - 25	25 - 28
Degami		
Series 106, 201 (6)	15 - 18	18 - 22
Series 250 (6) Longerie	15 - 20	20 - 25
G.B.T		
Series 3 (6) Nudes-semi nudes with Cupid	22 - 25	25 - 28
Rev. Stampa -- Ladies & Dogs		
Ladies & Dogs Series 316, 453, 491 (6)	15 - 18	18 - 22

G. Meschini (Unsigned)
MCA (Ars Nova)

G. Meschini (Unsigned)
MCA (Ars Nova)

Ladies & Horses **Series 383** (6)	15 - 18	18 - 22
MAYER, LOU (U.S.)		
K. Co., Inc. 207 "Vanity Fair"	10 - 12	12 - 15
Reinthal & Newman		
400, 500 Series	8 - 10	10 - 12
Fantasy Series (6) 878-883		
878 "The Pearl in the Oyster"	15 - 18	18 - 22
880 "Pond Lillies"		
881 "Grape Shot"		
882 "Bric-a-Brac"		
883 "Here's Looking at You"		
Ullman Mfg. Co. Pretty Girl Series	8 - 10	10 - 12
M.C. Beautiful Fashions	15 - 18	18 - 25
McFALL, J.V. (U.S.)	4 - 5	5 - 6
McLELLAN, CHAS. A.	4 - 5	5 - 6
McMEIN, NEYSA (U.S.)		
Novitas Series 15672 Head Studies (6)	10 - 12	12 - 15
Publisher at Polyphot (Finland)	12 - 15	15 - 18
Osh Kosh Pennant Girls (6)	10 - 12	12 - 15
MELASSO Series 125 Hats (6)	12 - 15	15 - 18
MERCER, JOYCE (G.B.) Art Nouveau	15 - 18	18 - 22
MESCHINI, G. (Italy) Art Deco		
G.P.M.		
Series 113 High Fur Collars, Hats (6)	40 - 45	45 - 50
Series Ars Nova	35 - 40	40 - 45
"Ultra" Series (6) Uns.	40 - 45	45 - 50

Ditta A. Guarneri, Milano

Series 2409 Lovers	25 - 30	30 - 35
Series 2411 Ladies/Dogs	35 - 40	40 - 50
Series 2443 Lovers Uns.	30 - 35	35 - 40
Ladies	32 - 35	35 - 40
Harlequins/Pierrot	40 - 45	45 - 50
Lovers	30 - 32	32 - 36
Series 48 Non Deco Ladies	15 - 18	18 - 22
MCA (Ars Nova) Uns.	35 - 40	40 - 45

METLOKOVITZ, LEOPOLDO or LM (Italy)

Art Nouveau Works	50 - 75	75 - 100
Art Deco	20 - 25	25 - 30
Ladies/Fashion	10 - 12	12 - 14
Bathing Beauties	10 - 12	12 - 15
Pierrot	25 - 28	28 - 32
Couples	8 - 10	10 - 12

MEUNIER, GEORGES (France)

Cinos and Collection des Cent	150 - 200	200 - 250

MEUNIER, HENRI (Belgium) Art Nouveau

"Four Seasons" (4)	60 - 70	70 - 80
"Les Grandes Femmes" (12)	200 - 250	250 - 300
"Inspiration"	100 - 110	110 - 120
"Zodiac" (12)	100 - 125	125 - 150

MEUNIER, SUZANNE   French Glamour

Marque L-E

No. 500-506	20 - 25	25 - 28
Series 11, 20, 22	18 - 22	22 - 26
Series 40 Semi-nude-Wild animals	32 - 35	35 - 40
Series 26, 42, 77	22 - 25	25 - 35
Series 29, 32, 35	20 - 25	25 - 30
Series 24, 52, 56, 74, 99	18 - 22	22 - 26
Series 60, 64, 69, 96, 98, 99	25 - 30	30 - 35
Series 96 (Smoking Ladies)	32 - 35	35 - 40
Delta - Series 90	20 - 22	22 - 26

MIGNOT, VICTOR (Belgium) Art Nouveau	30 - 35	35 - 40
MIKI (Finland) Art Deco	10 - 12	12 - 15
MILLER, MARION (U.S.)	3 - 4	4 - 5

MILLIERE, M. (France)   French Glamour

Series 6, 21, 30, 37	18 - 22	22 - 25
Series 34, 54, 65	25 - 30	30 - 35

MITCHELL, SADIE WENDELL (U.S.)

W.G. McFarlane

Fantasy Cupid Series	10 - 12	12 - 15
Valentine Series	8 - 10	10 - 12

"Troilene" American Girl Series (6)

"The Country Club Girl"	10 - 12	12 - 15
"The Automobile Girl"		
"The Summer Girl"		
"The Yachting Girl"		
"The Society Girl"		
"The Bathing Girl"		

German-American Art

Christmas & Easter Series	5 - 8	8 - 10

Suzanne Meunier, L-E 69-7
"Gestes frivoles"

Suzanne Meunier, L-E 99-7
"Les Boudoirs de Verre"

Lou Mayer, K. Company, Inc.
207, "Vanity Fair"

Sadie Wendell Mitchell, W.G.
McFarlane, "The Bathing Girl"

MOLINA, ROBERTO
"Diabolo" Series	10 - 12	12 - 15

MONESTIER, C. (Italy)   Art Deco

E. G. Falci
Series 27 Girl-Mask, Pierott	15 - 18	18 - 22
Series 830 Hats (6)	14 - 16	16 - 20
Others	8 - 10	10 - 12

Ladies & Dogs
Series 36 (6)	12 - 15	15 - 18

MONIER, MAGGY 15 - 18   18 - 22

MONTEDORO (Italy)   Art Deco

Rev. Stampa
Series A (6)	45 - 55	55 - 65
Series B (6)	65 - 70	70 - 75

MORAN, LEON (U.S.)   5 - 6   6 - 7

MORIN, LOUIS (France)
Collection des Cent No. 2b "Volupte"	300 - 325	325 - 350

MOSER, KOLOMAN (Austria)   Art Nouveau
Ackerman	225 - 250	250 - 275
Gerlach & Schenk "Ver Sacum"	1000 - 1500	1500 - 2500
Philipp & Kramer Series I - V	200 - 250	250 - 350

MOSTYN, MARJORIE   (G.B.)

Raphael Tuck
Series 108 Jewel Girls	12 - 15	15 - 18
Series 11 "Fair of Feature"	10 - 12	12 - 15
Water Color Series 2397 "A Maiden Fair"	8 - 10	10 - 12

MOUTON, Georges   (France)
Erotic	12 - 15	15 - 18
Others	20 - 25	25 - 30

MUCHA, ALPHONSE (Czechoslovakia)

French Issues

Home Decor, 1894
Store ad -- extremely rare; no recorded sales.

Collection Cinos, 1898
Waverley Cycles Advertising Bicycles
Last recorded sale in 1990; $13,500.
"Gismonda," "Samaritaine," "La Dame aux Camélias"	500 - 550	550 - 600
"Lorenzaccio"	650 - 700	700 - 750

Cocorico, 1900
Blue with rooster; horizontal.	650 - 700	700 - 750

Moet et Chandon, 1900
Menu designs (10)	250 - 300	300 - 350

F. Champenois
"Cartes Postales Artistiques"
First Series (C1-12), 1898
The Seasons (4)	125 - 150	150 - 200
The Flowers (4) The Ages of Man (4)	200 - 250	250 - 300

Second Series (C13-24), 1899
Byzantines (2)	125 - 150	150 - 200
The Seasons (4) The Arts (4)	175 - 200	200 - 225
Zodiac	250 - 300	300 - 350

Alphonse Mucha, F. Champenois
"The Flowers"

Alphonse Mucha, F. Champenois
"Printemps" (Spring)

Rêverie

Third Series (C25-36), 1900

Vignettes (3)	250 - 300	300 - 350
"Salomé"		
"L'aube" (Dawn), "Crepuscule" (Dusk)	350 - 400	400 - 450
"Le primevère" (Primrose)		
"La Plume" (Quill)		
Seasons, vertical (4)	200 - 250	250 - 300

Fourth Series (37-48), 1900

The Months of the Year (12)	150 - 175	175 - 200

Fifth Series (49-60), circa 1901

Sarah Bernhardt - "La Plume"	500 - 525	525 - 550
Austro-Hungarian Benefit Society	550 - 600	600 - 650
Cocorico (with Rooster, vertical)	500 - 550	550 - 600
Cocorico (lady in rectangle)	250 - 275	275 - 300
Cocorico (lady in oval)		
Menu for a Banquet	400 - 450	450 - 500
Menus (4)	225 - 250	250 - 300
Design for a Fan	475 - 500	500 - 525
Paris 1900 Exposition	400 - 450	450 - 500

Sixth Series (C61-72), circa 1901

Design for a Menu	325 - 350	350 - 375
Cover for the Champenois Catalog	350 - 375	375 - 400
"Papeterie" (Stationery)	325 - 350	350 - 375
Design for a Program (lady with harp)	350 - 375	375 - 400
"Les Moments de la Journée"		
(Times of the Day) (4)	250 - 300	300 - 350

Alphonse Mucha, F. Champenois
"Février" (Months of the Year)

Alphonse Mucha, F. Champenois
"Topaz"

Alphonse Mucha, F. Champenois
"Mai" (Months of the Year)

"Printemps" (Spring)	325 - 350	350 - 375
Lady with a Quill	500 - 550	550 - 600
"Nénuphar" (Water Lily)	400 - 450	450 - 500
"Fleur de cerisier" (Cherry Blossom)		
Seventh Series (C73-84), circa 1902		
Autumn	500 - 550	550 - 600
Lygie	450 - 500	500 - 550
Heather, Sea Holly		
Ivy, Laurel	500 - 550	550 - 600
Gemstones (4)		
Flowers	650 - 750	750 - 850
Fruits		
Collection des Cent, 1901		
No. 11a Peasant Woman	1500 - 2000	2000 - 2500
No. 11b Austro-Hungarian Benevolent		
Society	900 - 1000	1000 - 1200
Lygie, 1901		
B&W, same design as Champenois Ser. 7.	750 - 850	850 - 950
La Revue du Bien, circa 1903		
Photographic process	900 - 1000	1000 - 1200
Printed process		
Lefevre-Utile, 1904		
Biscuit advertisement	900 - 1000	1000 - 1200
Collection JOB (Cigarette Papers)		
"Femme Blonde"		
1903, horiz., plant motif background	350 - 375	375 - 400
1905, horiz., "Collection JOB" inscription	200 - 250	250 - 300

1908, horiz., "Bureau de Londres" inscript.	500 - 550	550 - 600
1911, horiz., "Collection JOB,		
Cigarettes JOB" inscription	400 - 450	450 - 500
1914, vertical	800 - 900	900 - 1000

"Femme Brune"

1905, horiz., "Collection JOB" inscription	200 - 250	250 - 300
1911, horiz., "Collection JOB,		
Cigarettes JOB" inscription	400 - 450	450 - 500
1915, vertical	800 - 900	900 - 1000

Vin Mariani, 1910   1000 - 1200   1200 - 1400

Cognac Bisquit, circa 1908

Horizontal, color   800 - 900   900 - 1000
  (w/cognac manufacturers adv. imprint;
    one recorded sale of $4,100 in 1993.)
Also comes in black & white in both vertical
and horizontal format. No recorded sales.
Extremely rare.

Rudolf Friml

Black & White	1000 - 1200	1200 - 1400
Color	1200 - 1500	1500 - 2000

U.S. Issues

Joan of Arc (Maude Adams) by Blanchard

Warner's Rust-Proof Corsets, 1909

No margin imprint	1000 - 1200	1200 - 1400
Three text paragraph & 4 text in margin	750 - 850	850 - 1000

Sarah Bernhardt American Tour

Four designs: "Gismonda," "Lorenzaccio,"
"Harriet," and "La Samartine." All in
single color but issued in different color
combinations and with repertories for
three different tours: 1905-6, 1910, and
1916-1917. Extremely rare; prices estimated at $10,000-20,000 each.

Czechoslovakian Issues

Advertisements

Dvacàtý Vek (20th Century), 1902,		
magazine cover	250 - 300	300 - 350
Slavia, 1909, insurance company		
Large Border	200 - 250	250 - 300
Small Border	250 - 300	300 - 3350
Krinogen, 1928, herbal hair preservative	400 - 450	450 - 500
The Kiss of Springtime, Fine Arts Society		
of Prague	250 - 300	300 - 350
Vopalka Textiles, attributed.		

Benefit Societies

The Moravian Teachers' Choir, 1911	200 - 250	250 - 300
Bohemian Heart Charity, 1912	250 - 300	300 - 350
Foundation for the Schools of Brno,		
circa 1912	350 - 400	400 - 450
Kamensky Society, 1920	250 - 300	300 - 350
Y.W.C.A., 1922	350 - 400	400 - 450
For the Blind, 1939	250 - 300	300 - 350

Festivals

Prague Sokol, 1901	350 - 400	400 - 450
Vyskov Exhibition of Agriculture,		
Industry and Ethnology, 1902	250 - 300	300 - 350
Vyskov Exhibition of Agri. & Ind., 1902	400 - 450	450 - 500
Student Festival, 1909	350 - 400	400 - 450
Ivancice Regional Fair, 1912-13	175 - 200	200 - 250
Prague Spring Festival, 1914		
Eighth Sokol Festival, 1926	150 - 175	175 - 200
Jubilee Festival, 1928	175 - 200	200 - 250
Fiftieth Anniversary of the Sokol at		
Ivancice, 1937	350 - 400	400 - 450
Czechoslovak Post, 1957; post-mortem.	175 - 200	200 - 250

Frescoes-Prague Municipal Building

Original 1909 Issue by Stenc (mark UP)

General views of the hall (2)	60 - 75	75 - 85
Ceiling circular frescoe (2)		
Mural frescoes (3)		
Cardinal virtues (8)	85 - 100	100 - 125

1919 Reissue by Amos Pesl

Cardinal virtues (8)	75 - 85	85 - 100
Others	50 - 60	60 - 75

Other Reissues

Cardinal virtues (8)	75 - 85	85 - 100
Others	50 - 60	60 - 75

The Beatitudes, 1909 (6)

Original 1909 Issue by Stenc (mark UP)	60 - 75	75 - 85
Circa 1919 Reissue by Amos Pesl	50 - 60	60 - 75

Slav Epic, 1928

Poster Design for the Exhibition of the		
Slav Epic	175 - 200	200 - 250
The Slkav Epic Paintings		
Published by Neubert, brown (6)	45 - 50	50 - 55
Photographic process (7)	50 - 55	55 - 60

Miscellaneous

Barcelona Expo, 1903 - Extremely Rare	Range	10-15,000
"Dance Soirée," 1899	750 - 850	850 - 950
Remembrance of Ivancice, 1909		
Color, large	175 - 200	200 - 250
Black & light brown, regular size	150 - 175	175 - 200
Defense of National Minorities, 1915	750 - 850	850 - 950
"Russia Restituenda," 1922	150 - 175	175 - 200
Reconciliation of Czechs & Slovaks, 1928	350 - 400	400 - 450
Château Emmahof, 1931	400 - 450	450 - 500
Nativity, 1934	175 - 200	200 - 250
Orphan	350 - 400	400 - 450

Other Countries

Barcelona Expo -- extremely rare		10000 - 15000
Bergamo Fair, 1900, Italy (2)	2000 - 2500	2500 - 3000
Zodiac, 1905		
Ad for English Clothiers in Germany (B&W)	500 - 600	600 - 700

* Listings for most Mucha cards are from Les
Illustrateurs, 1991 Edition, by **Neudin.**

MUGGIANI (Italy) Art Deco
Ladies/Heads/Fashion	12 - 15	15 - 18
Ladies/Animals	15 - 18	18 - 22

MUHLBERG, S. 8 - 10   10 - 12

MURCH, FRANK
Decorative Poster Co., Series HC 1-12   10 - 12   12 - 15

MUSSINO (Italy)   Art Deco

MUTTICH, C.V. (Czech.)
Head Studies   8 - 10   10 - 12

MYER (U.S.)   4 - 5   5 - 6

NP   Art Deco   12 - 15   15 - 18

NAILLOD, C.S. (France)   12 - 15   15 - 18

NAM, JAQUES (France)   12 - 15   15 - 18

NANNI, Giovanni (Italy)   Art Deco
   Rev. Stampa; Dell, Anna & Gasparini

Series 26-A, 597 Couples Kissing (6)	12 - 15	15 - 18
Series 373 Couples Kissing (6)		
Series 255 National Girls (6)	15 - 18	18 - 22
Series 529 Pajamas, Smoking (6)		
Series 21, 206, 253, 256, 304, 378 Hats (6)	18 - 20	20 - 25
Series 162 Hats and Ties (6)	20 - 22	22 - 27
Series 308, 376, 396 Heads (6)	12 - 15	15 - 20
Series 283 Fur Collar Hats (6)	18 - 20	20 - 25
Series 377, 521 Hats, Coats	15 - 18	18 - 22
Series 337 Playing Cards-Hats (6)	18 - 20	22 - 25
Series 372, 505 Heads, High Fash. (6)		
Series 480 In Buggy (6)	15 - 18	18 - 22
Series 494 With Hat Boxes (6)	20 - 22	22 - 25
Series 445 Lounging Around (6)		
Series 540 Heads (6)	22 - 25	25 - 28
Couples	10 - 12	12 - 15
Ladies/Animals	15 - 18	18 - 22
Pierrot/Harlequins	22 - 25	25 - 30
Soccer Series		
Erotic/Semi-Nudes	22 - 25	25 - 30

  Ladies & Dogs
Series 205, 300 (6)	15 - 18	18 - 22

  Ladies & Horses
Series 116, 257 (6)	12 - 15	15 - 20
Series 307, 374 (6)	15 - 18	18 - 22

   NASH, A.   (G.B.) (Ladies & Dogs)
   Heckscher   703 "Love Me, Love My Dog"   10 - 12   12 - 15

NAST, THOMAS, JR.
Tennis "Love Game"	18 - 22	22 - 25
Others	6 - 8	8 - 10

NEFF, GUY   2 - 3   3 - 4

NEWTON, RUTH   4 - 5   5 - 6

NEY (France) French Glamour
  Delta - Series 24   20 - 25   25 - 30

NICOLET, G.   8 - 10   10 - 12

NICZKY, R.   10 - 12   12 - 15

NIKOLAKI, Z.P.
  Reinthal & Newman Ladies Series   8 - 10   10 - 15

M. Pepin, Delta Series 23-114
"Porte-Bonheur"

L. Peltier, Delta Series 19-95
"Jour de I' An"

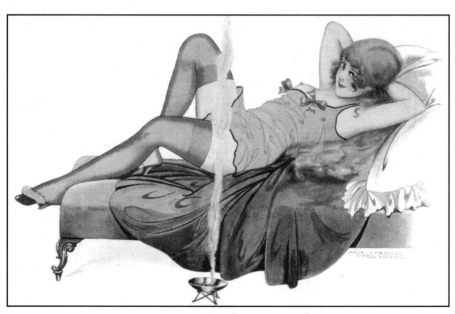

M. Pepin, Delta Series 21-005
"Les cinq sens de Pépinette"

NORMAN, S.		
Reinthal & Newman - **Series 1000** (6)	8 - 10	10 - 12
NOURY, GASTON (France) Art Nouveau	60 - 75	75 - 150
See Mermaids Section		
NYSTROM, JENNY (Sweden)	10 - 12	12 - 15
OCCHIPINTI, F.	8 - 10	10 - 12
OPLATEK (Ladies & Horses)	8 - 10	10 - 12
ORLANDI, V. (Italy)		
T.A.M. - **Series 7612** Couples Hugging (6)	8 - 10	10 - 12
OST, A. (Belgium) Art Nouveau	20 - 25	25 - 35
PAGNOTTA (Italy) Art Deco		
Series 494 High Fashion (6)	8 - 10	10 - 12
PAGONI (Italy) Art Deco	12 - 15	15 - 18
PALANTI, G. (Italy) Art Deco	12 - 15	15 - 18
PANNETT, R.	6 - 8	8 - 10
PATELLA, B. (Italy)		
Art Deco	15 - 20	20 - 25
Art Nouveau	35 - 40	40 - 45
PAWLOWSKI, J. (Poland)	10 - 12	12 - 15
PELLEGRINI, E.	12 - 15	15 - 18
PELLON, A. **Ideal Series** (6)	80 - 90	90 - 100
PELTIER, L. (France) French Glamour		
Delta		
Series 17	25 - 30	30 - 35
Series 28	18 - 20	20 - 22
PENNELL (U.S.) **Artist is actually Bennett**		
and was misnamed in previous editions.		
PENOT, ALBERT (France) French Glamour		
Series 10, 12, 16, 25, 28	18 - 22	22 - 26
Series 97, 98, 109		
PENTSY	8 - 10	10 - 12
PEPIN, MAURICE (France)		
Delta		
Series 21, 23 Semi-nudes	25 - 28	28 - 32
Series 16, 21, 30 French Glamour	20 - 25	25 - 30
PERAS (France) French Glamour		
Series 68	15 - 18	18 - 22
PERINI, T. (Italy) **Ladies & Horses**	10 - 12	12 - 15
PETER, OTTO (Germany)		
PETERSON, L. (U.S.) Cowboys/Indians		
H. H. **Tammen** -- Love & Life Series	6 - 8	8 - 10
PEW, G. L.		
Aquarelle Series 109, 2239	6 - 8	8 - 10
E.A.S.B. Series 108, 109	8 - 10	10 - 12
Leubrie & Elkus (L&E)		
Series 2221, 2223 (Heads)	8 - 10	10 - 12
PHILIPPI, ROBERT (Austria) Art Nouveau		
B.K.W.I. Cupid Series 3095 (6)	15 - 20	20 - 25

PHILLIPS, COLES (U.S.)

Coles Phillips' works are the most elusive of the famous U.S. illustrators, and his cards are rarely seen in auctions. The famous Fadeaway Girls, both signed and unsigned, are among the most beautiful ever published. His renderings of ladies for Community Plate are also very popular with advertising collectors. Relatively unknown are his set of six movie stars for C.P. & Company, New York. These also are extremely rare and hard to find.

COLES PHILLIPS

* **Cards Listed with an asterisk are Fadeaway Girls images.**

Life Publishing Co., 1907
   Life Series 1

"Her Choice"	40 - 45	45 - 55

Life Pub. Co., 1909

© **Coles Phillips Series**	50 - 55	55 - 65

   "Arms and the Man" *
   "Between You and Me ..." *
   "Home Ties"   *
   "Illusion"   *
   "Inclined to Meet" Series 2 *
   "The Sand Witch"
   "Such Stuff as Dreams are Made Of"
   "What Next?" Series 2
   "Which?" Series 2 *

Life Pub. Co., 1910

"A Call to Arms" *	50 - 55	55 - 65
"All Wool and Face Value" Series 2	45 - 50	50 - 55
"And Out of Mind as ..." Series 2		
"Discarding from Strength" Series 2	50 - 55	55 - 65
"Hers"	45 - 50	50 - 55

P.F. Volland & Co., Chicago
   © **by Life Pub. Co.**

"The Latest in Gowns, Good Night" *	45 - 50	50 - 55
"Long Distance Makes ..." *	55 - 60	60 - 65
"May Christmas Day Heap Up for You"	45 - 50	50 - 55
"Memories" *	50 - 55	55 - 60
"My Christmas Thoughts ..." *		
"Pals" *		
"The Survival of the Fittest" *		

C.P. Co., Inc., N.Y.
   Movie Star Series

"King Baggott," "Francis X. Bushman"	60 - 70	70 - 80
"Alice Joyce," "Blanche Sweet"		
"Rosemary Theby," "Lillian Walker"		

ADVERTISING

R. Stafford Collins, N.Y.

Community Plate	45 - 50	50 - 55

Community Plate
   Ad for Brunner Fl. Jeweler

Community Plate
   "A Case of Love at First Sight"
   "The Aristocrat of the Dining Table"

Book Advertisement

"The Dim Lantern," by Temple Bailey	60 - 65	65 - 75
"The Trumpeter Swan," by Temple Bailey		
Calendar Cards, With Verse (Uns.)	60 - 65	65 - 75

Unsigned Coles Phillips
SB 973, No Caption

Coles Phillips, Life Publishing Co.
"R.S.V.P."

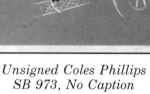

**Ten unsigned Fadeaway Girls have
been attributed to Coles Phillips.**

Values of these are:	30 - 35	35 - 40
PILLARD	5 - 6	6 - 7
PINKAWA, ANTON (Japan) Art Nouveau	25 - 30	30 - 35
PINOCHI (Italy) Art Deco		
Series 206 Hats (6)	10 - 12	12 - 15
Series 172 Lovers (6)		
Others	8 - 10	10 - 12
PIOTROWSKI, A. (Poland)		
PLANTIKOW	8 - 10	10 - 12
Ladies & Horses	10 - 12	12 - 14
POWELL, LYMAN (U.S.)		
"Eventful Days" Series		
"Graduation Day," "Engagement Day"	8 - 10	10 - 12
"Wedding Day," "Birthday"		
Flower Series 783, Fade-A-Way Series	6 - 8	8 - 10
Granbergs Konst.	8 - 10	10 - 12
PRESSLER, G. **Djer-Kiss Rouge**	6 - 8	8 - 10
PUTTKAMER Erotic Lovers Series 8027 (6)	15 - 18	18 - 22
QUINNELL, CECIL W.		
B.K.W.I.		
Series 258 "The Jewel Girls" (6)		
"Emerald," "Pearl," "Ruby," "Sapphire,"	12 - 15	15 - 18
"Topaz," "Turquoise"		
"Glad Eye" Series (6)	10 - 12	12 - 15

Cecil W. Quinnell, B.K.W.I. 258/3
"The Jewel Girls" – "Emerald"

Lyman Powell, Granbergs Konst.
No Caption

RABES, MAX (Germany)	8 - 10	10 - 12
RALPH, LESTER (U.S.)		
Reinthal & Newman		
"Dancing" Series 801-806		
801 "La Furlana"	18 - 22	22 - 25
802 "The Cortez"		
803 "The One Step"		
804 "The Half and Half"		
805 "The Maxie"		
806 "The Tango"		
813-818 Series* Love and Marriage Series		
813 "The Awakening of Love"	15 - 18	18 - 20
814 "The Stage of Life"		
815 "Up in the Clouds"		
816 "For All Eternity"		
817 "In Proud Possession"		
818 "The Home Guard"		
* With German Caption add $4.		
The Knapp Co., N.Y.		
Paul Heckscher (Distributed by)		
Series 302		
1 "Favored by Fortune"	10 - 12	12 - 15
2 "An Offer of Affection"		
3 "Weathering it Together"		
4 "His Proudest Moment"		
5 "Four-In-Hand"		

Lester Ralph, Knapp Co.
9523, "Fast Companions"

Lester Ralph
R&N 804, "The Half and Half"

6 "Her First Mate"			
7 "Two is Company Enough"			
8 "Fast Companions"			
9 "Fellow Sports"			
10 "Diana of the Shore"			
H. Import (Heckscher)			
Series 307			
1 "Take Me Along"		10 - 12	12 - 15
2 "Feathered Friends"			
3 "Wanted - A First Mate"			
4 "A Stroll Together"			
5 "Heart's Melody"			
6 "Speeding Her Up"			
H. Import (Heckscher)			
Series 308			
1 "Confidential Chatter"		10 - 12	12 - 15
2 "A Stroll Together"			
3 "A Social Call"			
4 "Playmates"			
5 "The Wings of the Wind"			
6 "A Surprise Party"		12 - 15	15 - 18
7 "Two is Company Enough"		10 - 12	12 - 15
9 "Fellow Sports"			
H. Import			
Series 335 No Caption			
1 Same as "Diana of the Shore"		8 - 10	10 - 12
2 Same as "Four in Hand"			

Lester Ralph
Knapp Co. Series 302-1
"Favored by Fortune"

Lester Ralph
Knapp Co. Series 302-2
"An Offer of Affection"

Lester Ralph
Knapp Co. Series 302-3
"Weathering it Together"

Lester Ralph
Knapp Co. Series 307-4
"A Stroll Together"

Lester Ralph
Knapp Co. Series 307-5
"Heart's Melody"

Lester Ralph
Knapp Co. Series 307-6
"Speeding Her Up"

3 Same as "Speeding Her Up"		
Hecksher Import		
Series 1026		
2 "Feathered Friends"	10 - 12	12 - 15
3 "Wanted - A First Mate"		
Calendar Cards With Advertising		
The Knapp Co.		
1913 (12)		
February "The Wings of the Wind"	18 - 22	22 - 25
April "Playmates"		
June "A Surprise Party"		
September "Speeding Her Up"		
October "Confidential Chatter"		
December "A Social Call"		

Others
Series 7 *   (12)
9523 "Fast Companions" January	10 - 12	12 - 15

9533 "Weathering it Together" February
9543 "Favored by Fortune" March
9553 "His Proudest Moment" April
9563 "Two is Company Enough" May
9573 "Her First Date" June
9583 "A Challenge from the Sea" July
9593 "A Game in the Surf" August
9603 "Diana of the Shore" September
9613 "Four-in-Hand" October
9623 "Fellow Sports" November
9633 "An Offer of Affection" December
* With advertising - Add $5-$10.
C.W. Faulkner
  Series 1314 (6)

B "Fast Companions"	10 - 12	12 - 15

C "Fellow Sports"
E "Her First Mate"
Series 1315 (6)

D "Her Proudest Moment"	10 - 12	12 - 15

McGowan-Silsbee Litho Co., N.Y.
  No Captions (B&W)
  Same as "An Offer of Affection"

RAPPINI (Italy) Art Deco and Glamour		
Series 2016 With Hand Mirror (6)	10 - 12	12 - 15
Ladies/Heads/Fashion	12 - 15	15 - 18
Ladies/Animals	15 - 18	18 - 22
Ladies/Sports		
Ladies & Horses		
Series 1002 (6)	10 - 12	12 - 15
Series 1092, 2019 (6)	9 - 11	11 - 13
RAUH, LUDWIG (Austria) Art Nouveau	25 - 30	30 - 35
READ, F. W. (U.S.) **Edward Gross Life Series 1**	4 - 5	5 - 6
READING	7 - 8	8 - 10
REED, MARION (U.S.)	3 - 4	4 - 6
RELYEA		
E. Gross		
Relyea Numbered Series	8 - 10	10 - 12
Relyea - No. 9 Golf	15 - 18	18 - 22
REYNOLDS, FRANK (U.S.)		
Anonymous		
Hat Series		
3701 "Ruth"	6 - 7	7 - 8
3702 "Helen"		
3703 "Rose"		
3706 "Grace"		
Cowgirl Series	7 - 8	8 - 9
REYZNER, M.	6 - 8	8 - 10
REZSO, KISS		
"Siren Lady" Series 68-73	10 - 12	12 - 15
RICCO, CARLO (Italy) Art Deco	10 - 12	12 - 15

RICCO, LORIS (Italy)   Art Deco

Ladies	18 - 22	22 - 26
Lovers	15 - 18	18 - 22
Pierrots/Harlequins	20 - 25	25 - 30

ROBERTY, L.
M. Munk, Vienna

Bather Series 1124	10 - 12	12 - 15
Fashion Series	15 - 20	20 - 25

RODE, G.

Rev. Stampa Series 6529 On Chair (6)	12 - 14	14 - 16
RODELLA, G.	4 - 6	6 - 8
RUMPEL, F.	6 - 8	8 - 10
RUNDALZEFF, M. (Russia)	6 - 8	8 - 10
RUSSELL, MARY LA F.	5 - 7	7 - 8

RYAN, C. (U.S.)
Art Nouveau

A633 "Folly" A634 "Joy"	12 - 15	15 - 18
A635 "Curiosity" A636 "Vanity"		
A637 "Harmony" A638 "So Lonesome"		
A639 "Love" A640 "Temptation"		
673 "Constancy" 674 "Sweet Memories"		
675 "Sweet Dreams"		
677 "Dreaming of Days Gone By"		
679 "May Success Be Thine"		
680 "Love's Token"		

Winsch Backs

Non-Art Nouveau, Glamour		
"Blissful Moments, etc."	5 - 6	6 - 8
RYLAND, H. (G.B.)	8 - 10	10 - 12
RYLANDER, CARL (Sweden) Art Deco	12 - 15	15 - 20

SACCHETTI, ENRICO (Italy)
E. Polenghi

Beautiful Ladies	20 - 25	25 - 28
Ladies & Dogs	15 - 18	18 - 22
Others	12 - 15	15 - 18

SAGER, XAVIER (France)
French Glamour/Fantasy
K.F., Paris

Series 4485, 4486 Ladies Fashions	20 - 22	22 - 25

A. Noyer, Paris

Series 61, 131 Pajamas	15 - 18	18 - 22
Series 84 "Proverbs Americans" (6)	18 - 22	22 - 25
Series 138 Lingerie		
Series 147 Semi-Nudes	22 - 25	25 - 28
Series 156 Lesbian Dancers	22 - 27	27 - 35
Series 690 "Peaceful Shells" (6)	18 - 22	22 - 25
Other Glamour Series		
Erotic/Nudes	20 - 25	25 - 30

ST. JOHN
National Art

"National Girls" Series	12 - 15	15 - 18
"Foreign Girls" Series	8 - 10	10 - 12
"The Four Seasons"	10 - 12	12 - 15
"State Girl" Series	8 - 10	10 - 12

Relyea, E. Gross Co., No. 9
No Caption

J. T. Sharpe, Carleton Pub. Co.
703/6, "Good-Bye"

Montgomery Co., Chicago
    103 "Shopping"
    104 "Promenade"
    106 "Beauties"

SALMONI, G. (Italy) Art Deco	10 - 12	12 - 15
SALVADORI (Italy) Art Deco		
Series 168 "The Wolf" Fur (6)	15 - 18	18 - 22
SAMSON, C. W.		
Valentine & Sons Bathing Girls	8 - 10	10 - 12
SAN MARCO (Italy) Art Deco		
P.A.R.		
Series 2037, 2082 Hats	12 - 15	15 - 20
Fantasy Series - Lady/Bubbles	15 - 20	20 - 25
Others	12 - 15	15 - 18
SAND, ADINA (Art Nouveau)	10 - 15	15 - 20
SANTINO, F. (Italy) Art Deco		
Rev. Stampa **Series 131** Fashion Pose (6)	12 - 15	15 - 20
Ladies & Dogs Series 6783 (6)	12 - 14	14 - 16
Ladies & Horses Series 68 (6)	8 - 10	10 - 12
SCATTINI (Italy) Art Deco		
Ladies	15 - 18	18 - 22
Pierrots/Harlequins	18 - 22	22 - 25
SCHIELE, EGON (Art Nouveau)	150 - 200	200 - 250
See Wiener Werkstätte Section		
SCHENK H.P., Praha Sporting Series (10)	12 - 15	15 - 20
SCHILBACH (Germany)	8 - 10	10 - 12

SCHLOSSER, R. (Germany)	5 - 6	6 - 8
SCHMUCKER, S. L. (U.S.)		
Detroit Publishing Co.		
"American Girl" or "Cosmopolitan" Series		
"England," "France," "Italy"	150 - 200	200 - 250
"Netherlands," "Norway," "Russia"		
"Spain," "Switzerland," "Turkey"		
"United States"		
SCHROCCHI (Italy) Art Deco		
Series 4360 Fashion (6)	10 - 12	12 - 14
SCHMUTZLER, L. (See Color Nudes)		
Moderne Kunst Series	8 - 10	10 - 12
SCHUBERT, H. (Austria)		
M. Munk, Vienna		
Glamorous Ladies	12 - 15	15 - 18
Ladies & Dogs		
SCHUTZ, ERIC (Austria)		
B.K.W.I. Series 128	12 - 15	15 - 18
See Fantasy Section		
SCHWETZ, KARL (Czech)		
See Wiener Werkstätte Section		
SHAND, C. E. (Art Deco)	25 - 30	30 - 35
SHARPE, J. T. (G.B.)		
Carleton Pub. Co.		
Series 703 Hats (6)		
4 "Memories"	10 - 12	12 - 15
6 "Good-Bye"		
SHERIE	6 - 8	8 - 10
SICHEL, N.	5 - 6	6 - 8
SIMM, PROF. FRANZ (Germahy)	5 - 6	6 - 8
SIMONETTI, A. (Italy) Art Deco & Glamour	12 - 15	15 - 18
Ladies & Horses		
Series 41 (6)	12 - 15	15 - 20
Series 90 (6)	10 - 12	12 - 15
SINGER, SUZI **See Wiener Werkstaette**		
SITSCHKOFF (Russia)	10 - 12	12 - 15
SOLDINGER, A. (Poland)	8 - 10	10 - 12
SOLOMKO, S. (Russia)		
Russian Backs (1901 era) (Sepia)		
Pen drawings, Heads of Beautiful Women (12)	60 - 70	70 - 80
Lapina, Paris		
"Country Series - War 1914-19"	15 - 18	18 - 22
Russian Princess 1600 Series*		
"Queen Aeviakovna"	22 - 25	25 - 28
"Wassilisa Mikoülichna"		
"Princess Apraksia"		
"Princess Warrior Nastasia"		
"Princess Mary, The White Swan"		
"Princess Zabava Poutiatichna"		
"Queen Azviakovna of the East"		
* Russian Backs - Add $4-5 each.		
T.S.N. (Theo. Stroefer, Nürnberg) *		
15 "Parisiene"	14 - 16	16 - 18
175 "Phantasy"	16 - 18	18 - 22

"SINGLE—ST. VALENTINE."

A. Simonetti, Rev. Stampa
218/5 – No Caption

Fred Spurgin, Novitas 51655/1
"Single – St. Valentine."

"Dream of Icarius"	14 - 15	15 - 18
"Pearl of Creation"	15 - 18	18 - 20
228 "Vanity" (Semi-nude)	15 - 20	20 - 25
"Circe" (Semi-nude)		
"The Tale" (Fantasy)	15 - 16	16 - 18
155 "The Blue Bird" (Fantasy)	18 - 20	20 - 22
"Magician Circle" (Semi-nude)	15 - 20	20 - 25
154 "Temptations" (Semi-nude)		
95 "Glow Worm" (Fantasy)	15 - 18	18 - 20
"Fortune Telling" (Fantasy)		
Other **T.S.N.** (Many)	8 - 10	10 - 12
* Russian Backs - Add $4-5 to prices.		
SOMERVILLE, H.	4 - 6	6 - 8
SONREL, ELISABETH (Art Nouveau)	75 - 100	100 - 150
Glamour	18 - 20	20 - 25
SOWERBY, AMY MILLICENT (G.B.) See Sowerby Chapter		
SPOTTI, F. (Ladies & Dogs)		
Rev. Stampa, Series 158	8 - 10	10 - 12
SPURGIN, FRED (Latvia)	5 - 7	7 - 10
STACHIEWICZ, P.	8 - 10	10 - 12
STAMM, MAUD	5 - 6	6 - 7
STANLAWS, PENRHYN (U.S.)		
Davidson Bros.		
Series 6079 Women of the Regiment (6)	18 - 22	22 - 25
Edward Gross Watercolors		
Stanlaws 1-12 No Captions		

One of the most beautiful sets ever!

1	Pink rimmed hat, facing left	20 - 25	25 - 28
2	Green cap, white blouse		
3	Queenly beauty with strand of pearls		
4	Young girl with blue headband		
5	Wide brim hat - beach background		
6	Toboggan ski cap, red stripes		
7	Large brim hat with roses		
8	Large hat, sailor shirt top		
9	Wide brim hat with pink plume		
10	Yellow hat, blue background		
11	Hat tied at chin, with pink roses		
12	Fur hat, with fox fur, snow		

Knapp Co., N.Y. Watercolors

900 Series

"A Midsummer Maid," "After the Matinee" 15 - 20 20 - 25
"Daisies Won't Tell," "Fair as the Lily"
"Fresh as the Morn," "Girl of the Golden West"
"Kissed by the Snow," "The Pink Lady"
"School Days"

K. Co.

Distributed by A.R. & C.i.B Watercolors

Series 500 Series 900 Reprints
"A Midsummer Maid," "Daisies Wont Tell" 15 - 20 20 - 25
"Fresh as the Morn," "Girl of the Golden West"
"The Pink Lady"

Series 544
5 "Among the Blossoms" 15 - 20 20 - 25

Series 550
"A Midsummer Maid," "Daisies Won't Tell" 15 - 20 20 - 25
"Fair as the Lily," "Fresh as the Morn"

Series 551 15 - 20 20 - 25
"After the Matinee"
"Kissed by the Snow"
"School Days"
"Fair as the Lily"

Series 1025
4 "The Pink Lady" 20 - 25 25 - 30

Reinthal & Newman

Military Ladies Series

981	U.S.	18 - 22	22 - 25
982	Serbia	12 - 15	15 - 20
983	Belgium		
984	France		
985	Italy		
986	Greece		
987	Great Britain		
988	Japan		
989	Russia		

H. Choate & Co.

Djer-Kiss Rouge & Face Powder Compacts
"Silver Blonde" 22 - 25 25 - 30

STEINLEN, A.T. (Switzerland)

Art Nouveau

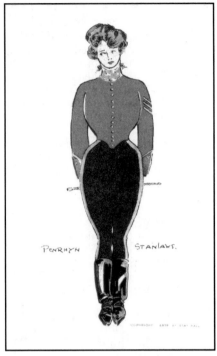

P. Stanlaws, R&N 981
"United States"

P. Stanlaws, Davidson Bros.
6079, "Women of the Regiment"

Better Issues	175 - 200	200 - 500
Others	30 - 35	35 - 45
STENBERG, AINA (Sweden) Art Deco	12 - 15	15 - 20
Art Nouveau issues	20 - 25	25 - 30
STOLTE, F. (Ladies & Horses)		
Series 25 (6)	10 - 12	12 - 15
F.T. **M. Munk Series 579** (6)	18 - 22	22 - 25
TACCHI, E. (Italy) Art Deco		
Series 494 High Fashion (6)	10 - 12	12 - 15
TAM, JEAN (France) French Glamour		
Series 39 "The Sammies in Paris" (6)	25 - 28	28 - 32
Series 47, 50, 70, 78, 81	18 - 22	22 - 25
Series 57, 67	20 - 25	25 - 30
TERZI, A. (Italy) Art Deco and Glamour		
Rev. Stampa; Dell, Anna & Gasparini		
Series 287, 299 Heads (6)	12 - 15	15 - 18
Series 322 Heads (6)	15 - 18	18 - 22
Series 323 Sitting (6)	12 - 15	15 - 18
Series 360, 486 Fashion (6)		
Series 454, 468 Fashion (6)	15 - 18	18 - 22
Series 482 Small Images (6)	8 - 10	10 - 12
Golf	20 - 25	25 - 30
Tennis	14 - 16	16 - 20
Couples	10 - 12	12 - 14
Ladies With Wild Animals	20 - 22	22 - 25

Jan Tam, L-E 78-7
"Femmes et Fruits"

F.T., M. Munk, 479
No Caption

Ladies & Dogs
    Series 341, 349, 399, 457, 482, 973 (6)   12 - 15   15 - 18
    Series 976, 559, 969 (6)
Ladies & Horses
    Rev. Stampa   **Series 320** (6)   12 - 15   15 - 18
TORNROSE, ALEX
    Welles Head Series (B&W)   6 - 8   8 - 10
    Others   6 - 7   7 - 8
TOULOUSE-LAUTREC, HENRI (France)
    "Cabaret Bruant"   600 - 800   800 - 900
    "La Goulue au Moulin Rouge"   1500 - 1600 1600 - 1800
    (Card recently sold for $1800.)
TRAVER, C. WARD (U.S.)
    H & S Art Co.
        "The Beauty of the Season"   8 - 10   10 - 15
        "Sweet Seventeen"
TRAVIS, STUART (U.S.)
    T.P. & Co.   **Series 727** Lovers   5 - 6   6 - 8
        Calendar Advert. "Dog Days"   10 - 12   12 - 15
TUHKA, A. (Finland) Art Deco   10 - 12   12 - 15
TURRAIN, E.D. Art Nouveau   25 - 30   30 - 35
TWELVETREES, C.   5 - 6   6 - 8

CLARENCE UNDERWOOD (U.S.)

Clarence Underwood was another of the more important illustrators of magazine covers and magazine fiction who benefitted from the great postcard era. This painter of beautiful ladies did work for Reinthal & Newman of New York, but his most beautiful images were published by the R. Chapman Co. (better known as the R.C. Co., N.Y.). They did the 1400 Series Water Colors of his ladies wearing big, beautiful, and colorful hats. These will always be some of the most beautiful renderings of the era.

CLARENCE UNDERWOOD

C.W. Faulkner		
Series 5	10 - 12	12 - 15
Series 1010		
1278 "A Symphony of Hearts"	8 - 10	10 - 12
"Their Search for Old China"		
National Art		
"Playing Card" Series	8 - 10	10 - 12
78 "Hearts" Two Men, Two Women		
79 "Poker" Five Men		
80 "Bridge" Four Women		
81 "Euchre" Five Men		
Reinthal & Newman		
300 Series Water Colors		
345 "The Flirt"	10 - 12	12 - 15
346 "Pretty Cold"		
347 "Her First Vote"	25 - 30	30 - 35
348 "It's Always Fair Weather"	10 - 12	12 - 15
349 "Rain or Shine"		
350 "Pleasant Reflections"		
R.C. CO., N.Y.		
Series 1400 Water Colors	18 - 22	22 - 28
1436 "Constance"		
1437 "Diana"		
1438 "Vivian"		
1439 "Phyllis"		
1440 "Celestine"		
1441 "Rosabella"		
1442 "Juliana"		
1443 "Victoria"		
1444 "Aurora"		
1445 "Sylvia"		
1446 "Virginia"		
1447 "Doris"		
Frederick A. Stokes Co.		
Series 1		
"A Problem of Income"	8 - 10	10 - 12
"Castles in the Smoke"		
"For Fear of Sunburn"		
"Knight Takes Queen"		
Series 2		
"Love Me, Love My Cat"	10 - 12	12 - 15
"Love Me, Love My Dog"		
"Love Me, Love My Donkey"		
"Love Me, Love My Horse"		

Series 3
"When We're Together Fishing"   10 - 12   12 - 15
"When We're Together at Luncheon"
"When We're Together Shooting"
"When We're Together in a Storm"
Series 4
"Beauty and the Beast"   10 - 12   12 - 15
"The Best of Friends"
"Expectation"
"The Promenade"
Series 5
"A Lump of Sugar"   10 - 12   12 - 15
"After the Hunt"
"The Red Haired Girl ..."
"Three American Beauties"
Series 6
"Feeding the Swans"   8 - 10   10 - 12
"A Pet in the Park"
"Posing"
"A Witch"   10 - 12   12 - 15
Series 7
"An Old Melody"   10 - 12   12 - 15
"Over the Teacups"
"The Opera Girl"
"The Violin Girl"
Series 8
"At the Races"   8 - 10   10 - 12
"Embroidery for Two"
"Out for a Stroll"
"Two Cooks"
Series 14
"Their First Wedding Gift"   8 - 10   10 - 12
"Their Love of Old Silver"
"Two and an Old Flirt"
"Vain Regrets"
Series 15
"A Lesson in Motoring"   10 - 12   12 - 15
"A Skipper and Mate"
Series 19
"The Only Two at Dinner"   8 - 10   10 - 12
"The Only Two at the Game"
"The Only Two at the House Party"
"The Only Two at the Opera"
Series 22
"The Greatest Thing in the World"   8 - 10   10 - 12
"The Last Waltz"
"Lost?"
"Love on Six Cylinders"   10 - 12   12 - 15
Series 377   Untitled   (4) B&W   5 - 6   6 - 8
Taylor, Platt & Co.
Series 782
"A Fisherman's Luck"   10 - 12   12 - 15
"A Heart of Diamonds"
"A Modern Siren"

1438, "Vivian"

1439, "Phyllis"

1440, "Celestine"

1442, "Juliana"

1444, "Aurora"

1446, "Virginia"

Six of Twelve Classics by Clarence Underwood
from R. C. Co.'s 1400 Series

"Daisies Won't Tell"
"The Glories of March"
"His Latest Chauffeur"
"Indicating a Thaw"
"The Magnet"
"Let's Paddle Forever"
"Love Has It's Clouds"
"Stolen Sweets"
"True Love Never Runs Smooth"
Osborne Calendar Co.
    Advertising Cards   30 - 35   35 - 40
    1521 "Fancy Work"
    1561 "Mary had a Little Lamb"

1571 "The Tongue is Mightier ..."
1601 "The Favorite's Day"
1621 "Music Hath Charm"

A.R. & Co.
1283 "Des Meeres und der Liebe Wellen"   10 - 12   12 - 15

M. Munk, Vienna
Series 303 (8)
Beautiful Ladies With Pets—No captions   10 - 12   12 - 15
Series 377, 385, 387, & 388   10 - 12   12 - 15
Ladies & Dogs   "My Companion"   10 - 12   12 - 15
Series 742 *
"Love Laughs at Winter"   8 - 10   10 - 12
"Love on Wings"   12 - 15   15 - 18
"Under the Mistletoe"   8 - 10   10 - 12
"The Sender of Orchids"
"The Last Waltz"
"The Greatest Thing"
* **Series 742** A,B,C,D,E,F,G & H.
All Same as Series 742 but with German
captions, add $3.
Series 832, 834, 837 & 860 *
"A Penny for Thought"   8 - 10   10 - 12
"A Problem of Income"
"Cherry Ripe"
"He Loves Me ..."
"How to Know Wildflowers"   12 - 15   15 - 18
"Only a Question of Time"   8 - 10   10 - 12
"The Sweetest Flower that ..."
"Skipper and Mate"   10 - 12   12 - 15
"Love and Six Cylinders"   12 - 15   15 - 18
With German Captions, add $3.

Novitas, Germany
400 Series
445   "Gestand nis"   8 - 10   10 - 12
447   "Einig"   10 - 12   12 - 14
449   "Zukunftplane"
Others, No Captions   8 - 10   10 - 12
20000 Series
20391 No Caption
20392 No Caption
20451 "Wer Wird Siegen"
20452 "Dem Fluck Entgegen"
20453 No Caption (Lovers of Beauty)
20454 "Liebe Auf Eis"
20455 "Abwesend, Aber Nicht Vergessen"
20456 No Caption
20457 "Zwei Seelen und ein Genankt"
20458 "Zukunpt Straune"
20459 No Caption
20460 "Glucklicht Tagt"

FINLAND
W. & G. (Weilin & Goos)
American Series N:0 7001 1-35
6 Cards with No Captions   20 - 22   22 - 25

RUSSIA
Richard or Phillips (Rishar)

"The Last Waltz Together"	25 - 30	30 - 40
UNIERZYSKI, J. (Poland)	6 - 8	8 - 10
UPRKA, JOZA (Czechoslavakia)	6 - 8	8 - 10

USABAL, L. (Italy)

P.F.B. (in Diamond) **Series 3796** (6)	12 - 15	15 - 18
Ladies & Dogs Series 3968 (6)	12 - 14	14 - 16
E.A.S.B.		
Series 111 Lovers under the Mistletoe	8 - 10	10 - 12
Series 103 Lovers Dancing		
Series 114, 370 Lovers Dancing	10 - 12	12 - 14
Erkal		
Series 301, 308, 315, 367 Hats (6)	8 - 10	10 - 12
Series 303 Smoking Ladies (6)	10 - 12	12 - 14
Series 336 Tennis (6)	20 - 22	22 - 25
Series 343 Skiing (6)	10 - 12	12 - 15
Series 318, 356 Lovers (6)		
Series 339 On Toboggan Sled (6)		
Series 347 Gypsy Heads (6)	8 - 10	10 - 12
Series 330, 337, 357 Dancing/Kissing (6)		
Series 1318 Lovers on Couch (6)	10 - 12	12 - 15
G. Kuais Series 1393 Hats	6 - 8	8 - 10
Gurner & Simon		
Series 2027 Lovers at the Bar (6)	6 - 8	8 - 10
S. & G. Series 694 Couples, Man in Uniform	6 - 8	8 - 10
S.W.S.B.		
Series 128 Lovers Kissing (6)	8 - 10	10 - 12
Series 1007, 1068, 1256 Couples Dancing (6)	10 - 12	12 - 15
Series 1091, 6380, 6383 Couples Dancing (6)		
Series 1070 Lesbian Dancers (6)	22 - 25	25 - 35
Series 1108 Nude in Fur (6)	12 - 15	15 - 20
Series 1295-1300 Dancing/Blacks (6)	20 - 22	22 - 25
Series 1356 Heads/Smoking (6)	10 - 12	12 - 18
Series 303 "Ladies Smoking" (6)		
Series 4668, 4669, 4670 (6)	10 - 12	12 - 15
Ladies & Dogs		
S.W.S.B.		
Series 1336, 4989 (6)	8 - 10	10 - 12
Series 1336 (6)		
Ladies & Horses		
S.W.S.B.		
Series 257, 328, 345, 5568 (6)	10 - 12	12 - 15
Erkal Series 307, 320, 335 (6)	10 - 12	12 - 15
S.W.S.B. Women in Uniform	10 - 12	12 - 15
Anonymous		
Series 20468 Couples Dancing	8 - 10	10 - 12
Art Deco		
Erkal		
Series 324 "Gypsy"	10 - 12	12 - 14
Series 363 Butterfly Ladies (6)	18 - 22	22 - 26
P.F.B. in Diamond		
Series 6073 Beauties on Pillows (6)	12 - 14	14 - 16

L. Usabal, S.W.S.B. 1246
No Caption

R. R. Wichera, M. Munk
Series 829

L. Usabal, S.W.S.B. 1244
No Caption

S.&G.S.iB.
    Series 6378, 6379, 6381, 6382 Dancing (6)   10 - 12   12 - 15
    Series 6384, 6387, 1071, 1091 Dancing (6)
    Series 1058, 1207, 1208,1330, 1333 Dancing (6)
Guner & Simon   Series 2027 Lovers Kissing 8 - 10   10 - 12
UZLEMBLO, HENRY (Poland)   12 - 15   15 - 18
VALLEE. A. Dancing   12 - 15   15 - 20
VALLET, L. (France)   French Glamour
    Lapina   Nude "La Douche" Series   22 - 25   25 - 28
    Collection des Cent 63b   150 - 175   175 - 200
VASSALO, A. (Italy) Art Deco   12 - 14   14 - 16
VENTURA, R.   10 - 12   12 - 15
VERNON, EMILE   3 - 4   4 -6
VILLON, JACQUES (France)   Art Nouveau
    Coll. des Cent   400 - 500   500 - 800
    Gala Henri Monnier   900 - 1000 1000 - 1100
VINCENT, RENE Art Deco   25 - 30   30 - 35
VILLA, A. (Italy)   10 - 12   12 - 15
VINNOY (France) Art Deco   12 - 14   14 - 18
VOGLIO, BENITO   (France)
WACHTEL, WILHELM (Germany)   6 - 8   8 - 10
WALLACE (U.S.) **Ladies & Horses**   10 - 12   12 - 15
WANKE, ALICE (Austria) Art Nouveau 50 - 60   60 - 75
WAPALLOKA (Russia)   6 - 8   8 - 10
WASILKOWSKI, K. (Poland)   8 - 10   10 - 12
WASKO, EDWARD G.   6 - 8   8 - 10

WEBSTER, W.E.		
WENNERBERG, B. (Sweden) Art Nouveau		
Lady Sports	12 - 15	15 - 25
Others	10 - 15	15 - 18
WEZEL, A. (Austria)	8 - 10	10 - 12
WFA Ladies & Horses Series 204 (6)	8 - 10	10 - 12
WICHERA, R. R. (Austria)		
M. Munk, Vienna		
Series 112, 224, 229, 322, 411, 450 (6)	10 - 12	12 - 15
Series 530, 633, 683, 1101, 1163 (6)		
Series 559, 5590 Big Hats (6)	12 - 15	15 - 18
Series 684 Semi-Nudes (6)	15 - 18	18 - 22
WIEDERSEIM, GRACE (also G. Drayton)		
Armour & Co.		
"American Girl" Series		
"The Wiederseim Girl"	30 - 35	35 - 40
"The Wiederseim Girl" (German Pub.)	35 - 40	45 - 50
WIMBUSH, WINIFRED		
Raphael Tuck		
Sporting Girls, Series 3603 (6)		
Bathing, Boating, Cricket	15 - 20	20 - 25
Golf	30 - 35	35 - 40
Skating	20 - 25	25 - 30
Tennis	25 - 30	30 - 35
WITT, MIA Art Deco	15 - 18	18 - 22
WUYTS, A.	4 - 6	6 - 8
YOBBI, L. (Italy)	10 - 12	12 - 15
ZABCZINSKY		
C.B.B.		
Series 21-1 Dancing (6)	15 - 18	18 - 22
Series 21-2 Standing (6)	18 - 20	20 - 25
Series 21-3 Dancing (6)	15 - 18	18 - 22
Series 21-4 Dancing (6)		
Series 21-5 Dancing (6)		
Series 21-6 Dancing (6)		
ZABCZOMSLU, W. Art Deco	8 - 10	10 - 12
ZANDRINO, A. (Italy) Art Deco		
Series 18 Nude With Wild Animals (6)	20 - 25	25 - 30
Series 17 Fans (6)	12 - 15	15 - 18
Series 23, 24, 30 Fashion (6)		
Series 94 Hats (6)		
Pierrots	20 - 22	22 - 25
ZELECHOWSKI, K. (Poland)	8 - 10	10 - 12
ZENISER, JOSEF	6 - 8	8 - 10
ZEUMER, BRUNO (Germany)	5 - 6	6 - 8
ZINI, M. Ladies	10 - 12	12 - 15
ZMURKO, FR. (Poland) See Color Nudes		
ANCZYC Series	8 - 10	10 - 12

BAUHAUS EXHIBITION

A continental-size series of 20 cards was issued for **"The Bauhaus Ausstellung"** of July-September, 1923 which was held in the German city

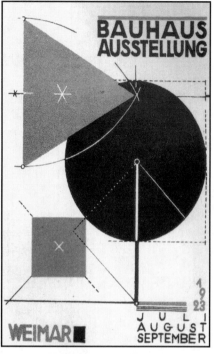

Paul Klee
4. "Die erhabene Seite"

Herbert Bayer
11. "Var. über Bauhaus-Signet"

of Weimar. These cards, drawn by 14 different artists, are among the most desired of all exhibition-type collectibles worldwide. Values are now in the $1500-5000 range and seem to rise each time they are offered at auction. Values are for only the EX-Mint issues. Artists and the number of their cards and price in Excellent condition are as follows:

Feininger 1. "Stadt" 2. "Kirche"	4,000.00
W. Kandinsky 3. "Komposition"	5,000.00
Paul Klee 4. "Die erhabene Seite"	
5. "Die heitere Seite"	5,000.00
Gerhard Marcks 6. "Hande, Hausmodell haltend"	2,000.00
Laszlo Moholy-Nagy 7. "Geometrische Formen"	2,500.00
Oskar Schlemmer 8. "Profile"	3,500.00
Rudolf Baschant 9. "Häuser und Mästen"	
10. "Variation über Bauhaus-Signet"	5,000.00
Herbert Bayer	
11. "Variation über Bauhaus-Signet"	3,000.00
12. "Geometrische Formen"	
P. Haberer 13. (Unknown)	1,500.00
D. Helm 14. "Variation über Bauhaus-Signet"	1,500.00
Ludwig Horschfeld-Mack 15. "Figur mit	
Spruchbandern" 16. "Komposition mit Lettern"	3,500.00
W. F. Molnár 17. "Architektur."	1,500.00
Kurt Schmidt 18. "Abstrakte Elemente"	
19. "Bäuhausler-Topografie"	1,500.00
Georg Teltscher 20. "Männchen"	1,500.00

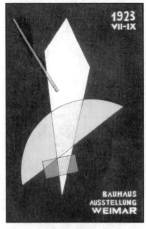  

Laszlo Moholy-Nagy	Gerhard Marcks	Rudolf Baschant
7. "Geometrische Formen"	6. "Hände, Hausmodell"	10. "V., Bauhaus-Signet"

WIENER WERKSTAETTE

The wonderful postcards of the Wiener Werkstaette were produced in the 1908-1912 era in Vienna during the "Secessionist" art movement. A group of approximately 50 talented artists began producing extremely beautiful works differing in style from the Art Nouveau works of their predecessors.

The **WW** series consisted of almost 1100 different cards, and production runs varied from a low of 200 to as many as 6000-7000 per card. Therefore, the number produced, the particular artist, and the number believed to still be in existence influence the price structure.

Most have the WW trademark in a box on the reverse side with the card number listed just below. The most popular artists were Oscar Kokoshka, Egon Schiele, Rudolf Kalvich, Moritz Jung, Mela Köhler, and Joseph Hoffman. Some of their cards have reached values as high as $3000 each. Others of notable importance, who are also well known for works by other publishers, are Mela Köhler, Suzi Singer, and Walter Hampel. Prices are for only the very best conditions...as less conditions are extremely lower.

WIENER WERKSTÄTTE (Vienna Workshops)

Beran, Otto Birthday, Easter (2)	400 - 500	500 - 600
Berger, Fritzi Fashion (3)	350 - 450	450 - 550
Böhler, Hans Japonism (6)	400 - 600	600 - 1000
Czeschka, Carl Otto New Year (1)	800 - 1000	1000 - 1200
Delavilla, Franz Karl		
Christmas, Easter, New Year (6)	400 - 500	500 - 700
Diveky, Josef		
City Sights (14)	200 - 500	300 - 700
Café Fledermaus (2)	1250 - 1500	1500 - 2000
1908 Kaiser Jubilee (6)	200 - 350	250 - 450
Christmas, Santa, Krampus (8)	250 - 600	400 - 800
Easter (1)	300 - 350	350 - 400
Fashion (8)	300 - 350	350 - 400

R.K. (Kalvach), W.W. No. 99
"Mutterglück"

O.K. (Kokoschka), W.W. No. 77
No Caption

Dolls (7)	500 - 700	600 - 800
Fantasy (6)	400 - 1200	600 - 1500
Drexler, Leopold City Sights (2)	150 - 200	200 - 250
Friedmann, Mizi		
Fantasy, Elves, Christmas (6)	300 - 400	400 - 500
Geyling, Remigius		
1908 Kaiser Jubilee (8)	150 - 350	200 - 400
Fashion (5)	150 - 350	200 - 400
Hoffmann, Josef		
Easter (1)	800 - 1000	1000 - 1200
Café Fledermaus (1)	1500 - 2000	2000 - 2500
Hoppe, Emil		
1908 Art Exhibition (4)	400 - 500	500 - 700
City Sights (7)	150 - 400	200 - 500
Janke, Urban		
Fantasy Jester (1)	300 - 400	400 - 500
Easter (1), Fashion (5), City Sights (9)	150 - 200	200 - 250
Jesser, Hilda Fashion (3)	400 - 500	500 - 700
Jung, Moriz		
Christmas (1)	600 - 650	650 - 750
Social Satire (34)	500 - 1500	750 - 2000
Aviation Fantasy (5)	700 - 900	800 - 1000
City Sights (4)	300 - 500	400 - 700
Music, Phonographs (10))	700 - 1000	800 - 1200
At the Zoo (9))	400 - 800	600 - 1000
Satirical Caricatures (6)	700 - 900	800 - 1000

O.K. (Kokoschka)
W.W. No. 73

O.K. (Kokoschka)
W.W. No. 147

O.K. (Kokoschka)
W.W. No. 152

Jungnickel, Ludwig Heinrich
Fashion (6)	300 - 400	400 - 500
Fantasy Animals (5)	400 - 500	500 - 600

Kalhammer, Gustav
Decorative (2), City Sights (13)	150 - 300	200 - 350

Kalmsteiner, Hans Puppet Shows (7) 500 - 700 600 - 800

Kalvach, Rudolf Birthday (1),
Christening (2), Fantasy (19) 1200 - 2500 1500 - 3000

Köhler, Mela
Children (24)	150 - 500	200 - 600
Easter (6)	200 - 250	250 - 300
Christmas (10)	150 - 800	200 - 1000
Santa, Krampus (6)	300 - 800	400 - 1000
New Year (5)	300 - 700	400 - 800
Fashion (89)	150 - 800	200 - 1000

Kokoschka, Oskar Fantasy (14),
Christmas (1), Easter (1) 1000 - 2000 2000 - 3000

Kolbe, Leopoldine Flower Baskets (6) 300 - 350 350 - 400

Krenek, Carl
City Sights (12)	150 - 400	200 - 500
Santa (1)	450 - 500	500 - 550

Kuhn, Franz
City Sights (33)	150 - 350	200 - 400
Easter (2), Fantasy (1)	800 - 1000	1000 - 1200

Lebisch, Franz Decorative (10), Easter (1) 100 - 250 150 - 300

Lendecke, Otto
Easter (2)	200 - 250	250 - 300
Fashion (12)	300 - 350	350 - 400

Leupold-Löwenthal, Alois City Sights (3) 200 - 250 250 - 300

Likarz, Maria
Easter (1), Christmas (1)	450 - 500	500 - 550
Krampus (2)	800 - 1000	1000 - 1200
New Year (5)	300 - 700	400 - 800
Decorative (1)	550 - 600	600 - 650
Woman w/Butterfly (1), Woman w/Beetle (1)	500 - 550	550 - 600

*Mela Köhler-Broman
W.W. No. 471*

*Mela Köhler-Broman
W.W. No. 346*

*Maria Likarz-Strauss
W.W. No. 772*

*Egon Schiele
W.W. No. 289*

*Egon Schiele
W.W. No. 290*

*Fritz Zeymer
W. W. No. 577*

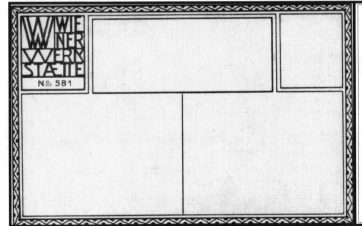

*Wiener
Werkstaette*

...

*One of the
Most Common
Postcard
Backs*

Masked Costumers (13)	150 - 350	200 - 400
Fashion (34)	200 - 700	300 - 800
Löffler, Berthold		
Easter (1), Good Luck (1)	150 - 200	200 - 250
1908 Kaiser Jubilee (4)	150 - 350	200 - 400
Fantasy (17)	150 - 700	200 - 800
Fledermaus Cabaret Advertisement (2)	3000 - 3500	3000 - 4000
Löw, Fritzi		
Easter (3), New Year (1)	400 - 450	450 - 500
Months of the Year (12)	300 - 350	350 - 400
Fashion (28)	75 - 250	100 - 300
Löwensohn, F. New Year (1)	750 - 800	800 - 850
Luksch-Makowska, Elena		
Social Satire of Russian Life (12)	400 - 700	500 - 800
Vienna Restaurant Interior (2)	400 - 450	450 - 500
Marisch, Gustav New Year (1),		
Sledding (1), Decorative (6)	300 - 350	350 - 400
Nechansky, Arnold		
Easter (5)	600 - 800	800 - 1000
Christmas (1), Santa/Krampus (2),		
New Year (6)	500 - 800	600 - 1000
Oswald, Wenzel		
Easter (2)	350 - 400	400 - 450
Fantasy (1)	200 - 250	250 - 300
Peche, Dagobert Harlequin (2)	350 - 400	400 - 450
Petter, Valerie Easter (1)	350 - 400	400 - 450
Schiele, Egon Women Portraits (3)	3500 - 5000	4000 - 6000
Schmal, Emil City Sights (8), Fashion (1)	150 - 200	200 - 250
Schwetz, Karl City Sights (61)	100- 250	150 - 300
Sika, Jutta		
City Sights (5)	300 - 350	350 - 400
Krampus (1)	550 - 600	600 - 650
Singer, Susi		
Fashion (5), Easter (1), Fantasy (1)	300 - 400	400 - 500
Christmas (3), Santa & Krampus (2)	500 - 1000	700 - 1200
Speyer, Agnes Fantasy (1)	900 - 1000	1000 - 1100
Teschner, Richard		
Fantasy (2)	150 - 200	200 - 250
Children with Toys (5)	300 - 500	400 - 600
Velim, Anton Christmas (5)	400 - 600	500 - 700
Wimmer-Wisgrill, Eduard Josef		
Fashion (10)	250 - 300	300 - 350
Zeymer, Fritz		
Easter (1), Christmas (1)	350 - 400	400 - 450
Fledermaus Cabaret	700 - 750	750 - 800
Zwickle, Hubert von 1908 Kaiser Jubilee (4)	150 - 350	200 - 400

There are an additional 100 known postcards by unknown artists. There are also 123 missing numbers which have not been found. The complete series runs from #1 through #1011. A few numbers have been used twice with different designs and artists. Much of the information here is taken from *Die Postkarten der Wiener Werkstätte* by Traude Hanse, which contains the most complete listing and illustrations of this series.

E. T. Andrews (Unsigned)
Anonymous

E. T. Andrews (Unsigned)
J. C. Schmidt

Mabel Lucie Attwell, R. Tuck
3715, "A Happy Easter"

Mabel Lucie Attwell, Valentines
3281, "Oh!-- Look at me ..."

F. Baumgarten, Meissner & Buch
3008, "Bonne Année"

F. Baumgarten, Meissner & Buch
Series 3044 (No Caption)

BEAUTIFUL CHILDREN

ALANEN, JOSEPH (Finland)		
Easter Witch Children	10 - 12	12 - 15
Miniature Easter Witch Cards	15 - 18	18 - 20
ALYS, M.	2 - 3	3 - 4
ANDERSON, ANNE	6 - 8	8 - 10
ANDERSON, V. C. (U.S.)	5 - 6	6 - 8
R. Tuck Series 7 – Leap Year (12)	8 - 10	10 - 12
ETA (E. T. ANDREWS)		
Early Chromolithographs		
B. Dondorf Series 173	25 - 30	30 - 40
Raphael Tuck		
Series 6615 (6) "Brown Eyes and Blue"		
ANTTILA, EVA (Finland)	6 - 8	8 - 10
ATTWELL, MABEL LUCIE (G.B.)		
Early Period, Pre-1915	15 - 18	18 - 22
Middle Period, 1915-1930	12 - 15	15 - 18
1930's-1950 Period	6 - 8	8 - 10
Valentine & Sons (See Blacks)		
Series 748 Golliwoggs	18 - 20	20 - 25
Series A561 Golliwoggs	15 - 18	18 - 22
Series A579 Golliwoggs	18 - 20	20 - 25
Suffragette "Where's My Vote"	30 - 35	35 - 40
AZZONI, N. (Italy) Art Deco		
Dell, Anna & Gasparini **Series 517** (6)	12 - 14	14 - 16

E. Bem, Lapina 612
Russian Caption

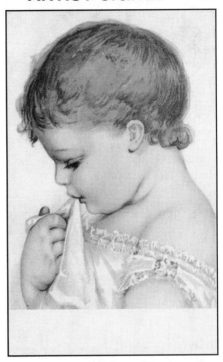

Frances Brundage (Unsigned)
Theo. Stroefer Series 115

BANKS, M. E.
   Raphael Tuck
      Dressing Doll Series 1, #3381 (6)

"Dolly Dimple"	150 - 175	175	- 185
"Jack at Play"			
"Little Pamela"			
"Our Jimmy"			
"Pretty Peggy"			
"Tommy Lad"			

BARBER, C. W. (G.B.)

Carleton Publishing Co.	8 - 10	10 - 12

BARHAM, SYBIL (G.B.) See Fairies/Fairy Tales

C. W. Faulkner Series 502, 701, 964 (6)	5 - 6	6 - 8
BARKER, C. M.	6 - 8	8 - 10

BARNES, G. L. See F. Tales/Nursery Rhymes, Cats

BARRIBAL, L. (G.B.)	8 - 10	10 - 12
BARROWS, ELIZABETH	5 - 6	6 - 7

BAUMGARTEN, FRITZ   (FB) (Germany)
   See Fairy Tales/Nursery Rhymes
   Meissner & Buch

Series 3008, 3044	12 - 15	15 - 20
Other Publishers	10 - 12	12 - 15
BAYER, CHARLES A.	2 - 3	3 - 4

BEM, E. (Russia)

Lapina Series	15 - 18	18 - 22
Russian Backs	18 - 22	22 - 26

Russian Alphabet Series	15 - 18	18 - 20
BERTIGLIA, A. (Italy) Art Deco		
Series 155 & 1053 Dutch Kids (6)	8 - 10	10 - 12
Series 1010 Playing War (6)	12 - 14	14 - 18
Series 1069 (6)	7 - 8	8 - 10
Series 2114 With Dolls (6)	10 - 12	12 - 16
Series 2428 Making Movies (6)	12 - 15	15 - 18
Series 2444, 2461, 2499 (6)	8 - 10	10 - 12
BLODGETT, BERTHA (U.S.)		
AMP Co.		
Series 209, Easter	7 - 8	8 - 10
Series 410, Christmas	5 - 6	6 - 7
Little Girls/Huge Hats Series	7 - 8	8 - 10
BOMPARD, L. (Italy) Art Deco		
Series 379, 454, 497 (6)	8 - 9	9 - 10
Series 523, 567, 906, 993 (6)	8 - 10	10 - 12
BONNE, SIGRID	5 - 6	6 - 7
BONORA (Italy)		
Boy Scout Series 760	20 - 25	25 - 28
BORISS, MARGRET (Art Deco)	10 - 12	12 - 15
Armag Co.		
"Occupation Series" (6)	8 - 10	10 - 12
See Fairy Tales/Nursery Rhymes		
BOWDEN, DORIS	6 - 8	8 - 10
BOWLEY, A. L. (G.B.)		
Early Unsigned Chromo-Lithographs	25 - 30	30 - 35
Raphael Tuck		
Series C218 Christmas Children	20 - 25	25 - 30
Series C1757 Children and Santa	25 - 30	30 - 35
Series C 3781, C3782		
Series 6037 Children and Snowman		
BOWLEY, MAY (G.B.)		
Early Unsigned Chromo-Lithographs	20 - 25	25 - 30
Others	15 - 18	18 - 20
BRETT, M. See Fairy Tales/Nursery Rhymes		
BRISLEY, NORA	6 - 8	8 - 10
BRUNDAGE, FRANCES (U.S.)		
Sam Gabriel		
New Year		
Series 300, 302, 316 (10)	10 - 12	12 - 15
St. Patrick's Day		
Series 140 (10) (Unsigned)	8 - 10	10 - 14
Memorial Day		
Series 150	12 - 15	15 - 18
"In that instant o'er his ..."		
"Would I could duly praise ..."		
"Enough of Merit has each ..."		
"Brave minds, howe'er at war ..."		
"One Flag, one Land, one Heart ..."		
"By fairy hands their knell ..."		
Valentine's Day Series 413 (6)	8 - 10	10 - 15
Halloween		
Series 120, 121 (10)	20 - 22	22 - 28
Series 123 (10)	12 - 15	15 - 20

Frances Brundage (Unsigned)
Anon. Ser. 434, "Mama lässt ..."

Frances Brundage (Unsigned)
Theo. Stroefer Ser. XXXX

Frances Brundage (Unsigned)
Anonymous, "Gruss"

Frances Brundage (Unsigned)
Theo. Stroefer Series 85-11

Series 125 (6)	20 - 22	22 - 25
Thanksgiving		
Series 130, 132, 133 (10)	8 - 10	10 - 12
Series 135 (6)	6 - 8	8 - 10
Christmas Series 200, 208, 219	10 - 12	12 - 15
Santas	15 - 18	18 - 22
Raphael Tuck		
New Year		
Series No. 12 (Uns.)	15 - 18	18 - 22
Series 601 (Uns.)	10 - 12	12 - 15
Series 1036	12 - 15	15 - 18
Valentine's Day		
Series 11 (4) (Uns.)	10 - 12	12 - 15
Series 20, 26 (Uns.)	12 - 15	15 - 18
Series 100, 101 (6) (Uns.)		
Series 107 and 117	10 - 12	12 - 15
Blacks	22 - 25	25 - 28
Series 102 (6)	12 - 15	15 - 20
Blacks	22 - 25	25 - 28
Series 115 (4)	10 - 12	12 - 15
Blacks	22 - 25	25 - 28
Series 118 (4)	10 - 12	12 - 15
Blacks	25 - 28	28 - 32
Easter Series 1049 (3)	8 - 10	10 - 15
Memorial Day		
Series 173 (12) (Uns.)	12 - 15	15 - 18
Halloween (See Halloween Greetings)		
Christmas		
Series 4 (12)	12 - 15	15 - 20
Series 165 (2)	10 - 12	12 - 15
Blacks	22 - 25	25 - 28
Series 1035 (2)	10 - 12	12 - 15
Blacks	22 - 25	25 - 28
Series 2723 "Colored Folks" (6)	50 - 60	60 - 70
Series 4096 "Funny Folks" (4)	30 - 35	35 - 40
Raphael Tuck, Paris		
Series 131 (B&W) (6)		
1 Girl leaning on big rock	25 - 30	30 - 35
3 Girl at brookside carrying large urn		
Early Foreign Publishers		
Carl Hirsch, W.H.B.,		
Theo. Stroefer (T.S.N.), Wezel &		
Naumann, C. Baum, & Anon.		
Large Images	35 - 40	40 - 50
Small Images	20 - 25	25 - 35
BURD, C. M. (U.S.) (See Advertising)		
Rally Day Series	8 - 10	10 - 12
Birthday Series		
BUSI, ADOLFO (Italy)		
Series 500 (6)	12 - 14	14 - 16
Boy Scout Series	16 - 20	20 - 25
CARTER, SYDNEY (G.B.)		
S. Hildesheimer & Co.		
"Children's Frolics" (6)	8 - 10	10 - 12

A. Busi, Degami Series 3544
No Caption (Easter)

Sofia Chiostri
Ballerini & Fratini, Series 365

Sofia Chiostri
Ballerini & Fratini, Series 268

Ellen H. Clapsaddle, Jmport
Series 5804, "Frohes Osterfest"

Ellen H. Clapsaddle, Wolf & Co.
106, "Woman's sphere is in ..."

"Romps" Series		
"A Morning Drive"	10 - 12	12 - 15
"Battledore"		
"Baby's New Ball"		
"Gee Up"		
"The Military Band"		
"Pickaback"		
Series 5246 "An Excursion on Bank Holiday"	8 - 10	10 - 12
Series 5188 "Months of the Year" (12)		
114 "March"	15 - 18	18 - 22
CARR, GENE		
Rotograph Co. Series 219 (4th of July)	8 - 10	10 - 12
CASTELLI, V. (Italy) Art Deco		
Ultra Series 533 (6)	8 - 10	10 - 12
C.B.T.	2 - 3	3 - 4
CENNI, E. (Italy) Art Deco	5 - 6	6 - 7
CHAMBERLIN (U.S.)		
Campbell		
310 "Suffrage First"	70 - 80	80 - 90
312 "Let's Pull ..." Suffrage		
CHIOSTRI, SOFIA (Italy) Art Deco		
Ballerini & Fratini		
Series 117, 362 (4) Children Pierrots	18 - 22	22 - 25
Series 184 Japanese (4)	12 - 15	15 - 18
Series 188, 268 (4)	10 - 12	12 - 15
Series 319 (4)	15 - 18	18 - 22

Series 365 (4)	22 - 25	25 - 30
CLAPSADDLE, ELLEN H. (U.S.)		
International Art. Publishing Co.		
Angels, Cherubs	6 - 8	8 - 10
Animals	4 - 5	5 - 6
Young Ladies, Women	6 - 8	8 - 10
Bells, Florals, Crosses, Sleds, etc.	2 - 4	4 - 5
Good Luck, Thanksgiving		
Thanksgiving Children	6 - 8	8 - 10
Indians		
Transportation	2 - 3	3 - 6
Christmas Children	10 - 12	12 - 15
Santas	18 - 22	22 - 25
Easter Children	8 - 10	10 - 15
Valentine Greetings	5 -6	6 - 8
Valentine Children	6 - 10	10 - 20
Series 941, 942, 944	8 - 10	10 - 15
Series 952, 953		
Series 1034, 1081 (Uns.)	6 - 8	8 - 10
Valentine Mechanicals	30 - 40	40 - 50
Series 16190 (4)		
"To My Valentine"		
"St. Valentine's Greeting"		
"To My Sweetheart"		
"Love's Fond Greeting"		
Series 51810	20 - 25	25 - 30
Memorial Day Series 973, 2444, 4397 (6)	8 - 10	10 - 15
Series 2935 (6)	12 - 14	14 - 16
Washington's Birthday		
Series 16208, 16209 (4)	8 - 10	10 - 12
Series 16250 (6)		
Series 51896 (6)		
Lincoln's Birthday	8 - 10	10 - 15
St. Patrick's Day	10 - 12	12 - 15
Independence Day		
Series 2443, 4398	8 - 12	12 - 15
Halloween (See Halloween Greetings)		
Wolf & Co.		
Large Children images	10 - 15	15 - 20
Small Children images	6 - 8	8 - 10
Later, smaller images	5 - 6	6 - 8
Suffragettes		
"Love Me, Love My Vote"	65 - 75	75 - 85
"Woman's Sphere is in the Home" (106)	40 - 45	45 - 50
Halloween (See Halloween Greetings)		
Foreign Publishers		
Signed issues: Add $5-$10 to above prices.		
Unsigned issues: Add $5-$7 to above prices.		
New discoveries: Add $10-$20.		
CLARK, A. (U.S.)	5 - 6	6 - 7
CLOKE, RENE (G.B.) See Fairies		
C. W. Faulkner Series (1930's)	8 - 10	10 - 15
Valentine's Series (1930's-40's)	8 - 10	10 - 12
Salmon Bros.		
Series (1930's-40's)	6 - 8	8 - 10

1950's Series	3 - 4	4 - 5
Medici Society Series (1950's-60's)	1 - 2	2 - 3
COLBY, V. (U.S.) (B&W)	2 - 3	3 - 4
COLEMAN, W. S.	6 - 8	8 - 10
COLOMBO, E. (Italy)		
A. Guarneri (Milano)		
Series 234 (6)	8 - 10	10 - 12
Series 454 (6)		
Series 618 (6)		
Series 665 Child With Dog (6)	8 - 10	10 - 12
Series 960, 1764, 1905, 1964 (6)		
Series 1968 (6)	10 - 12	12 - 14
Series 2007, 2140, 2141 (6)	6 - 8	8 - 10
Series 2033, 2044, 2181 (6)	8 - 10	10 - 12
Series 2223 (6)	10 - 12	12 - 14
Series 2252, 2426 (6)	6 - 8	8 - 10
G.P.M.		
Series 1693-2	8 - 10	10 - 12
Series 1964, 1996 (6)		
Ultra Series 2039 (6)	8 - 10	10 - 12
COOK, A. M.		
COOPER, PHYLLIS (G.B.) Art Deco		
Raphael Tuck		
Series 3463, 3464 "Happy Land" (6)	18 - 22	22 - 25
Doll-Toy Series (6)		
CORBELLA, T. (Italy)		
"Ultra"		
Series 2034, 2035, 2321	8 - 10	10 - 12
Series 2161 Dutch Kids		
Series 2182, 2221	10 - 12	12 - 15
CORBETT, BERTHA (U.S.)		
J.I. Austin Sunbonnet Children	8 - 10	10 - 15
CORY, F. Y.	2 - 3	3 - 4
COTTOM, C. M.	4 - 6	6 - 8
COWDEREY, K.		
COWHAM, HILDA (G.B.) (See Fairies)		
C.W. Faulkner Series 1618 (6)	10 - 12	12 - 15
Inter-Art		
Raphael Tuck		
Series 6076 "Humorous" (6)	15 - 18	18 - 22
Valentine's	10 - 12	12 - 15
CRAMER, RIE	15 - 18	18 - 22
CURTIS, E. (U.S.)		
McGowen Silbee Litho, N.Y. (B&W)	6 - 8	8 - 10
Raphael Tuck		
Garden Patch 2	8 - 10	10 - 12
"Apple" "Peach"		
"Beet" "Radish"		
"Cantelope" "Red Pepper"		
"Carrot" "Watermelon"		
Raphael Tuck		
Series 7 -- Leap Year (12)	8 - 10	10 - 12
"Valentine Maids" Series D12		
PC 1 "School Slates" (12)	6 - 8	8 - 10

PC 3 "Love's Labors" (12)
PC 4 "From Many Lands" (12)

CZEGKA, B. (Poland)

W.R.B. & Co. Series 22 (6)	8 - 10	10 - 12
DAWSON, MURIEL	4 - 6	6 - 8
DeGARMES	1 - 2	2 - 3

DEWEES, ETHEL, E.D., EHD (U.S.)

AMP Co	6 - 8	8 -10
Ernest Nister Series 2543	8 - 10	10 - 15
DEXTER, MARJORIE	4 - 5	5 - 6

DIXON, DOROTHY (U.S.)
Ullman Mfg. Co.

Sunbonnet Babies (6)	8 - 10	10 - 12

DRAYTON, GRACE - (Wiederseim) (U.S.)
A.M. Davis Co. (Quality Cards)

34 "Here's a load of Christmas Wishes..."	20 - 25	25 - 30

"Sing a song of Christmas"
"Though the weather's cold..."
"I told this Little Birdie..."
Baby Girl in Sled
"Pussy in the corner..."
Jack in the Box

Santa Pops up in mechanical version	40 - 45	45 - 55

Others
Series 143 Birthday Months (12)

"January," "February," "March"	35 - 40	40 - 45

"April sun or April showers"
"May," "June," "July," "August," "September"
"October," "November," "December"
Series 357

"As I pass upon the street..."	30 - 35	35 - 38

"Chubby leg and stubby toe..."
"I rode my cock horse"
"I sent a pretty blue bird"
"I told this little birdie"
"I took my bestest pen in hand"
"Jack in the box is full of glee"
"Pussy in the corner"

B.B., London (Birn Bros.) (6)	20 - 25	25 - 30

Reinthal & Newman, N.Y.
No No.

Dollie: "Dickey has had a accident..."	25 - 30	30 - 35

Eve: "Oh Adam! Wait!..."
306 "A Button Sewed on ..."
307 "Dressy Lady: "What are you crying..."
308 "I'd rather say Hello"
488 "Oh come and be my Lambey dear..."
489 "Oh dear me, what do I see..."
490 "It's nice to be a little boy..."
491 "Little maid neat and sweet..."
492 "Gee up Dobin - tried and true..." (Uns.)
493 The sun is shining warm and sweet..."
495 Teacher & Children
496 "Do you, or don't you?"
497 "I should worry"

Phyllis Cooper, Tuck Ser. 3463
"Fannie was as sweet a child ..."

G. Drayton, R&N 505
"The Honeymoon"

M. Dulk, Gibson Art 252
"I hope that you may always ..."

Pauli Ebner, M. Munk
Series 878, "Ein Traumichnicht."

498 "I Love to Dance with You"		
499 "I think I'd Rather..."		
500 "More of All"		
502 "Love at first sight" *	30 - 35	35 - 38
503 "The Trousseau" *		
504 "The Wedding" *		
505 "The Honeymoon" *		
506 "First Night in their New Home" *		
507 "Their New Love" *		
* Easel Cut-outs - add $5-10		

Raphael Tuck

Series 223 (6) (Unsigned)	20 - 25	25 - 30
Series 241 "Bright Eyes" (Uns.) (6)	20 - 25	25 - 30
"I'se Awful Sweet ..."		
"I'm Your Little Darling Boy ..."		
"The Boys About Me Rant ..."		
Others		
Series 242 (Unsigned) (6)		
Children with Pets		
Girl with drum and Teddy Bear	30 - 35	35 - 38
Others		
Series 243 "Love Message" (Uns.) (6)	20 - 25	25 - 30
Series 244 "Sweet Bliss" (Uns.) (6)		
Series 1002 "Happy Easter" (Uns.) (6)	20 - 25	25 - 28
See Blacks		
See Halloween		

Advertising

"Adam and Eva" A Comedy Play	50 - 60	60 - 70

Minneapolis Tribune

North American Co. "I'm Kaptin Kiddo"	70 - 80	80 - 100
DUDDLE, JOSEPHINE (G.B.)	8 - 10	10 - 12

DULK, M.

Gibson Art   Series 252

Fantasy Flower Girls, Birthday	10 - 12	12 - 16

"Daffodil"	"Rose"
"Pansy"	"Sweet Pea"
"Forget me Not"	"Violet"
"Poppy"	"Red Rose"
"Pussy Willow"	"Tulip"

Valentine Series - Girls (6)	8 - 10	10 - 12
E.H.S. (Ellen H. Saunders) (U.S.)		
M.T. Sheahan, Boston	6 - 8	8 - 10

EBNER, PAULI (Germany)

Early - Signed **PE**	15 - 18	18 - 22
Santas	22 - 25	25 - 28

M. Munk, Vienna

Series 878 Toys	15 - 18	18 - 22
Series 1126 Victorian Children	10 - 12	12 - 15
Series 1129 Birthday	10 - 12	12 - 15
Series 403, 986, 1019 New Year	12 - 15	15 - 18
Series 550, 1136, 1269 New Year	15 - 17	17 - 20
Series 1044 Winter	12 - 14	14 - 16
Series 1158, 1263		
Series 1106 Christmas		

K. Feiertag, B.K.W.I., Ser. 881-5
"Treue Freunde."

W. Fialkowska, AVM 846
"A Ladies' Man"

Series 1227 Christmas, w/Santa	22 - 25	25 - 28
August Rokol, Vienna or AR		
Series 1428 Birthday	12 - 15	15 - 20
Series 1375, 1440 Toys	15 - 18	18 - 22
Series 1321	12 - 15	15 - 20
"Puppet Marriage Series"	18 - 22	22 - 28
E.F.D. or ELLEN F. DREW		
M.A.P. Co.	4 - 6	6 - 8
Ernest Nister	6 - 8	8 - 10
EGERTON, LINDA (G.B.)		
ELLAM, WILLIAM (G.B.)	10 - 12	12 - 15
ELLIOTT, KATHRYN (U.S.)	4 - 5	5 - 6
Gibson Art Co. Halloween Series (10)	6 - 8	8 - 10
F.B. (not Brundage)	5 - 6	6 - 8
F.S.M.		
Heininger **"Courtship & Marriage"** Series	8 - 10	10 - 12
FEDERLEY, ALEXANDER (Finland)	5 - 6	6 - 8
FEIERTAG, K. (Austria)		
B.K.W.I.	5 - 6	6 - 8
Tennis, Golf, Santas	10 - 12	12 - 15
FIALKOWSKA, WALLY (Germany)		
Large Children, Comical	10 - 12	12 - 15
Small Children & Babies	6 - 8	8 - 10
Black Children	12 - 15	15 - 22
FLOWERS, CHARLES (U.S.)	5 - 6	6 - 8
FOLKARD, CHARLES (G.B.)		

A & C Black
  "Nursery Rhymes & Tales"
  Series 91 (6)   15 - 18   18 - 22
  "Beauty and the Beast"
  "Cinderella"
  "Little Bo Peep"
  "Tom, Tom, the Piper's Son"
  "Red Riding Hood"
  "Sleeping Beauty"
FRANK, E. (Germany)   6 - 8   8 - 10
GASSAWAY, KATHARINE (U.S.)
  Julius Bein & Co.
  Series 55, "Full Day" Series (6)
    550 "Rising Time"   8 - 10   10 - 12
    551 "Bath Time"
    552 "Study Time"
    553 "Play Time"
    554 "Dinner Time"
    555 "Bed Time"
  Series 75 "Courtship" Series (6)
    750 "Rising Time"   10 - 12   12 - 14
    751 "The Introduction"
    752 "The Proposal"
    753 "The Engagement"
    754 "The Marriage"
    755 "The Honeymoon"
  Edward Gross, N.Y.
  "Butterfly"   Series   8 - 10   10 - 12
  "Ailments of Childhood" Series
  "Hives," "Mumps," "Measels"   10 - 12   12 - 15
  D. Hillson   6 - 8   8 - 10
  National Art Co.
    169 "This is so sudden"   6 - 8   8 - 10
    170 "I Send my Love by Mail"
    171 "My heart is All for You"
  Raphael Tuck
    Series 113   Bridal, Valentines (6)   6 - 8   8 - 10
    Series 130   Easter Series (12)   6 - 7   7 - 8
    Series 2495 "The New Baby" (6)   6 - 8   8 - 10
         Blacks   15 - 18   18 - 22
  The Rotograph Co.   "F. L" precedes numbers
    100 "New York"   8 - 10   10 - 12
    101 "Boston"
    102 "Chicago"
    103 "St Louis"
    104 "Philadelphia"
    105 Black Girl, "I'm scared I'll..."   15 - 18   18 - 22
    106 "What are little girls made of..."   8 - 10   10 - 12
    107 "What are little boys made of..."
    113 "Beware of the Dog"
    108-116
  "Age" Series   10 - 12   12 - 15
    117 "1 Year"
    118 "2 Years"

119 "3 Years"		
120 "4 Years"		
121 "5 Years"		
123 Black girl: "I wish I was in Dixie"	15 - 18	18 - 22
124 Black boy: "Thought I heer'd de boss..."		
125-138	6 - 8	8 - 10
139-158 Occupation Series	8 - 10	10 - 12
The Sports images in this series	10 - 12	12 - 15
159-186	6 - 8	8 - 10
193 Black boy: "New Orleans"	15 - 18	18 - 22
214 "Don't cry little girl..."	6 - 8	8 - 10
National Girls		
220 "America"	8 - 10	10 - 12
221 "Ireland"	7 - 8	8 - 10
222 "England"		
223 "Germany"		
224 "France"		
225		
226 "Italy"		
227 "Sweden"		
American Kid Series (6)	6 - 8	8 - 10
GEORGE, MARY ELEANOR		
Ernest Nister		
1858 "Dear Valentine, you're..."	18 - 22	22 - 25
1862 "Telling the Secret..."		
2117 "For my own love"		
2182 "The surest way to hit a woman's heart..."		
2183 "Choose your Love..."		
3119 "You've got me on the string"		
GILSON, T. (U.S.)		
Black Children Comics	12 - 15	15 - 18
GOLAY, MARY	3 - 4	4 - 5
GOODMAN, MAUDE		
Raphael Tuck		
Series 824-833	12 - 15	15 - 20
Early Chromolithographs	25 - 30	30 - 35
GOLIA, E. (Italy) Art Deco		
Series 102 War-time Children	18 - 20	20 - 25
GOVEY, A. (G.B.)		
Humphrey Milford, London		
"Dreams and Fairies" Golliwoggs	18 - 22	22 - 25
GRASSETTI (Italy) Art Deco	6 - 8	8 - 10
GREINER, MAGNUS (U.S.) See Blacks		
International Art Pub. Co.		
Dutch Children Series 491, 692 (6)	8 - 10	10 - 12
"Molly & the Bear" Series 791	12 - 15	15 - 20

IMPORTANT NOTE

Re: Price Quotations for Cards Listed in This Price Guide

For a card, or series, that has no value listed at the end of the line, please
refer to the entry just above.

HBG, L. & E., Series 2243
"I've Lost My Heart and As I ..."

Mary Eleanor George, E. Nister
2182, "The surest way to hit..."

GRIGGS, H. B. (also H.B.G.)

L & E (Leubrie & Elkus)		
Christmas Series 2224, 2264, 2275	10 - 12	12 - 15
New Year's Series 2225, 2266, 2276		
Easter Series 2226, 2254, 2271		
Valentine's Day		
Series 2218, 2243, 2244, 2267		
Series 2217, 2219, 2248		
Blacks	20 - 22	22 - 25
St. Patrick's Day		
Series 2230, 2232, 2253, 2269	8 - 10	10 - 12
Thanksgiving		
Series 2212, 2213, 2233, 2263, 2273	6 - 8	8 - 10
George Washington's Birthday		
Series 2242, 2268	8 - 10	10 - 12
Halloween		
Series 2214, 2216, 2262	12 - 15	15 - 18
Series 2263, 2272		
Series 2231, 7010	15 - 16	16 - 18
Birthday Series No No, 2232	6 - 8	8 - 10
Anonymous Publisher Series		
Series 2215, 7010	12 - 14	14 - 16
GRILLI, S. (Italy) Art Deco **Series 1839** (6)	10 - 12	12 - 15
GRIMBALL, Meta M. (U.S.)		
Gutmann & Gutmann		
203 "Our Flag at the Pole"	30 - 40	40 - 50

*M. M. Grimball, Gutmann &
Gutmann, "Have some?"*

*M. M. Grimball, Gutmann &
Gutmann 705 (No Caption)*

210	"The Top of the World"		
604	"Fired"	25 - 30	30 - 35
701	"Have Some?"		
Same - no number			
702	"The Kidnapper"		
703	"Some Dog Biscuits Please"		
705	"Help"		
Same - No Caption		30 - 35	35 - 40
"A Good Catch"		20 - 25	25 - 28
"A Welcome Guest"			
"And They Say School Days..."			
"The Advance Guard"			
"The Captive"			
"The Champion"			
"The Christmas Spirit"		40 - 45	45 - 50
"The Convalescent"		20 - 25	25 - 30
"The Grand Finale"			
"Guess Who?"			
"He Won't Bite"			
"The Loving Cup"			
"Love at First Sight"			
"Now Don't You Tell"			
"Rivals"			
"Stolen Sweets"			
"Sweethearts"			
"Verdict - Love for Life"			

"A Call to Arms"	40 - 50	50 - 65
Reinthal & Newman	10 - 20	20 - 25
FOREIGN ISSUES		
Novitas (N in star)		
Series 542		
1 "Dollie's Bonnet	35 - 40	40 - 50
Series 10543		
3 "The Introduction"	25 - 30	30 - 35
Series 10726		
"Puppen Mutterchen's Einkauf"	25 - 30	30 - 35
"Storenfried"		
"Leckerbissen"		
Series 10930 (R & N)		
"Say Das Nicht Noch Mal!"	25 - 30	30 - 35
"Und da sagen sie mir..."		
"And They Say School Days..."	20 - 25	25 - 30
Series 10966		
"Kinderlieb"	25 - 30	30 - 35
Series 20607		
"Delighted"		
1 "He Won't Bite" (Ger. Caption) Uns.	25 - 30	30 - 35
Also U.S. Caption	20 - 25	25 - 30
5 "The Grand Finale"		
Series 20608		
4 "The Champion"		
Series 21681		
"Fired"	25 - 30	30 - 35
"Love at First Sight"		
Others with German Captions	25 - 30	30 - 35
Rishar (Russia) (Phillips or Richard)		
453 "The Grand Finale"	30 - 35	35 - 40
GROSS, O.	2 - 3	3 -5
GUARINO, ANTHONY	3 - 4	4 - 5
GUASTA (Italy) Art Deco	6 - 8	8 - 10
GUTMANN, BESSIE PEASE (U.S.)		
Gutmann & Gutmann		
No No.		
"Autumn"	35 - 40	40 - 45
"Baby's First Christmas"		
"Blue Bell"		
"Fall"		
"Falling Out" **S/Bessie C. Pease**	25 - 30	30 - 35
"Feeling"		
"The First Born"	35 - 40	40 - 45
"The First Lesson"		
Girl in Hat		
"Love at First Sight"	25 - 30	30 - 35
"Love is Blind"		
"Making Up" **S/Bessie C. Pease**		
"Ragtime"	30 - 35	35 - 40
"S.O.S" (C.Q.D.)	40 - 45	45 - 50
Skater		
"Spring"		
"Summer"		

B. P. Gutmann (Unsigned)
Novitas 20559, "Ihr Liebling."

B. P. Gutmann, Novitas 20556
"Das Bild des Zukünftigen."

B. P. Gutmann, Rishar 135
"The Intruder."

H. Gutmann, Rishar 234
"The Poodle-Mobile."

B. P. Gutmann, Novitas 20607-3
"Love is Blind" (Liebe Macht Blind)

200 Series - Children

200	"The New Love"	25 - 30	30 - 35
201	"The Lone Fisherman"	30 - 35	35 - 40
211	"The Happy Family"	35 - 40	40 - 45

500 Series - Beautiful Women

500	"Rosebuds"	40 - 45	45 - 50
501	"Senorita"		
502	"Waiting"	50 - 55	55 - 60
503	"Daydreams"		
504	"Poppies"		
505	"I wish you were here"		
704	"The Foster Mother"	25 - 30	30 - 35

800 Series - Young Girls

800	"Margaret"	30 - 35	35 - 40
801	"Betty"		
802	"Virginia"		
803	"Alice"		
804	"Lucille"		
805	"Dorothy"		

900 Series - Babies

900	"Contentment"	35 - 40	40 - 45
901	"Come play with me"		
902	"All is Vanity"		
903	"His Majesty"		
904	"Dessert"		

1000 Series - Baby/Mother

1000	"Sunshine"	40 - 45	45 - 50
1001	"I love to be loved by a baby"		
1002	"In Slumberland"		
1003	"Baby mine"		
1004	"The Sweetest Joy"		

1100 Series - Young Women

1100	"Repartee"	70 - 75	75 - 80
1101	"Sweeheart"		
1102	"Sweet Sixteen"		
1103	"Speeding"	50 - 55	55 - 60
1104	"Happy Dreams"		

1200 Series - The Five Senses

1200	"Tasting"	30 - 35	35 - 40
1201	"Seeing"		
1202	"Smelling"		
1203	"Hearing"		
1204	"Feeling"		

1300 Series - A Woman's Life

1300	"The Baby"	40 - 45	45 - 50
1301	"Off to school"		
1302	"The Dubutante"		
1303	"The Bride"		
1304	"The Mother"		

Metamorphic

B505	"Love or Money" S/BCP	175 - 200	200 - 225

FOREIGN
W. de Haan, Utrecht

3004 "Het Gezicht" Girl sits at mirror	45 - 50	50 - 55

De Muinck & Co., Amsterdam
54 "Liefde is Blind" (Love is Blind) Sepia

M.J.S., Bulgaria   Johnson listed as artist

011 Images in water "Cupids Reflection"	60 - 65	65 - 70

Novitas - N in Circle

No No. Girl with muffler and Holly	60 - 65	65 - 75

Series 542

4 Little girl sits in big hatbox	35 - 40	40 - 45
10357 "Come Play With Me" Baby/butterfly		
10357 "His Magesty"	30 - 35	35 - 40

Series 10930
"Zwietracht" Same as "Falling Out" (S/B.C.P.) 50 - 55   55 - 60
"Eintracht" Same as "Making Up" (S/B.C.P.)
"Hoppa Hoppa Reiter!" Same as "Strenuous"

Series 15727

"Rosebuds"	35 - 40	40 - 50

Series 20360 (6)
Same cards as **G&G 1300 Series**

"A Woman's Life"	40 - 45	45 - 50
Series 20361 - Sunshine Series	40 - 45	45 - 50
20556 "Das Bild des Zukunftigen" ("Cupid's Reflection")	65 - 75	75 - 85
20557 "Der Dritteim Bunde" ("Tie that binds")	55 - 60	60 - 65

20558 "Aufbruch in der Krieg" Mother on
knees kisses boy
20559 "Ihr Liebling" Boy kissing mother

Series 20607

"Love at First Sight"	35 - 40	40 - 45
3 "Love is Blind"		
Also German caption "Liebe Macht Blind"	40 - 45	45 - 55
4 "The First Lesson"	35 - 40	40 - 45
Also German caption "	40 - 45	45 - 55
"The New Love"	35 - 40	40 - 45

Series 20608 (6)
1 "Music Hath Charm"
3 "Ragtime"

"My Bruzzer has a fever..."	40 - 45	45 - 50
5 "Puppenmutterchen" Girl with many dolls	45 - 50	50 - 60

6 "The Lone Fisherman"

Series 20697 (6)

Same cards as **G&G 200 Series**	35 - 40	40 - 45

Others

"All is Vanity"	40 - 50	50 - 55
"Feeling"	35 - 40	40 - 45

"Delighted"
"The Foster Mother"
"Guess Who?" Unsigned
"Love is Blind"
"Margaret"
"Stolen Sweets" Unsigned
"Strenuous"
Others

C.Q.D.
"S.O.S." Crying baby standing in bed   45 - 50   50 - 60

RUSSIAN

Richard (Rishar, Petrograde or St. Petersburg)

91	"The New Love"	40 - 50	50 - 55
93	"A nice family" Little girl w/many dolls		
	Also has German and Russian captions	50 - 60	60 - 70
95	"Die Liebe ist blind" Little girl kisses doll		
	with broken head. (Love is Blind)	45 - 50	50 - 60
99	"Die Perle" Mermaid in large clam shells	75 - 85	85 - 100
100	"Wasserlilie" Mermaid sits on lily pad		
135	"The Intruder" Boy kisses white bunny	45 - 50	50 - 55
136	"The Strenuous Life"		
137	"Making Up" Girls with umbrella		
138	"Falling Out" Girls with umbrella		
150	"Delighted" Boy with rifle and Teddy		
	Bear by foot. A take off on Teddy Roosevelt.		
155	Little Girl with many dolls	50 - 55	55 - 65
234	"The Grand Finale"	45 - 50	50 - 55
1277	"Good Night" Woman holding candle	65 - 70	70 - 80
	Others		

Russian/Universal Back
173 Boy kissing rabbit (The Intruder)   45 - 50   50 - 55
Leningrad Society
  Russian/French Back
  Series 15104 20000 (Print run) Oversize
  248 No Caption - Same as "Feeling"   55 - 60   60 - 65
Other Foreign Publishers & Distributors   40 - 45   45 - 50

ADVERTISING

Brown & Bigelow Calendars (12)
  Misspelled artist name - (Gutman)
  Months of the Year (Various Advertisers)

120	"The Defenders" January 1911	75 - 85	85 - 100
121	"Allow Me"		
122	"A Little Breezy" March 1910		
123	"Which Hand?" August 1909		
124	"New Arrivals" May 1910		
125	"Easter Boy"		
126	"First Aid" July 1910		
127	"Vacation" August 1909		
128	"School Days"		
129	"His First Attempt" October 1909		
130	"Who's Afraid" November 1909		
131	"Tired Out" December 1909		

GUTMANN, BERNHARDT (Bessie's brother-in-law)
Gutmann & Gutmann

B502	"In the Midst of Life..." Metamorphic	90 - 100	100 - 125
B503	"The Breakers" Comical cooks	40 - 50	50 - 60
B504	"Coming events cast their shadows..."		
	This G&G card was signed by George Blake	20 - 25	25 - 35

Rishar (Russia)

234 "The Poodle-Mobile" (S/H. Gutmann)	90 - 100	100 - 110
HALLOCK, RUTH	5 - 6	6 - 8

HARDY, FLORENCE (G.B.)

C.W. Faulkner & Co.	8 - 9	9 - 10
Dancing Series 914 (6)	12 - 14	14 - 16
M. Munk, Vienna		
Series 352 (6)	8 - 10	10 - 12
Others	6 - 8	8 - 10
R. Tuck		
Series 9694 (6)	8 - 10	10 - 12

HAYS, MARGARET G. (U.S.)

Ernest Nister		
Big Eyes Series	25 - 30	30 - 35
"Miss Polly Pigtail" Series (6)	25 - 30	30 - 35
2748 Dressed in Pink		
2749 Dressed in Green		
2750 Dressed in Purple		
2751 Dressed in Red		
2752 Dressed in Yellow		
2753 Dressed in Blue		
Series 3059 Valentine Children	15 - 18	18 - 22
Series 3061 (6) Large Images		
3463 Dressed in pink hat, roses, white dress		
The Rose Co.		
Christmas Series (6)	15 - 17	17 - 20
Anonymous		
Paper Doll Series 3, 6 (6)	75 - 85	85 - 100

HEINMULLER, A.

International Art Pub. Co.		
Series 1002, Halloween (6)	12 - 15	15 - 18
Series 1003, St. Patrick's Day (6)	6 - 8	8 - 10
Series 1004, Thanksgiving (6)	4 - 5	5 - 6
Series 1620, Valentines (6)	5 - 6	6 - 7
HOLLYER, EVA	6 - 8	8 - 10
HORSFALL, MARY (G.B.)	4 - 6	6 - 8

HUMMEL

Pre-1950	12 - 15	15 - 18
Later Period	5 - 6	6 - 7

HUMPHREY, MAUD (U.S.)

V. O. Hammon Pub. Co.	125 - 150	150 - 175

"Children of the Revolution" (all Signed)

576 "Benjamin Franklin Entering Phila."
577 "Boston Tea Party"
578 "Bunker Hill"
579 "Washington's Courtship"
Total of 12 possible as prints seen in the book,
"Children of the Revolution," by Maud H.
and Copyright 1900 by Frederick A. Stokes Co.
contain the 4 listed above. Captions are:

"Martha Washington Pouring Tea" **If so:**	125 - 150	150 - 175

"The Surrender of Cornwallis"
"LaFayette Dancing the Minuet"

M. Humphrey, V. O. Hammond
578, "Bunker Hill"

E. P. Kinsella, Rishar, No. 103
No Caption

"Paul Revere's Ride"		
"Betsy Ross"		
"Paul Jones"		
"Moll Pitcher"		
"Washington Crossing the Delaware"		
R. L. Conwell Co. (Unsigned)	10 - 12	12 - 15
Anonymous Publisher		
Signed M.H. -- "The Four Seasons" (4)	50 - 60	60 - 75
Gray Lithograph Co. (Unsigned)		
43, 44, 45, 46, 47, 48, 49, 50, 54	12 - 15	15 - 20
Rotograph		
Series F457	12 - 15	15 - 20
HUMPHREYS, L. G.	2 - 3	3 - 4
HUTAF, AUGUST (U.S.)		
Ullman Mfg. Co.		
"A Little Odd Fellow"	6 - 8	8 - 10
"A Little Shriner"	6 - 8	8 - 10
Other	6 - 8	8 - 10
Other Publishers	4 - 6	6 - 8
I.M.J. (I.M. JAMES) (G.B.)		
M. Munk		
Children Series	6 - 8	8 - 10
JACKSON, HELEN (G.B.) (See Fairy Tales)		
Others	10 - 12	12 - 15
JACOBS, HELEN (G.B.)	6 - 8	8 - 10

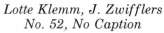

Lotte Klemm, J. Zwifflers
No. 52, No Caption

Maison Kurt, AVM 998
German Caption

K.V.
  LP Co.

Kewpie-like Children	8 - 10	10 - 12
Black Children (or Mixed)	12 - 15	15 - 18

KASKELINE, FRED

Silhouette Series 9033 (6)	6 - 8	8 - 9
Others	6 - 7	7 - 8

KEMBLE, E. B.   (U.S.) See Blacks

Comic Children	3 - 4	4 - 5

KENNEDY, T. R. or TK   (See Fairy Tales)

KIDD, WILL (U.S.)	3 - 5	5 - 6
KER, MARY SIGSBEE (U.S.)	4 - 5	5 - 6
KING, HAMILTON (U.S.)	8 - 10	10 - 12

KINSELLA, E. P.

Tennis Series	18 - 20	20 - 25
Others	12 - 15	15 - 18

KIRK, M. L. (U.S.)
  National Art Co.

Birthday Signs (7)	8 - 10	10 - 12

KLEMM, LOTTE

J. Qwifflers	10 - 12	12 - 15

KNOEFEL
  Illuminated Appearance
  Novitas

Series 664 (6)	8 - 10	10 - 12
Series 656 With Phones (6)	10 - 12	12 - 15

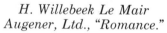

H. Willebeek Le Mair
Augener, Ltd., "Romance."

Beatrice Mallet, R. Tuck 3610G
"Gefalle ich Ihnen?"

Series 15834, 20887 (Mother/Child) (6)	8 - 10	10 - 12
KÖHLER, MELA (Austria) Art Deco	25 - 30	30 - 35
KURT, MAISON (Germany)		
AVM **Series 998**	12 - 15	15 - 18
K.V.i.B. Series 100, 1842 Deco Children		
LeMAIR, H. WILLEBEEK (G.B.)		
Augener, Ltd.		
Children's "Pieces of Schumann"		
"Catch Me if You Can," "Dreaming"	12 - 15	15 - 20
"Perfect Happiness," "Melody"		
"The Merry Peasant," "First Loss"		
"The Poor Orphan." "Romance"		
"Roundelay," "Sicilienne"		
"Soldier's March," "Vintage"		
The Children's Corner		
"Baby's Fright," "Dreadfully Busy"	8 - 10	10 - 12
"Fishing Boats," "Greedy"		
"Hair Cutting," "Last Year's Frock"		
"Out of the Snow," "Preserving Dickey"		
"Poor Baby," "Queen of the Birds"		
"The Dove's Dinner Time," "The Garden City"		
"The Invalid's Birthday"		
LEVI, C.		
Suffragette	20 - 22	22 - 28
Series 210, 3308 "Komical Koons"	12 - 15	15 - 18

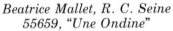

Beatrice Mallet, R. C. Seine
55659, "Une Ondine"

H.G.C. Marsh-Lambert
562, "Children of the Empire"

LEWIN, F.G. (See Blacks)		
Bamforth Co.		
Children Comics	6 - 8	8 - 10
LINDEBERG		
Head Studies	8 - 10	10 - 12
LD Meissner & Buch	8 - 10	10 - 15
LANDSTROM, B. (Finland) Fairy Tales	6 - 8	8 - 10
MAILICK, R. (German)		
Angels, Children	8 - 10	10 - 15
MAISON-KURT		
Fantasy Bear Set with Girl (4)	15 - 18	18 - 22
MALLET, BEATRICE (G.B.)		
R. Tuck "Cute Kiddies" Oilette Series		
Series 3567, 3568, 3628, 3629 (6)	8 - 10	10 - 12
Others		
MARCELLUS, IRENE		
E. Nister		
Series 3215, Child's Head in Pie, etc.	15 - 18	18 - 22
Series 736, 737, 1885, 3097		
MARGOTSON, H.	6 - 8	8 - 10
MARSH-LAMBERT, H.G.C. (G.B.)		
BD		
Child and Teddy Bear	10 - 12	12 - 15
"Wee Willie Winkle"	8 - 10	10 - 12
"Curly Locks"	7 - 8	8 - 10
Series 389, 562 (6)	10 - 12	12 - 15

C. W. Faulkner, Series 962 (6)	10 - 12	12 - 15
MARSHALL, ALICE (G.B.)	8 - 10	10 - 15
MART, L.	5 - 6	6 - 7
MARTINEAU, ALICE	6 - 8	8 - 10
MAYBANK, THOMAS (See Fairies)	8 - 10	10 - 12
McCUTCHEON, JOHN T. (U.S.)	6 - 8	8 - 10
MAUZAN, L. A. (Italy) Art Deco		
Series 45 With Dogs	10 - 12	12 - 15
M.D.S. (U.S.) See Blacks and Teddy Bears		
M.E.P. (see MARGARET EVANS PRICE, MP)		
Others	6 - 8	8 - 10
M.M.S.		
G.K. Prince Series 421	6 - 8	8 - 10
M.S.M.		
A.V.M.	10 - 12	12 - 15
Meisner & Buch	12 - 15	15 - 20
MERCER, JOYCE (G.B.)	12 - 15	15 - 18
MILLER, HILDA T.		
MITCHELL, SADIE	4 - 5	5 - 6
NASH, A. (U.S.)		
Heckscher		
Series 704	6 - 8	8 - 10
NIXON, K. See Fairy Tales		
NORFINI (Italy) Art Deco	8 - 10	10 - 15
NOSWORTHY, FLORENCE E. (G.B.)	6 - 8	8 - 10
See Fairy Tales		
NUMBER, JACK		
PFB (in Diamond) German Captions		
Series 2068, 2070, 2076 (4)	8 - 10	10 - 12
NYSTROM, JENNY (Sweden)		
BKWI - New Year Children	15 - 18	18 - 22
Others	10 - 12	12 - 15
See Fairy Tales		
NYSTROM, KURT (Sweden)	6 - 8	8 - 12

O'NEILL, ROSE (U.S.)

One of the most popular of all artists was Rose O'Neill, who created and drew the lovable Kewpie doll. The Kewpies delighted children and adults during the period after World War I through the Depression of the thirties.

Her first works were for advertising, covers and inside illustrations for some of the leading magazines. All showed the adorable Kewpies collection. The Gibson Art Company published many of O'Neill's designs on postcards for most holiday seasons. Her most popular were probably of Christmas. The Edward Gross Co. did a great set of six large image Kewpies and the Suffrage issues of Campbell Art and National Publishers Suffrage group have become the most famous of all her works. She also did two series of blacks that were published by Raphael Tuck which are extremely scarce and are avidly pursued by many collectors.

Rose O'Neill also did illustrations for advertisements as well as illustrated books. The book signatures sometimes used her married name, Latham.

ROSE O'NEILL

Campbell Art Co.		
"Klever Kards" Folds to form easel-stands up.		
Dated 1914 **(29)**	50 - 55	55 - 60
Dated 1915 **(30+)**	55 - 60	60 - 65
Miniature Klever Kards (3 x 4.5)	80 - 90	90 - 100
Suffrage Klever Kard		
228 "Votes for Women-Do I get your Vote?"	150 - 175	175 - 200
Gibson Art Co. (64 in all)	30 - 35	35 - 45
New Years (9)		
Valentine (18)		
Easter (13)		
Christmas (18)		
Miscellaneous types (6)		
Edward Gross Co.		
Large Image Kewpies (6)		
100 "The Kewpie Army"	90 - 100	100 - 120
101 "The Kewpie Carpenter"		
102 "This Kewpie wears overshoes"		
103 "The Kewpie Cook"		
104 "This Kewpie careful of his voice"		
105 "The Kewpie Gardener"		
National Suffrage Pub. Co.		
"Votes for Women - Spirit of '76"	300 - 400	400 - 500
"Votes for our Mothers" (not Kewpies)	450 - 600	600 - 750
Raphael Tuck Black Comics		
Series 2483 "Pickings from Puck" (4)		
"One View"	60 - 70	70 - 80
"Better than a Sermon"		
"A Brain Worker"		
"Ne Plus Ultra"		
Series 9411 "High Society in Coontown" (6)		
"All that was Necessary"	100 - 110	110 - 120
"Taken"		
"A Provisional Finance"		
"A Misunderstanding"		
"Finis"		
"Has Limited Provisioning Capacity"		
Series 9412 "Coontown Kids" (6)	80 - 90	90 - 100
Rock Island Line, Advertising	45 - 50	50 - 60
Parker-Bruaner Co. Ice Cream Ad.	100 - 150	150 - 200
OUTCAULT, R. (U.S.)	8 - 10	10 - 12
See Artist-Signed Comics		
OUTHWAITE, IDA R. (See Fantasy Fairies)	10 - 12	12 - 15
PALMER, PHYLLIS (U.S.)	4 - 6	6 - 8
PARKINSON, ETHEL (G.B.)		
BC **Series 745** (6)	8 - 10	10 - 12
BD **Series 475** (6)	10 - 12	12 - 14
C. W. Faulkner Series 951	12 - 14	14 - 16
M. Munk, Vienna		
Series 132, 380, 488 (6)	10 - 12	12 - 15
Series 191, 232, 234, 502, 554 (6)	8 - 10	10 - 12

Rose O'Neill, National Suffrage
Pub. Co., "... The Spirit of '76"

Rose O'Neill, Campbell Art 245
"Don' know where I'm going..."

Series 531 (6)		
Days of the Week (Dutch Children)	12 - 15	15 - 18
Others	8 - 10	10 - 12
PARTLETT, HARRY (COMICUS) (G.B.)	5 - 6	6 - 7
PATERSON, VERA (G.B.)	6 - 7	7 - 8
Golf Series	10 - 15	15 - 20
PEARSE, S. B. (Susan) (G.B.)		
M. Munk, Vienna		
Series 563, 727, 728 (6)	12 - 15	15 - 18
Series 635 (6) Dolls	18 - 20	20 - 25
Series 679, 712, 713 (6)	12 - 15	15 - 18
Series 758 (6) Dancing		
Series 844, 922, 925 (6)		
Series 856 (6) With Toys	18 - 20	20 - 25
Series 862 (6)	8 - 10	10 - 12
PEASE, BESSIE COLLINS (U.S.) See Gutmann		
PETERSEN, HANNES (Belgium)	6 - 8	8 - 10
HMB		
Series 3708 In the kitchen	8 - 10	10 - 12
Series 3710, 3978 First Day of School (6)	10 - 12	12 - 15
Others	8 - 10	10 - 12
PHILIPP, FELICIEN	6 - 8	8 - 10
PIATTOLI, G. (Italy) Art Deco		
PINOCHI, E. (Italy) Art Deco		
PITTS, JOHN E. J.E.P. (U.S.)	5 - 6	6 - 10

R. F. Outcault, R. Tuck
"I Adore You"

POWELL, LYMAN (U.S.)
    Series 82 (6) Watercolors

"Baby Sends Love"	8 - 10	10 - 12
"Introducing Baby"		

PRESTON, CHLOE (G.B.)   Art Deco

A. R. & Co. **Series 1587-4**	22 - 25	25 - 28
B. R. Co. **Series E** (Black Background) (6)	12 - 15	15 - 20
Raphael Tuck **Series 461** (6)	12 - 15	15 - 18
Valentines **Series 1022** (6)		

PRICE, MARGARET EVANS **M.E.P & MP** (U.S.)
    Stecher Litho Co.

Series 413, 415, 417 Christmas (6)	8 - 10	10 - 12
Series 648, 656, 657, 749, 875 Christmas (6)	10 - 12	12 - 15
Series 517, 628, 821 Valentine's (6)		
Series 503, 750, 783 Easter (6)		
Series 98 Flower Children (6)		
Series 403 St. Patrick's (6)		
Girl Scouts	12 - 15	15 - 18
See Halloween		
Note: Many of the **Stecher** Series were		
reprinted in the 40's & 50's.	2 - 3	3 - 4

R.R.

M. Munk, Vienna **Series 1030**	8 - 10	10 - 12
RACKHAM, ARTHUR (G.B.)	12 - 15	15 - 20
RICHARDS, EUGENIE (G.B.)	6 - 8	8 - 10

RICHARDSON, AGNES   (G.B.)

Charles Hauff **No No. Series**	12 - 15	15 - 18
C. W. Faulkner **Series 126, 6126** (6)	15 - 18	18 - 22
M. Munk, Vienna **Series 706** (6)	8 - 10	10 - 12
International Art Co.		
1958 "My Love is Like ..."	8 - 10	10 - 12

Vera Paterson, Humoresque 2687
"You seem so near and yet so ..."

Vera Paterson, Salmon 5035
"I know a feller can't always..."

G. Piattoli, Ballerini & Fratini
439, No Caption

S. B. Pearse, M. Munk 862
No Caption

Vera Paterson, Valentine's 1090
"A Few Bits of BUDE"

S. B. Pearse (Uns.), M. Munk
862, No Caption

Quadrille.

Chloe Preston, A. R & Co.
1587-4, No Caption

Susan B. Pearse, Series 758
"Quadrille."

M.E.P. (Margaret Evans Price)
Stecher 413E, "Merry Christmas"

1959 "I'll Take Care of Mummy"		
Photo Chrom Co.		
"Celesque" Series		
1425 "Anxious to start"	15 - 18	18 - 22
1426 "When the heart is young"		
1427 "Happy Days"		
1428 "The Riding Lesson"		
1430 "News for Daddy"		
Raphael Tuck (See Blacks)		
Series 9982 "Little Tots" (6)	18 - 22	22 - 25
Series C3609, 8670 (6)	10 - 12	12 - 15
Series 1262 (6) Golliwoggs	20 - 25	25 - 30
Series 1232 "Rescued" (6) Golliwoggs		
Series 1397 (6) Golliwoggs	22 - 25	25 - 30
Series C-1420, C-1421, C-1422	15 - 18	18 - 22
Valentine & Sons		
Series C2006 (6) Golliwoggs	22 - 25	25 - 30
Others	8 - 10	10 - 12
ROBINSON, ROBERT (U.S.)		
Edward Gross Series 205 Boy Ball Player	15 - 20	20 - 25
ROWLES, L. Art Deco	8 - 10	10 - 12
RUSSELL, MARY LA FENETRA (U.S.)		
Sam Gabriel Co.		
Children	4 - 6	6 - 8
Halloween	8 - 10	10 - 12
Salke "Brick Wall" Children	6 - 8	8 - 10

A. Richardson (Unsigned)
Photo Chrom, No No.

Chicky Spark, AVM 1178
"Fröhliche Weihnachten!"

Fröhliche Weihnachten!

SANDFORD, H. DIX (G.B.) See Blacks		
SANFORD, M. (G.B.) See Blacks		
SAUNDERS, E. H. (U.S.)	5 - 6	6 - 8
SHEAPHEARD		
M. Munk Series 185 (6) Dutch Children	6 - 8	8 - 10
S.K. Art Deco	8 - 10	10 - 12
SGRILLI (Italy) Art Deco	8 - 10	10 - 12
SMITH, JESSIE WILCOX (U.S.)		
Reinthal & Newman		
"Garden" Series 100	18 - 18	18 - 22
"Among the Poppies," "Five O'Clock Tea"		
"The Garden Wall," "The Green Door"		
"In the Garden," "The Lily Pool"		
SMITH, MAY	6 - 8	8 - 10
SOWERBY, AMY MILLICENT (G.B.)		
(See Chapter on Sowerby)		
SPARK, CHICKY (Germany)	8 - 10	10 - 15
SPURGIN, FRED (G.B.) See Blacks	6 - 8	8 - 10
STENBERG, AINA (Sweden)	12 - 15	15 - 18
STOCKS, M. (G.B.)		
H.K. & Co. "Jack in the Box" (Golliwoggs)	12 - 15	15 - 20
SURR, RUTH WELCH (U.S.)	2 - 3	3 - 4
R.T.	2 - 3	3 - 4
TARRANT, MARGARET (G.B.) (See Nursery Rhymes)	6 - 8	8 - 12
TEMPEST, DOUGLAS (G.B.) (See Blacks)		
Bamforth Co. Comic Kids and Animals (30's)	3 - 4	4 - 6

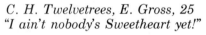

C. H. Twelvetrees, E. Gross, 25
"I ain't nobody's Sweetheart yet!"

C. H. Twelvetrees, E. Gross
"I have no desire to put out ..."

Raphael Tuck **Series 3** (6) "Dainty Dimples"		6 - 8	8 - 10
TEMPEST, MARGARET (G.B.)		4 - 6	6 - 8
THOMAS, V. (Germany)		4 - 5	5 - 8
TWELVETREES, CHARLES (U.S.)			
Ullman Mfg. Co.			
"National Cupid" Series 75			
1877 "United States"		20 - 25	25 - 30
1878 "England"		15 - 20	20 - 25
1879 "Ireland"			
1880 "Scotland"			
1881 "Germany"			
1882 "Mexico"			
1883 "Holland"			
1884 "Spain"			
1885 "Canada"			
1886 "France"			
1887 "China"			
1888 "Italy"			
Edward Gross, N.Y.			
Comical Kids		6 - 8	8 - 10
Wedding Series		10 - 12	12 - 15
1050 "Infant Series"		5 - 7	7 - 8
"Am I crying..."			
"I'm a war baby, but..."			
"I'm the family darling..."			
"Folks all say..."			

"Our baby can't talk..."
"Watch your step..."
National Art
 Days of the Week Series   5 - 7   7 - 8
 Morning-Noon-Night Series   6 - 8   8 - 10
UPTON, FLORENCE K. (G.B.)
 Raphael Tuck
  Golliwogg Series
  Series 1252, 1281, 1282, 1397 25 - 30 30 - 40
  Series 1782, 1785   30 - 35 35 - 40
  Series 1791, 1792, 1793, 1794 35 - 40 40 - 45
VOIGHT, C.A.   3 - 4   4 - 5
VON HARTMANN, E.   2 - 3   3 - 4
WALL, BERNHARDT C. (U.S.) See Blacks
 Ullman Mfg. Co.
  "Overall Boys"   6 - 8   8 - 10
  92 "Young America"
  93 "Me and Jack"
  94 "Leap Frog"
  95 "A Rough Rider"
  "The Senses"   10 - 12 12 - 15
  1716 "Feeling"
  1717 "Smelling"
  1718 "Tasting"
  1719 "Hearing"
  1720 "Seeing"
  "Nursery Rhymes" Series (Unsigned) 15 - 18 18 - 22
  1664 "Little Bo Peep"
  1665 "To Market, To Market"
  1666 "Rain, Rain Go Away"
  1667 "See Saw, Marjorie Daw"
  1668 "Come, Let's Go to Bed"
  Sunbonnet Months of the Year
   Unsigned, 1633-1644   8 - 9   9 - 12
  Sunbonnet Girls' Days of the Week
   Unsigned, 1408-1410, 1491-1494 10 - 12 12 - 15
  Sunbonnet Seasons
  1901 Spring   10 - 12 12 - 15
  1902 Summer
  1903 Autumn
  1904 Winter
  "Mary and Her Lamb" Sunbonnets
   1759-1762   8 - 10 10 - 12
  Sunbonnet Twins
  1645 "Give us this Day ..."   10 - 12 12 - 15
  1646 "The Star Spangled ..."
  1647 "Should Auld Acquaintance ..."
  1648 "A Good Book is ..."
  1649 "Now I Lay Me Down ..."
  1650 "Be It Ever So Humble ..."
  Sunbonnet Girls   10 - 12 12 - 14
  1765 "6 A.M., Milking Time"
  1766 "7 A.M., Breakfast Time"
  1767 "10 A.M., Mowing Time"

1768 "12 N., Noon Time"			
1769 "3 P.M., Haying Time"			
1770 "6 P.M., Home, Sweet Home"			
Sunbonnet Girls Nursery Rhymes		10 - 12	12 - 15
1664 "Little Bo Peep"			
1665 "To Market, to Market"			
1666 "Rain, Rain, Go Away"			
1667 "See Saw, Marjorie Daw"			
1668 "Goosey, Goosey, Gander"			

Bergman
 Suffragettes
  "Votes for Women" Series 30 - 35 35 - 40
  Unnumbered Sunbonnet Series 8 - 10 10 - 12
Schlesinger Bros., N.Y.
 Dutch Kids (6) (B&W) 3 - 4 4 - 5
No Publisher
 Animated Fruit & Vegetable Set

"Apple"	"Cabbage"	8 - 10	10 - 12
"Karat"	"Ears"		
"Cucumber"	"Lemon"		
"Melon"	"Onion"		
"Pair"	"Peach"		
"Pine"	"Potato"		
"Pumpkin"	"Turnip"		

WANKE, ALICE 8 - 10 10 - 12
WHEELER, DOROTHY (See Fairy Tales)
WHITE, FLORA (See Fairy Tales-Nursery Rhymes)
 W.E. Mach Pub. Co. "Musical Children" (6) 8 - 10 10 - 12
WICHERA, R. R. (Austria) 6 - 8 8 - 10
WIEDERSEIM, GRACE (also Grace Drayton)
 Reinthal & Newman
  No Number 20 - 25 25 - 30
 "A button sewed on..."
 "Blow"
 Bobby: "I brought your birdie..."
 Dressy Lady: "What are you crying for...?"
 "Everybody loves me"
 "I think I'd rather..."
 "The more I see ..."
 "Nothing doing"
 "You're going to get ..."
 98 "Nothing doing"
 98 "Happy Days"
 99 "Where's oo hanky"
 110 "What you don't know ..."
 112 "No Ma'am, we ain't ..."
 113 "So near & yet so far"
 114 "Tis better to have loved and lost..."
 115 "Curfew shall not ..."
 116 "I'm so discouraged ..."
 117 "Courage"
 120 "I hate a spanking ..."
 121 "Stung!"

174 "Here's How"
175 "Don't wake me up ..."
176 "I wish somebody was ..."
177 "And what did Mamma's boy do..."
178 "Mr. Moon Man, turn..."
179 "Music Hath Charms"
249 "Gee! but this is ..."
250 "Wanted! Somebody ..."
308 "I'd rather say Hello ..."
310 "All I want is you"
493 Skipping Rope
· 495 "Why do we place a hyphen..."
496 "Do you or don't you"
500 "More of all"

A. G. Taylor (Orthochrome Series) **(Schweizer)**

"Help the Poor"

"His First Case"	35 - 40	40 - 45

"I don't think..."
"Two Hearts that beat as one"
"Weary Willy and Appy Ann"

Raphael Tuck

"Bright Eyes" Series (Uns.)	30 - 35	35 - 38

"Sweet Bliss" Series
"It fills my heart..."

"In Arcady"	25 - 30	30 - 35
Series 200 "Cunning Cupids"	40 - 50	50 - 60

Series 223 (6)
Series 242 "Childhood Pets" (Uns.)
Series 243 "Love's Messages" (Uns.)
Series 244 "Masquerade Children" (Uns.)
Halloween Series 807 (Uns.) (4)

"Hallowe'en. Look in the glass..."	80 - 90	90 - 100

"Jack O'Lantern"
"O-o-o The Witches Brew"
"The Witch!"

"In Arcady"	25 - 30	30 - 35
Series 2914 "Cunning Cupids"	40 - 50	50 - 60

Armour & Co.

American Girl Series "The Wiederseim Girl"	30 - 35	35 - 40

Fairman Co.

"Everything goes wrong when you're away"	20 - 25	25 - 28

C.W. Faulkner
Series 1281 (Uns.)

"Dressed in his best"	32 - 35	35 - 38

North American

"What-che-know- 'bout that"	30 - 35	35 - 38

Anonymous
Series 38 "Days of Week" (Uns.)

Campbell Art Co.	30 - 35	35 - 40

Campbell Soup Co. - Advertising
Campbell Soup Kids

Horizontal - (4) (with variations) (1909)	35 - 40	40 - 50

Vertical - (10¢ a can) -- (24) * **

Series 1-12 With **No Series No.** (1912)	125 - 150	150 - 175

G. Wiederseim, Alfred Schweizer
"His First Case"

Grace Wiederseim, Russian   *G. Wiederseim, Alfred Schweizer*
Real Photo No. 279   *Set 10, No Caption*

Series 1 Numbered 1 thru 6 (1912)	120 - 140	140 - 160
Series 2 Numbered 7 thru 12 (1912)		
Card 7 with Suffragette jingles (2)	150 - 175	175 - 200
Series 3 Numbered 13 thru 18 (1913)	120 - 140	140 - 160
Series 4 Numbered 19 thru 24 (1913)		

* The 24 images have from 3 to 4 different
jingles on each card...meaning there could be
as many as 80 to 96 different total cards.
** Grace Wiederseim remarried in 1911 so
any of these cards with copyright after that
would be by Grace Drayton. Nos. 1 thru 24
were copyright 1912-1913.
Swift & Co.

"Days of the Week" With Ads on Reverse (7)	40 - 45	45 - 50

Alfred Schweizer Co., Hamburg

No No.		
"I Don't Think!"	35 - 40	40 - 45
Set 10 (Signed)		
Boy pulls girl on sled		
Series 8 "Tit for tat"		
Series 9 Girl walking Poodle		
Series 10596		
Boy/Girl under Mistletoe	30 - 35	35 - 40
"Beware of Dog" Sign		
"Chase Me"		
"Help the Poor"		

"Jilted"
"Time is money"
"Weary Willie and 'Appy Ann"
"You mustn't kiss me!"

Russian Real Photo, No. 279 (Russian Caption)	50 - 60	60 - 75
WOODWORTH, JULIA (U.S.)	3 - 4	4 - 5
WUYTS, A. (Austria)	4 - 6	6 - 8

COMICS

ANDERS, O. (G.B.)	5 - 6	6 - 8
ANDERSON, M. (CYNICUS) (G.B.)	6 - 8	8 - 10
ARIS, ERNEST (G.B.)	5 - 6	6 - 8
BAIRNSFATHER, BRUCE (G.B.)	6 - 8	8 - 10
BARNES, G. L. (G.B.)	3 - 5	5 - 8
BATEMAN, H. M. (G.B.)	4 - 5	5 - 7
BIGGAR, J. L. (G.B.)		
BIANCO, T. (Italy)		
Political Comics	15 - 20	20 - 25
BISHOP, P. (U.S.)	4 - 5	5 - 7
BLACK, W. M. (W.M.B.) (G.B.)	5 - 6	6 - 8
BLOODGOOD, DON (U.S.) Chromes		
Outhouses	3 - 5	5 - 7
BOULANGER, MAURICE (See Animals)	10 - 12	12 - 15
BRADSHAW, P.V. (G.B.)	6 - 8	8 - 10
BRILL, GEORGE R. (U.S.)	6 - 7	7 - 10
Rose Co. "Ginks" Series	8 - 10	10 - 12
BROWNE, TOM (G.B.)		
Davidson Bros.		
Each Series Contains 6 Cards:		
Series 2525 "Golf"	15 - 18	18 - 22
Series 2575 "Seaside Comfort"	6 - 8	8 - 10
Series 2578 "Billiards Made ..."	10 - 12	12 - 15
Series 2585 "Amateur Photographer"		
Series 2587 "Cycling"		
Series 2594 "Kissing"		
Series 2598 "Are We Downhearted ..."	5 - 8	10 - 15
Series 2618 "Baseball III"	20 - 25	25 - 30
Series 2619 "Baseball III"		
Series 2627 "Diabolo"	12 - 15	15 - 18
Series 2637 "New Compensation Act"	8 - 10	10 - 12
Series 2642 "Joys of the Ocean"	6 - 8	8 - 10
BUCHANAN, FRED (G.B.) (See Blacks)	6 - 8	8 - 10
BULL, RENE (G.B.)	5 - 6	6 - 8
BUXTON, DUDLEY (G.B.)	5 - 6	6 - 8
CADY, HARRISON (U.S.) **"QUADDY" Series 10**	35 - 40	40 - 45
CARMICHAEL (U.S.)		
S.K. Simon		
Series 200 "You Look Good to Me" (6)	6 - 8	8 - 10
S.B. Co.		
Series 261 "Would You?" (12)		
Series 262 "If" (12)		
Anonymous		
Series 310 "Why?" (12)		

Don Bloodgood, HSC-47
"Made to Order"

George R. Brill, Rose Co.
"I'm the Gink wot reads your..."

Tom Browne, Davidson Brothers
2525-2, "A Grand Day for Golf."

Series 311 "There are Others" (6)			
Series 315 "Don't Marry" (12)			
T.P. & Co.			
Series 565 "I love my wife, but oh you kid" (12)			
Series 568 "I wish I had a beau" (12)			
Series 620 Playing Card Series (12)			
Series 621 "Your Fortune" (12)			
Series 668 "Anybody here seen Kelly?" (12)			
Series 669 Fish Series (12)			
Series 761 Stork Series (12)			
Bamforth Co. **Series 262** "If" **(12)**		5 - 7	7 - 8
CARR, GENE (U.S.)			
Bergman Co.			
Series 2003, 2004, 8515 Easter		6 - 8	8 - 10
Rotograph Co., N.Y.			
Series 218 Mosquitos (4)		6 - 8	8 - 10
Series 219 4th of July Series (5)			
St. Patrick's Series 187-192 (6)			
Comic Series 201-213 (12)			
CARTER, REG. (G.B.)			
Early Issues		8 - 10	10 - 12
After 1920 Issues		3 - 4	4 - 6
CARTER, SYDNEY (G.B.)		8 - 10	10 - 12
CAVALLY, FRED L. (U.S.) Also See Teddy Bears		2 - 4	4 - 6

Harrison Cady, "Quaddy"
"Peter Rabbit"

G. F. Christie, Photochrom Co.
"I'm Having a Long Spell Here."

CHANDLER, E.	5 - 6	6 - 8
CHRISTIE, G. F. (G.B.)	8 - 10	10 - 12
COCK, STANLEY	4 - 5	5 -8
COMICUS (HARRY PARTLETT) (G.B.)	2 - 3	3 - 4
COLBY, V. (U.S.)	1 - 2	2 - 3
COOK, C. K. (G.B.)	6 - 8	8 - 10
COWHAM, HILDA (G.B.)	4 - 5	5 - 6
CROMBIE, CHARLES (G.B.)		
Valentine		
"Rules of Golf" Series	15 - 20	20 - 25
"Rules of Cricket" Series	10 - 12	12 - 15
"Humors of Fishing" Series		
Others	4 - 6	6 - 8
DARLING, JAY (U.S.)	10 - 12	12 - 15
DAVEY, GEORGE (G.B.)	5 - 6	6 - 8
DENSLOW, W. W. (U.S.) Thanksgiving	10 - 12	12 - 15
See Teddy Bears		
DIRKS, GUS (G.B.) Comic Insects	8 - 10	10 - 12
DIRKS, R. (Germany)		
American Journal Examiner		
Katzenjammer Kids	6 - 8	8 - 10
DISNEY, WALT (U.S.)		
Foreign Issues		
French, 30's Era	20 - 25	25 - 35

DWIG, Raphael Tuck
"Cheer Up!!" Series

DWIG, Raphael Tuck
"Smile" Series

DWIG, Raphael Tuck
"If" Series

German, 30's Era		
Czech., 30's Era		
Hungarian, 30's Era		
Other 30's Era Issues	15 - 20	20 - 25
Felix the Cat		
DONADINI, JR. (Italy) See Blacks)		
A-H Motoring Comics (6)	6 - 8	8 - 10
German-American Novelty Art Co.		
Series 491 Driving Comics (6)	12 - 15	15 - 18
"What is worth doing..."		
K. & B. D.		
Boating Comics, Series 1660 (6)	10 - 12	12 - 15
Driving Comics, Series 3033 (6)	12 - 15	15 - 18
Driving Comics, Series 202 (6)	8 - 10	10 - 12
Drunk Comics, Series 357 (6)		
Lover Comics, Series 362 (6)	10 - 12	12 - 15
Seashore Comics, Series 393 (6)		
"Sell Well" Comics Series 14 (6)	6 - 8	8 - 10
Children Comics, Series 201 (6)		
Ottmar Ziehr Mountain Climbing Series 129	10 - 12	12 - 15
Anonymous		
Driving Comics, Series 652 (6)	10 - 12	12 - 15
Easter Comics, Series 787 (6)	6 - 8	8 - 10
Farm Life, Series 239 (6)		
Men at Seashore Series (6)	8 - 10	10 - 12
Funny Children Head Studies (6)		
DUNCAN, HAMISH	3 - 4	4 - 6
DWIG (C.V. DWIGGINS) (U.S.)		
J. Marks Series 981 "Halloween" (6)	25 - 30	30 - 35
Raphael Tuck		
"Cheer Up" Series (24)	6 - 8	8 - 10

"Don't" Series (24)		
"Everytime" Series (24)		
"Follies" Series (12)		
"If" Series (24)		
"Ophelia" Series (24)		
"Pipe Dreams" Series 122 (12)	12 - 15	15 - 18
"Help Wanted" Series (12)	6 - 8	8 - 10
"Never" Series (24)		
"Jollies" Series (12)		
"School Days" Series (24)		
"Smiles" Series (24)	8 - 10	10 - 12
Series 127 "Toasts For Today" (12)	12 - 15	15 - 20
Series 128 "Toasts for Occasions" (12)		
"Zodiac" Series (12)	50 - 60	60 - 70
Charles Rose		
"Baby" Series (6)	8 - 10	10 - 12
"Figures in Mountains" Series (6)	10 - 12	12 - 15
"Moon" Series (6)		
"Moving" Series (6)	8 - 10	10 - 12
"New York" Series (6)	12 - 15	15 - 18
"Oyster Girl" Series (6)	10 - 12	12 - 15
"Sandwich" Series (6)	8 - 10	10 - 12
"Superstition" Series (6)		
"What are Wild Waves ..." Series (6)	10 - 12	12 - 15
"The Wurst Girl" Series (6)	12 - 15	15 - 18
"The Frankfurter Girl" Series (6)	10 - 12	12 - 15
R. Kaplan		
"Fortune Teller" Series (12)	8 - 9	9 - 10
"How Can You Do It?" Series (24)	6 - 7	7 - 8
"Mirror Girl" Series (24)	8 - 10	10 - 12
Sam Gabriel		
"If's & And's" Series (6)	6 - 7	7 - 8
"Leap Year" Series 401 (12)	9 - 10	10 - 12
"Fortune Teller" Series 55 (12)	6 - 8	8 - 10
Edward Gross		
"What's the Use?" Series (6)	6 - 7	7 - 8
Cardinell-Vincent Co. © 1910 Ninon Traver		
Series 101 "Widow's Wisdom" (12)		
EDWARDS, LIONEL	4 - 6	6 - 8
ELLAM (W.H.) (See Teddy Bears)		
"Breakfast in Bed" Series	20 - 22	22 - 25
Others	10 - 12	12 - 15
FOX, CRAIG (Linens)	1 - 2	2 - 3
FISHER, BUD (U.S.)		
Mutt and Jeff (Unsigned)	12 - 15	15 - 20
FLEURY, H.	4 - 6	6 - 8
FULLER, EDMUND G.	5 - 7	7 - 8
GIBBS, MAY	18 - 22	22 - 26

PFB, Series 6310
"Love's golden dream!"

HBG, L. & E., 2242
"Here's to Columbia's Favorite..."

GIBSON, CHARLES DANA (U.S.)		
Henderson Co. Sepia Comics (36)	5 - 6	6 - 7
Detroit Publishing	8 - 10	10 - 12
Golf	15 - 18	18 - 22
GILL, ARTHUR (G.B.)	4 - 5	5 - 6
GILSON, T. (G.B.) (See Blacks)	4 - 5	5 - 6
GLADWIN, MAY (G.B.)	4 - 5	5 - 6
GOLDBERG, RUBE (U.S.)		
Albie the Agent	8 - 10	10 - 12
Barton & Spooner		
Series 212 "The Ancient Order"	6 - 8	8 - 10
Series 213 "Foolish Questions"	5 - 6	6 - 8
Dreamland Skating Rink -- Advertising	15 - 18	18 - 22
GOODYEAR, ARCHIE	4 - 5	5 - 6
GRIGGS, H. B. and HBG		
L & E		
Halloween (See Halloween)		
George Washington Women's Suffrage	70 - 80	80 - 90
Others	8 - 10	10 - 12
HAMISH (G.B.)	4 - 5	5 - 6
HARDY, DUDLEY (G.B.)	6 - 8	8 - 10
HASSALL, JOHN (G.B.)	6 - 8	8 - 10
HORINA, H. and H.H. (U.S.) (See Blacks)		
Illustrated P.C. Co.	5 - 6	6 - 8

Phil May, R. Tuck, "Write Away" Series 1008
"I miss you awfully"

HURST, HAL (U.S.)	4 - 5	5 - 6
HUTAF, AUGUST (U.S.) (See Blacks)		
P.C.K. "Advice to Vacationists"	5 - 6	6 - 8
IBBETSON, ERNEST (G.B.)	6 - 8	8 - 10
KENNEDY, A. E. (G.B.)		
KINSELLA, E. P. (See Sports and Blacks)		
KYD, J.C.C. (G.B.)		
Raphael Tuck "Dickens Characters"		
"The Artful Dodger" -- Oliver Twist	8 - 10	10 - 12

"Mrs. Bardell" -- Pickwick Papers
"Bikes" -- Oliver Twist
"Bumble" -- Oliver Twist
"Captain Cuttle" -- Dombey & Sons
"Dick Swiveller" -- Old Curiosity Shop
"Fat Boy" -- Pickwick Papers
"Mr. Jingle" -- Pickwick Papers
"The Little Marchioness" -- Old Curiosity Shop
"Mr. Micawber" -- David Copperfield
"Mr. Pecksniff" -- Martin Chuzzlewit
"Mr. Peggotty" -- David Copperfield
"Mr. Pickwick" -- Pickwick Papers
"Quilp" -- Old Curiosity Shop
"Sam Weller" -- Pickwick Papers
"Samson Brass" -- Old Curiosity Shop
"Mrs. Sarah Gamp" -- Martin Chuzzlewit
" Sergeant Buzfuz" -- Pickwick Papers
"Toots" -- Dombey & Sons

"Trotty Veck" -- The Chimes
"Uriah Heep" -- David Copperfield
"Mr. Weller" -- Pickwick Papers
"Whackford Squeers" -- Nicolas Nickleby

LEWIN, F.G. (See Blacks)	5 - 6	6 - 8
LEVI, C. (See Blacks)	4 - 5	5 - 6
LUDOVICI, A.	8 - 10	10 - 12
MARTIN, ABE (U.S.)		
Illustrated P.C. Co.	5 - 6	6 - 8
"Leap Year"	6 - 8	8 - 10
Other "Leap Year" Issues		
F.L.		
"Comical Types" (The Strong Man, etc.)	6 - 8	8 - 10
Others	5 - 6	6 - 8
HYDE, GRAHAM		
MASON, GEORGE W.		
MAY, PHIL (G.B.)	6 - 8	8 - 12
Raphael Tuck		
Series 1008 (6) Golf	20 - 22	22 - 25
Series 1295 (6)	8 - 10	10 - 12
Series 1775 (6) Drunks	6 - 8	8 - 10
McCAY, WINSOR (U.S.)		
Raphael Tuck		
"Little Nemo" Series	25 - 30	30 - 35
McGILL, DONALD (G.B.) See Blacks		
Pre-1914	6 - 8	8 - 10
Others	2 - 3	3 - 4
McMANUS, GEORGE (U.S.)		
"Bringing Up Father" Series	35 - 40	40 - 45
MORELAND, ARTHUR	5 - 6	6 - 8
MORGAN, F. E. Golf	12 - 15	15 - 18
MORGAN, F. R. Question Series	8 - 10	10 - 12
MUNSON, WALT (Linens) (See Blacks)	1 - 2	2 - 3
MYER Aurochrome Series	4 - 5	5 - 6
NEWELL, PETER (U.S.)		
Detroit Publishing Co. Series 14169-14178		
"Bigger-than-Weather-Boys"	10 - 12	12 - 15
OPPER, FRED (U.S.)		
"Happy Hooligan" Series	8 - 10	10 - 12
"Alphonse & Gaston" Series	6 - 8	8 - 10
"And Her Name Was Maud" Series	6 - 8	8 - 10
Others	5 - 6	6 - 8
Add $3 for Tuck Issues.		
OUTCAULT, R. F. (U.S.)		
The American Journal Examiner		
Buster Brown Series (8)		
"Look at Santa Claus"	15 - 20	20 - 25
"Oh, See the Sea Serpent"	12 - 15	15 - 18

F. E. Morgan, J. Salmon Ltd.
"I can't finish the rahnd wiv ..."

Walt Munson, 68039
"Hey Pop -- I made it! ..."

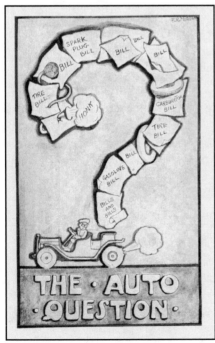

F. R. Morgan, A-415
"The Labor Question"

F. R. Morgan, A-417
"The Auto Question"

"Resolved: Nothing Can Stop Us"	10 - 12	12 - 15
"Say! Mary Jane ..."	12 - 15	15 - 18
"What Enormous Bill on Legs ..."	10 - 12	12 - 15
"Who is Buster Posing?"	15 - 18	18 - 22
"Who is Buster Getting Away From?"	12 - 15	15 - 18
"Who is the Laugh On?"	12 - 15	15 - 18
"A Smooth Bit of Road" (Blacks)	20 - 25	25 - 30
"The Constable"	20 - 25	25 - 30
"All Over"	15 - 20	20 - 25

Bloomingdale Brothers, 1902
   Buster Brown Adv. Series (6)   70 - 80   80 - 90
Bloomingdale Brothers
   Buster Brown Santa Claus Card   100 - 115   115 - 125
Brown Shoe Company, 1909
   Buster Brown Blue Ribbon Shoes   20 - 25   25 - 30
     Months of Year (12)
Burr-McIntosh, 1903
   "Buster Brown and His Bubble" (10)   *

"A Quiet Day in Town"	15 - 20	20 - 25
"Hands Up"		
"Black or White?" (Blacks)	28 - 32	32 - 35
"Looking for Trouble"	15 - 20	20 - 25
"A Good Bump"		
"Over the Bounding Main" (Blacks)	28 - 32	32 - 35
"A Rise in Bear"	15 - 20	20 - 25
"A Smooth Bit of Road" (Blacks)	28 - 32	32 - 35
"The Constable"		
"All Over"	15 - 20	20 - 25

* Set also by I.H. Blanchard Co. and by
  Souvenir P.C. Co. - Appr. same values.
Kaufmann and Strauss, 1903
Advertising Cards with Imprints of
     Various Firms (16+)   12 - 15   15 - 18
J. Ottman, 1905
   Comic Series (40+)   10 - 12   12 - 15
J. Ottman, 1906
   Christmas Card Set (4?) Unsigned   12 - 15   15 - 18
F. A. Stokes, 1906
   Buster Brown Outcault Cartoon Lectures   15 - 18   18 - 22
   "Come on Tige"
   "Gee, What's Playing?"
   "Give it to Mary Jane, Buddy"
   "If Tige Would Only Go Away"
   "Where Are You Going?"
H. H. Tammen, 1906
   Buster Brown Series (Embossed) *   15 - 18   18 - 22
   "Come and Join Us in a Blowout"
   "I Ain't Got no Time ..."
   "Hurry Back with the Answer"

"It was de Dutch"		
"Way Down in My Heart ..."		
* Reduced Series of Above Set, 1908	20 - 25	25 - 30
Raphael Tuck, 1903		
Valentine Series (12)	10 - 12	12 - 15
Raphael Tuck, 1904		
Valentine Scroll Series (6)	10 - 12	12 - 15
"Can you Guess the One ...?"		
"Don't Monkey with this Heart of Mine"		
"Here's a Wireless Telegram ..."		
"I am Perfectly Willing ..."		
"Why Don't Someone Ask ...?"		
"Won't You be my Honey ...?"		
"There's a Certain Person ..."		
"Will you be my Valentine ...?"		
Raphael Tuck		
New Outcault Series 7		
Valentine Postcards	12 - 14	14 - 16
Buster Brown		
Series 8 Valentine Postcards (10)	10 - 12	12 - 15
"Bear, Bear, Don't Go Away"		
"Honey, How Your Eyes Do Shine"		
"I Am Perfectly Willing ..."		
"I Dreams Erbout Yo' Eb'ry Night ..."		
"Laugh, Laugh and be Merry ..."		
"Love Me, and the World is Mine"		
"Now How Do Little Birdies Know ..."		
"Of All the Days in the Year ..."		
"Oh, Maid, Take Pity ..."		
"Someone Has Asked Someone ..."		
Buster Brown Postcards	12 - 15	15 - 18
Love Tributes Series 5	10 - 12	12 - 15
Ullman Mfg. Co., 1906 *		
Series 76 "Darktown" (4)		
"Darktown Doctors"	22 - 25	25 - 30
"Darktown Dames"		
"Deed, I Dun Eat No Chicken"		
"Koontown Kids"		
* **American Postcard Co.** also did Ser. 76		
Buster Brown Co., Chicago, 1906		
Buster Brown 1906 Calendars	15 - 18	18 - 22
Buster Brown 1907 Calendars		
Outcault Adv. Co., Chicago, 1907		
Buster Brown 1908 Calendars	18 - 22	22 - 25
Buster Brown 1909 Calendars		
Buster Brown 1910 Calendars		
Buster Brown 1911 Calendars		
R. F. Outcault, New York, 1907		
Little House Maid 1908 Calendars	12 - 15	15 - 20

Little House Maid 1909 Calendars
Little House Maid 1910 Calendars
Little House Maid 1911 Calendars
Mr. Swell Dresser 1908 Calendars
Mr. Swell Dresser 1909 Calendars
Mr. Swell Dresser 1910 Calendars

R. F. Outcault, N.Y., 1908-11
Bank Series 1909-11 Calendars   12 - 15   15 - 18
R. F. Outcault, N.Y., 1909
Bank Series 1912-13 Calendars
Rockford Watch 1909-10 Calendars   25 - 30   30 - 35
R. F. Outcault, N.Y., 1911
Yellow Kid 1910 -12 Calendars   80 - 100   100 - 125
Yellow Kid 1913 Calendars
R. F. Outcault, Copyright
Blue Boy 1912-14 Calendars   12 - 15   15 - 20
Buster Brown 1912-15 Calendars
Furniture 1912-15 Calendars
Mary Jane 1911-13 Calendars
Yellow Kid Look-a-Like 1914-15 Calendars

PARLETT, HARRY (G.B.)
Taylor's Orthochrome
Series 2830 (6) Roller Skating   10 - 12   12 - 15
PHIZ (H.K. BROWNE)   8 - 10   10 - 12
PIPPO (France)
Big Eyed Man Series   10 - 12   12 - 15
Barber   Blacksmith
Cook   Doctor
Gambler   Musician
Richman   Sculptor
POULBOT, F. (France)   10 - 12   12 - 15
RAEMAKERS, LOUIS (Netherlands)   6 - 8   8 - 10
REYNOLDS, FRANK (U.S.)   5 - 6   6 - 8
REZNICEK (Denmark)   12 - 15   15 - 18
ROBERTS, VIOLET
ROBIDA (France)   10 - 12   12 - 15
ROBINSON, W. HEATH (U.S.)   6 - 8   8 - 10
ROCKWELL, NORMAN (U.S.)   30 - 40   40 - 50
ROWNTREE, HARRY (G.B.) See Teddy Bears   6 - 8   8 - 10
SANDFORD, H. DIX (See Blacks)   6 - 7   7 - 8
SCHONFLUG, FRITZ (Austria)   10 - 12   12 - 20
SCHULTZ, C. E. (Bunny)
"Foxy Grandpa" Series   6 - 8   8 - 10
SHEPHEARD, GEORGE E.   5 - 6   6 - 7
SHINN, COBB and TOM YAD (U.S.)   3 - 4   4 - 5
See Art Nouveau
H. A. Waters Co.
"Foolish Questions" Series   3 - 4   4 - 6

I'M DER FELLER DAT MAKES DIS WORLD GO ROUND AND DER PEOPLE SQUARE. BY HECK!

lead, kindly light!

Cobb Shinn, TP & Co., 903
"I'm der feller dat makes dis ..."

PFB, Series 6895
"Lead, kindly light!"

"Ford" Comics	8 - 10	10 - 12
"Charlie Chaplin" Cartoons		
SPURGIN, FRED (Latvia) See Blacks		
Series 956 "Leap Year"	8 - 10	10 - 12
Others	5 - 6	6 - 8
STUDDY, G. E. (G.B.)		
"Bonzo"	8 - 10	10 - 12
Golf	12 - 15	15 - 20
Others	4 - 5	5 - 6
SWINNERTON		
American Journal Examiner	6 - 7	7 - 10
TAYLOR, A. (G.B.) (1950's)	1 - 2	2 - 3
TEMPEST, D. (G.B.) (See Blacks)		
Others	2 - 3	3 - 5
THACKERAY, LANCE (G.B.)		
Raphael Tuck		
"At the Seaside" (6)	8 - 9	9 - 12
"Game of Golf" (6)	15 - 18	18 - 22
Series 9088 "Weather Reports" (6)	7 - 8	8 - 10
THIELE, ARTHUR See Blacks, Cats, etc.		
L & P		
Fat Lady Series	10 - 12	12 - 15
Bathing Girls Series	12 - 15	15 - 18
Others	10 - 12	12 - 15

A.T. (A. Taylor), Bamforth 13546
"It'sh gonna be a tight game, ..."

Lawson Wood, Valentine & Sons
"Gran'pop" Series, "Tough Nuts."

Walter Wellman (Uns.), 1480
"Excuse My Haste! This Ain't ..."

UPTON, FLORENCE (G.B.) (See Golliwoggs)	30 - 35	35 - 40
WAIN, LOUIS (G.B.) See Cats, Dogs		
"Charlie Chapman Cats"	200 - 225	225 - 250
WALL, BERNHARDT (U.S.)		
Many Sets and Series	5 - 6	6 - 10
WARD, DUDLEY	3 - 4	4 - 5
WEAVER, E. (U.S.)		
Ford Comics	8 - 10	10 - 12
Others	1 - 2	2 - 3
WELLMAN, WALTER (U.S.)		
"Try Dan Cupid" Series (32)	5 - 7	7 - 10
"Merry Widow Wiles" (8)		
"Last Will & Testament" Series (8)	6 - 8	8 - 10
"Weaker Sex" Series (12)		
"Hand" Series (12)	5 - 6	6 - 8
"The Suffragette" Ser. (16) See Suffragettes		
"Life's Little Tragedies" (16)	5 - 6	6 - 8
Linen Comics (See Blacks)	1 - 1.50	1.50 - 2
WELLS, C.		
Lounsbury		
Series 2025		
"Lovely Lilly"	6 - 8	8 - 10
WITT, MIA "Ford Booster" Comics (10)	7 - 8	8 - 10

WOOD, LAWSON (G.B.)		
Chimps, Parrots, etc.	6 - 8	8 - 10
See Suffragettes		
YAD, TOM (Also **COBB SHINN**)	1 - 2	2 - 3
ZIM	4 - 5	5 - 6

PUBLISHERS

Bauman (Unsigned)		
Ugly Girls - Days of the Week (6)	6 - 8	8 - 10
Gartner & Bender		
Water Color Sets (6)	6 - 8	8 - 10
"Amy Bility"		
"Antie Quate"		
"Gee Whiz"		
"Gee Willikins"		
"Jimmy"		
"Optimistic Miss"		
"Phil Os Opher"		
Irwin Kline (Unsigned)		
Masonic (No Numbers) (6)	6 - 7	7 - 8
P.F.B. (Unsigned)		
Series 5897 Mother-in-Law (6)	8 - 10	10 - 15
Series 6307 Comic Lovers (6)		
Series 6538 Domestic Riot (6)		
Many Others	6 - 8	8 - 10

SILHOUETTES

ALLMAHER, JOSEFINE	6 - 8	8 - 10
BECKMAN, JOHANNA		
BURKE, PAUL	5 - 7	7 - 8
BORRMEISTER, R. (Germany)	6 - 8	8 - 10
BRENING, H.	10 - 12	12 - 15
DIEFENBACH, K.W. (Germany)		
B. G. Teubner Fantasy Children	12 - 15	15 - 18
FORCK, ELSBETH (Germany)		
GRAF, MARTE (Germany)		
Art Deco Series 1, 2, 3, 4 (743-754)	8 - 10	10 - 15
Others	8 - 10	10 - 12
GROSS, CH.	5 - 7	7 - 8
GROSZE, MANNI (Germany)		
P.F.B. (In Diamond)		
Deco Series 2041 "After Bath"	12 - 15	15 - 20
Nude Series 2042		
Series 2043	10 - 12	12 - 15
Nude Series 3339	12 - 15	15 - 20
Series 3341 & 3342	10 - 12	12 - 15
K.M.H.	8 - 10	10 - 12

Trebicky
Kleiner, 3318

G. L. Schmidt
Meissner & Buch, 2615

KASKELINE
Art Deco, Ladies/Children	8 - 10	10 - 15

LAMP, H.
Series 3, Deco Dancing	12 - 15	15 - 20
Series 4, Bathing	12 - 15	15 - 18

PHILIPP, FELICIEN	8 - 10	10 - 12
PEANITSCH, LEO	10 - 12	12 - 15
ROBA (Deco Fantasy)	12 - 15	15 - 20
SACHSE-SCHUBERT, M.	10 - 12	12 - 14
SCHIRMER (See Fairy Tales/Nursery Rhymes)	10 - 12	12 - 15
SCHÖNPFLUG, FRITZ (Austria)	12 - 15	15 - 20
SCHMIDT, GERDA LUISE (Germany)	12 - 15	15 - 18
STUBNER, LOTTE (Germany)	8 - 10	10 - 12

S.K.
Meissner & Buch	8 - 10	10 - 12

SUSS, PAUL	10 - 12	12 - 15

TREBICKY (Germany)
Kleiner 3318 (Tennis)	20 - 25	25 - 28
Others	12 - 15	15 - 18

BLACKS, SIGNED

ATTWELL, MABEL L. (G.B.)
Valentine & Sons	22 - 25	25 - 28

Others

Early Period, Pre-1915	22 - 25	25 - 28
Middle Period, 1915-30	16 - 18	18 - 22
Late Period, 1930-50	10 - 12	12 - 15

B.   See Bonte

T.S.N. Series 440 (N1-N20?)	30 - 35	35 - 45
BENSON, HENRY (U.S.) **Ullman Mfg. Co.**	6 - 8	8 - 10

BERTIGLIA, A. (Italy)

Series 518 (Blacks/Whites)	15 - 18	18 - 22
BISHOP (U.S.)	8 - 10	10 - 12

BONTE or B

E. Nister   (UndB)

Series 71, 72, 73, 74	25 - 30	30 - 35

Theo Stroefer (T.S.N.)   **Series 404**

BORISS, MARGRET Amag Series 0322	12 - 15	15 - 18

BROWNE, TOM (G.B.)

BRUNDAGE, FRANCES (U.S.)

Raphael Tuck

Oilette Series "Christmas Greetings"

"The Night Before Christmas"	25 - 28	28 - 32

Series 2723 "Colored Folks" (6)

"The Christening," "Church Parade"	50 - 60	60 - 70

"De Proof of de Puddin'"

"Don't took de las' piece"

"The Village Choir," "You is a Chicken"

Series 2816 The "Connoisseur" Series (6)

   Duplicates **Series 2723**

Series 100 "Valentine" (Uns.)

"Loving Thoughts"	22 - 25	25 - 28

Series 102 "Valentine" (1)

"To Ma Honey"	22 - 25	25 - 28

Series 103 "Valentine" (1) (Uns.)

"Git a Move On..."

Series 107 "Valentine" (2) (Uns.)

"To My Heart's Beloved"

"To My Loved One"

Series 108 Valentines (4) (Uns.)

Girl - "Does yo' reckon I would do..."

Boy - "I'm cuttin up now..."

Boy - "I lubs yo' deah, and dats why..."

Girl - "I lubs yo' deah, wid my hearts..."

Series 115 "Valentine" (2) (Uns.)

Boy Angel "To My Valentine"

Lovers - "My little love..."

Series 118 "Little Loves & Lovers"(2) (Uns.)	25 - 28	28 - 32

Girl - "Waiting fo' Mah Sweetheart"

Boy - "To Greet Mah Valentine"

Series 165 (2)	22 - 25	25 - 28

Series 1035 (2)

Margret Boriss, AMAG 0322
No Caption

E. Colombo, GMB "Ultra" 2224
No Caption

"B." (Bonte)
Theo. Stroefer 440, N-17

Series 4096 "Funny Folk" (4)		
"I'se Just Been Married"	40 - 50	50 - 60
"The Pickaninnies Bedtime"		
"Preparing for the Party"		
"Tubbing Time in Darkie Land"		
Series 6616 "Humorous" (Uns.)		
"Get a move on..."	20 - 25	25 - 28
Series 8201 Black Angels		
T.S.N. (Theo Stroefer, Nürnberg)		
Series 664 Girl looks through picket fence	15 - 20	20 - 30
Other Signed Brundage	15 - 18	18 - 25
Unsigned	12 - 15	15 - 20
BUCHANAN, FRED (G.B.)		
Raphael Tuck "Write Away"		
Series 9309 (6)	20 - 25	25 - 30
CARTER, SYDNEY (G.B.)		
Hildesheimer & Co.		
Series 5232 "The Dance" Series	12 - 15	15 - 20
CHIOSTRI, SOFIA (Italy)		
Ballerini & Fratini Series 242 (4)	40 - 50	50 - 60
CLAPSADDLE, ELLEN H. (U.S.)		
Int. Art. Pub. Co.		
Mechanical Series 1236		
"A Jolly Halloween" Black Child	350 - 400	400 - 450

Ellen Clapsaddle, Int. Art 780
German Caption

A. M. Cook, B. Dondorf 636
No Caption

No Number Valentine, New Year, Christmas 22 - 25   25 - 28
Series 780 (6) **"Love's Fair Exchange"**
1 - Boy offers ice cream to girl   22 - 25   25 - 30
"To My Valentine" (2)
1 - Boy with Banjo
2 - Boy with top hat and cane
"With Love's Greeting" (3)
1 - Boy with Straw Hat Walking Left
2 - Boy offers watermelon to girl
3 - Girl in blue dress sits on wooden box
Series 781 (4)
"Affectionate Greetings"
"My Love to You"
"True Love"
"With Fondest Love"
Unsigned: Elegant boy/girl do cake walk   18 - 22   22 - 25
Kopal
New Year Series (4)   30 - 35   35 - 40
No Captions (2)
Stewart & Woolf, London
Series 696
"A Happy Christmas" (2)   22 - 25   25 - 28
"A Joyful Christmas"

"With Best Christmas Wishes"
Boy and girl with slice of watermelon
Anonymous, Germany
  Cotton background, Embossed, (Uns.)
  Same images as Series 780 (6)

"My Love to You"	30 - 35	35 - 40
"My Valentine Think of Me"		
"To my Valentine"		
"To the One I Love"		
"With Fondest Love"		
Others	20 - 25	25 - 30
CLARK, ROSE (U.S.)		
Ullman "Kute Koon Kids" Series 165 (4)	15 - 18	18 - 22
COCKRELL	10 - 12	12 - 15
COLOMBO, E. (Italy)	15 - 18	18 - 22
COOK, A. M. (G.B.)		
C.W. Faulkner Series 1413 (6)	18 - 22	22 - 25
COWHAM, HILDA (G.B.)	15 - 18	18 - 22
CRANE	8 - 10	10 - 12

CURTIS, E.
DONADINI, JR.
  Series 454 (6)

"The Voice that breathed o'er Eden"	30 - 35	35 - 40

  Tall Lady with hurt child walking behind
  Lovers under red umbrella
  Surprised man washes foot
  Well dressed Dude with suitcase
  Man singing from "Sleep, Darling Sleep"
There is also an anonymous, unsigned series
  of series 454

FASCHE, HANS (Austria)		
"SECT" Black & White Dancers	20 - 25	25 - 28
F.E.M. R. Tuck	12 - 15	15 - 18
FERNEL (F in circle) (France) Cakewalks	40 - 45	45 - 50
FIALKOWSKA, WALLY (Austria)	12 - 15	15 - 18
FYCH, C. D. (G.B.)		
Valentine & Sons	8 - 10	10 - 12

GASSAWAY, KATHARINE
  Rotograph Co.

105 "I Scared I'll Get Sunburned"	12 - 15	15 - 18
123 "I Wish I was in Dixie"		

GILSON, T. (G.B.)
  E. J. Hey & Co.

Series 151, 262, 378, 410, 474	12 - 15	15 - 18
J. Salmon		
Series 2571, 2580	10 - 12	12 - 15
British Manufacturer & Ludgate Series	10 - 12	12 - 15

F (Fernel), Anonymous
"Cake Walk"

O. Merté
A.M.S. Series 589

Publisher O.P.F.
Sack Background, Cake Walk

GREINER, MAGNUS (U.S.)
  International Art

Series 701-710	22 - 25	25 - 28
701 "A Darktown Trip"		
702 "The Serenade"		
704 "A Lad and a Ladder"		
707 "A Darktown Idyl"		
708 "A Feast"		
709 "A Darktown Lover"		
710 "A Darktown Philosopher"		
Series 780	15 - 18	18 - 22

H.G.B. (H.B. GRIGGS) (U.S.)
  L & E

Series 2217 (6)	18 - 22	22 - 25
Series 2224	15 - 18	18 - 22

H.H. (H. Horina)

J.I. Austin Co. Sepia Series	12 - 15	15 - 20
White City Art Co. Series 234	15 - 18	18 - 22

H.H. (H. Herman) (U.S.)
  (Correction from "Black Americana" P.C.P.G.)
  Ullman Mfg. Co.

Series 85 Thanksgiving	15 - 18	18 - 22
Series 103 2082 "Gin"	22 - 25	25 - 28
Series 106 "In the Colored Swim" (4)	20 - 25	25 - 30

Series 109 "The National Game" (4)	35 - 40	40 - 45
Series 116 Skaters (4)	20 - 22	22 - 25
HARLOW, GRACE (U.S)	10 - 12	12 - 15
HARTMAN, E. VON	18 - 22	22 - 25
HUTAF, AUGUST (U.S.)		
Ullman Series 113 "Blacktown Babies"	20 - 22	22 - 25
HYDE, GRAHAM (G.B.)		
R. Tuck Series 9094 "Coons Motoring" (6)	20 - 25	25 - 28
K.V.		
L.P.		
Series 205, 206, 227 Black-White Kewpies	12 - 15	15 - 18
Series 210 Black Kewpies		
KEMBLE, E. B. (U.S.)		
Detroit Pub. Co.		
"Kemble's Coontown" (10) (B&W)	28 - 32	32 - 35
Fairman Co. (B&W)	8 - 10	10 - 12
Gibson Art (B&W)		
KENNEDY, T. R. or TRK (G.B.)		
A.M. Davis Co.		
Series 521 "Little Darkies" (6)	15 - 18	18 - 22
Gale & Polden Series 2143 (6)		
KINSELLA, E. P.		
Langsdorf & Co. Series 713 (6) "Diabolo"	25 - 30	30 - 35
KOCH, LUDWIG "...2000 jahre karikatur"	50 - 60	60 - 70
LEVI, C. (U.S.)		
Ullman Mfg. Co.		
Series 165 "Kute Koon"	12 - 15	15 - 18
Series 210, 3308 "Suffragette"	25 - 30	30 - 35
LEWIN, F. G. (G.B.)		
Inter-Art Co.		
"Artisque" Series	12 - 15	15 - 18
Others		
W.E. Mack	10 - 12	12 - 15
M. Munk (Signed/Unsigned FGL)		
Series 244, 416 (6)	35 - 40	40 - 45
J. Salmon	10 - 12	12 - 15
Bamforth Co.		
"Black Kid Comics"	10 - 12	12 - 15
Florence House		
L.N.S. (Dutch Publisher)	8 - 10	10 - 12
Geo. Pulman	12 - 15	15 - 18
E.W. Savory, Bristol	18 - 22	22 - 25
LEWIS		
Inter-Art	8 - 10	10 - 12
Ullman Mfg. Co. Series 165 "Cute Coon Kids"	12 - 15	15 - 18
LONG, F. G. (U.S.)		
Kaufmann & Strauss, 1904		
49-56 (UndB)	20 - 25	25 - 30

T. Gilson, Salmon
"If dems what you use then I'll..."

T. R. Kennedy, "Comique" 6130
"I'se gwine back to Dixie!"

H.H. (Herman), Ullman Ser. 109
2153, "Out on a Fly"

H.H. (Herman), Ullman 106
2095, "We're Off"

A. Hutaf, Ullman Series 113
2175, "Don't Wake the Babies"

Ludwig Koch.

Wien. Künstlerfest „2000 Jahre Karikatur".
Schützenkränzchen.

F. G. Lewin, Geo. Pulman 443
"There's no place like Home."

Ludwig Koch, Anonymous
"...2000 jahre karikatur"

F. G. Lewin (FGL), M. Munk
Series 416 (The Cake Walk)

Series 60 Valentines	18 - 20	20 - 25
LUZE (France)	10 - 12	12 - 15
M.D.S.		
Ullman Mfg. Co. Series 81 "Happy Day"	12 - 15	15 - 18
American P.C. Co. Series 165	8 - 10	10 - 12
M.M.S.		
G.K. Prince Co.	10 - 12	12 - 15
MALLET, BEATRICE (G.B.)		
MARQUIS (France)		
IMP American Series 14		
"Black and White" Nursing Black Baby	35 - 40	40 - 50
MAURICE, REG (G.B.)		
Regent Series 501, 4137	12 - 15	15 - 18
McGILL, DONALD (G.B.)		
J. Asher & Co.	10 - 12	12 - 15
Bamforth Co.		
D. Constance, Ltd.	6 - 8	8 - 10
Inter-Art Co.	10 - 12	12 - 15
MINNS, B. E. (G.B./Australia)		
Carlton Publishing Co. "Glad Eye" Series (6)	15 - 18	18 - 22
MUNSON, WALT (U.S.) Linens	5 - 6	6 - 8
O'NEILL, ROSE (U.S.)		
Raphael Tuck "Pickings from Puck"		
Series 2482 "High Society in Coontown"		

"A Misunderstanding" (Uns.) | 80 - 100 | 100 - 110

Series 2483 "Pickings from Puck"
"A Brain Worker" | 60 - 70 | 70 - 80
"Better than a Sermon"
"Ne Plus Ultra"
"One View"
Series 9411 "High Society in Coontown" (6) | 100 - 110 | 110 - 120
"A Matrimonial Alliance"
"A Misunderstanding"
"A Provisional Finance"
"All that was Necessary"
"Finis"
"His Limited Provisioning Capacity"
Series 9412 "Coontown Kids" (6) * | 35 - 45 | 45 - 55
* Reprinting of Series 2483

OUTCAULT, RICHARD F. (U.S.)
I.H. Blanchard Co.
"Buster Brown & His Bubble" *
3 "Black or White" | 28 - 32 | 32 - 35
6 "A Good Bump"
8 "A Bit of Smooth Road"
* Same series also by **Souvenir P.C. Co.**
J. Ottoman | 12 - 15 | 15 - 20
Ullman Mfg. Co.
Series 76 "Darktown" *
1889 "Koontown Kids" | 22 - 25 | 25 - 30
1890 "Deed, I dun eat no Chickun"
1891 "Darktown Doctors"
1892 "Darkytown Dames"
• **American P.C. Co.** also published this series.
H.H. Tammen
Buster Brown Series 1001 (Emb.) | 15 - 20 | 20 - 25
Raphael Tuck
Und/Back Valentines | 15 - 18 | 18 - 22
Buster Brown and His Bubble (3, 6 & 8) | 25 - 30 | 30 - 35

A.S. Hildesheimer & Co.
Series 5268 (No Captions) | 8 - 10 | 10 - 12

PARKINSON, ETHEL
B. Dondorf Series 517 | 15 - 18 | 18 - 22

PETERSEN, HANNES (Denmark) | 10 - 12 | 12 - 15

PHIFER, L. C. (U.S.)
Theo Eismann
Baseball Song Series 1820 (4) | 40 - 50 | 50 - 60
De Witt C. Wheeler Same with blue borders | 35 - 40 | 40 - 45
Note: Also issued in strip form | 25 - 30 | 30 - 35

RICHARDSON, AGNES (G.B.)
Photochrome "Celesque" Series | 18 - 22 | 22 - 25
Unsigned Children Series | 15 - 18 | 18 - 22

RYAN, C. (U.S.) **Winsch Backs   A100 Series** | 20 - 25 | 25 -30

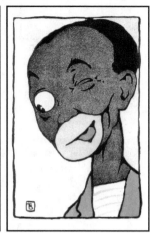

TB, BKWI 753-5   *TB, BKWI 753-6*   *TB, BKWI 753-1*

SANDFORD, H. DIX (or H.D. or H.D.S.)
   Raphael Tuck
      Series 6891, 8457 "Happy Little Coons" (6)   18 - 22   22 - 25
      Series 8457 "Happy Little Coons" (6)
      Series 9003, 9048 "Happy Little Coons" (6)
      Series 9049, 9050 "Happy Little Coons" (6)
      Series 9093 "Curley Coons" (6)   20 - 25   25 - 28
      Series 9227 "Happy Little Coons" (6)   18 - 22   22 - 25
      Series 9228, 9229 "Happy Little Coons" (6)
      Series 9299 "Happy Little Coons" (6)   22 - 25   25 - 28
      Series 9819 "Seaside Coons" (6)   18 - 22   22 - 25
      Series 9427 "More Coons" (6)   10 - 12   12 - 15
      Series 9428, 9489
         "Dark Girls & Black Boys" (6)   15 - 18   18 - 22
      Series 9457 "Happy Little Coons" (6)
      Series 9761 6)   18 - 22   22 - 25
      Series 9968, 9969 "Seaside Coons" (6)
   Hildesheimer & Co. Series 5268 "Negroes"   18 - 22   22 - 25
SANFORD, M. Raphael Tuck Series   10 - 12   12 - 15
SHEPHEARD, GEORGE E. (G.B.)
   Raphael Tuck
      Series 9068, 9536 "Coon's Cooning" (6)   22 - 25   25 - 30
      Series 9297 "Among the Darkies" (6)
      Series 740 French Tucks (6)
SHINN, COBB (U.S.)   8 - 10   10 - 12
SPARKUHL & SPARKY
   AVM Series 636 White/Black   12 - 15   15 - 18
SPURGIN, FRED (Latvia/G.B.)
   J & A Co. "Coon Series" **405**
      "Am My Nose Still Shiny?"   12 - 15   15 - 18
      "Golly! You are Looking Pale"
      "Things are Looking Black"
   Inter-Art Series "One-Four-Nine"

"BLACKMAIL"

Arth. Thiele, F.E.D. Series 306
No Caption

C. Twelvetrees, R&N 706
"Blackmail."

T.B. **B.K.W.I. Series 753** (6)	25 - 30	30 - 35
T.R. **A.M. Davis Co.**	10 - 12	12 - 15
TEMPEST, DOUGLAS (G.B.)		
Bamforth Co. "Kiddy Comics"		
"Look me over, buddy ..."	8 - 10	10 - 12
"Oh, Honey! If ..."		
"I'se Black all over ..."	6 - 8	8 - 10
"Full on top -- cooler than riding inside!"	8 - 10	10 - 12
"Here's a Quaint Coon"		
Other Publishers	8 - 10	10 - 12
THIELE, ARTHUR (Germany)		
FED **Series 306** Head Studies (6)	30 - 35	35 - 40
Theo. Stroefer **Series 871** Sports (6)		
German-American Novelty Art Co.		
Series 871 duplication	25 - 30	30 - 35
TIMMONS, JR. (Linens)	4 - 5	5 - 6
TWELVETREES, CHARLES (U.S.)		
Bergman Co.	6 - 8	8 - 10
Edward Gross Co. *	8 - 10	10 - 12
* Add $2-3 for die-cut stand-up types.		
R&N Series 706 "Blackmail"		
TYRRELL, E. R. (U.S.) **S. S. Porter**	10 - 12	12 - 15
USABAL, LOTTE (Germany) Series 1295-1300	18 - 20	20 - 22

WALL, BERNHARDT　(U.S.)

Bamforth Co. (Back) "I'm Your Melon Honey"	20 - 25	25 - 30
Bergman Co.	8 - 10	10 - 12

Ullman Mfg. Co.

Series 59 "Little Coons"	10 - 12	12 - 14
1660 "You all can hab de Rine"		
1661 "Deed, I didn't steal um"		
1662 "Who's dat say chicken?"		
1663 "Just two Coons"		
Series 70 "Cute Coons"	10 - 12	12 - 14
1852 "A chip off the old Block"		
1853 "Whose Baby is OO?"		
1854 "He lubs me"		
1855 "I's so happy"		
Series 81 "Happy Day"	10 - 12	12 - 15
Series 143 Black Halloween	20 - 25	25 - 30
Series 173	8 - 10	10 - 12
Series 127 Thanksgiving	10 - 12	12 - 15
Series 155 Automobiles	10 - 12	12 - 15

WIEDERSEIM, GRACE　(U.S.)

Hand-made of Black & White kids	50 - 60	60 - 75

WELLMAN, WALTER　(U.S.)

Manhattan P.C. Co. Art Deco types (Uns.)	8 - 10	10 - 12
Colourpicture (Tichnor) (Linens)	8 - 10	10 - 12
WHITE, E. L. (Linens)	3 - 4	4 - 5
WHITE, FLORA (G.B.)	10 - 12	12 - 15
WITT, MIA　Series 2002	6 - 8	8 - 10

WUYTS, A.　(Austria)

A. Noyer Series 76 (6)	10 - 12	12 - 14

ZA, NINO　(Italy)

A74 Josephine Baker (Continental)	120 - 130	130 - 140

ZAHL

Poster Series	12 - 14	14 - 18
"Othello"		
"Be's Jst Du?"		

BLACKS, UNSIGNED

Albertype Co.　**PMC**

"Greetings from the Sunny South" (12)	30 - 35	35 - 40

AMAG

Series 0260 Blacks courting white girls	15 - 18	18 - 22
A.M.P. Series 70 "Cute Coons"	12 - 15	15 - 18

Joseph Asher & Co.

"Two Blacks don't make a White"	25 - 30	30 - 35
J.I. Austen	15 - 18	18 - 22

Barton & Spooner

Series 142, 495, 6505 and CS528	10 - 12	12 - 15

Bergman Co.		
Julius Bien "Comic Series"	12 - 15	15 - 18
G. B. Co.		
Series G Husband & Wife (6)	8 - 10	10 - 12
H.M.B. Series 2847	25 - 30	30 - 35
Franz Huld		
Cake Walk, "Darkey Series" (PMC)	12 - 15	15 - 18
Ill. P.C. Co. Series 78 "Darkies"	8 - 10	10 - 12
E.C. Kropp, Milwaukee Comics	12 - 15	15 - 18
Langsdorf		
"Greetings from the Sunny South"	10 - 12	12 - 15
Livermore & Knight	18 - 22	22 - 25
Arthur Livingston Black Comics	10 - 12	12 - 15
Moore & Gibson, New York		
15 "Brushing up on Acquaintance"	12 - 15	15 - 18
26 "The Whole Black Family"	20 - 25	25 - 30
31 "A Souther Bird Fancier"	15 - 18	18 - 22
32 "I Take This Opportunity"		
34 "The pearly gates ajar"		
35 "It's the Little Things in Life..."		
36 "A Sudden Rise in Wool"		
Evolution Comic		
2 "Evolution of a Coon"	90 - 100	100 - 120
E. Nash		
Series 31 "Sporting Girl" (Emb.) (6)		
Baseball Girl, Football Girl	25 - 30	30 - 35
Chorus Girl, Yachting Girl, others	20 - 25	25 - 30
E. Nister		
Unsigned G.H.T. George H. Thompson		
294 "Golly, but I wish I could grow..."	40 - 50	50 - 60
297 "Why do folks call me Jim Crow..."		
303 "I see Mr Possum up de Tree..."		
304 "Watermelons Juicy and Ham is..."		
Quality Valentines, Unsigned		
Series 1270, 1280	20 - 25	25 - 28
O.P.F. Cake Walkers on sack cloth B.G.	35 - 40	40 - 50
P.F.B.		
Series 7179, 7942	22 - 25	25 - 28
Black Gents & Ladies (6)		
Series 7946 (6)		
Charles Rose Co. Series 11 Song Cards	15 - 18	18 - 22
S&M Series 1515 (Unsigned Donadini, Jr.)	25 - 28	28 - 32
Schlesinger Bros. Children Comics (B&W)	10 - 12	12 - 15
Theo. Stroefer, Nürnberg (T.S.N.)		
Series 440 (6) Classical Blacks	25 - 30	30 - 35
Taggart		
Red Background Series N-24 (6)	25 - 30	30 - 35
Thanksgiving Series 608 (6)	12 - 15	15 - 18
Others	10 - 12	12 - 15

Anonymous, 109
A Surprise

Anonymous
Black & White Lovers

H.M.B., Series 2847
No Caption

Curt Teich (Linens)

"C.T. Jitterbug Comics" (10)	25 - 30	30 - 35

Raphael Tuck   Most have 6-card sets

Series **100** "Love Songs"	22 - 25	25 - 28
Series **115** "Little Wooers"	15 - 18	18 - 22
Series **368M** (French) "Cake Walk"	22 - 25	25 - 28
Series **970** "Write Away" Minstrels	22 - 25	25 - 28
Series **1043** "Calendar"		
Series **1794** "Write Away" Cake Walk	25 - 28	28 - 32
Series **1819** "Cake Walk"	22 - 25	25 - 28
Series **6706** "Humorous Series" Cake Walk	25 - 28	28 - 32
Series **6813** Sophisticated, well dressed	18 - 22	22 - 25
Series **2398, 6909** Negro Melodies	15 - 18	18 - 22
Oilette Series 9297		
"Coontown Kids" Series **2843, 9092, 9412**	15 - 18	18 - 22

Ullman Mfg. Co.

"Little Coons," Series **59** (6)	10 - 12	12 - 15
Series **81** Valentine "Happy Days"	12 - 15	15 - 18
"Kute Koon Kids," Series **165** (6)	15 - 18	18 - 22
Mechanical - "Pick the Pickaninnies"		
Puzzle	50 - 55	55 - 60
Suffrage Series 210		
3308 "De Suffre-Jet"	25 - 30	30 - 35

Valentine & Sons
"Christmas in Coon Land"
"We've Come to Meet Yo' Massy Santy..."   300 - 400   400 - 500
Others in series
"Little Nigger" Series (6)   12 - 15   15 - 18
"Coonville" Series (6)
Series 602
Black Santa with black-white kids   175 - 200   200 - 225
Real Life Blacks (1900-1915)   10 - 15   15 - 20
White Border, Real Life   (1915-1930)   5 - 7   7 - 10
Linen Cards (1930-1949)   2 - 3   5 - 8

For a more comprehensive listing of all blacks see *"Black Americana
Postcard Price Guide."* It contains over 560 photos, has 352 pages, 6x9.
by J. L. Mashburn. ISBN: 1-885940-01-7 - $19.95. Can be obtained from
bookstores or may be ordered from Colonial House, P.O. Box 609, Enka, NC
28728. Please add $3 postage.

COWBOYS & INDIANS

BETTS, HAROLD (U.S.)
    Detroit Pub. Co. - Fred Harvey
        New Mexico Indian scenes   6 - 8   8 - 10
CRAIG, CHARLES (U.S.)
    Williamson-Hafner Indian Series   8 - 10   10 - 12
CURTIS, E. S. (U.S.)   Sepia
    Indian Series
        "Hopi Girl"   40 - 45   45 - 50
        "Zuni Water Carriers"   .
        Others
DAVENPORT, R. A.   Cowboys   6 - 8   8 - 10
FELLER, FRANK (U.S.)   8 - 10   10 - 12
GOLLINS   8 - 10   10 - 12
GREGG, PAUL   (U.S.)
    H. H. Tammen Co. Cowboy Series   8 - 10   10 - 12
INNES, JOHN   (U.S.)
    Western Art Series (6)
        "The Bad Man," "Pack Train"   10 - 12   12 - 15
        "The Portage," "Prairie Schooner"
        "Roping Bronco," "Warping the Fur Barge ..."
    MacFarlane Pub. Co.
        Troilene Series   10 - 12   12 - 15
        "Cattle Girl," "Indians in a Snow Storm"
        "Indian Pony Race," "Fur Canoe"
        "Roping a Steer," "The Town Marshall"
        "The War Canoe"
        "Warping the Air Barge Upstream"
G. de L.
    R. Tuck, Series 8668, "Muscalero Apache" 12 - 15   15 - 18

G. de L., Raphael Tuck, American Indians 8668
"Muscalero Apache"

LARSEN, DUDE AND DOT (U.S.)
 Linens of 30's and 40's   1 - 2   2 - 3
MAY, KARL (Germany)
 Cowboys and Indians   10 - 12   12 - 15
PAXSON, E.S.
 McKee Printing Co.
 Northwest Postcard and Souvenir Co.
  "Apache," "Crow," "Curley," "Custer's Scout"   10 - 12   12 - 15
  "Flathead," "Mis-sou-la"
  "A Nez Perce," "Northern Indian"
  "Sioux"
PAYNE, HARRY (G.B.)
 Raphael Tuck
  Series 9530 "The Wild, Wild West" (6)   12 - 15   15 - 20
  Series 9531 (I) "The Wild, Wild West" (6)
  "A Prairie Belle," "The Bucking Bronco"   12 - 15   15 - 20
  "Cowboy Fun," "A Scamper Across the Prairie"
  "Neck or Nothing," "Throwing the Lariat"
  "Sounding the 'Turn Out' "
  Series 9532 (II) "The Wild, Wild West" (6)
  "The Abduction," "The Scout"   12 - 15   15 - 20
PETERSON, L. (U.S.)
 H.H. Tammen Co.
  Indian Series
   3420 "Chief Sitting Bull"   10 - 12   12 - 15
   3421 "Chief Geronimo"
   3422 "Chief Yellow Hawk"   8 - 10   10 - 12
   3423 "Chief Eagle Feather"

Harry Payne, R. Tuck 9532-II.
"The Avenger"

F. W. Schultz, W-H 1729
"Go It, You —!"

3424 "Chief High Horse"		
3425 "Starlight"		
3426 "Chief Big Feather"		
3427 "Sunshine"		
3428 "Fighting Wolf"		
3429 "Minnehaha"	10 - 12	12 - 15
3430 "Hiawatha"		
3431 "Chief Red Cloud"		
3432 "Eagle Feather & Squaw"	8 - 10	10 - 12
3433 "Chief Black Hawk"	10 - 12	12 - 15
Unsigned Series	8 - 10	10 - 12
H. H. Tammen Co. **"Cow Girl Series"**	6 - 8	8 - 10
REISS, WINOLD (Germany-U.S.)	15 - 18	18 - 22
REMINGTON, FREDERIC (U.S.)		
Detroit Publishing Co.		
14179 "Evening on a Canadian"	35 - 45	45 - 55
14180 "His First Lesson"	30 - 35	35 - 45
14181 "A Fight for the Water Hole"	35 - 45	45 - 55
14182 "An Argument with the Marshal"	35 - 45	45 - 55
14183 "Calling the Moose"	30 - 35	35 - 45
Taylor Publishing		
1012 "Pony War Dance"	80 - 90	90 - 100
1022 "The Sun Fisher"		
1027 "The Punchers"		

REYNOLDS

Cowboy Series 4400	5 - 6	6 - 8
Cowgirl Series 4406	5 - 6	6 - 8

RINEHART, F.A. (U.S.)

Indian Series	8 - 10	10 - 12

"Rain in the Face" (Sioux)
"Big Man"
"Chief Wolf Robe" (Cheyenne)
"Chief Red Cloud" (Sioux)
"Chief Sitting Bull" (Sioux)
"Wa-ta-Waso" (Sioux)
"Sioux Squaw and Papoose"
"Two Little Braves -- Sac and Fox"
"Lost Bird" (Sioux)
"Annie Red Shirt" (Sioux)
"Eagle Feather & Papoose"
"Two Little Braves" (Sioux & Fox)
"Chase-in-the-Morning"
"Hattie Tom" (Chiricahua, Apache)

ROLLINS, W. E. (U.S.) 6 -10 10 - 12

RUSSELL, CHARLES M. (U.S.)

Ridgley Calendar Co. (In Color)	25 - 30	30 - 35

"All Who Know Me ..."
"Antelope Hunt"
"Are You the Real Thing?"
"A Bad Bronco"
"The Bear in the Park ..."
"Better than Bacon"
"Blackfeet Burning ..."
"Bold Hunters ..."
"Boss of the Herd"
"Cowboys Off for Town"
"Elk in Lake McDonald"
"The First Furrow"
"Have One on Me"
"I Savvy These Folks"
"Jerked Down"
"Lassoing a Wolf"
"Lone Wolf - Piegan"
"Powderface -- Arapahoe"
"Rainy Morning in a ..."
"Red Cloud"
"Roping a Grizzly"
"Roping a Wolf #2"
"The Round Up #1"
"The Round Up #2"
"Scattering the Riders"
"The Scouts"

"Stay With Him!"
"Sun Shine and Shadow"
"A Touch of Western ..."
"Waiting for a Chinook"
"Where Ignorance is Bliss"
"White Man's Skunk ..."
"Wild Horse Hunters #1"
"Wild Horse Hunters #2"
"Women of the Plains"
"Wound Up"
"A Wounded Grizzly"

(In Sepia or Black and White)	10 - 12	12 - 15

"The Buffalo Hunt #28"
"Buffalo Protecting Calf"
"The Christmas Dinner" (B/W)
"Cowboys off for Town"
"Gnome with Lantern"
"Holding up the ... Stage" (B/W)
"Indian Dog Team"
"Initiated" (B/W)
"The Initiation of ..." (B/W)
"The Last of the Buffalo" (B/W)
"Nez Perce"
"An Old Fashioned ..."
"Painting the Town" (B/W)
"Powderface -- Arapahoe"
"A Roper"
"The Shell Game" (B/W)
"The Trail Boss" (B/W)

Printed Photograph (Head in Oval)	6 - 8	8 - 10

(Black ink on pale green silk)
a.   "A Christmas Dinner"
b.   "The Initiation of the Tenderfoot"
c.   "The Last of the Buffalo"
d.   "Painting the Town"
e.   "The Shell Game"
f.   "The Trail Boss"

C.A. Read & Co.

"Hold her Zeb, I'm Coming"	6 - 8	8 - 10

Roberts, Helena, Montana

"Waiting for a Chinook"	6 - 8	8 - 10

Souvenir of Circus & Wild West Show

Southhampton, LI, NY, July 2-4, 1910	10 - 12	12 - 15

SCHULTZ, F. W. (U.S.)

Cowboy Series 1728-1746

1728 "The Outlaw"	8 - 10	10 - 15

1729 "Go It, You —!"
1730 "Alkalai Ike"
1741 "Roping the Bull"

F. A. Rinehart
"Chief Red Cloud"
(Sioux)

F. A. Rinehart
"Wa-tah-Waso"
(Iroquois)

F. A. Rinehart
"Rain in the Face"
(Sioux)

E. C. Kropp, 273
"Medicine Man"

E. C. Kropp, 271
"Kicking Bear"

Real Photo, AZO
"Chief Manitou"

    1744 "Roping the Broncho"
    "Shooting the Town"
PUBLISHERS
  Detroit Publishing Co.
    13941 "Montera Cabezon (Apache)"   12 - 15   15 - 18
    13943 "A Jicarilla Apache Chief, Arizona"
    13943 "Buffalo Calf (Jicarilla Apache)"
  Fred Harvey, for Detroit Pub Co.
    Hopi Indians, etc.   5 - 10   10 - 15
  Franz Huld
    Indian Chiefs, 1906
    1 "George Standing Bear"   10 - 12   12 - 15
    4 "Tsi-Loya-Greatest Chief

Illustrated Post Card Co.
    Series 183 Cowboys and Indians   5 - 7   7 - 12
E. C. Kropp
    271 "Kicking Bear"   12 - 15   15 - 18
    273 "Medicine Man"
F.E. Moore   **"Hiawatha Series"** (12) (B&W)   3 - 5   5 - 8
A. Selige, St. Louis
    Indian Chief Series
        "Chief Black Hawk"   10 - 12   12 - 15
        "Chief Afraid of Eagle"
        "Chief Fleet of Foot"
        "Chief Bear Goes Inwoods"
        "Chief Yellow Hair"
Curt Teich   Seminole Indians   6 - 8   8 - 12
Raphael Tuck
    Series 2171 "Indian Chiefs" (12)
        "Chief Charging Bear"   10 - 12   12 - 15
        "Chief Yellow Thunder"
        "Chief Yellow Horn"
        "Chief White Swan"
        "Chief Shooting Hawk"
        "Chief Black Thunder"
        "Chief Eagle Track"
        "Chief Red Owl"
        "Chief Black Chicken"
    Series 9131   (6)   10 - 12   12 - 15
        "Chief Charging Bear"
        "Chief Not Afraid of Pawnee"
        "Chief Black Chicken"
        "Chief Eagle Track"
        "Chief Black Thunder"
        "Chief White Swan"
    Series 9011 "Hiawatha" (6) (II)   10 - 12   12 - 15
    Series 1330 "Hiawatha" (6)
    Series 3495 "Indian Chiefs" (6)
    Cowboy Series 2499   5 - 6   6 - 8
Weiners, Ltd. "Buffalo Bill's Wild West" (6)   20 - 25   25 - 30

ANIMALS

CATS

ALDIN, CECIL (G.B.)   6 - 7   7 - 8
BARNES, G. L. (G.B.)
    Raphael Tuck
        Series 9301, 6495 "Cat Studies" (6)   8 - 10   10 - 12

BOULANGER, MAURICE (France)

International Art Publishing Co.

Series 586 (6)	6 - 8	8 - 10
Series 472 Large Image (6)	12 - 15	15 - 20
Series 473 Large Image (6)	15 - 18	18 - 22

K.F. Editeurs Series 586	18 - 20	22 - 25
Kopal Series 417	12 - 15	15 - 18

Raphael Tuck

Series 122 "Humorous Cats" (6) (Uns.)	12 - 15	15 - 18

BROWNE, TOM (G.B.)

Davidson Brothers

Series 2509 (6) "Funny Cats"	8 - 10	10 - 12
Series 2528 (6) "Comic Cats"		

CLIVETTE	6 - 8	8 - 10

COBBE, B. (G.B.)

Raphael Tuck

Series 9099, 9157, 9436　Oilettes (6)	10 - 12	12 - 14
DAWSON, LUCY	5 - 6	6 - 8
FEIERTAG (Austria)	6 - 8	8 - 10

FREES, H. W.

Rotograph Co.

Real Photo Cat Comics	6 - 8	8 - 12

GEAR, MABEL

Valentine & Sons	6 - 8	8 - 10
HOFFMAN, A. (Germany)	5 - 8	8 - 10

KASKELINE (Germany)

S.W.S.B. Series 4370	5 - 8	8 - 10

LANDER, EDGAR (G.B.)

Raphael Tuck

Real Photo Studies

Series 5088, 7006 (6)	4 - 5	5 - 8

MAC or HENRY SHEPHEARD (G.B.)

Valentine & Sons

Cat Studies	6 - 8	8 - 10

SCHWAR

Cat Studies	6 - 8	8 - 10
SPERLICH, T. (G.B.)	6 - 7	7 - 8

German-American Novelty Co.

Series 648 (6)	8 - 10	10 - 12

Langsdorf Co.

Series 3047	8 - 10	10 - 12
STOCK, A.	5 - 6	6 - 7
STOCKS, M.	6 - 8	8 - 10

H.K. Co.

Series 217, 3237, 381 (6)	6 - 8	8 - 10

THOMAS, PAUL

Raphael Tuck

Series 1196 (6)	8 - 10	10 - 12

Anonymous
A.&M.B. 4169

Sperlich, German-American
Novelty Art, 768

DOGS

BARTH, KATH	6 - 8	8 - 10
BUTONY		
B.K.W.I. Series 859 (6)	8 - 10	10 - 12
C.A.	6 - 8	8 - 10
CORBELLA, TITO (Italy)		
Series 378 (6)	12 - 15	15 - 18
Others	10 - 12	12 - 15
DONADINI, JR. (Italy)		
Dog Studies (6)	10 - 12	12 - 15
Series 235 (6)	12 - 14	14 - 16
DRUMMOND, NORAH (G.B.)		
Raphael Tuck		
Series 3599 (6) "All Scotch"	8 - 10	10 - 12
Series 9105 (6)		
"Sporting Dogs"	12 - 14	14 - 16
"Faithful Friends"	7 - 8	8 - 12
Series 772 Dachshunds	8 - 10	10 - 12
FREES, H.W.		
Rotograph Co. Comic Dog Photos	4 - 6	6 - 8
GAULIS, R. E.		
S.T.Z.F. 111 Wire Haired Fox Terrier	8 - 10	10 - 12

Fromme Troody, Anonymous
German Shepherds

R. E. Gaulis, S.T.Z.F. 111
Wire Haired Fox Terrier

GREINER, A.
 Series 726 (Dog Studies) (6) 8 - 10 10 - 12
 Series 727 (6)
GROSSMAN, A.   6 - 8 8 - 10
GROSSMAN, M.   8 - 10 10 - 12
HANSTEIN
 Raphael Tuck
 Series 4092 "Favorite Dogs" (6) 8 - 10 10 - 12
HARTLEIN, W.   6 - 7 7 - 8
HERZ, E.W. (Austria)   7 - 8 8 - 10
KENNEDY, A. E. (G.B.)
 C. W. Faulkner Series 1424 8 - 10 10 - 12
KIENE   10 - 12 12 - 15
KIRMBE
 Raphael Tuck
 Series 3586 "Racing Greyhounds" (6) 12 - 15 15 - 18
KLUGMEYER (Austria)   6 - 8 8 - 10
MacGUIRE (G.B.)
 Head Studies (Pastels) 8 - 10 10 - 12
MAILICK, A. (Germany)
 Dog Studies 10 - 12 12 - 15
MOODY, FANNIE (G.B.)   6 - 8 8 - 10
MÜLLER, A. (Germany)
 Series 3956 (6) Dachshunds 12 - 15 15 - 18

REICHERT, C. (Austria)
  T.S.N.

Series 923, 1280 (6)	7 - 8	8 - 10
Series 1336, 1337 (6)	8 - 10	10 - 12
Series 1851 (6)	8 - 10	10 - 12

SCHONIAN (Germany)
  German American Art

Series 1961	8 - 10	10 - 12
T.S.N. Series 1961	8 - 10	10 - 12

SPERLICH, SOFIE (Germany)   5 - 6   6 - 8

STOLZ, A. (Austria)

Series 772 Dachshunds	8 - 10	10 - 12

STUDDY (G.B.)

"Bonzo" Issues	8 - 10	10 - 12
With Tennis or Golf	12 - 15	15 - 20
With Black Dolls	12 - 15	15 - 18

THOMAS (G.B.)
  Raphael Tuck

Series 6990 "French Poodles" (6)	10 - 12	12 - 14

WATSON, MAUDE WEST (G.B.)
  Raphael Tuck
    "Dog Sketches"

Series 3346, 8682, E8837, 9977 (6)	8 - 10	10 - 15
Series 3103 (6)	10 - 12	12 - 15

WOMELE
  M. Munk, Vienna

WUNDERLICH, A.

Dachshunds	12 - 15	15 - 18

HORSES

ADAMS (Germany)
  Meissner & Buch   8 - 10   10 - 15

BARTH, W. (Germany)

BRAUN, LOUIS (Germany)

CASTALANZA

Series 342	8 - 10	10 - 12

CORBELLA, TITO (Italy)

Series 316 (6)	12 - 14	14 - 18

DONADINI, JR. (Italy)

Star Series 237 Racing	12 - 15	15 - 18

DRUMMOND, NORAH
  Raphael Tuck

Series 9065, 9138 (6)	8 - 10	10 - 15
Series 9561 (6)	12 - 15	15 - 18
Series 3109, 3194, 3603 (6)	8 - 10	10 - 12

FENNI (Racing Series)   10 - 12   12 - 15

FRIEDRICH, H. (Germany)

Series 464 (6)	6 - 8	8 - 10

HANSTEIN
  Raphael Tuck
    Series 810 Steeple Chase (6)   8 - 10   10 - 15
HERMAN
  Raphael Tuck Oilettes
    "The Horse" (6)   10 - 12   12 - 14
KOCH, LUDWIG (Austria)
  B.K.W.I.
    Series 493, 948 (6)   10 - 12   12 - 15
    Series 830, 865 (6)   12 - 15   15 - 20
    Series 1447, 1470 (6)   10 - 12   12 - 15
    Series 372, 377, 473 (6)   12 - 14   14 - 18
    Series 566, 660, 739
    Series 966 Circus Studies (6)   12 - 15   15 - 20
  O.F.Z.-L   Series 280-285   10 - 12   12 - 15
KOCH, PROF. G.
  Raphael Tuck   Series 588B (6)   10 - 12   12 - 15
KOLB
  Raphael Tuck
    Series 4084 Oilette (6)   10 - 12   12 - 15
KROMBACK
MATHEUSON   8 - 10   10 - 12
MAUZAN   Series 383 (6)   10 - 12   12 - 16
MERTÉ, O. (Austria)
  A.M.S.
    Series 589, 599, 660 (6)   10 - 12   12 - 15
    Series 623 - Circus Horses (6)
    Series 729 (6)   8 - 10   10 - 12
  Raphael Tuck
    Series 9946 - Circus Horses (6)   10 - 12   12 - 15
MÜLLER   (Germany)
  T.S.N.
    Series 128, 133 (6)   8 - 10   10 - 12
    Series 333, 411, 509 (6)   10 - 12   12 - 15
  S.W.S.B.   Series 6919 (6)   6 - 8   8 - 10
NANNI, G. (Italy)   **Series 257, 307** (6)   8 - 10   10 - 15
PAYNE, HARRY (G.B.)
  Raphael Tuck
    Series 550, 553 (6)   12 - 15   15 - 20
    Series 544 "Animal Life" **(6)**
R.K.
  B.K.W.I.   Series 350, 380, 386 (6)   8 - 10   10 - 12
RANKIN, GEORGE (G.B.)   6 - 8   8 - 10
REICHERT, C.
  T.S.N.
    Series 934, with dogs (6)   10 - 12   12 - 15
    Series 1359 (6)
    Series 1605, 1606, with dogs (6)   8 - 10   10 - 12

Donadini, Jr.,
Star Series 237

Nora Drummond, R. Tuck
Hunting Series 3194, "Tally Ho"

Anonymous
A.&M.B. 593

Series 1732, with dogs (6)		
Series 1782, 1870 (6)	10 - 12	12 - 15
Series 1422, Unsigned (6)	6 - 8	8 - 10
M. Munk, Vienna		
Series 268, 771 (6)	8 - 10	10 - 12
Series 1165 (6)	10 - 12	12 - 14
SHILLING, F.		
A.R. & C.i.B. Series 1136 (6)	8 - 10	10 - 12
SCHONIAN (Germany)		
T.S.N.		
Series 1838, 5826 (6)	10 - 12	12 - 15
Series 1935, with dogs (6)	12 - 14	14 - 16
Series E1935 (6)	10 - 12	12 - 14
SCHUTZ Series 972 (6)	6 - 8	8 - 10
Alfred Stiebel Co. Series 430, 438 (6)	10 - 12	12 - 15
STOKES, VERNON		
Photochrom Co. "Celesque" Series (6)	7 - 8	8 - 10
TENNI Harness Racing Series	8 - 10	10 - 15
TERZI, A. Series 320 (6)	10 - 12	12 - 15
THAMES Raphael Tuck	6 - 8	8 - 10
THOMAS, J.		
Raphael Tuck		
Series 353, 529 (6)	10 - 12	12 - 15
Series 1182, 9254 (6)	12 - 15	15 - 20

Series 575-B - Trotters (6)	10 - 12	12 - 15
Series 579 - Steeplechase (6)	8 - 10	10 - 15
Racing Series	10 - 12	12 - 15
Series 9254 (6)	8 - 10	10 - 12
W&L, Berlin Series 1182	10 - 12	12 - 14
TRACHE, E.		
Series 464, 466, 788 (6)	8 - 10	10 - 12
Series E463, 1175 (4)	8 - 10	10 - 12
VELTEN		
A.B.D. Series 775	8 - 10	10 - 12
W.F.A.	7 - 8	8 - 10
WALKER		
Raphael Tuck Series 9544 (6) "Chargers"	8 - 10	10 - 12
WRIGHT, ALAN Series 12219 (6)	10 - 12	12 - 15
WRIGHT, GEORGE		
E. W. Savory, Ltd. Series 2118 (6)	8 - 10	10 - 12

OTHER ANIMALS

CANTLE, J. M. (G.B.)	6 - 7	7 - 8
COBBS, B. (G.B.)		
Raphael Tuck Series 9539 (6) "Bunnies"	5 - 6	6 - 8
DONADINI, JR. (Italy) Animal Studies	10 - 12	12 - 16
DRUMMOND, NORAH (G.B.)		
Raphael Tuck		
Series 9507 (6) "Famous British Cattle"	7 - 8	8 - 10
Series 3297 (6) "Faithful Friends"	7 - 8	8 - 12
EARNSHAW, HAROLD C.		
Millar & Lang (Comic Animals)	4 - 6	6 - 8
Gottschalk, Dreyfus & Davis	4 - 6	6 - 8
GEAR, MABEL (U.S.)	5 - 8	8 - 10
GREEN, ROLAND (G.B.)	5 - 6	6 - 7
HARVEY		
Charles Reed Co. (18) "Nurse Guinnipen"	5 - 6	6 - 8
JAMES, FRANK (G.B.)		
KEENE, MINNIE (G.B.)		
KENNEDY, A. E. (G.B.)	5 - 8	8 - 10
LANDSEER, SIR EDWIN (G.B.)	8 - 10	10 - 15
MAGUIRE, HELENA (G.B.)	5 - 6	6 - 7
Raphael Tuck		
Series 6713, 6714 (6) "Animal Studies"	7 - 8	8 - 10
MÜLLER, A. (Germany)	5 - 6	6 - 8
PERLBERG, F.		
Raphael Tuck Art Series 991 (6)	6 - 7	7 - 8
POPE, DOROTHY (G.B.)	4 - 5	5 - 6
RANKIN, GEORGE (G.B.)		
SCRIVENER, MAUDE (G.B.)	6 - 7	7 - 10
VALTER, EUGENIE (G.B.)	5 - 6	6 - 8
WEST, A. L. (G.B.)	5 - 6	6 - 7

3
FANTASY

Fantasy postcards have become one of the great demand types of all motifs of the hobby. Collectors of the 70' and 80's had little interest in fantasy types because good material was very limited. This, however, was before the beautiful and desirable English, German and other European imports began appearing in U.S. dealer stocks and at auction. Now it seems that everyone has discovered them.

What is fantasy? To children and adults alike it is the result of varied imaginations. They can be wild or visionary fantasies, unnatural or bizarre, or they can flourish in the daydreams and playmaking of children. Because of the thousands of artists in the postcard "golden years" who were highly imaginative, today's collector has been left with a plethora of wonderful and colorful fantasy postcards.

Most of the fantasies bring back the treasured days of youth...of diminutive fairies, of nursery rhymes, and scary fairy tales...of stories of teddy bears and dressed animals acting like people. Fantasy worlds change as the youth grows to more mature heights, and it is notable that imagined fantasies remain, good and bad, and continue throughout life. All are chronicled and portrayed on postcards that make a wonderful fantasy world for us all!

FAIRIES

The Fairy family includes Brownies, Elves, Gnomes, Goblins, Fairies, Leprechauns, Pixies, Sprites and other dimunitive unnamed creatures.

	VG	EX
ANDERSON, FANNIE MAY (G.B.)		
Vivian Mansell & Co.		
Series 2115 (6)	$20 - 25	$25 - 28

ANICHINI, EZIO (Italy)		
Ballerini & Fratini Series 351	18 - 22	22 - 25
ATTWELL, MABEL L. (G.B.)		
Valentine & Sons	18 - 22	22 - 25
BARHAM, SYBIL (G.B.)		
C. W. Faulkner		
Series 1859 (6) "Fairies"	10 - 12	12 - 14
BAUMGARTEN, FRITZ (Germany)		
Oppel & Hess, Jena		
Series 1502, 1509, 1514, 1534 (6)	12 - 15	15 - 18
Series 5179, 5192, 5195, 6182 (6)		
Other Publishers	10 - 12	12 - 15
BERGER Series 116 (B&W)	15 - 20	20 - 25
BOWDEN, DORIS (G.B.)	18 - 22	22 - 25
CHECKLEY, GLADYS (G.B.)	12 - 15	15 - 18
CLOKE, RENE (G.B.)		
Valentine & Sons "Fairies"		
Series 1002, 1183, 1848, 1851 (6)	15 - 20	20 - 25
Series 5372-77 (6)		
J. Salmon, Ltd.	6 - 8	8 - 10
COWHAM, HILDA (GB)		
C. W. Faulkner		
Series 1918 "Fairies" (6)	18 - 22	22 - 25

Fannie Mae Anderson, Vivian Mansell & Co. 2115, "Fairy Revels"

Anonymous Meissner & Buch

Anonymous Meissner & Buch

F. B. (Fritz Baumgarten)
Oppel & Hess 6182

THE SPEEDWELL FAIRY

Rene Cloke, Valentine's 1851
"The Speedwell Fairy"

Elsbeth Forck, H. A. Peters 537
German Caption

"The Fairy Glen" Series (6)		
DAUSTY		
C. & P. & Co. Series 704 "Nymphs" (6)	8 - 10	10 - 12
DIELITZ "Alpen Fairy"	12 - 15	15 - 18
DUDDLE, JOSEPHINE (G.B.)	15 - 20	20 - 25
FORCK, ELSBETH (Germany) Silhouettes	12 - 15	15 - 18
GIRIS, CESAR		
Raphael Tuck Series 2365 "Madame Butterfly"	18 - 20	20 - 25
GOVEY, A. (G.B.)	25 - 28	28 - 32
F.H. (G.B.)	15 - 18	18 - 22
HAIG, BERYL (G.B.)	12 - 15	15 - 18
HINE, L. M. (G.B.)	32 - 35	35 - 38
KENNEDY, TOM or TK (G.B.)	15 - 18	18 - 22
KONEWKA, PAUL (Germany)		
Series 110 "Titania" (12) Silhouettes	22 - 25	25 - 28
MARGOTSON, HESTER (G.B.)		
Series 2127, 2129 (6)	15 - 18	18 - 22
MARSH-LAMBERT, H.G.C. (G.B.)		
A. M. Davis & Co.		
Series 519 "Flower Fairies" (6)	15 - 18	18 - 22
C. W. Faulkner Series 1400, 1510 (6)	12 - 15	15 - 18
MARSHALL, ALICE (G.B.)		
Raphael Tuck		
Series 3489 "Fairyland Fancies" I (6)	30 - 35	35 - 38
Series 3489 "Fairyland Fancies" II (6)		

Thomas Maybank, R. Tuck
"Midsummer Dreams" 6683

Paul Müller, Fingerle Co. 326
No Caption

MAUSER, PHYLLIS
   P. Salmon
      Series 5159 "Brownies & Fairies" (6)   8 - 10   10 - 12
MAYBANK, THOMAS (G.B.)
   Raphael Tuck
      Series 6683 "Midsummer Dreams" (6)   25 - 28   28 - 32
MILLER, HILDA T. (G.B.)
   C. W. Faulkner
      Series 1690, 1693 "Fairies" (6)   22 - 25   25 - 28
      Series 1822 "Peter Pan" (6)   15 - 18   18 - 20
MÜLLER, PAUL LOTHAR (Germany)
   Oscar Heierman, Berlin (Novitas)
      Series 550 "Gnomes"   10 - 12   12 - 15
   Fingerle Co. Series 326
OUTHWAITE, IDA R. (Australia)
   A. & C. Black Ltd., London
      Series 71 "The Enchanted Forest" (6)
         by I. R. & G. Outhwaite
      "The Butterfly Chariot"   22 - 25   25 - 28
      "Good-bye to Patty"
      Others
      Series 71-A "Elves & Fairies" (6)
      "Fairy Frolic"   25 - 28   28 - 32
      "The Glowlamp Fairy"
      "The Nautilus Fairy"
      "Serena's Wedding"
      "They stood still in front of her"
      "The Witch"
      Series 72 "Fairyland" (6)
      "Butterfly Ferry"   25 - 28   28 - 32
      "Catching the Moon"
      "Listening to the Nightingale"
      "Tossing up the Rainbow Bubbles"
      Others
      Series 73 "Bunny and Brownie" (6)
      "Driving the others with reins..."   28 - 32   32 - 35
      "Fairies were dancing in and out."
      "Playing with the bubbles"   30 - 35   35 - 40
      "Round the grass-tuft...a Pearly Shell" 28 - 32   32 - 35
      "She was rather severe with George"

I. R. Outhwaite, A. & C. Black 75   *I. R. Outhwaite, A. & C. Black 79*
"Periwinkle Painting the Petals"   *"Anne Rides on a Nautilus..."*

Series 79 "The Little Road to Fairyland" (6)
   by A.R. Rentoul and I. R. Outhwaite

"Anne rides on a Nautilus Shell"	28 - 32	32 - 35
"The farthest one looked like..."		
"The little one took it's paws..."		
"She flew through the window..."		
"What a fright she got"		
PEYK, H. (Germany)	10 - 12	12 - 15
PLUMSTEAD, JOYCE (G.B.)		
PURSER, PHYLLIS M. (G.B.)	8 - 10	10 - 12
RICHARD, J. (G.B.)	22 - 25	25 - 28

RICHARDSON, AGNES
   Raphael Tuck

Series 1649 "Fairies"	22 - 25	25 - 28
Series 1650, 1850, 3244 3447 (6)		
ROSE, FREDA M. (G.B.)	12 - 15	15 - 18
SCHERMELE, WILLY (Netherlands)	10 - 12	12 - 15

SCHMUCKER, SAMUEL L. (U.S.)
   Detroit Publishing Co., 1907 (Uns.)
      "Fairy Queen" or "Mottos" Series (6)

14659 "Roses" - by Rosseth	250 - 300	300 - 350
14660 "Harmony" - by Thomas Moore		
14661 "Captive" - by Coleridge		
14662 "Youth's Garden" - by Herrick		
14663 "Unafraid" - by Shakespeare		
14664 "Philomeis" - by Byron		

   "Gnome" Series (6) *

1 Hummingbird	150 - 175	175 - 200
2 Bee		
3 Mouse		
4 Frog		
5 Beetle		
6 Owl		

   * Same series with short quotation
      instead of one-word title. Value: $1500 - 1650

SCHUTZ, E. (Austria)
   B.K.W.I.

Series 165 "Fairy Nudes" (6)	28 - 32	32 - 35
Series 391 (6)	18 - 20	20 - 25

   M. Munk, Vienna

Series 1363, 1364, 1365 (6)	15 - 18	18 - 22
Series 435 (6) Uns. Andersen's Fairy Tales	18 - 20	20 - 25

SHERBORNE, M. (G.B.)

Salmon & Co. Series 4239 "Fairies of the Wood"	10 - 12	12 - 15

SOWERBY, AMY MILLICENT
   See SOWERBY Chapter

STEELE, L. R. (G.B.)
   Salmon & Co.

Series 4964-4969 "Peeps at Pixies"	10 - 12	12 - 15
Series 5050-5055 "Famous Fairies"		
Series 5172-77		

SYMONDS, CONSTANCE (G.B.)
   C. W. Faulkner & Co.

Constance Symonds, C. W. Faulkner 1957, "Blue Periwinkle"

C. Symonds, C. W. Faulkner 1958, "Welcome Stranger"

L. R. Steele, J. Salmon 4965 "The Hat Shop"

Series 1645 (6)		
"Do you love Butter?"	15 - 18	18 - 20
"The Duet"		
"Fairy Piper"		
"The Morning Walk"		
"The Punt"		
"Wake Up"		
Series 1926, 1957 (6)	18 - 22	22 - 25
Series 1958 (6)		
American Starwort - "Welcome Stranger"	18 - 22	22 - 25
Blue Convolvuloua - "Night"		
Bundles of Reeds - "Music"		
Guelder Rose - "Snow"		
Heather - "Solitude"		
Michaelmas Daisies - "Farewell		
TARRANT, MARGARET (G.B.)		
Medici Society		
PK 120 "The Fairy Troupe"	8 - 10	10 - 12
PK 184 "The Enchantress"		
Others	8 - 10	10 - 12
UNTERSBERGER, ANDREAS (Germany)		
Emil Kohn, München		
Fairy and Gnome Series (12)	12 - 15	15 - 18
WATKINS, DOROTHY (GB)		
Valentine & Sons		
Series 6 "The Dance of the Elves"	8 - 10	10 - 12

WEIGAND, MARTIN (Austria)

Gnomes & Mushroom Series	15 - 20	20 - 25
Gnomes, Mushroom Series (12)	15 - 18	18 - 20

Raphael Tuck

Oilette Series 6683 (6)	15 - 18	18 - 22
"Mid-Summer Dreams" (6)	15 - 20	20 - 25
Valentine & Sons Series 108 (6)	10 - 12	12 - 14

WHEELER, DOROTHY (G.B.)

Bamforth & Co.

Series 1 "Fairy Secret" (6)	12 - 15	15 - 18

WHITE, FLORA (G.B.)

P. Salmon Series 4419 (6)	18 - 22	22 - 25
WIELANDT, MANUEL (Germany)	12 - 15	15 - 18

WILLIAMS, MADGE (G.B.)

J. Salmon, Ltd.	12 - 15	15 - 18
Raphael Tuck Series 1160 (6)	8 - 10	10 - 12
Valentine & Sons "Fairy" Series 6044-6049	12 - 15	15 - 18

ANONYMOUS

Elves	5 - 8	8 - 15
Fairies	8 - 10	10 - 15
Gnomes	6 - 8	8 - 12
Goblins (Usually Halloween)	6 - 8	8 - 12
Leprechauns	5 - 7	7 - 12
Pixies	8 - 10	10 - 15
Sprites	7 - 8	8 - 10
Russian Real Photo Types	10 - 12	12 - 15

FAIRY TALES AND NURSERY RHYMES

ATTWELL, MABEL LUCIE (G.B.) (Uns.)

R. Tuck Series, 3328, 3376 (6)	20 - 25	25 - 30

BANKS, M. E. (G.B.)

R. Tuck

"Paper Dolls" Series 3381-I, 3382-II,		
3383-III, 3384-IV (6 in each series)	125 - 150	150 - 175

BARHAM, SYBIL (G.B.)

Series 1734 "The Pied Piper of Hamelin"	10 - 12	12 - 14

BARNES, G. L. (G.B.)

Cats - Fairy Tales-Nursery Rhymes

Raphael Tuck

Series 5600 "Cat Studies" (6)	15 - 18	18 - 22
Series 5625 "Pussy in Fairyland" (6)	18 - 22	22 - 25
Series 9301 (6)		
"Little Bo Peep"	15 - 18	18 - 22
"Little Boy Blue"		
"Old King Cole"		
"The Queen of Hearts"		
"Red Riding Hood"		
"Tom, Tom, Piper's Son ..."		

BAUMGARTEN, FRITZ (FB)   Germany

Oppel & Hess Series 1487, 1516	10 - 12	12 - 15

BILIBIN, IVAN (Russia)

Russian Fairy Tales, Art Nouveau Style	75 - 100	100 - 125

Margret Boriss, AMAG 0413
"Rotkäppchen"

BORISS, MARGRET (Netherlands)
    AMAG

"Hansel and Gretel" (6)	10 - 12	12 - 15
"Pied Piper of Hamelin" (6)		
"Puss in Boots" (6)		
"Rotkäppchen" (6)		

BOWLEY, A. L. (G.B.)
    R. Tuck

Series 3386 **"Paper Doll Punch-outs"** (6)	150 - 175	175 - 200

BRETT, MOLLY
    The Medici Society, Ltd., London

Series 1, 145, 147, 155, 168, 179, 185	6 - 8	8 - 10

BRUNDAGE, FRANCES (U.S.)
    R. Tuck

Series 4095 **"Little Sunbeams"** (8)		
"Little Bo Peep," "Little Milk Maid"	35 - 40	40 - 50
"Little Miss Muffet," "May Blossoms"		
"Polly and her Kettle," "Rosy Apples"		
"The Snow Maiden," "Summer at Sea"		

BURD, C. M. (U.S.)

Series 18 "Nursery Rhymes" (Fralinger's) (24)	30 - 40	40 - 50

CALDECOTT, RANDOLPH

F. Warne & Co. 48-card Set	8 - 10	10 - 12
1970's Reprint of the 48 card set	3 - 4	4 - 5

CARTER, SYDNEY (G.B.)

"Hans Andersen's Fairy Tales" (6)	15 - 20	20 - 25

COMMIEHAU, A. Series 48

	6 - 8	8 - 10

COOPER, PHYLLIS (G.B.)
    R. Tuck

Phyllis Cooper, R. Tuck 3164
"Up goes our pretty ball ..."

Elsbeth Forck, Oppel & Hess
1230/4, "Hansel and Gretel"

KG (Kate Greenaway), Anon.
"Humpty Dumpty sat on a ..."

Series 3482 **"Happy Land" V** (6)	25 - 28	28 - 32
Series 3487 **"Happy Land" VI** (6)	20 - 25	25 - 28
Series 3486 **I, II, III, IV, V, VI** (6 each)	25 - 28	28 - 32
Nursery Rhymes III Series 3488 (6)	20 - 25	25 - 28

DOCKAL, H.
    UVACHROM Series 407   8 - 10   10 - 12

DRAYTON, GRACE (U.S.)
    Reinthal & Newman Nursery Rhymes
        488 "O come and be my Lambey dear..."   40 - 45   45 - 50
        489 "O dear me, what do I see..."
        490 "It's nice to be a little boy..."
        491 "Little maid neat and sweet..."
        492 "Gee up Dobbin -- tried and true..."
        493 "The sun is shining warm and sweet..."

EDGERTON, LINDA
    Mansell & Company Series 1111 (6)   10 - 12   12 - 15

GREENAWAY, KATE (U.S.)

Postcards relating to the works of Kate Greenaway were published after
her death in 1901, and were adapted from her images and rhymes in
Rutledge & Sons' *Mother Goose* and *Old Nursery Rhymes* books which
appeared before 1900. Two series have surfaced. One is black and white and
the other colored, and both are signed KG. Each has a small verse along
with the image. These are extremely rare, and few have been seen for sale
or in auctions for many years.

The cards have undivided backs, are not numbered, and can only be identified by the verse and Kate's easily recognized images and initialed signature. There are no publisher bylines.

KATE GREENAWAY
  Colored Series (Signed KG)

German Undivided Back	150 - 200	200 - 300

  Black & White Series (Signed KG)

"A dillar, a dollar..."	90 - 100	100 - 125

    "As Tommy Snooks, and Bessie Brooks..."
    "Little Boy Blue..."
    "Cross Patch, lift the latch..."
    "Elsie Marley has grown so fine..."
    "Girls and boys come out to plat..."
    "Goosey, goosey, gander..."
    "Hark! Hark! The dogs bark..."
    "Here am I, little jumping Joan..."
    "Humpty Dumpty sat on a wall..."
    "Jack and Jill went up the hill..."
    "Johnny shall have a new bonnet..."
    "Little Betty Blue lost her..."
    "Little Jack Horner sat in a corner..."
    "Little lad, little lad..."
    "Mary, Mary, quite contrary..."
    "Polly put the kettle on..."
    "Ride a cock-horse to Banbury-cross..."
    "Ring-a-ring-a-roses..."
    "Rock-a-bye baby..."
    "There was an old woman..."
    "Tom, Tom, the piper's son..."

HERRFURTH, OSCAR (Germany) Several other artists are represented in sets below.
  UVA Chrom, Stuttgart
  Brothers Grimm Fairy Tales (6 per Series)

125	"Hansel & Gretel"	6 - 8	8 - 10
128	"Rotkäppchen"		
	(Little Red Riding Hood)	7 - 8	8 - 10
139	"Frau Holle" (Lady Hell)	4 - 5	5 - 6
140	"Dornröschen" (Sleeping Beauty)	7 - 8	8 - 10
147	"Schneewittchen" (Snow White)	7 - 8	8 - 9
154	"Aschenbrödl" (Cinderella)	6 - 7	7 - 10
223	"Der Gestiefelte Kater" (Puss in Boots)	5 - 6	6 - 7
241	"Die Gansemagd" (The Goose Maid)		
242	"Der Rattenfanger von Hameln"		
	(Pied Piper)	7 - 8	8 - 10
252	"Der Schweinhirt" (The Pig Herdsman)	5 - 6	6 - 7
254	"Siebenschön" (Seven Lovelies)		
264	"Der Tannenbäum" (The Fir Tree)	4 - 5	5 - 6
265	"Der Wolf und die Sieben Geisslein"		
	(The Wolf and the Seven Goats)		
266	"Marienkind"		
267	"Tischlein deck dich"		

Anon., No. 57/7
(Hansel and Gretel)

Hilda T. Miller, C. W. Faulkner
1784, "See-Saw, Margery Daw"

Frisch-Liemerk, Deutscher
Schulverein 60, "Der Froschkönig"

268	"Die Sieben Schwaben"	5 - 6	6 - 7
269	"Bruderchein und Schwesterchen"	6 - 7	7 - 8
285	"Die Bremer Stadtmusikanten"	5 - 6	6 - 7
298	"Hans im Gluck" (The Lucky Hans)		
299	"Das Tapfere Schneiderlein"		
311	"Der Kleine Daumling" (Tom Thumb)	6 - 7	7 - 10
319	"Hase und Igel - Das Lumpengesindel"	5 - 6	6 - 7
320	"Die Sieben Raben" (The Seven Ravens)	6 - 7	7 - 8
324	"Münchhausen I"	4 - 5	5 - 6
325	"Münchhausen II"		
354	"Das Schlaraffenland" (Milk & Honey Land)		
355	"Der Frosch König" (The Frog King)	6 - 7	7 - 10
363	"Die Heinselmannchen"	5 - 6	6 - 7
369	"Till Eulenspiegel" (12 cards)	4 - 5	5 - 6
376	"Schneewittchen und Rosenrot -- Die Sterntaler"	6 - 7	7 - 8
379	"Konig Drosselbart"	4 - 5	5 - 6
387	"Caliph Stork"		
388	"Aus Flem deutschen Marchenwald I"		
406	"Aus Flem deutschen Marchenwald II"		
407	"Rumpelstilken"	6 - 7	7 - 8
413	"Marchen-Elfen"	5 - 6	6 - 7

Tales (Sagen) Other than Grimm (6-Card Series)
Sage - A fantastic or incredible tale.

127	"Die Nibelungen - Sage"	6 - 7	7 - 8

141	"Parsival" (Parsifal)	7 - 8	8 - 10
157	"Rubezahl I"	4 - 5	5 - 6
158	"Wilhelm Tell" (12)	5 - 6	6 - 7
161	"Rubezahl II"	4 - 5	5 - 6
239	"Die Tristan - Sage"	6 - 7	7 - 8
247	"Die Parsival - Sage I"		

HEY, PAUL (Germany) Fairy Tales — 10 - 12 — 12 - 15

HUTAF, AUGUST W. (U.S.)

Series 105 (Little Bakers) — 6 - 8 — 8 - 10

2089	"Pat-a-Cake"	
2090	"Make Me a Cake ..."	
2091	"Criss It and Cross It ..."	
2092	"Put It in the Oven ..."	
2093	"Put on the Chocolate ..."	
2094	"Icing and Candles ..."	

JACKSON, HELEN

  Raphael Tuck   Art Series 6749 (6) — 18 - 22 — 22 - 25

JUCHTZER (Germany) — 7 - 8 — 8 - 10

KENNEDY, A. E. (G.B.)

  C. W. Faulkner   Series 1633 (6) — 12 - 15 — 15 - 18

KOCH, A. O. (Germany) — 15 - 18 — 18 - 22

KUBEL, OTTO (Germany)

  UVA Chrom   Brothers Grimm Tales — 10 - 12 — 12 - 14

KUTZER, ERNST (Austria)

  Der. Sudmark Poster Series — 18 - 22 — 22 - 25

248	"Walther von der Vogelweide"
253	"Die Parsival - Sage II"
258	"Die Lohengrin - Sage"
259	"Die Tannehäuser - Sage"
263	"Aus der Zeit der Minnesanger"
361	"Der Lichtenstein" (12) 4 - 5 5 - 6

  Bund Der Deutschen

    373 "Rotkäppchen" (Red Riding Hood) — 12 - 15 — 15 - 18

    Others

LANDSTROM, B. (Finland) — 6 - 8 — 8 - 10

LEEKE, Ferdinand (Germany)

  H.K. & M. Co.

    "Siegfried" Poster Cards (6) — 12 - 15 — 15 - 18

LeMAIR, WILLIBEEK (G.B.)

  Augener, Ltd.

    Our Old Nursery Rhymes (12)

    "Baa Baa Black Sheep" — 15 - 18 — 18 - 22

    "Hickory, Dickory, Dock"

    "Georgy Porgy"

    "Here We Go Round the Mulberry Bush"

    "I Love Little Pussy"

    "Little Bo Peep"

    "Mary Had a Little Lamb"

    "Oranges and Lemons"

    "O Where is My Little Dog Gone"

    "Pat a Cake"

    "Pussy Cat, Pussy Cat"

    "Sing a Song of Sixpence"

    Old Rhymes With New Pictures (12)

"Humpty Dumpty"	12 - 15	15 - 18
"Little Boy Blue"		
"Little Miss Muffet"		
"Lucy Locket"		
"Polly Put the Kettle on ..."		
"Twinkle Twinkle"		
"Jack & Jill"		
"Little Jack Horner"		
"Little Mother"		
"Mary, Mary ..."		
"Three Blind Mice"		
"Yankee Doodle"		

Little Songs of Long Ago (12)

"Dame Get Up and Bake Your Pies"	12 - 15	15 - 18
"I Had a Little Nut Tree"		
"I Saw Three Ships a Sailing"		
"Little Polly Flinders"		
"Little Tom Tucker"		
"London Bridge Has Broken Down"		
"Old King Cole"		
"Over the Hills and Far Away"		
"There Came to My Window"		
"The North Wind Doth Blow"		
"Young Lambs to Sell"		
"Simple Simon"		

Little People (6)

"Evening Prayer"	12 - 15	15 - 18
"In the Garden"		
"Good Evening, Mr. Hare"		
"Little Culprit"		
"In the Belfrey"		
"Time to Get Up"		

More Old Nursery Rhymes (12)

"A Frog He Would a Wooing Go"	15 - 18	18 - 22
"A Happy Family"		
"Bed Time"		
"Curley Locks"		
"Girls and Boys Come Out to Play"		
"Hush-a-by Baby"		
"Ride a Cock Horse"		
"The Crooked Man"		
"There Was a Little Man"		
"Three Little Kittens"		

Old Dutch Nursery Rhymes

"Follow the Leader"	15 - 18	18 - 22
"Our Baby Prince"		
"Polly Perkin"		
"The Little Sailor"		
"The Marionettes"		
"The Tiny Man"		
"Turn Round, Turn Round"		

Small Rhymes for Small People

"Dance-a-Baby Ditty"	12 - 15	15 - 18

H. Willibeek Le Mair

The North Wind doth blow.

H. Willibeek LeMair, Augener, Ltd.
"The North Wind doth blow"

"Dance to Your Daddy"
"Goosey Gander"
"Lavender Blue"
"Lazy Sheep"
"Little Jumping Joan"
"Sleep, Baby, Sleep"
"The Babes in the Woods"
"Three Mice Went to a Hole to Spin"

M.M.H. (G.B.)	10 - 12	12 - 15
MARSH-LAMBERT, H.G.C. (G.B.)		
A.M. Davis & Co.		
Series 518, 550 Nursery Rhymes (6)	20 - 22	22 - 25
MILLER, HILDA T. (G.B.)		
C. W. Faulkner & Sons		
Fairy Tale Series 1784 (6)	15 - 20	20 - 25
MILLER, MARION		
Ernest Nister	10 - 12	12 - 15
MÜHLBERG, GEORG (Germany)	8 - 10	10 - 12
NIXON, K. (G.B.)		
C. W. Faulkner & Co.		
"Alice in Wonderland" (6)	12 - 15	15 - 18
NOSWORTHY, FLORENCE E.		
F. A. Owen Series 160	10 - 12	12 - 14
NYSTROM, JENNY (Sweden)		
Axel Eliason, Stockholm	20 - 22	22 - 25
Unsigned Issues	10 - 12	12 - 14
PAYER, E. (Germany)	12 - 15	15 - 18
PEZELLERZ, F. (Germany) Silhouette Fairy Tales	12 - 15	15 - 18
PINGGERA, HEINZ (Austria)		
Posters	22 - 25	25 - 28

239 "Sans Däumling" (Tom Thumb)		
240 "Schneewittchen" (Snow White)		
241 "Das Tapfere Schneiderlein und die Riefen"		
242 "Siegfried"		
243 "Frauhitt"		
245 "Aschenpuitel" (Cinderella)		
246 "Rübezahl"		
248 "Herr Olof"		
249 "Parsifal"		
250 "Tannhäuser"		
251 "Jung Frau"		
Others		
ROWLAND, FR. (Germany)	12 - 15	15 - 18
RYAN, C. (U.S.)	10 - 12	12 - 15
SCHIRMER, ANNA (Germany)	8 - 10	10 - 12
SCHUTZ, E. (Austria)		
B.K.W.I.		
Poster Cards		
Series 435 (6) Andersen's Fairy Tales	15 - 18	18 - 22
Series 885 Poster cards of Fairy Tales (6)	25 - 30	30 - 35
Deutscher Schulverein		
Poster Cards		
319 "Rumpelstilzchen"	15 - 20	20 - 25
320 "Schneewittchen" (Snow White)		
321 "Rotkäppchen" (Red Riding Hood)		
322 "Die Sieben Raben" (Seven Ravens)	15 - 18	18 - 22
564 "Aschenbrödel" (Cinderella)	20 - 22	22 - 25
653 "Der Froschkönig" (The Frog King)		
862 "Dornröschen" (Sleeping Beauty)	18 - 20	20 - 22
SOWERBY, AMY MILLICENT (G.B.)		
(See SOWERBY Chapter)		
TARRANT, MARGARET (G.B.)		
T. P. & Company, N.Y.		
"Story Book Series"	6 - 8	8 - 10
TYPO, Boston		
"Tell Me a Story"	6 - 8	8 - 10
VALENTINE'S Series (6)	6 - 8	8 - 10
THIELE, ARTH. (Denmark)		
Series 1180 (6)	20 - 25	25 - 28
WAIN, LOUIS (G.B.)		
Raphael Tuck		
Calendar Series 304 (6)	100 - 125	125 - 150
"Oilette" Series 3385 "Paper Doll Cats"		
"Aladdin"	300 - 350	350 - 400
"Beauty and the Beast"		
"Cinderella"		
"Little Red Riding Hood"		
"Robinhood"		
"Dick Whittington"	300 - 400	400 - 600
WALL, BERNHARDT		
Ullman Mfg. Co.		
"Nursery Rhymes" Series 1664-1668	15 - 18	18 - 22
"Red Riding Hood" Series		
1752 "Take Some Cakes ..."		

"Multiplication is vexation, ..."

"Tom, Tom, the Piper's son, ..."

"Mary had a little lamb, ..."

Hush Baby my dolly, I pray you don't cry..."

"Little Bo-Peep Has lost her sheep ..."

"I had a little hobby-horse ..."

**The Wonderful Nursery Rhymes of H.G.C. Marsh-Lambert
Series 518 -- by A. M. Davis & Company**

WHITE, FLORA (G.B.)

Ilfracombe Mermaid, "Who are You?"	20 - 25	25 - 30

J. Salmon Poster Series

"Cinderella"	10 - 12	12 - 15
"Dick Whittington"		
"Goose Girl"		
"Hop-O-My-Thumb"		
"Peter Pan"		
"Puss in Boots"		

WINKLER, ROLF — 7 - 8 — 8 - 10

Anonymous   Same images as those by
M. E. Banks and published by R. Tuck
Paper Doll Cut-outs

Series 3382 "Little Bo-Peep"	125 - 150	150 - 175
Series 3383 "Little Boy Blue"		

PUBLISHERS

Bien, Julius Series 40 (6)	10 - 12	12 - 15
A. & C. Black		
Series 44, 45 "English Nursery Rhymes" (6)	12 - 15	15 - 18
Series 80 "Alice in Wonderland"	20 - 25	25 - 28
Clark, C. S. Series	6 - 8	8 - 10
F.A.S. Co. Series 9 (6)	8 - 10	10 - 12
Fairman Co. Series 625 B&W		
Paul Finkenrath (P.F.B.)		
Series 3714 (6)	25 - 30	30 - 35
Series 6943 (6)	22 - 25	25 - 28
Series 8666 (6)	25 - 30	30 - 35
F. Firth & Co. Rhymes	8 - 10	10 - 12
German-American Novelty Art		
Series 307, 397 (6)	8 - 10	10 - 12
Gottschalk & Dreyfuss (German)		
Series 2114 and 2115	10 - 12	12 - 15
Mansell, A. Vivian & Co., London		
Series 1067, 2105 (6)	8 - 10	10 - 12
Misch & Stock		
Series 120 "Fairy Tales & Pantomines" (6)	10 - 12	12 - 15
National Art Company		
Series 308 - 314 (6)	10 - 12	12 - 15
Newman, Wolsey & Co.		
Nursery Rhymes, Signed MMH	8 - 10	10 - 12
F. A. Owen Series 160, 161 (6)		
Salmon & Company Fairy Tale Series	10 - 12	12 - 15
Tuck, Raphael		
Series IX Glosso "Happy Childhood" (B/W)	6 - 8	8 - 10
Series 12 "Nursery Don'ts" (12)	12 - 15	15 - 18
Series 132 "Lovers in Nursery Land"		
Series 3376 "Nursery Rhymes" (6)	10 - 12	12 - 18
Series 3328, 3379, 3488 (6)		
Series 5579 "Happy Childhood"	8 - 10	10 - 12
Series 5600 "Cat Studies" (6) B/W	12 - 15	15 - 18
Series 5629 "Pussy in Fairyland"	10 - 12	12 - 14
Series 6496 "Landor's Cat Studies" (B/W)	6 - 8	8 - 10

Series 8484 Oilette "Aesop's Fables" (6)	15 - 18	18 - 22
T.P. & Co., New York "Story Book" Series	10 - 12	12 - 15
Tullar-Meredith "This Little Pig" (5)	8 - 10	10 - 12

Anonymous
Eagle on back Series, Lacy Border (10)

"Cock-a doodle-doo..."	10 - 12	12 - 15

"Little Bo Peep has lost her sheep..."
"Little Boy Blue..."
"Little Jack Horner..."
"Mary, Mary, quite contrary..."
"Old Mother Hubbard..."
"Pussy Cat, Pussy Cat..."

Advertising

Dr. Swett's Root Beer Nursery Rhymes	25 - 30	30 - 35
Fralinger's Original Salt Water Taffy (24)		
Series 18 "Nursery Rhymes" by C. M. Burd	30 - 40	40 - 50
Minneapolis Knitting Nursery Rhymes (6)	15 - 20	20 - 25
Swift's Premium, 1918 Nursery Rhymes (6)	15 - 18	18 - 22

DRESSED ANIMALS

(Non-Dressed Animals Listed in Artist-Signed Animal Section)

BARNES, G. L. (G.B.) **Cats See Nursery Rhymes**
BARNES-AUSTIN, EDGAR (G.B.)

Raphael Tuck "Piggie-Wiggie" Series (6)	12 - 15	15 - 18

BAUMGARTEN, FRITZ (F.B.) **(Germany)**

Meissner & Buch Frogs	15 - 20	20 - 25
Dogs	12 - 15	15 - 18

Oppel & Hess

Series 1457, 1458, 1486, 1511 (Bears) (6)	12 - 15	15 - 20

BOULANGER, MAURICE (France)

H & M Co. Series 104 "In Catland" (12)	12 - 15	15 - 18

International Art Pub Co.

Series 472 (6)	20 - 25	25 - 28
K. F. Editeurs, Paris Series of 6	22 - 25	25 - 28

R. Tuck

Series 122 "Humorous Cats" (6)	25 - 30	30 - 35
"Months of the Year" (12)	30 - 35	35 - 40
Series 6878 "Humorous Cats" (6)		

Anonymous Series 417 Chromolithos (6)
CADY, HARRISON (U.S.)

Quaddy Plaything Co.

"Quaddy" Postcards (10)	90 - 100	100 - 125
CHARLIN, F. Bears	12 - 15	15 - 18

CLARK, ROSE

National Art Co. Chicks Series	12 - 15	15 - 18

Rotograph Co. Frogs Series

F.L. 379 "Officer Stout Frog"	30 - 35	35 - 40

F.L. 380 "Dew-Drop Frog"
F.L. 381 "Will B. Stout Frog"
F.L. 382 "Mrs. Hoppin Frog"
F.L. 383 "Leap Frog"

F.L. 384 "Hammersly Frog, the Village.."
F.L. 385 "Grandmother Bullsie"
F.L. 386 "Lily-Pad Frog"
F.L. 387 "Professor Singer Frog"
F.L. 388 "Captain Skippin Frog..."
F.L. 389 "Brassie Frog"
F.L. 390 "I M. De Bull Frog"   40 - 45   45 - 50
R. Tuck
  Series 36, 4121, 4122 Chicks (6)   15 - 18   18 - 22
CLIVETTE
  Series 619 Dancing Cats (6)   12 - 15   15 - 18
CLOKE, RENE (G.B.)
  J. Salmon Co. Squirrel Series   8 - 10   10 - 12
COBBE, BERNHARD
  R. Tuck
    Series 9539 Bunnies (6)   8 - 10   10 - 12
    Cats, Dogs   6 - 8   8 - 10
COWELL, CYRIL (G.B.) **"Squirrilquins"** (6) 8 - 10   10 - 12
CRANE, D. P. Baby Duckling Series (6)   20 - 22   22 - 25
CRITE
  HSV Litho Co.
    "Billy Possum Political Series" (12)
    "Are you Dead - or Just Playing Possum/"   20 - 25   25 - 28
    "Aw don't play possum"
    "The Boogie Man'll Get You..."
    "Dear Friends, My Home Address..."
    "Dear, Am unavoidably detained..."
    "Do it Now! Don't Play Possum: But..."
    "Give My Regards to Bill!"   25 - 30   30 - 35
    "Good Eating Here!"   30 - 35   35 - 40
    "I'm having a high old time..."   20 - 25   25 - 35
    "It' a Great Game..."   Golf   30 - 35   35 - 45
    "Oo's 'ittle' possum is 'oo?"   20 - 25   25 - 35
    "Very Busy; Both Hands Full..."
DE WEES, ETHEL (U.S.)
  A.M.P. Co. "Billy Possum" Series
    "Arrived here just at right time"   25 - 30   30 - 35
    "I'll make another drive..."
    "I'm going to make a record..."
    "It's a bad thing to put off..."
    "Just a few lines before game..."   28 - 32   32 - 35
    "Yale's Favorite Son"
DOD, GIL (G.B.)
  S. Hildesheimer Series 5244 "Sports Meet" (6) 20 - 25   25 - 28
DOVIE, E. H. (G.B.) Squirrels   8 - 10   10 - 12
ELLAM, WILLIAM HENRY (G.B.)
  B. Dondorf Bear Series (6)   15 - 18   18 - 22
  R. Tuck
    "Breakfast in Bed"
    Series 9321 I & II   20 - 22   22 - 25
    Series 9953, 9784, 9793
    Series 574B With German Captions   15 - 18   18 - 22

F. Baumgarten (Uns.) Meissner &
Buch, "Gelukkig Nieuwjaar"

Rose Clark, Rotograph Co.
F.L. 381, "Will B. Stout Frog"

"Mrs. Caudle's Lectures"		
Series 8683, 8684	15 - 18	18 - 22
F.D.S. (Bears)		
FEIERTAG, K. (Austria)		
B.K.W.I. Series 160 (Bears) (6)	12 - 15	15 - 18
Dogs		
FIALKOWSKA, WALLY or **WF** (Austria)		
Cats, Dogs, Frogs	12 - 15	15 - 18
FREES, H. W.		
Rotograph Co. Real Photo Dress Dogs & Cats	8 - 10	10 - 12
GOVEY, L. A. (G.B.) The Little Mouse Family" (6)	22 - 25	25 - 28
GRATZ, THOMAS (Germany)	10 - 12	12 - 15
GROSMANN, M. B.K.W.I. Series 797 Dogs (6)		
GUGGENBERGER, I. G. (Germany) Mice	20 - 25	25 - 30
G.H.T. (THOMPSON, G. H.) (G.B.)		
Ernest Nister, London Signed & Unsigned		
Series 6 Hippo Series (6)	35 - 40	40 - 50
Series 179 "The Animals' Trip to the Sea" (6)	40 - 50	50 - 60
Series 180 "The Animals' Picnic" (6)		
Series 181 "The Animals' Rebellion" (6)		
Series 70 (6)		
Series 172 Hippo Head Series (6) Signed		
Series 354 "The Animal's School"		

Note: Uns. large images were then made from the
small images on the above series into individual
series by E. Nister & Theo. Stroefer listed below.

Gil Dod, S. Hildesheimer 5244
"Obstacle Race"

Rene Cloke, J. Salmon Ltd.
"A Pennyworth, Please"

W. H. Ellam, R. Tuck 9562
"Mixed Bathing"

Nister - Series 316, 328, 331, 333 (6)	35 - 40	40 - 50
Series 330 Bunny Series (6)	30 - 35	35 - 40
T.S.N. (Stroefer) - Series 319, 325, 330, 441 (6)	30 - 35	35 - 40
Series 757 (Same as Series 179; **Series 965** (6)		
HANKE, H. or H.H. (Germany)		
Series 4056 Dressed Dachshunds (6)	15 -18	18 - 22
HORINA, H. (U.S.)		
Ullman Co.		
Series 91 "Jimmy Pig" (10)	15 - 18	18 - 22
HUDSON, G. M.		
R. Tuck **Series 8648 "Guinnipens"** (6)	30 - 35	35 - 40
JIRAS, A. (Austria?) Dressed Donkeys	25 - 30	30 - 35
HY-M (Henry Mayer) (Germany)		
E. Nister "Jumbo" Elephant Series		
Series 186 "Jumbo" (6) (Uns.)	30 - 35	35 - 40
Series 187, 188, 189 (6)		
MAINZER, ALFRED (40's - 60's)		
Cats, Dogs	4 - 5	5 - 6
Golf or Tennis themes	8 - 10	10 - 12
MANASSE, A. Bears	10 - 12	12 - 15
MARTIN, L. (G.B.) Bears		
MEGGENDORFER, L. (Germany)		
H.K.C.M. Monkey Series		
Series 224, 263, 264, 265 (6)	18 - 22	22 - 25
MÜLLER, A. (Germany) **Dog Series 3908**	15 - 20	20 - 25
MÜLLER, R. (Austria) Frogs	18 - 22	22 - 25

GHT (G. H. Thompson), T.S.N. Series 757
and From Series 179 "The Animals Trip to the Sea"

OHLER, C. (Hungary)		
B.K.W.I. Series 4678 (6)	20 - 25	25 - 28
Birds Series, Duck Series, Comical Dogs (6)	6 - 8	8 - 10
OPSWALD, EUGEN (Germany)		
"Animal Sports" (6)	35 - 50	50 - 75
ONSLOW, LOLA (G.B.)		
Mack Co. "Storybook" Series Bunnies	8 - 10	10 - 12
PANKRATZ Comical Dachshunds	10 - 12	12 - 15
PAYER, E. (Austria)		
B.K.W.I. Series 1748 Frogs (6)	15 - 20	20 - 25
Others (The Frog King)		
P.O.E. (Germany) Dressed Dogs	12 - 15	15 - 18
REICHERT, C. Dressed Dogs		
ROGER (France)		
K.F. Editeurs		
Series 590 Elephants in Restaurant (6)	15 - 20	20 - 25
ROGIND, CARL (Denmark) Pig Sports Series	20 - 25	25 - 28
ROWNTREE, HARRY (G.B.)		
"Sporting Duckling" Series	15 - 18	18 - 22
SCHNOPLER, A. (Austria) Comical Dachshunds	12 - 15	15 - 18
A.S.M. Series 625 Dressed Cats (6)	15 - 18	18 - 22
SCHONIAN, ALFRED (Germany)		
Elf and Frog Series	18 - 22	22 - 25
SCHUTZ, ERIC (Austria)		
B.K.W.I. Poster 41 "The Froschkönig"	25 - 30	30 - 35
STUDDY, GEORGE (G.B.)		
B.K.W.I. Bonzo Series	10 - 12	12 - 15
Golf & Tennis themes	15 - 20	20 - 25
Valentine's Bonzo Series	10 - 12	12 - 15
Golf & Tennis themes	15 - 20	20 - 25

Anonymous, H. & L., 1286
"Glückliches Neu-Jahr!"

Anonymous, EAS 6272
"Herzlichen Pfingstgrusse"

Anonymous, Meissner & Buch
1897, Maikäfer Man

Anonymous
"Frohe Pfingsten"

TEMPEST, MARGARET
    Medici Society Series 61 (Bears)   6 - 8   8 - 10
THIELE, ARTH. (Denmark)
    F.E.D.
        Series 160, 474 (6)   20 - 25   25 - 28
    German American Art
        Series 789 Dressed Hog Head Studies (6)   20 - 25   25 - 30
        Series 806 Dressed Dog Head Studies (6)   20 - 25   25 - 30
    T.S.N.
        Series 710, 861, 947, 995, 1412, 1424 Cats (6) 30 - 35   35 - 40
        Series 1468 (Cats) (6)
        Series 962, 975, 1012, 1077, 1194 (Cats) (6) 15 - 20   20 - 25
        Series 1326, 1423, 1403, 1405, 1423 (Cats) (6)
        Series 1438, 1601, 1602, 1646, 1852 (Cats) (6)
        Series 1880, 1881, 1882, 3575 (Cats) (6)
        Series 1010, 1229 Cats (6)   22 - 25   25 - 28
        Series 1020, 1021 Bunnies (6)   15 - 20   20 - 25
        Series 1240, 1355, 1451 Bunnies (6)   20 - 25   25 - 28
        Series 1021, 1165, 1352, 1452 Chicks (6)   15 - 18   18 - 25
        Series 843, 946 Dogs (6)   18 - 22   22 - 25
        Series 1215 Horse Head Studies (6)   30 - 35   35 - 40
        Series 781, 844 Monkeys (6)   22 - 25   25 - 30
        Series 1413 Animal Head Studies (6)
TWELVETREES, CHARLES H. (U.S.)
    National Art Co. Frog Series
        136 "Matinee Idol"   20 - 25   25 - 30
        137 "Paul and Virginia"
        138 "Come in the Water's Fine"
        139 "The Bride"
        140 "The Groom"
WAIN, LOUIS (G.B.)
    Max Ettlinger
        Series 5376 Cat Santas   400 - 450   450 - 500
    R. Tuck Cats
        Series 3551-Cats, 3552-Dogs "Mascots" (6) 150 - 175 175 - 200
        Series 3553, 3554 "Mascots" (6)
        Series 8612, 8615 "Taking the Waters" (6) 100 - 125 125 - 150
        Series 8613, 8614 "Taking the
            Harrogate Waters" (6)
        Series 9396 (6)   60 - 75   75 - 100
        Charlie Chaplin Series (6)   250 - 275 275 - 300
        Many others   60 - 75   75 - 150
WESSEL, E. (Germany)
    B. Dondorf Series 28 "Sporting Frogs"   20 - 25   25 - 30
WEIGAND, MARTIN (Germany)
    Emil Kohn "The Frog King"   25 - 28   28 - 32
        Others   12 - 15   15 - 20
WINKLER, ROLF (Germany) Dressed Dogs   20 - 22   22 - 25
WOOD, LAWSON (G.B.)
    Valentine Pub. Co. Monkey Series   12 - 15   15 - 18
        Golf   15 - 20   20 - 25

PUBLISHERS
    A. & M. B. Series 47 Chromolithos Fish   20 - 25   25 - 30

Louis Wain, Anonymous
"Who said Ghosts?"

Arth. Thiele, T.S.N. 1215
No Caption

Louis Wain, R. Tuck 9396
"Marketing"

Series 113,170, 283 Frogs (6) Chromolithos	25 - 30	30 - 35
AMAG Series 2143 Bunnies (6)	12 - 15	15 - 18
A.R. Company Series 1394-1	20 - 22	22 - 25
Birn Brothers (B.B. London)		
Series E243 "We love Billy Possum..."	28 - 32	32 - 36
Frank J. Cohen & Son, Atlanta		
"Billy Possum" (B&W)	100 - 125	125 - 150
E.A.S. Series 1044 "The Frog Gardener"	20 - 25	25 - 28
H.H.i.W. Dog Series 459 (6)	12 - 15	15 - 20
H.W.B. Pig Chimney Sweeps	15 - 18	18 - 22
Lester Book & Stationery, Atlanta		
Taft with Possum "Beat it Teddy Bear"	300 - 350	350 400
Fred C. Lounsbury		
Series 2515 (6) Sepia "Billy Possum"		
"The only Possum that escaped"	20 - 25	25 - 28
"Billy Possum and Jimmy P. on the links"	28 - 32	32 - 35
"Good Bye Teddy"		
"Moving day in Possum Town"	20 - 25	25 - 28
"The Nation's Choice"	28 - 32	32 - 35
Series 2517 (6) Blue tone		
"Billy Possum to the Front"		
"Columbia's Latest 'Possum and Taters"		
"Uncle Sam's New Toy"		
"The Nation's Choice"		
Meissner & Buch Series 2960 Bunnies (6)	15 - 18	18 - 22
Misch & Co. Series 420 "Fishy Customers" (6)	20 - 25	25 - 28

Series 403 Frogs (6) Chromolithos	20 - 25	25 - 30
M. Munk, Vienna Bear Series	12 - 15	15 - 18
Series 420 Frogs Dance Series (6)	22 - 25	25 - 28
Series 729 Bunnies (6)		
O.P.F. Dressed Frogs Very high quality	40 - 50	50 - 60
F. A. Owen Co. "Billy Possum" (B&W)		
"Hurrah for Bill and Old Eli"	40 - 50	50 - 60
P.F.B. Dog Series 5957, 8168 (6)	20 - 25	25 - 28
Series 3903 Animals do Cake Walk (6)	20 - 22	22 - 25
S.W.S.B. Series 8837 Bears	12 - 15	15 - 18
Novitas Series 80607 Courting Birds	6 - 8	8 - 10
R. Tuck		
Series 294, 4089 (6) Frogs	22 - 25	25 - 30
Series 1723 Chromolithos (6)		
Series 2598 (6)	18 - 22	22 - 25
Ullman Mfg. Co.		
Series 72 "Jungle Sports" Various animals	15 - 18	18 - 22
Series 84 "Bunny Girl"	10 - 12	12 - 15
Series 112 "Br'er Rabbit"	12 - 15	15 - 18
Series 196 "Monkey Doodle"	8 - 10	10 - 12
Albert Hahn "Kaatskill Cats"	10 - 12	12 - 15
ADVERTISING		
Robeson Cutlery Co. Red Pig Knives (10)	50 - 75	75 - 100
OTHER ARTIST DRESSED ANIMALS, ETC.		
Note: Average values. Values reflect the particular card and prominence of artist.		
BIRDS	5 - 6	6 - 8
BUGS	8 - 10	10 - 15
CATS	6 - 8	8 - 10
COWS, BULLS, ETC.	10 - 12	12 - 15
DOGS	8 - 10	10 - 12
DUCKS, GEESE, CHICKENS		
ELEPHANTS, GIRAFFES	12 - 15	15 - 22
FROGS		
GOATS	12 - 15	15 - 18
GRASSHOPPERS	10 - 12	12 - 15
HIPPOPOTAMUS, GROUNDHOGS	15 - 20	20 - 25
HORSES, BURROS, DONKEYS, ZEBRAS	12 - 15	15 - 18
MAY BUGS (MAIKÄFERS), BEETLES, INSECTS	12 - 15	15 - 22
MONKEYS	8 - 10	10 - 12
OPOSSUMS	12 - 15	15 - 20
PARROTS, OWLS	8 - 10	10 - 12
PIGS	10 - 12	12 - 18
PIG CHIMNEY SWEEPS	12 - 15	15 - 20
RABBITS, SQUIRRELS	6 - 8	8 - 15
RATS/MICE	10 - 12	12 - 15

See Animal Section for Animals not Dressed or
   doing People things.

MISCELLANEOUS FANTASY

AUTOS FLYING ABOVE CITY	8 - 10	10 - 12
BUSI, ADOLFO		
Series 3059 Women/Snowmen (6)	18 - 20	20 - 25

Anonymous, A. R. Company, 1394-1
"Fröhliche Pfingsten"

P/Kaplan
    Series 57 Women's Heads in Clouds (12)   12 - 15   15 - 20
CORBELLA, TITO
    Uff. Rev. Stampa, Milano
       Series 268   Death and Edith Cavell   15 - 20   20 - 25
        1 - "Cavell Standing over the Conquered
           Figure of Death ..."
        2 - "Death Offering Head of Cavell ..."
        3 - "Death and Arrogant German Officer ..."
        4 - "Cavell Standing Before Death ..."
        5 - "Death Hovers as Cavell Gives Water ..."
        6 - "Death Plays Piano as Cavell Lies ..."
DEATH HEADS   8 - 12   12 - 18
ELVES, GNOMES   5 - 6   6 - 10
FACES IN MOUNTAINS   10 - 12   12 - 18
FLOWER FACES   6 - 8   8 - 12
    Ernest Nister, London   10 - 12   12 - 15
    The Standard, London (Multi-Baby) **Series 67**   6 - 8   8 - 10
GIANT PEOPLE   5 - 6   6 - 7
GOLLIWOGGS
    ATTWELL, MABEL L. (G.B.)
       Valentine's
       Series A551 (6)   18 - 22   22 - 25
       Series A579 (6)
       689 "Golly, It's Nice!"   22 - 25   25 - 28
       Series 7346 (6)
    GOVEY, A. (G.B)
       Humphrey Milford
       "Dreams & Fairies" Series (6)   15 - 18   18 - 22
    KENNEDY, T. R. (G.B.)   15 - 20   20 - 25

*Fritz Baumgarten (Uns.), M&B
3179, German Greeting*

*Agnes Richardson, A.R. & Co.
1511-3, German Caption*

MARSH-LAMBERT, H.G.C. (G.B.)
A.M. Davis Co.
    Series 501 "Round the Clock"
    "I'll play, I think, with Sambo..."   18 - 22   22 - 25
    "At nine my breakfast is over..."
    "Oh Dear! How quickly six has come..."
RICHARDSON, AGNES (G.B)
Raphael Tuck
    Series 1232 **"Rescued"** (6)   22 - 25   25 - 28
    Series 1262, (6)
    Series 1397 (6)
    Card C1420 "Little Snowflakes..."
    Card C1421 "My Greeting is Loving..."   18 - 22   22 - 25
    Series C2005   22 - 25   25 - 28
    Series 8688
    "I'm down here with the family"   25 - 30   30 - 35
Valentine & Sons
    Series C2006 (6)   18 - 22   22 - 25
STOCKS, M. (G.B.)
H.K. & Co.
    "Jack-in-the Box" with Golliwogg   15 - 18   18 - 22
UPTON, FLORENCE (G.B.)
Raphael Tuck
    Series 1252   30 - 35   35 - 40

Anonymous, P.F.B., Series 11144
"Viel Glück im neuen Jahre"

Series 1281 "Art" Series
"Golliwogg and his Auto-Go-Cart"   35 - 40   40 - 45
"Golliwogg taken to Prison"
"Golliwogg and his Auto...applying pump"
Series 1282 "Art"
  Golliwogg w/Dutch Dolls
"The Golliwogg"   30 - 35   35 - 40
"Golliwogg and the Highwayman"
"Golliwogg Rescued"
"Golliwogg Introducing Himself"
"Golliwogg Taken to Prison"
"Golliwogg Escapes from Prison"
Series 1397 "Humorous" (6)   30 - 35   35 - 40
Series 1782 "New Year" (6)
Series 1785 "New Year" (6) Signed
"Golliwogg introduces himself
"Highwayman"   35 - 40   40 - 45
Series 1791 (6) Signed
Golliwogg and His Auto Car   35 - 40   40 - 45
Series 1792 Christmas, New Year (6) Signed
Golliwogg and the Highwayman
Series 1793 (6) Signed
Golliwogg in Prison
Series 1794 (6) Signed
Series 6065 "Humorous" (6)
Series 8063 "New Year" (6)
Davidson Bros. Series   22 - 25   25 - 30

Anonymous
Stick People

Anonymous, B.K.W.I., 893-1
The Foot Family

Regent Publishing Co.
A. C. Redmon Co.
OTHERS
B.B., London (Birn Bros.) Anonymous Artist
    Series 10 Silver Background
    Courtship-Marriage w/Stickgirl

At the Beach	20 - 25	25 - 28
In Row Boat		
In Automobile		
On Park Bench		
Playing Cards		
The Family Outing		
Series X296	20 - 22	22 - 25
C. W. Faulkner		
Series 996	18 - 22	22 - 25
Series 1136 (6)		
Raphael Tuck		
Series 507 (6)	15 - 18	18 - 22
John Winsch		
1910 Issue	15 - 18	18 - 20
1912 Issue (Santa)	18 - 22	22 - 26
1913 Issue (Santa) (2)	40 - 50	50 - 60
Anonymous **Series 733**	15 - 18	18 - 22
DEPICTING THE FUTURE	7 - 8	8 - 10

EGG OR FOOT PEOPLE	15 - 18	18 - 22
MAN IN THE MOON	5 - 8	8 - 10
MAPS-BODIES MAKING UP COUNTRIES	8 - 9	9 - 10
METAMORPHICS See Topicals		
MUSHROOMS, GIANT	6 - 8	8 - 12
MUSHROOM PEOPLE	8 - 10	10 - 15
SKELETONS, DEPICTING DEATH	8 - 10	10 - 12
SNOWMEN	6 - 10	10 - 20
S/A. Thiele Snowman Series 1297 (6)	15 - 18	18 - 22
P.F.B. Series 11144	20 - 22	22 - 25
SOLOMKO		
UN		
1015 "Dream of Icarius"	12 - 15	15 - 18
1019 "Blue Bird"	15 - 18	18 - 20
STICK OR WOOD PEOPLE	12 - 15	15 - 18

WAGNER OPERA FIGURES

Many think the German composer, Richard Wagner, was the greatest composer who ever lived. He died in 1883 but left a legacy that would live forever. It is believed that he alone fundamentally changed European musical, literary, and theatrical life. To Germans and other Europeans he was a great man, and at the turn of the century his operas continued to be a passion for all who loved music and the theatre.

Wagner's first opera was *Rienzi* and then *The Flying Dutchman.* Later came his famous *Tannhäuser* and *Löhengrin*, which were operas concerning the romantic views of medieval life. His greatest creation, however, was *The Ring of the Nibelungs*, which was four operas in one...*The Rhine Gold, The Valkyrie, Siegfried,* and *The Twilight of the Gods*.

The love story of *Tristan and Isolde* was one of his most popular, and *The Mastersingers of Nürnberg* was his only mature comedy. Wagner's final work was *Parsifal*, a religious story of early Spain and the Holy Grail.

German artists, because of their great love for the works of Wagner, painted many beautiful fantasy sets and series about the heroes and heroines of his operas. The great poster-type cards by Hanns Printz, Heinz Pinggera, and Eric Schutz are certainly of epic proportions. Also, the works by R. Tuck and ESD of paintings by Stassen are among the best in a very wide field.

AIGNER		
Series 259 (6) 4490 "Tannhäuser"	8 - 10	10 - 12
AUBERT, PAUL (Germany)		
27 "Tannhäuser" B&W	8 - 10	10 - 12
BAUFCHILD "Löhengrin" (6)	10 - 12	12 - 15
BERGMULLER, C. W. Nude "Walküre"	12 - 15	15 - 20
BRAUNE, ERWIN (Germany)		
Nude "Walküre"	12 - 15	15 - 20
DOUBEK, F. (Germany)		
Ackerman Ladies in Wagner Operas	15 - 18	18 - 22

H. Fründt, M. Kimmelstiel & Co.
"Fliegender Holländer"

ERLAND, P. V. (Germany)	8 - 10	10 - 12
FAHRENKROG, LUDVIG (Germany)		
298 "Parsifal"	8 - 10	10 - 12
520 "Parsifal"		
FRÜNDT, H. (Germany)		
M. Kimmelstiel & Co.		
"Walküre," "Fliegende Hollander," Others	20 - 22	22 - 25
GEIGER, C. A.		
Marke J.S.C. 6108 "Tannhaüser"	12 - 15	15 - 18
GLOTZ, A. D. (Germany)		
"Parsival" Series	10 - 12	12 - 15
Series 22	8 - 10	10 - 12
GOETZ (Germany)	8 - 10	10 - 12
HENDRICHS (Germany)		
Poster "Siegfried's Tod"	15 - 18	18 - 22
HOFFMAN, H. (Germany) "Siegfried" (6)	12 - 15	15 - 18
JANOWITSCH		
B.K.W.I. 3219 "Parsifal"	8 - 10	10 - 12
KLIMESOVA, M.		
KUDERNY, F. (Austria)		
Deutsch. Dereines fur Osterreich		
"Die Nibelungen" Posters		
"Kriemfild," "Siegfried"	15 - 18	18 - 22
Others		
KUTZER, E. (Austria)		
B.K.W.I. Series 438 Poster Cards (6)		
1 "Tannhäuser"	20 - 25	25 - 28

C. A. Geiger, Marke J.S.C. 6108
"Tannhaüser"

2 "Der Fliegende Holländers"
3 "Meistersinger"
4 "Parsifal"
5 Wagner's "Rienzi"
6 "Löhengrin"
Vereines Sudmark
    245 "Die Meistersinger von Nürnberg"   22 - 25   25 - 28
    246 "Die Meistersinger von Nürnberg"
    247 "Die Meistersinger von Nürnberg"
    248 "Löhengrin"
    249 "Tristan und Isolde"
    252 "Tannhäuser"
    253 "Die Walküre"   22 - 25   25 - 28
    254 "Das Rheingold"
    255 "Siegfried"
    256 "Siegfried"
Schulverein fur Osterreich
"Die Nibelungen" Poster Cards (8)
    "Siegfried und der Trache" (Dragon)   18 - 22   22 - 26
L.R.
    1096 "Parsifal"   10 - 12   12 - 15
    1097 "Siegfried"
    Others
LEEKE, FERDINAND (Germany)
  M. Munk, Vienna
    Series 861 (12)
    "Die Feen"   8 - 10   10 - 12

F. Leeke, L. Pernitzsch 2
"Der Fliegende Holländer"

E. Kutzer, Vereines Südmark 247
"Die Meistersinger von Nürnberg"

"Die Meistersinger" (The Master Singer from Nürnberg"		
"Die Walküre" (The Valkyrie)		
"Götterdämmerung" (Twilight of the Gods)	10 - 12	12 - 14
"Löhengrin"	8 - 10	10 - 12
"Parsifal"	10 - 12	12 - 14
"Rienzi"	8 - 10	10 - 12
"Rheingold"	10 - 12	12 - 14
"Siegfried"	8 - 10	10 - 12
"Tannhaüser"		
"Tristan und Isolde"	10 - 12	12 - 14
"Tristan und Isolde"		
Series 982 (12)		
Same images as **Series 861**	8 - 10	10 - 12
984 and E984 (12) Reprint of **Series 861**	6 - 8	8 - 10
Hanfstaengl's Kunstlerkarte or **H.K.M. Co.**		
Series 72 (6)		
"Die Walküre," "Götterdämmerung"	10 - 12	12 - 15
"Löhengrin," "Siegfried"		
"Tannhäuser," "Tristan und Isolde"		
H.K.M. Co.		
Series 12 Same as series 72	10 - 12	12 - 15
Poster Cards		

L. Pernitzch
"Richard Wagner's Heldengestalten" (24)

1	"Rienzi"	15 - 18	18 - 22
2	"Der Fliegende Holländer"		
	(The Flying Dutchman)		
3	"Der Fliegende Holländer"		
4	"Tannhäuser"		
5	"Tannhäuser"		
6	"Tannhäuser"		
7	"Löhengrin"		
8	"Löhengrin"		
9	"Tristan und Isolde"		
10	"Tristan und Isolde"		
11	"Tristan und Isolde"		
14	"Die Walküre"		
15	"Die Walküre"		
16	"Die Walküre"		
17	"Siegfried		
18	"Siegfried"		
21	"Götterdämmerung"		
22	"Götterdämmerung"		
23	"Götterdämmerung"		
24	"Götterdämmerung"		

LEFLER, PROF. HEINRICH   (Austria)
  M. Munk, Vienna
    Wagner's Frauengsetalten Series 1281 (6)

"Brünhilde" - Götterdämmerung	15 - 18	18 - 22
"Elisabeth" - Tannhäuser		
"Elsa" - Löhengrin		
"Eva" - Die Meistersinger		
"Fricka" - Die Walküre		
"Isolde" - Tristan and Isolde		
"Ortrud" - Löhengrin		

LUDVIG

Series 718 (6)	8 - 10	10 - 12

NOWAK, OTTO   (Germany)
  B.K.W.I.

Series 1412 "Parsival"	8 - 10	10 - 12
Series 2352 "Wotan"		

PEETE "Siegfried" and the Dragon	12 - 15	15 - 18

PETER, O. (Germany)

Series 399 "Brünhilde"	12 - 15	15 - 18
PILGER "Tannhaüser" (With Music)	10 - 12	12 - 15

PINGGERA, HEINZ   (Austria)
  Bund der Deutchen in Niederösterrich
    Series 242-252   Poster cards

242 "Siegfried"	18 - 22	22 - 25
248 "Herr Olof"		

Heinrich Lefler, M. Munk 1281
"Eva" (Die Meistersinger)

E. Schutz, B.K.W.I. 438-1
"Tannhäuser"

250	"Tannhaüser im Sorfelberg"		
750	"Götterdämmerung"		
751	"Die Walküre"		
752	"Tannhaüser"		

PRINTZ, HANNS (Austria)

  T.S.N. (Theo. Stroefer, Nürnberg)

Series 1370 (6) Chromolithographs		
"Das Rheingold" Mermaid	30 - 35	35 - 40
"Die Meistersinger von Nürnberg"	25 - 30	30 - 35
"Die Walküre"		
"Löhengrin"		
"Parsival"		
"Tannhäuser"		

ROWLAND, FR. (Germany)

Series 258 "Parsifal"	18 - 22	22 - 25

SCHLIMARSKI

Series 420 (6)		
1 "Parsifal"	10 - 12	12 - 15
Others		

SCHUTZ, ERIC (Austria)

  B.K.W.I.

Series 205 Musical Posters (6)		
1 "Wagner - Parsifal"	22 - 25	25 - 28
4 "Wagner - Parsifal"		

6 "Wagner - Parsifal"
Series 438 Posters
1 "Tannhäuser"   22 - 25   25 - 28
2 "Der Fliegende Holländers"
3 "Meistersinger"
4 "Tristan & Isolde"
5 "Rienzi"
6 "Löhengrin"
SINZ, MAX   8 - 10   10 - 12
SPIELZ, A.
Series 247 (6)
4423 "Parsival"   10 - 12   12 - 14
STASSEN, FRANZ   (Germany)
H & A Bruning
Richard Wagner Series   (6)
5990 11 "Elsa"   20 - 25   25 - 28
6991 III "Venusburg"
6992 IV
6993 V "Brünhild"
6994 XIV "Senta"
Raphael Tuck
"Wagner" Series
Series 690 "Siegfried"   22 - 25   25 - 28
Series 691 "Löhengrin"
Series 692 "Götterdämmerung"
Series 693 "Tristan and Isolde"
Series 694 "The Rheingold"
Series 695 "The Flying Dutchman"
German "Modern Meister" XX, 1219 (6)
"Götterdämmerung," "Löhengrin"   15 - 20   20 - 25
"Parsifal," "Rheingold"
"Siegfried," "Tristan und Isolde"
E.S.D. (Unsigned Stassen)*
German and American Art Nouveau Series
8157 "Die Walküre" (6)   18 - 22   22 - 25
8158 "Siegfried" (6)
     Add $5 for Dragon Images.
8159 "Das Rheingold" (6)
     Add $10 for Mermaid Images
8160 "Götterdämmerung" (6)
8161 "Die Meistersinger" (6)
8162 "Tristan und Isolde" (6)
8163 "Der Fliegende Holländer" (6)
8164 "Löhengrin" (6)   12 - 15   15 - 18
* Same caption number on both U.S. and German
TOEPPER, HANS (Germany)
F. A. Ackerman, München (Continental size)
Series 625 "Ring des Nibelungen" (12)   12 - 15   15 - 18

TOUSSAINT "Isolde"	8 - 10	10 - 12
WEISLEIN "Barbarossa" Poster	10 - 12	12 - 15

PUBLISHERS

B. & W. 271 "Siegfried's Death"	12 - 15	15 - 18
B.K.W.I. Series 206, 438 (6)	12 - 15	15 - 18
Wilhelm Boehme		
"Altgermanische Gotter" 625-630 (6	12 - 15	15 - 18
F.M.K. 3153 "Löhengrin" (6)		
FRG		
Series 247 "Parsifal" (6)	12 - 15	15 - 18
Series 258 "Löhengrin" (6)		
C. W. Faulkner 1401 "Die Feen"	12 - 15	15 - 18
M. Munk, Vienna **Wagner's Series 28**		
Ricordi & Co.		
"Siegfried & the Dragon"	8 - 10	10 - 12
Ladies in Wagner's Operas	12 - 15	15 - 18
T.S.N. (Theo. Stroefer)		
Series 141 "Löhengrin" (6)	15 - 18	18 - 22
Raphael Tuck *		
"Wagner" Series See Franz Stassen		
* Same as E.S.D. Series Above		
Series XX, 1219 "Modern Meister" (6)		
Same Captions as "Wagner" Series (6)	18 - 22	22 - 25
Stengel & Co.		
29132 "Die Walküre"	8 - 10	10 - 12
Ottmar Zieher Wagner's Operas (6)	25 - 28	28 - 32

DEATH FANTASY

Death is a process of nature for all mankind and, in that vein, it certainly is not a fantasy. However, some of the events that precede it make it so. The fears and anguish of growing old, the thoughts of wars and pestilence, and the torment of dying with a deadly, lingering disease all bring fantastic thoughts and dreams which are indeed Death Fantasy.

Death, while feared by many, may be relatively calm and peaceful for those with very little to live for. Death, in myth and literature, has been portrayed by writers and artists as one of the greatest enemies of man. Picture the black-hooded Grim Reaper with his merciless scythe...a skeleton on a black horse with eyes of madness and nostrils flaring...or a smiling death head so sure of his prey...and a cynical staring death head laughing at the foolish as they drink and revel. These are the epic images in a fantasy world.

DEATH FANTASY

BALUSCHECK
"Ghost and Death"	10 - 12	12 - 15

BÖCKLIN, A. (Germany)
  Julius Bard, Berlin
    "Der Kreig"   15 - 18   18 - 22
  F. Bruckmann, München
    "Selfportrait mit Tod"
BÜRFEL, G. (Germany)
  Death in Black   12 - 15   15 - 20
CIEZKIEWKZ, E.
  "Girl in Red"   12 - 15   15 - 18
  "Woman & Skull"
  "Le Nocturne de Chopin"   15 - 18   18 - 20
  Girl looks at death
CHOPIN, FR.
  Series 116 "Playing Death"   10 - 12   12 - 15
CORBELLA, TITO (Italy)
  Uff. Rev. Stampa, Milano Series 268
    Death and Edith Cavell   20 - 25   25 - 28
    1 - "Cavell Standing over the Conquered
       Figure of Death ..."
    2 - "Death Offering Head of Cavell ..."
    3 - "Death and Arrogant German Officer ..."
    4 - "Cavell Standing Before Death ..."
    5 - "Death Hovers as Cavell Gives Water ..."
    6 - "Death Plays Piano as Cavell Lies ..."
ERLANG
  "Die Vision," Nude and Death Head   15 - 18   18 - 22
FAHRENKROG, LUDVIG (Germany)
  Wilhelm Hartung   104 "Fate"   15 - 18   18 - 22
FISCHER, J. (Czech.)
  Minerva, Prague
    40 "Spectre de la guerre"   15 - 18   18 - 22
GASSNER
  Death on a Black Horse   12 - 15   15 - 20
GOLTZ, A. D. (Germany)
  "Illusion"   12 - 15   15 - 20
HERING, ADOLF (Germany)
  Arthur Rehn & Co.
    "Der Tod and das Madchen"   18 - 22   22 - 25
KELLER, FERDINAND (Germany)
  Franz Hanfstaengl   "Finale"   12 - 15   15 - 18
JUNG, F.
  Ghost in the swamp   8 - 10   10 - 12
KLAKARSCHEVA   "Ikarus"   10 - 12   12 - 15
KORPAK, T.
  Ghost and Death   12 - 15   15 - 20
LAMM, ERICH (Austria)
  B.K.W.I.
    1521 Death in the Field   10 - 12   12 - 15

Lionel Royer, Salon de Paris 734
"La Sirene"

G. Bürfel, Runftler
"Das Buch für Alle"

LEOPAROVA "Fable"	12 - 15	15 - 18
LIST, FR. (Hungary)		
Series 116/2		
"Rhapsodie Hongroise"	10 - 12	12 - 15
MANDL, J. "The End"	12 - 15	15 - 18
NEJEDLY		
Salon J.P.P.		
"Inspiration"		
PETER, O. (Germany)		
400 Burning Nudes	12 - 15	15 - 20
PODKOWINSKI (Poland)		
Nude on Fiery Horse	15 - 18	18 - 22
REASTELLI "The Coming Storm"	12 - 15	15 - 18
WACHSMUTH, M. (Germany)		
P.F.B. in diamond "Die Beute"	12 - 15	15 - 20
WILFE Poster "Der Walschrat"	15 - 18	18 - 22
WOLFF, H. (Germany)		
P.F.B. in diamond		
4480 Death Rides a Horse	12 - 15	15 - 20
WOLLNER, H. (Germany)		
B.K.W.I.		
2402 "Seduction"	15 - 18	18 - 25
P.F.B., Series 226	15 - 20	20 - 25
Anonymous		
Death Fiddles while Clowns Dance (Und.)	20 - 25	25 - 30

DEATH HEADS

Novitas		
21101 Death Head on car body	18 - 22	22 - 25
21102 Death Head with 2 Drinkers		
Rotophot		
09-585 Death Head; Man-Woman cooking	22 - 25	25 - 28
SB Death Head; Lovers Drinking (6)	18 - 22	22 - 25
Schweizer		
129 Death Head - "All is Vanity"	20 - 22	22 - 25
Real Photos Types		
"L'amour de Pierrot"	25 - 30	30 - 35
P.F.B. 226 "Lettre d'adieu"		
"Napoleon" (2)		
Rarer Publishers	35 - 50	50 - 100

NUDE FANTASY

BENDER, S.
H.R. "La Femme" Series

Reclining nude with animals (12)		
1217 With parrot	$ 20 - 25	$ 25 - 28
1220 With monkey and spider		
1222 With cat		
Others		
(Snakes)	12 - 15	15 - 18

BEROUD, L.
    Salon 1901

Series 201-20 "Fantasie" Tiger and nude	15 - 18	18 - 22

BÖCKLIN, A. (Germany)
    Bruckmann A. G.

6 "Die Nereide"	12 - 15	15 - 18
16 "Im Meere" (Nude and Merman)	10 - 12	12 - 15
21 "Triton & Nereide" (Merman)	10 - 12	12 - 15
"Spiel der Wellen" Nudes and Horse-man	12 - 15	15 - 20

BRAUNE, E. (Austria)

Amag Kunst 63. "Walküre" (Horse)	12 - 15	15 - 18

CABANEL, A.
    Salon J.P.P.

2206 "Nymph & Faun" (Man-Goat)	15 - 18	18 - 22

COURSELLES DUMONT, H. (France)

Lapina 564. "In der Arena" (Lion)	12 - 15	15 - 20
Salon de 1912 47. "In the Arena" (Lion)		

DE BOUCHE, A. (Germany)

Moderner Kunst, Berlin 2516 "Salambo"	15 - 18	18 - 22

DUSSEK, E. A. (Austria)

J.K. 69 "Froschkönigs Braut" (Frog)	22 - 25	25 - 28

FIDUS

Among the most beautiful fantasy real photo nudes on postcards are the graphic works of Hugo Hoppener (who used the pen name of Fidus). He did great drawings of nude and sometimes erotic young ladies and young boys, plus many others, for his books, posters and magazines. In most of his works he used very precise graphic border illustrations which greatly enhanced their beauty.

To advertise and sell these works he published real photo advertising postcards, describing each of them, and distributed the cards widely. It is not known just how successful he was in selling his works with the cards, but the cards themselves have become extremely popular with collectors. The series entitled "Tempeltanz der Seele" (Temple Dance of the Soul) of young maidens standing on fantasy petals, leaves, stems and the Universe, is probably the most sought after by today's collector. However, Fidus did many others in the fantasy vein that are also in great demand.

FIDUS or **Hugo Hoppener**   (Germany)
    N.B.C. (Real Photos)

2 "Drachen Kampfer" Nudes and Dragon	25 - 28	28 - 32

101	"Tempeltanz Der Seele I"	30 - 35	35 - 40
102	"Tempeltanz Der Seele II"		
103	"Tempeltanz Der Seele III"		
104	"Tempeltanz Der Seele IV"		
105	"Tempeltanz Der Seele V"		
106	"Tempeltanz Der Seele VI"		
134	"Erwartung" Nude in white birch grove	20 - 25	25 - 30
135	"Sterntänzerin" Nude standing on globe	30 - 35	35 - 40
393	Nude and statue of Wagner	20 - 25	25 - 30
515	"Neapmierinatais Lucifers" Satan	20 - 25	25 - 30
	Many other Fantasy types		
	Others - non Fantasy	12 - 15	15 - 18

FISCHER-COERLINE   (Germany)
  M.K.B.   2475. "Salome" (Severed Head)   18 - 22   22 - 25
GEBHARDT, CARL   (Germany)
  E.M.   132. "Loreley"   20 - 25   25 - 28
GEIGER, C. A.   (Hungary)
  Marke J.S.C.
    6109 "Liebeskampf" (Man-Sea Beast)   18 - 22   22 - 25
    6112 "Salome" (Severed Head)
GIOVANNI, A.   (Italy)
  ARS Minima   119. "Salome" (Severed Head)   12 - 15   15 - 20
GLOTZ, A. D.   (Germany)
  B.K.W.I.   1009 "Lebensluge" (Ghost of Dead)   12 - 15   15 - 18
HIRSCH   10 - 12   12 - 14
HOESSLIN, GEORGE
  NPG   491 "Die Schaumgebstene"
    (Nude in Oyster Shell)   10 - 15   15 - 18
HORST   (Germany)
  P.F.B. in Diamond
    4323   Semi Nude and Horse Drink   12 - 15   15 - 18
ICHNOWSKI, M.   (Poland)
  Series 90   16. Nude and Lion   18 - 22   22 - 25
KANDLER, V.   (Germany) Nude and Snake   15 - 18   18 - 22
KELLER, F.   (Germany)
  Russian Publisher 076. "Finale" (Death Head)   15 - 18   18 - 22
KOMINEL   15 - 18   18 - 22
KORPAL
LAMM
LANGENMANTEL
  Nude on Bull   12 - 15   15 - 20
LEEKE, F. (G.B.)
  Münchener Kunst
    3113 "Nidre und Wasserman"
      (Water Creature)   12 - 15   15 - 20
    3114 "Gefangene Nymphe" (Dwarfs)
    3117 "Triton Belaufde Nereide" (Merman)   15 - 18   18 - 22
LENOIR, CH.   (France)
  Lapina   5122 "Victory!!" (Octopus)   22 - 25   25 - 28

Fidus, St. Georgs-Bundes 135
"Sterntänzerin"

Fidus, St. Georgs-Bundes 102
"Tempeltanz der Seele II"

LEOPAROVA
KV
    1183 "Salome" (Severed Head)   12 - 15   15 - 20
LINS, ADOLF
    EAS   607 "Faun and Nymphe"   12 - 15   15 - 18
MANDL, J.
    Minerva 177 "Printemps" (Wings)   10 - 12   12 - 15
MASTAGLIO
    Galerie Münchener Meister
    380 "Duell" (Nudes Fencing)   12 - 15   15 - 20
MASTROIANNI, C. (Italy)
    198 "Fievre d'Amore" (Waterfall)   10 - 12   12 - 15
MEUNIER, SUZANNE (France)
    MARQUE L. E.
    Series 64 (6) Nudes & big snakes   35 - 40   40 - 45
MICHAELIS, O.
    P.F.B.   **Series 4416** "Centaur und Nymphe"   20 - 25   25 - 30
MÜHLBERG, GEORG (Germany)
    Nude Riding a Seahorse   12 - 15   15 - 18
MÜLLER, PROF. RICH (Austria)
    251 Nude riding goldfish "Perlen"   20 - 22   22 - 25
    252 Nude with red Ibis
MÜLLER-BAUMGARTEN (Germany)
    FEM   161 "Faun & Nymphe" (Man-Goat)   10 - 12   12 - 15

MUTTICH, C. V.   (Czech)
   V.K.K.V.   2077 "Sulejka" (Peacock)   12 - 15   15 - 20
OKON, T.
   Stella, Bochina   1233 Nude and black cat   12 - 15   15 - 20
PENOT, Albert   (France)
   Lapina
      1340 "Red Butterfly" (Red-Winged Nude)   12 - 15   15 - 20
PIOTROWSKI, A.   (Poland)
   Minerva
      505   Woman/Children/Serpent   15 - 20   20 - 25
      1028 "Salome" (Severed Head)   18 - 22   22 - 25
   Marke J.S.C.
      6082 "Charmeuse de Serpents" (Snake)   15 - 18   18 - 22
PODKOWINSKI   (Poland)
   Nude on wild Horse   18 - 22   22 - 25
REINACKER, PROF. G.   (Germany)
   PFB
      6082 "Schlangen-Bandigerin" (Snake)   15 - 18   18 - 22
   Marke J.S.C.
      6082 Same as above
ROTHAUG, ALEX   (Germany)
   LP   2815 "Pan and Psyche" (Man-Beast)   15 - 18   18 - 22
   W.R.B. & Company   No. 4 "Nymphe"   12 - 15   15 - 18
ROWLAND, FR.   (G.B.)
   SVD   379 "Sirenen" (Snakes)   18 - 22   22 - 25
ROYER, L.   (France)
   Salon de Paris   374 "La Sirene" (Death Head)   12 - 15   15 - 18
RÜDISÜHLI, EDUARD
   K.E.B.   "The Demon of Love"   12 - 15   15 - 18
SAMSON, E.   (France)
   A.N., Paris
      243 "Diane" (Wolf Dogs)   15 - 18   18 - 22
SCALBRET, J.
   S.P.A.
      48 "Leda & the Swan"   10 - 12   12 - 15
SCHIFF, R.   (Germany)
   W.R.B. & Co.
      22-74 "Leda & the Swan"   15 - 18   18 - 22
      22-74 "Head in Clouds"   12 - 15   15 - 18
SCHIVERT, V.   (Germany)
   Arthur Rehn & Co.   "Die Hexe"   20 - 25   25 - 28
SCHMUTZLER, L.   (Germany)
   Russian Publisher, Richard
      245 "Salome" (Severed Head)   12 - 15   15 - 20

SCHNEIDER, S.   (Germany)

Little is known of the artist S. Schneider. His real photo and real photo-type images, mainly of male nudes being confronted by strange and eerie

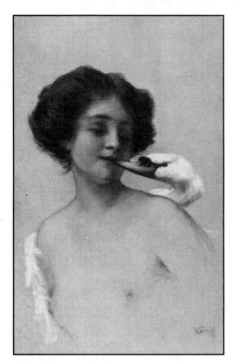

S. Schneider, Russian Publisher
No. 1245

R. Schiff, W.R.B. & Co. 22-74
"Leda and the Swan"

Jules Scalbret, S.P.A. 48
"Leda and the Swan"

supernatural animals and beings, have become extremely popular with the Fantasy postcard collector.

A large percentage of his works appeared on cards that were issued in Russia, and have divided and undivided Russian backs. However, many also have German, French and bilingual backs for use in other countries. Schneider's works are definitely "stranger-than-fiction" fantasy renditions, and many appear to emit implications of bondage in strange ways. For collectors who search for something different, this type material will be a fascinating change from the normal fare.

S. SCHNEIDER

182 Nude adorned with thorny shoots	30 - 35	35 - 40
1085 Flying man-bull and student		
1088 Supernatural animal, angel, corpse		
Death mourner and huge breasted beast		
1216 Nude with torch & eerie monster		
1235 Nude in chains & eerie monster		
1245 Nude bird-man with slave		

SCHUTZ, ERIC (Austria)
B.K.W.I. Poster Cards

41 "The Frog King" (Big Frog)	18 - 22	22 - 25
885 Goethe's "Der Fischer" (Mermaid)	30 - 35	35 - 40

885 "Der Gott und Der Baiadere"	20 - 25	25 - 30
979 "Die Forelle" (Mermaid)	30 - 35	35 - 40
205 Wagner's "Parsival"	15 - 18	18 - 22
557 "Lotusblume" (Nude in flower)	25 - 30	30 - 35
Series 165 (6) (Nudes on Giant Flowers)	25 - 30	30 - 35

SETKOWICZ
Music, Harp and Snakes	18 - 22	22 - 25

SIMONSON-CASTELLI, PROF.

Hans Friedrich
565 Nude and big snake	15 - 18	18 - 22

SOLOMKO, S. (Russia)

TSN
"The Blue Bird," "Circe," "Dream of Icarius,"	15 - 20	20 - 25
"Fortune Telling," "Glow Worm," "Phantasy"		
Semi-Nude in Peacock Feathers	18 - 20	20 - 25
"The Tale"		

STANKE, W. (Germany)

S.W.S.B.
4776 "Das Marchen" Nude with horse	10 - 12	12 - 15
4777 "Das Geheimnis" Nude with horse		

STELLA, EDUARD (Germany)
B.R.W. 354 "Diana" (Dogs)	18 - 22	22 - 25

STRNAD, JOS. Anonymous 255 "Nymphe" 12 - 15   15 - 18

STUCK, FRANZ VON (Germany) 10 - 12   12 - 15

STYKA, JAN (France)
Lapina 810 "Good Friends" (Horse)	10 - 12	12 - 15

SZYNDIER, P. (Poland)
Mal. Polske 22 "Éve" (Snakes)	20 - 25	25 - 30

THOMAS "Leda" Nude and Swan 12 - 15   15 - 18

VEITH, E. (Austria)
B.K.W.I. 1101 "Teasing" (Man-Goat)	10 - 12	12 - 15

WACHSMUTH, M. 10 - 12   12 - 14

WARZENIECKI, M.

WILSA
90 "Une Nouvelle Esclave" (Death)	12 - 15	15 - 18

WOLLNER, H. (Austria)
B.K.W.I. 1101 "Sadismus" (Death Head)	12 - 15	15 - 18

ZANDER (Germany)
S.S.W.B. 4790 "Sieg der Schonheit" (Tiger)	12 - 15	15 - 18

ZATZKA, H. (The Netherlands)
Panphot, Vienne 1284 "La Lerle"		
(Nude in Large Oyster Shell)	15 - 18	18 - 22

ANONYMOUS

Russian
Real Photo 752 Nude with Snake	18 - 22	22 - 25
Real Photo No No. Centaur and Nude		

MERMAIDS

The mermaid was a mythical creature that lived in the seas and streams. According to popular belief they had bodies that were half human and half fish. Their beauty and mystique, as they sang and combed their long hair, was a great attraction for mortal men. A magical cap always lay beside them, and when the man they wanted appeared they would slip the cap on his head and take him away with them. A human being could live in the sea by wearing this cap. There were, on the other hand, mermen who also captured mortal maidens.

Through the years, mermaids and mermen have continued to be painted or dramatized in art and poetry. Certain sea animals; e.g., seals, look a little like humans from a distance. This similarity may explain the myths related to them.

The most beautiful mermaids on postcards are the works of Eric Schutz and Sofia Chiostri, "The Mermaid" series by Raphael Tuck, the Art Nouveau series by Gaston Noury, and the great early anonymous German chromolithographs. All are extremely scarce and are in great demand. Although there is no actual mermaid (with the upper body of a girl and lower body of a fish) shown, the Detroit Publishing Co. "Mermaid" series by S. L. Schmucker must be placed in this section. This series of six, with various fish and heads of beautiful ladies, are masterworks of art, and the best by any U.S. artist.

ADOLF, T. (Germany)	15 - 18	18 - 22
ATTWELL, MABEL LUCIE (G.B.)		
Valentine & Sons 951 (With Black Doll)	25 - 30	30 - 35
E.B. (Germany)		
M. L. Cartlens, Hamburg		
Series 5508 "Ein Guter Fang"	15 - 18	18 - 22
BENEZUR "Der Kampf"	16 - 18	18 - 22
BERNHARD, L. (Austria)		
Karl H. Detlefsen		
Series 3156 B&W "Ein Stelldichen"	12 - 15	15 - 18
BÖCKLIN, A. (Germany)		
F. Bruckmann AG		
"Play of Naiads"	12 - 15	15 - 18
"Im Spiel der Wellen"		
BOISSELIER (France)		
Salon des Paris 1143 "Les Nerides"	8 - 10	10 - 12
BRUNNER		
Art Moderne Series 715 (6)	12 - 15	15 - 18
BUXTON, DUDLEY (G.B.)		
Bamforth Co. "Ye Gods: It's the Missus!"	8 - 10	10 - 12
CARTER, REG. (G.B.)		
Max Ettlinger & Co.		

Series 4453 (Diver Series) (6)		
"A Diver walked along one day..."	18 - 22	22 - 25
"They fell in love..."		
"Things cannot go on like this..."		
"They went for a walk..."		
"But true love not always runs smooth..."		
"Her father passed by that way..."		
CHIOSTRI, SOFIA (Italy)		
Ballerini & Fratini		
Series 238 Cupid and Mermaid (4) Deco	50 - 60	60 - 75
Series 317 (4) Deco		
CLAY, JOHN CECIL (U.S.)		
Alfred Schweizer		
Gibson Karte 1018 No Caption, Sepia	15 - 18	18 - 22
COT, WILLIAM (France)		
AN, Paris Real Photo #224	15 - 18	18 - 22
DUBOSCLARD, PAUL (U.S.)		
M.A. Sheehan (Serigraphs)	10 - 12	12 - 15
FITZPATRICK (G.B.) **Bamforth & Co.**	8 - 10	10 - 12
FULLER, EDMUND G. (G.B.)		
"Midsummer Nights Dream" Series	15 - 18	18 - 22
GEO. Valentine's "Mr. Popple sees a Mermaid"	15 - 18	18 - 22
GIBBS, MAY (Australia)		
Western Mail Postcards (B&W)		
"Pearling in the Norwest"	80 - 90	90 - 100
GIRARDOT, GEORGES (France?)		
Societe des Artistes Francais		
"Siren at the mirror" (R.P.)	12 - 15	15 - 18
GOHLER, H.		
"Rishar" Russian		
566 "Du Nixlein Wunderhold..."	30 - 35	35 - 40
GRIMM (Austria)	12 - 15	15 - 18
GUILLAUME, ALBERT A. (France)		
A.N., Paris "The Wreck"	20 - 25	25 - 30
Art Moderne Series 764 "Seetrift"	18 - 20	20 - 25
GUTMANN, BESSIE PEASE		
Rishar (Russian) Russian Caption		
99 "Die Perle"	75 - 85	85 - 100
100 "Wasserlilie"		
H.F.	10 - 12	12 - 15
H.N.		
Rud. Stolle 472 "Kuste bei Georgenwalde"	10 - 12	12 - 15
IRWIN	6 - 8	8 - 10
JACOBS, HELEN (G.B.)		
C. W. Faulkner Series 1764 (6)	18 - 22	22 - 25
KASPARIDES "Bath of Water Fairy"	15 - 18	18 - 22
KENNEDY, C. N. (G.B.)		
Leeds Gallery "The Mermaid"	5 - 6	6 - 8

B. Gutmann, Russian Rishar 100
"Wasserlilie"

B. Gutmann, Russian Rishar 99
"Die Perle"

KIRCHNER, RAPHAEL (Austria)
Anonymous "Flussnixe"	150 - 200	200 - 250
Marque L-E "Ondine"	100 - 125	125 - 150

KLEY, H. (Germany)
EDM 366 "Rheingold, Rheingold!" (B&W)	10 - 12	12 - 15

LA PIERRE-RENOUARD (France)
Lapina, Paris 1312 "Idyll"	12 - 15	15 - 18

LEEKE, F. (Germany)
Munchener Kunst
3116 "De Taufe des Fawn"	15 - 18	18 - 22

LIEBENWEIN, M. (Austria)
B.K.W.I. 1028 "Der Verrufene Weiher"	18 - 22	22 - 25

LUPIAC, A. P. (France)
A.N., Paris 79 "Centaur and sea-maid"	25 - 28	28 - 32
M. I. W. de Haan Series 1020 (6) (B&W)	10 - 12	12 - 15

MARAPAN
Vetta "The Neptune Myth" (1945)	10 - 12	12 - 15

MILLER, HILDA T. (G.B.)
C. W. Faulkner Series 1822 (6)	22 - 25	25 - 30

MUNSON, WALT (U.S.)
Tichnor (Linen) 70327 "Fresh Guy"	6 - 8	8 - 10
E. C. Kropp (Linen)		
C43 "Believe it or not"		

NOURY, GASTON (France)
Anonymous Series (8) Chromolithos	125 - 150	150 - 175

O'NEILL, ROSE (U.S.)
Gibson Art Co.
96014 "For the Rainy Day"	40 - 45	45 - 50

OUTHWAITE, IDA R. (Australia)
A. & C. Black, London
Series 73 "Playing with Bubbles"	25 - 30	30 - 35

PAPPERITZ, G. (Germany)
Real Photos 151-12	10 - 12	12 - 15

M.E.P. (PRICE, MARGARET EVANS) (U.S.)
C.M. Klump
Zodiac, Pisces (February & March)	12 - 15	12 - 18

PRINTZ, HANNS (Austria)
   T.S.N. Series 1370 "Das Rheingold"   40 - 45   45 - 50
RICHARDSON, AGNES (G.B.)
   Photochrom Co.
     2018 "Now I've caught you"   20 - 25   25 - 30
ROTHAUG, ALEX (Germany)
   W. R. B. Co. No. 4 "Nymphe"   20 - 22   22 - 25
SADKO (Russia) "Canko" and Alexander III   20 - 25   25 - 30
SAGER, XAVIER (France)
   Big Letter Card "Un Baiser D'Ostende"   25 - 30   30 - 35
SCHMUCKER, S. L. (U.S.)
   Detroit Publishing Co., 1907
     "Mermaid" Series (6)
     Fish and girl facing front   200 - 225 225 - 250
     Trout and girl facing left
     Sea Horse and head of beautiful girl
     Fish and girl facing right
     Lobster and head of beautiful girl
     Goldfish and head of beautiful girl
SCHMUTZLER, L. (Germany)
   Hanfstaengl Co.   18 - 22   22 - 25
SCHREKHASSE, P. (Germany)
   S. Hildesheimer & Co., Series 5317 (6)   8 - 10   10 - 12
   Hans Kohler, Series 329 (6)   12 - 15   15 - 18
SCHUTZ, ERIC (Austria)
   B.K.W.I. Poster Cards
     203   "Flame of Love"   30 - 35   35 - 38
     391-3 Heine - "Der Mond ist ..."
     434-4 Andersen's Märchen
     766-2 Schubert - "Das Wasser ..."   35 - 40   40 - 50
     885-5 Goethe - "Der Fischer"
     979-5 Schubert - "Die Forelle"
SHINN, COBB and **YAD** (U.S.)
   Anonymous (B&W)   10 - 12   12 - 15
SOLOMKO, SERGE (Russia)
   T.S.N.
     93 "The Tale"15 - 18   18 - 25
STUDDY, GEORGE E. (G.B.)
   Bonzo Series by Valentine's
     Series 2982 "I'm a poor fish..."   12 - 15   15 - 18
TOLNAY (Hungary)
   Rotophot, Budapest
     "Die Quelle" (B&W)   15 - 18   18 - 22
WARNER, CHET (U.S.) Linens   8 - 10   10 - 12
WEISS, R. (Switzerland)
   A.W.R., Zurich "Auf Der Meersgrund"   12 - 15   15 - 18
WELLMAN, WALTER (U.S.)
   1026 "Beauty isn't all on the surface"   10 - 12   12 - 15

Six of Eight Cards from the Exquisite Anonymous Series of Chromolithic Mermaids by the French Artist, Gaston Noury

WHITE, FLORA (G.B.)
   W. E. Mack, Hampstead "The Little Mermaid" 18 - 20   20 - 25
   Photochrom Co. "Who are You?"
   J. Salmon Co. (6) (Uns.) 3820 "My Hat"   18 - 22   22 - 25
WILKIN, BOB   6 - 8   8 - 10
WINK
   L.P.   2772 "Auf Stiller Flut"   12 - 15   15 - 18
WIWEL, KIRSTEN (Germany)
   Eneret   **Series 5047** (6) 1950's   8 - 10   10 - 12

PUBLISHERS
   American P. C. Co. Series 1319 (6)   10 - 12   12 - 15

E.S.D. "Wagner" Series (Uns. Stassen)

Series 8158 Scenes from Opera "Seigfried"	25 - 30	30 - 35
Series 8159 From Opera "Das Rheingold"		
No captions	30 - 35	35 - 40
Series 8160 (Embossed) (6)		
Scenes from "Das Rheingold"		
Series 8164 Scenes from Opera "Löhengrin"	25 - 30	30 - 35

S. Hildeshimer & Co.

Andersen's "The Little Mermaid"	20 - 25	25 - 30

E. S. Lyon Series 122 (B&W) 8 - 10   10 - 12

M. N. Co., 1910

Unsigned and Unnumbered (10)

"Come around and play with me"	20 - 22	22 - 25
"Every Queen needs a King"		
"I want you and I want you right away"		
"If music be the food"		
"I'm leading an easy life"		
"I'll take another chance"		
"I'm going some nowadays"		
"I's Oo's little mermaid"		
"I'm hooked at last"		
"I'm looking for a partner"		
"Just meet me at the same old place"		
"Tag - You're it!"		

M.&L.G.

National Series, Untitled

Art Nouveau -- With Seashell	25 - 30	30 - 35
Mutoscope Co. Navy comics with mermaids	4 - 5	5 - 6

P.F.B. in Diamond

S/R. Kammerer Series 6097	12 - 15	15 - 18
Percy, McG. Mann, Philadelphia (B&W)	10 - 12	12 - 15
S.W.S.B. Children Series	8 - 10	10 - 12
Salis, München (UndB) Chromolithos	40 - 50	50 - 60

Theo. Stroefer

Series IV 314 Mermaid in shell	15 - 18	18 - 22
H. H. Tammen "Here's to the girl..."	8 - 10	10 - 12

Curt Teich Linens

3C-H549 Ad for Shedd Aquarium	12 - 15	15 - 20

Tichnor Bros.   Linens

"What I saw at..."	8 - 10	10 - 12

Raphael Tuck

Series 3027 "Fun at the Seaside" (6)	12 - 15	15 - 18
Series 6822 "Mermaid" Series (6)	30 - 35	35 - 40
Series 694 "Wagner" Series "Rhine Gold"	30 - 35	35 - 40

Typo, Boston

207 "There's something fishy"	6 - 8	8 - 10

Anonymous

Art Nouveau Series 643 (6)	50 - 55	55 - 65

R. Tuck, 6822
"Mermaid"

S.W.S.B., 9209
No Caption

Copenhagen Statue (Early Real Photo)		
"La Petite Sirene"	4 - 5	5 - 6
1 er Avril (French April Fool) Montage	15 - 20	20 - 25
Japanese back, Unknown Artist	40 - 50	50 - 60
Montage (B&W)		
Series 12, #2, Girl's head/Mermaid body	15 - 18	18 - 22
Private Mailing Card (Chromolitho)		
Mermaid & Singing Frog	60 - 70	70 - 80
Real Photo Montage	18 - 22	22 - 25
Color Montage	15 - 18	18 - 22
Silhouette Poster "Die Rheintochter"	20 - 25	25 - 30
Series 643 German Chromolithos		
"Wassernixen" (6)	60 - 70	70 - 80
ADVERTISING		
Ackers Chocolates	30 - 35	35 - 40
Fish & Chips (A California Dish)		
Longshaw Card Co. Linen	12 - 15	15 - 18
Hartman Litho	10 - 12	12 - 15

SUPERIOR WOMEN/LITTLE MEN FANTASY

COLLINS, SEWELL		
Henderson & Sons		
"**Humorous**" Series B-8	10 - 12	12 - 15

Sewell Collins, Henderson & Sons
B-8, "'Play'-things"

C. Giris, ATV, Paris
135-2, "Domination"

FASCHE, TH.   (Germany)
  M. Munk, Vienna

"Diabolo" Series (6)	15 - 18	18 - 22

GIRIS, C.   (France)
  ATV, Paris

Series 135 (6) 2 "Domination"	20 - 25	25 - 28

KYOPINSKI
  Peter Triem   Little Men   (6)

162 "Der Schuchferne"	12 - 15	15 - 18
163 "Der Eifersuchfige"		

KURDNEY, F.   (Austria)
  M. Munk, Vienna

Series 556, 606, 699 (6)	12 - 15	15 - 20

  N.F.

Series 160-165 (6)	10 - 12	12 - 15

MAUZAN, L.   (France)

Series 83, Little Men (6)	12 - 15	15 - 18

PEANITSCH, LEO
  L.P.

Series 105 "Ihr Spielzeug" Silhouettes	15 - 20	20 - 25

PENOT, A.

Lapina Little Men Series (6)	15 - 18	18 - 22

SAGER, XAVIER

Series 43 Soldiers/Little Women (6)	18 - 20	20 - 25
SCHEUERMANN, W. (Germany)		
S.W.S.B.		
Series 6582 "Proving his hearts"	10 - 12	12 - 15
SCHÖNPFLUG		
B.K.W.I. **Series 4132** (6)	10 - 12	12 - 15
TAM, JEAN (France)		
Marque L.E. 70-4	18 - 22	22 - 25
VINCENTINI (Italy)		
Deco Ladies in Spider Webs, Little Men	15 - 18	18 - 22

PUBLISHERS

B.G.W. **Series 123/1233** (6)	8 - 10	10 - 12
Marks, J. **Series 155 "Summer Girl"** (8)	10 - 12	12 - 15
B.K.W.I. **Series 136** (6)	8 - 10	10 - 12
WBG **Series 123** (6)	7 - 8	8 - 10

TEDDY BEARS

The lovable and ever-popular Teddy Bears are very much in demand by postcard collectors who search for both artist-signed, unsigned, and real-photo types. Many great sets and series were published during the 1905-1914 era, both in the U.S. and Europe, and are extremely popular with today's fantasy enthusiasts. A considerable number in this group are unsigned and, because of inadequate records by publishers, the artists have not been identified.

Collectors are indebted to Teddy Roosevelt and the U.S. press for the Teddy Bear. We are told that Mr. Roosevelt was invited to go bear hunting by some of his friends. After some period of time with no apparent success in finding bear meat, someone supposedly spotted one, but it turned out to be a little cub. Roosevelt refused to shoot the bear, and afterwards the press picked up on this unusual story of "Teddy's Bear." Thus, the Teddy Bear legend was born and the fad grew worldwide.

Books were written about the adventures of Teddy Bear, and toys and novelties of all types were generated. Publishers of postcards also took advantage of the terrific interest in the new fad. The resulting output of collectible cards was enormous, and many remain for the collectors of today. The "Roosevelt Bears," named after the President, are perhaps the most recognized of the sets or series and "The Cracker Jack Bears" are perhaps the most popular.

BAUMGARTEN, FRITZ (FB) (Germany)		
Meissner & Buch Series 1974	12 - 15	15 - 18
BEM, E. (Russia)		
Russian "Rishar"	20 - 25	25 - 30
Russian Red Cross Soc. (St. Eugenia)		
Other Russian Publishers		

Lapina, Paris	15 - 20	20 - 25

BUSY BEARS (12)

J. I. Austen Co.	15 - 18	18 - 22

    427 Monday (Washing)
    428 Tuesday (Ironing)
    429 Wednesday (Cleaning)
    430 Saturday (Mopping the Floor)
    431 Thursday (Mending)
    432 Saturday (Sewing)
    433 "Learning to Spell"
    434 "Playing Leap Frog"
    435 "Off to School"
    436 "Getting it in the Usual Place"
    437 "Something Doing"
    438 "Vacation"

CAVALLY BEARS (Nursery Rhymes)

  CAVALLY, FRED (U.S.)

Thayer Publishing Co., Denver	18 - 22	22 - 25

    "See-saw, Margery Daw"
    "Rain, rain, go away"
    "To make your candles last for aye"
    "Cock crows in the morn"
    "Little Red Snooks was fond ..."
    "What are little Ted Boys made of?"
    "As I went to Bonner"
    "Nose, nose, jolly red nose"
    "Dame Bear made a curtsy"
    "Wash me, and comb me"
    "Ding dong bell"
    "Little Ted Grundy"
    "Teddy be nimble"
    "Multiplication is vexation"
    "Tell Tale Tit!"
    "Little Ted Horner"

ROSE CLARK BEARS (12)

  CLARK, ROSE (U.S.)

Rotograph Co., N.Y.	18 - 22	22 - 25

    307 "Bear Town Cadet"
    308 "Is That You Henry?"
    309 "Henry"
    310 "The Bride"
    311 "The Groom"
    312 "A Bear Town Sport"
    313 "A Bear Town Dude"
    314 "I'm Going a-Milking"
    315 "I Won't be Home ..."
    316 "C-c-come on in"
    317 "Fifth Avenue"
    318 "Hymn No. 23"

F.B. (Fritz Baumgarten), Meissner & Buch 1974

COLLINS BAKING CO. (4)		25 - 30	30 - 35
CRACKER JACK BEARS (16)			
B. E. MORELAND (U.S.)			
Rueckheim & Eckstein			
1	At the Lincoln Zoo	30 - 40	40 - 50
2	In Balloon	30 - 35	35 - 40
3	Over Niagara Falls		
4	At Statue of Liberty		
5	At Coney Island		
6	In New York		
7	Shaking Teddy's Hand (Roosevelt)	35 - 45	45 - 50
8	At Jamestown Fair		
9	To the South	35 - 40	40 - 45
10	At Husking Bee		
11	At the Circus		
12	Playing Baseball	45 - 50	50 - 60
13	Cracker Jack Time	35 - 40	40 - 50
14	Making Cracker Jacks		
15	At Yellowstone		
16	Away to Mars		
CRANE BEARS CRANE, D. P. (U.S.)			
H.G.Z. & Co. (ZIM)			
"Days of the Week" (7)		15 - 18	18 - 22
"Months of the Year" (12)		18 - 22	22 - 25
DENSLOW, W. W. "TEDDY BEAR" BREAD (4)			
Kolb's Bakery			
1	"Is there anything in it?"	30 - 45	45 - 60
2	"I'll See!"		

D. P. Crane, H.G.Z. & Co.
Days of the Week -- "Sunday"

Cracker Jack Bears, Rueckheim
& Eckstein 8, "On Ship Board..."

3 "Why, It's 'Teddy Bear' Bread!"		
4 I'll buy it!"	50 - 60	60 - 75
DOGGEREL DODGER BEARS		
WHEELAN, A. R. (U.S.)		
Paul Elder Co. (6)		
"This Bear's Witness..."	18 - 22	22 - 25
Others		
ELLAM BEARS		
B. Dondorf		
Series 347 (6) No Captions	15 - 18	18 - 22
Series 370 (6)	18 - 22	22 - 25
Raphael Tuck		
Series 9793 (6)	15 - 20	20 - 25
Series 9794 (6)		
Others		
FEIERTAG, K. (Austria)		
B.K.W.I. Series 609	12 - 15	15 - 18
HAHN BEARS		
SHEARER (U.S.)		
Albert Hahn Co. (A.H. in Trademark) (8)		
"En Route"	10 - 12	12 - 15
"Happy"		
"In Court"		
"In War"		

Denslow, Kolb's Bakery
"Is there anything in it?"

Rose Clark, Rotograph Co. 312
"A Bear Town Sport."

Denslow, Kolb's Bakery
"I'll See!"

"Just too Late"
"Look Pleasant"
"On Duty"
"Painting the Town"

HEAL DAYS OF THE WEEK
William S. Heal (U.S.)

"Sunday" Going to Church	10 - 12	12 - 15
"Monday" Washing Clothes		
"Tuesday" Ironing		
"Wednesday" Mending		
"Thursday" Baking		
"Friday" House Cleaning		
"Saturday" Shopping		
Same Series in Leather	12 - 15	15 - 18

HILDEBRANT (G.B.)
Raphael Tuck
Series 9792

Teddy Bears (6)	15 - 18	18 - 22

HILLSON DAYS OF THE WEEK
D. Hillson

"Monday" Washday	10 - 12	12 - 15
"Tuesday" Ironing		
"Wednesday" Mending		
"Thursday" Baking		

"Friday" Cleaning
"Saturday" Shopping
"Sunday" Church

KENNEDY, A. E.   15 - 18   18 - 22
    C. W. Faulkner & Co., Ltd.
      "Somebody's been sitting on my chair!"

LANGSDORFF BEARS
    G. S.
      Teddy Bear Orchestra, No. 4   15 - 20   20 - 25

LITTLE BEARS
    Raphael Tuck
      Series 118 (12)   20 - 25   25 - 30
      "A Morning Dip"
      "A Very Funny Song"
      "Breaking the Record"
      "Kept in at School"
      "Missed Again"
      "Oh! What a Shock"
      "Once in the Eye"
      "The Cake Walk"
      "The Ice Bears Beautifully"
      "The Jolly Anglers"
      "Tobogganing in the Snow"
      "Your Good Health"

MARY'S BEARS
    C.L. (U.S.)
    Ullman Mfg. Co. (4)
      Series 119 (4)
      "Mary had a little bear..."   10 - 12   12 - 15
      "Everywhere that Mary went..."
      "It followed her to school one day..."
      "It made the children laugh..."

McLAUGHLIN BROS. BEARS
    McLaughlin Bros.   15 - 18   18 - 22

MOLLY & TEDDY BEARS
    GREINER, M. (U.S.)
    International Art Co.   Series 791 (6)   15 - 18   18 - 22

OTTOMAN LITHOGRAPHING BEARS
    Ottoman Lithographing Co., N.Y.   15 - 18   18 - 22
      "Come Birdie Come"
      "Good Old Summertime"
      "Is Marriage a Failure?"
      "Many Happy Returns"
      "Never Touched Me"
      "Please Ask Pa"
      "Right Up-To-Date"
      "Well, Well, You never can Tell"
      "Where am I at?"

K. Feiertag, B.K.W.I. 609-2
"La Fille à l'Ours."

Anonymous, Wildt & Kray 1838
No Caption

"Will She Get the Lobster"

PILLARD (U.S.)
   S. Langsdorf & Co. Series 730

Teddy at Golf	22 - 25	25 - 28
Teddy at Soccer	18 - 22	22 - 25
S. S. PORTER BEARS (6)	8 - 10	10 - 12

ROMANTIC BEARS
   M.D.S. (U.S.)
   Ullman

Series 88 (4)	15 - 18	18 - 22

     1950 "Too Late"
     1951 "Who Cares?"
     1952 "The Lullaby"
     1953 "A Letter to My Love"

ROOSEVELT BEARS
   E. Stern Co. (First Series, 1906)

1 "At Home"	25 - 30	30 - 35

     2 "Go Aboard the Train"
     3 "In Sleeping Car"
     4 "On A Farm"
     5 "At a Country School"
     6 "At the County Fair"
     7 "Leaving the Balloon"
     8 "At the Tailors"

9 "In the Department Store"
10 "At Niagara Falls"
11 "At Boston Public Library"
12 "Take an Auto Ride"
13 "At Harvard"
14 "On Iceberg"
15 "In New York City"
16 "At the Circus"
Second Series
17 "Out West"   60 - 70   70 - 80
18 "Put out a fire"
19 "At the Wax Museum"
20 "At West Point"
21 "As Cadets"
22 "In New York"
23 "In Philadelphia"
24 "At the Theatre"
25 "Swimming"
26 "At Independence Hall"
27 "Celebrate the Fourth"
28 "At the Zoo"
29 "Go Fishing"
30 "Bears on a Pullman"
31 "Hunters"   80 - 90   90 - 100
32 "At Washington" (With Roosevelt)   35 - 40   40 - 50
Third Series (no captions)
17 "Lighting Firecracker" (horizontal)   250 - 275   275 - 300
18 "Celebrating the Fourth" (horizontal)
19 "Waving Flags"
20 "Ringing Liberty Bell"
No No. Series
Roosevelt Bears in Canada   250 - 275   275 - 300
Roosevelt Bears in England
Roosevelt Bears in Ireland
Roosevelt Bears in Scotland
Roosevelt Bears in Switzerland
The Roosevelt Bears "Return from abroad"
ROWNTREE, HARRY (G.B.)
  C. W. Faulkner & Co. Series 236 (6)
  "I am collecting"   22 - 25   25 - 28
  "I am coming up to see you"
  "I'm feeling a bit off color"
  "The Weather is Perfect"
  Others
  Williston Press
    Same images as Series 236   15 - 18   18 - 22
SPORTY BEARS
  M.D.S. (U.S.)

Ullman Mfg. Co.   Series 83 (7)

1923 "Love All"	12 - 15	15 - 18
1924 "Here's for a Home Run"	15 - 18	18 - 22
1925 "Out for Big Game"	10 - 12	12 - 15
1926 "King of the Alley"		
1927 "A Dip in the Surf"		
1928 "An Unexpected Bite"		

ST. JOHN BEARS   ST. JOHN
Western News Co.

161 "Spring"	12 - 15	15 - 18
162 "Summer"		
163 "Autumn"		
164 "Winter"		

V.O.H.P. Co.
Series X40

Days of the Week (7)	10 - 12	12 - 15

TEMPEST, MARGARET
Medici Society

Series 61 (6)	10 - 12	12 - 15

TOWER TEDDY BEARS

Tower M. & N. Co. (30)	10 - 12	12 - 15

"Beary Well, Thank You"
"But We Are Civilized"
"Did You Ever Wear..."
"Don't Say a Word"
"Here's to the Stars and Stripes ..."
"Hurrah for - Eagle"
"Hurrah for the..."
"I'm Waiting For You"
"Our Birth, You Know"
"We Wear Pajamas"
"You Don't Say"
Others

T. P. & CO. TEDDY BEARS

T. P. & Co.	10 - 12	12 - 15

"Out for Airing"
"I Wonder if He Saw Me?"
"Isn't He a Darling"
"How Strong He Is"
"Oh! My! - He's Coming!"
"Off for the Honeymoon"
"Little Girl with Teddy"
"Dolly Gets an Inspiration"
"Lost, Strayed, or Stolen"

TWELVETREES BEARS
TWELVETREES, CHARLES

National Art Co. (6)	10 - 12	12 - 15

206 "Little Bear Behind"
207 "Stung"

Real Photo, ca 1915

Bernhardt Wall, Ullman Co. 1907
"Tuesday"

208 "The Bear on Dark Stairway"
209 "How can you Bear this Weather?"
210 "A Bear Impression"
211 "The Seashore Bear"

National Art Co.

271 "It's Up to You"	10 - 12	12 - 15

WALL, BERNHARDT

Ullman "Busy Bears" Series 79	10 - 15	15 - 18

1905 Sunday
1906 Monday
1907 Tuesday
1908 Wednesday
1909 Thursday
1910 Friday
1911 Saturday

Ullman "Little Bears" Series 92	12 - 15	15 - 18
WELLS BEARS (7)	8 - 10	10 - 12

ANONYMOUS

(Vine Through Post Card) Flat Printed

241 "I am in a whirl"	6 - 8	8 - 10

242 "I'm certainly enjoying myself"
243 "I never expected to meet you"
244 "Oh my but you are sweet"
245 "I have not had much luck so far"

Real Photo, AZO
Twins and their Teddy Bear

246 "I am not going anywhere..."
247 "The joys of a bachelor's life"
248 "It was a touching scene"
249 "Stuck again"
250 "I have been hunting for you"

REAL PHOTO TEDDY BEARS

With Children (Large Bears)	25 - 35	35 - 45
With Children (Small Bears)	20 - 25	25 - 30
With Ladies (Large Bears)	18 - 22	22 - 28
With Ladies (Small Bears	12 - 15	15 - 20
Bears Alone (Large)	15 - 20	20 - 25
Bears Alone (Small)	12 - 14	14 - 16
Bears and Movie Stars	10 - 12	12 - 15

OTHER ARTIST-SIGNED TEDDY BEARS

With Children (Large Bears)	10 - 15	15 - 20
With Children (Small Bears)	8 - 12	12 - 15
With Ladies (Large Bears)	10 - 12	12 - 18
With Ladies (Small Bears)	8 - 12	12 - 15

Additional listings of Bears can be found under "Bears" in the Dressed Animals Section.

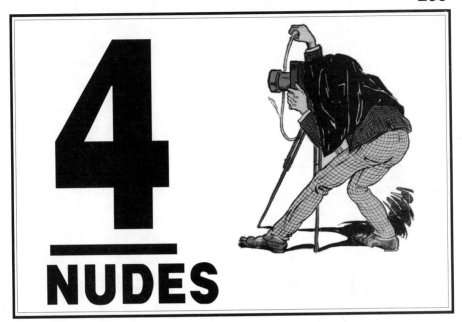

NUDES

COLOR NUDES

Color nudes have now been discovered! For many years color nudes were completely neglected by the American postcard collector. Until recently, the only issues available were those of the Great Masters' reproductions of paintings from big museums and art galleries throughout the world. Stengel Art Co. of Dresden, Germany was the major publisher.

These museum reproductions gave color nudes a bad impression and repressed their growth until it was finally realized that there were hundreds of other beautiful nudes and semi-nudes that were not museum reproductions. During postcards' Golden Years, European artists—especially the French and Germans—painted beautiful nudes relating to mythical, historical, Biblical, fairy tales, and fantasy motifs that were beautifully adapted to postcards. These cards have become highly collectible and are pursued by many American deltiologists.

Since there was no demand in the United States from 1900 to 1920, color nudes by American artists are very rare. Therefore, most all of the nudes listed here are from Europe. Many artists painted only a limited number of different nudes; therefore, very few sets or series are available. Nude Fantasy types of most all artists are very desirable. Beginning to catch on also are the Real Photo types of some of the more prominent works.

	VG	EX
ALLEAUME, L.		
Lapina		
59 "In the Rose"	$15 - 18	$18 - 22
201 "Offering"	12 - 15	15 - 20
ASTI, ANGELO		
JL & W 36/25, No Caption, Unsigned	15 - 20	20 - 25

Salon 1897, "Songeuse" — 18 - 22 — 22 - 25
AUER, R.
Salon J.C.Z. 4 "Tender Flower" — 15 - 18 — 18 - 22
1 "Delight" — 12 - 15 — 15 - 18
AXENTOWICZ, T. (Poland)
ANCZYC
10 "Noc" — 20 - 25 — 25 - 30
110 "Noc" — 18 - 20 — 20 - 25
D.N. 29 "Studjum"
BARBER, COURT (U.S.)
S.& G.S.i.B
1283 "Nach dem Bade" — 12 - 15 — 15 - 20
1284 "Der Goldene Schal"
BEAUFEREY, M. LOUISE (France)
A.N., Paris 89 "The Rest" — 12 - 15 — 15 - 18
BECAGLI, P. (France)
Salon de Paris "Paressguse" — 12 - 15 — 15 - 20
BENDER, S.
H.M., "La Femme" Series (12) — 15 - 18 — 18 - 22
MEYER-BERNBURG, A. (Germany)
O.G.Z-L, 1132 "Erwacht"
BERNHARD, LEO (Germany)
"Bachante" — 12 - 15 — 15 - 18
BIESSY, GABRIEL (France)
Salon de Paris "The Model" — 12 - 15 — 15 - 20

J. Cayron
Lapina 5433, "Repose"

Mme. Th. Croy, Lapina
"The Model"

BORRMEISTER, R. (Germany)
  Herman Wolff
    1128 "Morgengruss"   12 - 15   15 - 18
    1093 "Wald Marchen"
    1094 "Versuchung"   15 - 18   18 - 22
BOTTINGER, H. (Germany)
  J.P.P. 1074 "Marchen"   12 - 15   15 - 18
BOULAND, M. (France)
  A.N., Paris 446 "Femme a l'echape"
BRICHARD, X. (France)
  A.N., Paris 404 "After the Bath"
BRUNNER (Germany)   15 - 18   18 - 22
  Art Moderne 717 "Wassernymphe"
BUBNA, G. (Germany)
  Hermann Wolff 1135 "Ein Neugierger" 10 - 12   12 - 15
BUKOVAC, V. (Czech)
  Minerva
    21 No Caption
    28 "Koketa"
  Lapina 825 "The Dream of Love"
BUSSIÈRE, GASTON (France)
  Salon de Paris 744 "Salome"   10 - 12   12 - 15
CAYRON, J. **Lapina** 5433 "Repose" 12 - 15   15 - 18
CHANTRON, A. J.
  Salon de Paris 993 "The Bind Weed" 12 - 15   15 - 20
  A.N., Paris 38 "Spring"
  Lapina 5016 "Woman with a Parrot"
CHAPIN
  Stengel 29920 "Souvenirs"   8 - 10   10 - 12
CHERY "The Source"   12 - 15   15 - 18

J. Corabceuf, A. N., Paris, "Awaking"

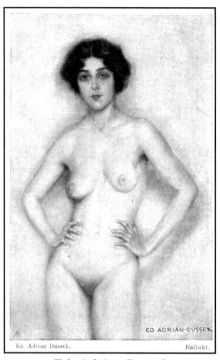 

Ed. Adrian Dussek
Kilophot Co., J.K. 66, "Halbakt"   *Ed. Adrian Dussek*
Kilophot Co., J.K. 67, "Erwachen"

COLLIN, R. **Lapina** 408 "Floreal"	8 - 10	10 - 12
COMERRE, LEON		
Palais des Beaux Arts "The Golden Rain"	10 - 12	12 - 15
A.N., Paris 164 "While the Artist ..."	8 - 10	10 - 12
Musee de Luxembourg		
411 "The Spider"	10 - 12	12 - 15
CORABCEUF, J. **A. N., Paris,** "Awaking"	18 - 22	22 - 25
COURTEN (France)		
Salon J.P.P. 1015 "La Source"	15 - 18	18 - 22
COURTOIS, G. **Lapina** 526 "La Lecture"	10 - 12	12 - 15
CROY, Mme. Th. (France)		
Lapina 5289 "The model"		
CROZAT **Galerie d'Art** 117 "Apres le bal"	12 - 15	15 - 20
CUNICEL, EDW. **O.F.Z.-L** "Coquetry"	10 - 12	12 - 15
CZECH, E. (Bulgaria)		
"Apollon Sophia" 70 "Temptation"	10 - 12	12 - 15
DE BOUCHE, A.		
E.K.N. 1050 "The New Ornament"	8 - 10	10 - 15
DERVAUX, G. (France) **Lapina** 5412 "Naughty"	10 - 12	12 - 15
DEWALD, A.		
Emgre-Sabn 229 "Eve"	12 - 15	15 - 20
DOLEZEL-EZEL, P. (France)		
F.H. & S. 5221 No Caption	10 - 12	12 - 15
DOMERGUE, JEAN-GABRIEL (France)		
A. N. Paris Real Photo Art Deco Nudes	30 - 35	35 - 40
(Also see Artist-Signed)		

DUPUIS, P.
    Hanfstaengel 199 "The Wave"   12 - 15   15 - 18
DUSSEK, ED. ADRIAN (Austria)
    Kilophot Co.

JK18	"Das Neue Modell"	15 - 18	18 - 22
JK25	"Modelpause"	12 - 15	15 - 20
JK51	"In Gedanken"	15 - 18	18 - 22
JK52	"Im Atelier"	20 - 22	22 - 25
JK53	"Studie"		
JK54	"Das Model"	12 - 15	15 - 20
JK55	"The Hat"	15 - 18	18 - 22
JK56	"Studie"	18 - 20	20 - 25
JK57	"The Model"	12 - 15	15 - 20
JK58	"The Hat"	15 - 18	18 - 22
JK59	"In Gedanken"		
JK60	"Schwuller Tag"	12 - 15	15 - 18
JK61	"Koketterie"	15 - 18	18 - 22
JK62	"Die Gold Gube"		
JK63	"Vertraumt"		
JK64	"Jugendstil Akstudie"	18 - 20	20 - 22
JK65	"Im Abendlicht"	15 - 18	18 - 22
JK66	"Halbakt"	25 - 28	28 - 32
JK67	"Erwachen"	18 - 22	22 - 25
JK68	"Blonder Akt"	22 - 25	25 - 28
JK69	"Frosch Koenigs Bride"	25 - 28	28 - 32
JK70	"Gross Toilette am Land"	12 - 15	15 - 18

DU THOIT (France)
    A.N., Paris 338 "Fair Haired Woman"   15 - 18   18 - 22
EICHLER, MAX
    O.G.Z-L 291 "Nach Dem Bade"   12 - 15   15 - 18
EINBECK "Nana"
ENJOLRAS, D. (France)
    Lapina
        718 "Repose"   12 - 15   15 - 20
        "Ruth"   10 - 12   12 - 15
        "Rest"
        1401 "Nude"   12 - 15   15 - 20
        1696 "Pearls"
EVERART, M.
    A.N., Paris 7 "The Woman With Ribbons"   12 - 15   15 - 18
    E.S., Paris 37 "On the Telephone"
    SPA
        4059 "The Woman With Lamp"   10 - 12   12 - 15
        76 "Young Woman at Mirror"   12 - 15   15 - 20
FAR-SI (France)
    A.N., Paris "Oriental Perfume"   12 - 15   15 - 18
FAUGERON, A. (France)
    Lapina, Paris
    5913 "Nayade"   12 - 15   15 - 18
FEIKL, S. (Germany)
    J.K.P. 236 "Akt"   10 - 12   12 - 15
FENNER-BEHMEL, H.
    Hanfstaengel's 194 "Ysabel"   15 - 18   18 - 22

FERRARIS, A.V. (Austria)
B.K.W.I. "Leda"	12 - 15	15 - 18
FOURNIER "Woman Bathing"	10 - 12	12 - 15

FREAND, E. (France)
Lapina 5415 "Familiar Birds"	8 - 10	10 - 12

FREISKE (France)
Lapina 546 "A Woman Sleeping"	12 - 15	15 - 18

FRIANT, E. (France)
Salon de 1911 "Forest's Echo"

FRIEDRICH, OTTO (Austria)
B.K.W.I. 1541 "Eitelkeit"	10 - 12	12 - 15

FRONTE, M. (France)
Lapina "Woman Lying Down"	12 - 15	15 - 18

FUCHS, RUDOLPH (Germany)
W.R.B. & Co.
738 "Blaue Augen"	10 - 12	12 - 15

GALAND, LEON
Salon de Paris "A Sleeping Woman"	12 - 15	15 - 18

GALLELLI, M.
P. Heckscher
143 "The First Pose"	10 - 12	12 - 15

GEIGER, C. AUG.
NPG 453 "Eva"	10 - 12	12 - 15
GERMAIN "First Session"	12 - 15	15 - 18

GERVEX, HENRI (France)
Palais des Beaux-Arts
261 "Birth of Venus"	10 - 12	12 - 15

GITTER, H. (Germany)
Galerie Munchen Meister
"Morgen"	8 - 10	10 - 12
"Tag"	6 - 8	8 - 10

GLUCKLEIN, S. (Germany)
Hanfstaengel's 202 "Reposing"	10 - 12	12 - 15

GLUCKLICH, S. (Germany)
Herman Wolff 1188 "Quellnymphe"	15 - 18	18 - 22

GODWARD, J.W.
Russia **Richard**
295 "A Fair Reflection"	10 - 12	12 - 15

GOEPFART, FRANZ
301 "Ruhender Akt"

GOROKHOV
N.P.G., Berlin "Wassernixe"	12 - 15	15 - 18

GRENOUILLOUX, J. (France)
Lapina
"The Fair Summer Days"	12 - 15	15 - 18
"The Nymph with Flags"		

Apollon
78 "Speil der Wellen"	8 - 10	10 - 12

Salon de Paris
"The Nymph with Flags"	12 - 15	15 - 18

GSELL, HENRY (France)
A.N., **Paris** 435 "Summer"

GUETIN, V.
Lapina 799 "Das Bad"	8 - 10	10 - 12

Henry Gsell, A. N., Paris
435, "Summer"

O. Herrfurth, N.P.G.
489, "An der Quelle"

GUILLAUME, R.M.
  Lapina
    1400 "The Repose of the Model"   8 - 10   10 - 12
    1083 "Rapid Change"   10 - 12   12 - 15
    1523 "Rubbing the Leg"
  Soc. des Artistes 58 "The Fly"   8 - 10   10 - 12
A.H.
  K.th W.II 636 "Lybelle"   10 - 12   12 - 15
HERRFURTH, O. (German)
  N.P.G. 489 "An der Quelle"   15 - 18   18 - 22
HERVÉ, GABRIEL (France)
  Lapina
    44 "Resting"   12 - 15   15 - 20
    813 "Farniente"   12 - 15   15 - 18
    "My Model and My Dog"   8 - 10   10 - 12
HEYMAN, RICHARD
  Heinrich Hoffman "Psyche"   10 - 12   12 - 15
HILSER (Czech)
  Minerva
    83 No Caption   10 - 12   12 - 15
    1130 "Siesta"
HOESSLIN
  NPG 491 "Die Schaumgeborene"   12 - 15   15 - 18
JANUSZEWSKI, J. (Poland)
  ANCZYC
    185 "Akt"   10 - 12   12 - 15
    455 No Caption

JOANNON, E. (France)

Salon de Paris 5331 "Lassitude"   15 - 18   18 - 22

KÄMMERER, PAUL

E.M.M. Poster 255 "Frühling"   25 - 28   28 - 32

KASPARIDES, E.

B.K.W.I.

161-4 "A Warm Summer Morning"   8 - 10   10 - 12

164-3 "The Airbath"   10 - 12   12 - 15

164-10 "Forest Silence"   8 - 10   10 - 12

Others

KIESEL, C.

A.R. & C.i.B 463 "Salome"   8 - 10   10 - 12

KLIMES

Minerva 1227 "Nymphe"   10 - 12   12 - 15

KNOBLOCH, J.R.

O.G.Z.-l 1700 "Tired"

KNOEFEL (Germany)

Novitas

668 (4) Illuminated Nudes   15 - 18   18 - 22

866 (4) Illuminated Nudes

KORPAL, T.

ANCYZ 16 Bather "Au Ete"   10 - 12   12 - 15

KOSEL, H.C. (Austria)

B.K.W.I.

181-3 "Kungstgeschlchte"   8 - 10   10 - 12

181-8 "Nach im Bade"

181-9 "Lekture"

181-10 "Sklavin"   10 - 12   12 - 15

KRENNES, H. C1-12 "Danse"   8 - 10   10 - 12

KRIER, E.A. (France)

Salon de Paris 5379 "Folly at Home"

KUTEW, CH.

Frist

Series 90, 8 No Caption   10 - 12   12 - 15

Series 90, 10 No Caption   12 - 15   15 - 18

A.F.W.

111-2 "Ondine"   10 - 12   12 - 15

"Nymph"   12 - 15   15 - 18

LANDAU, E.

Lapina 979 "Putting things in order"   10 - 12   12 - 15

LANDROW, F. (Germany)

S.V.D. 416 "Meereslockung"

LANZDORF, R.

R. & J.D. 501 "Young Bedouin Girl"   8 - 10   10 - 12

LAURENS, P.A. (France)

Lapina 2032 "Didon"

LEEKE, F. (Germany)

Munchener Kunst

3114 "Bad de Bestalin"   12 - 15   15 - 18

Hans Koehler & Co.

76 "Bacchantalin"

LEFEBRE, J.

Salon J.P.P. 2215 "Es werde Licht!"   15 - 18   18 - 22

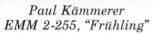

Paul Kämmerer
EMM 2-255, "Frühling"

M. Muller, Anonymous
6, "Le Peignoir-Chemise"

LEFFEBURE, J.
  Musee de Luxembourg
    500 "Woman Warming Herself"   6 - 8   8 - 10
LENDIR P. Heckscher 366 "Die Sofe"   10 - 12   12 - 15
LENOIR, CH. (France)
  Lapina 853 "Stream Song"   12 - 15   15 - 18
  A.N., Paris 19 "Tanzerin"   8 - 10   10 - 12
L'EVEIL (France)
  Salon 1914 304 "The Awakening"   12 - 15   15 - 18
LIEBERMAN, E. (Germany)
  Emil Kohn 890 "At the Window"   8 - 10   10 - 12
LINGER, O. (Germany)
  G. Liersch & Co.
    537 "Susses Nichtshen"   10 - 12   12 - 15
LOUP, EUF. (France)
  A.N., Paris 292 "Study"   18 - 22   22 - 25
LUCAS, H.
  Lapina 890 "Happy Night"   10 - 12   12 - 15
MAKOVSKY, C. (Russia)
  Russia 539 "Dans ie Boudoir"
MALIQUET, C. (France)
  Lapina "Voluptuousness"   12 - 15   15 - 18
  Salon de Paris
    56 "At the Hairdresser"   10 - 12   12 - 15
MANDL, JOS.
  Salon J.P.P. 2056 "L'Innocence"   8 - 10   10 - 12

MARECEK
   KV 1335   "Nach dem Bade"   8 - 10   10 - 12
   VKKA 1201   "Toileta"   6 - 8   8 - 10
MARTIN, F. (Germany)
   AR & CiB 395   "Vom dem Spiegel"   8 - 10   10 - 12
MARTIN-KAVEL
   Lapina
      "Nude on Tiger Rug"   8 - 10   10 - 12
      934   "Surprised"
MAX, G. (Bulgaria)
   Apollon Sophia   68   "Bacchante"   10 - 12   12 - 15
MENZLER, W. (Germany)
   NPG   512   "Akt"   8 - 10   10 - 12
MERCIER
   Art Moderne
      748   "Nymphe Endormie"   10 - 12   12 - 15
      "Nymph Reclining"
MERLE, K.
   Moderner Kunst 2355   "After the Bath"   8 - 10   10 - 12
MIASSOJEDOW, J.
      224 Russian   "Arabian Tanzerin"   12 - 15   15 - 18
MOHN, ROTER
   Moderner Kunst
      245   "Feuerlilien"   8 - 10   10 - 12
      246   No Caption
MORIN
   Salon J.P.P.   1124   "Feu Follet"   8 - 10   10 - 12
MÜLLER, A.
   Anon. Watercolor No. 6   "Le Peignoir-Chemise"   25 - 30   30 - 35
MÜLLER, RICH.
   Malke & Co.
      25   "My Models"   18 - 22   22 - 25
   SPGA
      251   "Gold Fish"
      252   "Der Rote Ibis"
   Others
NAKLADATEL, J.
   Salon J.P.P.
      440-445 (6)   Semi-Nudes   15 - 18   18 - 22
NEJEDLY   Salon J.P.P.   "Erwachen"   10 - 12   12 - 15
NEMEJC, AUG.   Polish   "Tragedie"   8 - 10   10 - 12
NISSL, RUDOLF (Germany)
   Novitas 388   "Akt im Mantel"   10 - 12   12 - 15
NONNENBRUCH, M. (Germany)
   Salon J.P.P. 2187   "La Sculpture"
   O.G.Z.-L. 1174   "After Dancing"
   Hanfstaengel's 49   "Flora"
OSTROWSKI, A.J. (Russia)
   Russian, **Rishar** 2172   "The Model"   12 - 15   15 - 18
OTTOMAN   Lapina   "The Sleeping Courtesan"   8 - 10   10 - 12
PAPPERITZ, G. (Bulgaria)
   Apollon
      84   "Boa Neuf"   12 - 15   15 - 18
      237   "Bayadere"

A. Penot, Lapina
1226, "The Charm of Spring"

A. Penot, Lapina
1227, "A Young Girl"

Hanfstaengel's 197   "Chrysanthemums"   12 - 15   15 - 18
PAUSINGER   Russian   063 "Salome"   15 - 18   18 - 22
PENOT, A.
   Lapina
     "Water Flower"   15 - 18   18 - 22
     "Bayadera"
     "Libelle"   10 - 12   12 - 18
     1223   "Repose"
     1226   "The Charm of Spring"   12 - 15   15 - 20
     1227   "A Young Girl"
     1340   "Red Butterfly"
     1345   "The Fur Stole"   15 - 18   18 - 22
   A.N., Paris
     27   "Frolicsome"
     229   "Repose"
     408   "Fariente"
PERRAULT   (France)
   Salon de Paris
     727   "Der Erste Mai"   12 - 15   15 - 18
   S.V.D.
     291   "Einheisser Sommertag"   12 - 15   15 - 20
     292   "Das Kunstler Modell"
PIOTROWSKI, A.   **Minerva**   1028 "Salome"
PRICE, J. M.
   Hanfstaengel's   117   "Odaliske"   12 - 15   15 - 18

R.R.
M. Munk Series **684** (6)	18 - 22	22 - 25

RASCH, PROF. (Germany)
N.P.G. 42 "Akt"	10 - 12	12 - 15
Series **873** (6)	18 - 22	22 - 25

REINACKER, G. (Germany)
M.K.B.
2517 "Triumphant Love"	12 - 15	15 - 18

Marke JSC
6054 "Am Morgen"	10 - 12	12 - 15
6055 "Verkauft"	12 - 15	15 - 18
6083 "Der Neue Schmuck"		
PFB 6034 "Die Favoritin"	10 - 12	12 - 15

REIFENSTEIN, LEO (Germany)
Galzburger Kunst 45 "Schönhut"	12 - 15	15 - 18

RETTIG, H. (Germany)
Munchener Meister 568 "Im Spiegel"	10 - 12	12 - 15

RIESEN, O. (Germany)
A. Sch. & Co. 7152 "Unschuld"		
S. & G. S.i.B. 1471 "Am Morgen"	12 - 15	15 - 18

RITTER, C.   Novitas 397 "Im Gotteskleid" | 10 - 12 | 12 - 15 |

ROTMANNER, ALFRED (Germany)
Hans Kohler 71 "Beim Lampenschein"

ROUSSELET, E. (France)
Lapina
1129 "Bathing"	12 - 15	15 - 18
"The Dream"	8 - 10	10 - 12

ROUSTEAUX-DARBOURD
Salon 1912 571 "Am Feuer"	10 - 12	12 - 15

SAIZEDE
Lapina "A Woman & Statuette"	8 - 10	10 - 12

SALIGER
Haus der D. Kunst "Die Sinne"	10 - 12	12 - 15

SCALBERT, J.
A.N., Paris
422 "The Shift"	8 - 10	10 - 12

Lapina
795 "The Toilet"	10 - 12	12 - 15
1329 "An Ugly Fellow"		
5158 "Hesitation"	10 - 12	12 - 15
SPA 30 "Satisfaction"	8 - 10	10 - 12

Salon de Paris
1570 "Five O'Clock Tea"	10 - 12	12 - 15
5085 "The Looking Glass"		

SCIHLABITZ, A.   NPGA 30 "Akstudie"
SCHIVERT, V.
TSN 801 "Der Liebestraube"	6 - 8	8 - 10

NPG
237 "Susanne"	10 - 12	12 - 15
238 "Akt"	12 - 15	15 - 18

Munchener Kunst
193 No Caption	12 - 15	15 - 18
199 No Caption		
PFB 42291 "Das Modell"	15 - 18	18 - 22

Arthur Rehn & Co.
   "Die Quelle"   15 - 18   18 - 22
   "Die Rivalin"   12 - 15   15 - 18

SCHLEMO, E.
  TSN
    888   "Schonheit ist alles"   12 - 15   15 - 18
    889   "Beauty"   10 - 12   12 - 14

SCHLIMARSKI, H.
  B.K.W.I. 1805   "Vanity"   10 - 12   12 - 15

SCHMUTZLER, L.
  O.G.Z.L. 364   "Courtezan"   15 - 18   18 - 22
  E.N. 810   "Passion"

SCHNEIDER, E.
  "Die Windsbraut"   10 - 12   12 - 15
  NPGA 54   "Halbakt"
  AMAG Kunst 51   "Bacchantin"

SCHUTZ, E. (Austria)
  B.K.W.I.
    Series 165 (4)   22 - 25   25 - 30
    885-1   Gothe's "Der Got und Baidere"   15 - 18   18 - 22

SCHWARZSCHILD, A.
  Munchener Kunst "Ball Spiel" 10 - 12   12 - 15

SEEBERGER, J.
  A.N., Paris
    368   "A Dragon-Fly"   18 - 20   20 - 22
    466   "After the Bath"   10 - 12   12 - 15
    470   "Smit with Love"   12 - 15   15 - 18

SEIGNAC, G. (France)
  A.N., Paris
    "Gachucha"   8 - 10   10 - 12
    470   "Smit with Love"   12 - 15   15 - 20
    597   "A Sprightly Girl"   10 - 12   12 - 15
    760   "Indolence"   12 - 15   15 - 20
  Art Moderne 760 "Indolence"
  Lapina "The Birth of Venus"

SEZILLE, D.E. (France)
  Lapina 913 "Annoying Accident"

SIEFERT, PAUL (France)
  A.N., Paris "Diana"   15 - 18   18 - 22
  Salon de Paris 746, "Diana"

SKALA
  Minerva
    1069   "Susses Nichtstun"   10 - 12   12 - 15
    1117   "Eva"

SOLOMKO, SERGE (Russia)
  TSN 153   "Circe"   15 - 18   18 - 22

STACHIEWICZ, P. (Poland)
  Wydann. Salon
    152/23   "Kwiat Olean"
    152/24   "Zloty Zawoj"   12 - 15   15 - 18
    "Ruth"

STELLA, EDUARD
  BRW
    353   "Madame Sans Gene" 18 - 20   20 - 22

J. Seeberger, A. N., Paris
470, "Smit with Love"

A. Subbotin, Granbergs
577, "Im Harem"

354 "Diana"	18 - 20	20 - 22
STEMBER, N.K.		
Richard (Rishar) 1078 "Elegie"	18 - 20	20 - 25
Hanfstaengel's 56 "Jugend"		
STYKA, JAN (France)		
Lapina "Harmony in yellow"	15 - 18	18 - 22
STYKA, TADE (France)		
Lapina 183 "Cinquecento"	6 - 8	8 - 10
SUBBOTIN, A. (Russia)		
NPG 87 "Studie"	15 - 18	18 - 22
Granbergs, Stockholm		
577 "Im Harem"		
SUCHANKE		
VKKA		
1336 "Fruhlingslied"	6 - 8	8 - 10
SYKORA, G.		
G.Z. 032 "Der Necker"	8 - 10	10 - 12
TABARY, E. (France)		
A.N., Paris		
115 "An Actress"	12 - 15	15 - 18
139 "Curious"		
906 "The Pendant"		
TARDIEU, VICTOR (France)		
Salon de Paris 168 "Study in Nude"		
TOLNAY (Hungary)		
Rotophot, Budapest "Venus Anadyomene"		

P. Du Thoit, A.N., Paris
338, "Fair-Haired Woman"

Fr. Zmurko, Anczyg
448, No Caption

URBAN, J.
D.K. & Co. 678		12 - 15	15 - 20
J.P.P. 42		12 - 15	15 - 18

VACHA, L. Minerva 1170   "Suzanne"   8 - 10   10 - 12

VALLET, L. (France)
    Lapina
      2498   "The Gourmet"   15 - 18   18 - 22
      2506   "Luxury"
      2507   "Pride"

VASNIER, E.
    Lapina 779   "The Toilet"   12 - 15   15 - 18

VASSELON, H. (France)
    A. Noyer   "The Spring"   12 - 15   15 - 20

VEZIN, F.
    Salon J.P.P. 1004 "Danse aux voiles"

VOLKER, ROB. (Germany)
    Munchener Kunst
      385   No Caption   10 - 12   12 - 15
      386   No Caption

VOWE, P.G.
    MBK 2546   No Caption   8 - 10   10 - 12

WALLIKOW, F.B.
    GK. v., Berlin 432   "Reifers Obst"   10 - 12   12 - 15

WEBER, E. (Germany)
    B.K.W.I. 2363 "Akt"

WITTING, W. (Germany)		
S.V.D. 358 "Auf Freier Hohe"	12 - 15	15 - 18
Dresdner KK · "Jugend"	10 - 12	12 - 15
WOBRING, F. (Germany)		
S.W.S.B. 4771 "Morgentau"	10 - 12	12 - 15
ZIER, ED. (Germany)		
Russian, **Rishar** "La Siesta"	12 - 15	15 - 18
ZMURKO, FR. (Poland)		
ANCZYC		
291, 297, 355, 448, 516	12 - 15	15 - 20
280, 347, 449, 510, 648	10 - 12	12 - 15
ZOPF, C. (Germany)		
O.G.Z.-L 865 "Curious"	8 - 10	10 - 12
ZWILLER, A. (France)		
Salon de Paris "The Rest"	10 - 12	12 - 15

PUBLISHERS

STENGEL NUDES		
Various Artists	8 - 10	10 - 12

REAL PHOTO NUDES

Real photo nude postcards were first made famous by French publishers who selected bountiful beauties of the day to pose sans clothes. The more important publishing Salons were **AN, Corona, Noyer, PC, SAPI,** and **Super.** Others such as **AG, BMV, CA, ER, GP, JA, JB, JOPA, J.R., Leo, Lydia, MAH, SDK, S.I.C., S.O.L., Star, VC,** and **WA** added to the many cards produced.

Although not always the norm, many publishers used airbrushing to obliterate any pubic or underarm hair from the photos and painted on lingerie for the prudish buyers in some markets. Tinting, especially those by **S.O.L., Paris,** enhanced the eye appeal and quality of selected series but, for today's collector, these are not quite as popular as the untouched material.

The cards were usually published and sold in sets of 6, 10 or 12, and from these many classical nudes exist. Various studio props were used for background affect. Chairs, tables, chests with mirrors, hanging tapestries, vases, and statues were among the favorites.

The most popular nudes, however, are those that were not professionally posed...where hair was not airbrushed away, and therefore nothing was left to the imagination. Although the French did their share, cards of this particular type were produced mainly in Germany and Austria, and normally do not have publisher by-lines. A small number of cards in this group may also have been done in the United States. Many cards do not have postcard backs, but this apparently has not made a difference to collectors in relation to the pricing structure. It is becoming extremely hard to find good quality nudes and prices continue to rise.

Professionally Posed
Waverly, Paris, 514

Professionally Posed
Waverly, Paris, 514

Non-Professionally Posed

Full Frontal, with pubic hair	35 - 40	40 - 45
Semi-Nude, with underarm hair	25 - 30	30 - 35
Semi-Nude, no underarm hair in view	20 - 25	25 - 30
Rear View	15 - 20	20 - 25
Lesbian Types	25 - 30	30 - 35

Add $5 to $10 to above for nicely tinted cards.

Professionally Posed

Full Frontal, with pubic hair	25 - 30	30 - 35
Full Frontal, no pubic hair	20 - 25	25 - 30
Semi-Nude, with underarm hair		
Semi-Nude, no underarm hair	18 - 22	22 - 25
Rear View	15 - 18	18 - 20
Lesbian Types	20 - 25	25 - 30

Add $5 to $10 for nicely tinted images.

Cheese-cake Types, showing lingerie, etc.   10 - 15   15 - 18

AFRICAN AND ASIAN SEMI-NUDES

Ethnic African and Asian nude postcards continue to be very popular with collectors and there seems to be and abundent supply. A quality group entitled "Afrique Occidentale" appears to be the most popular. Cards are lightly colored and numbering has been seen from 1 up into the 1400's. The

Professionally Posed
Waverly, Paris, 119

Professionally Posed
P.C., Paris, 2060

Professionally Posed
S.O.L., Paris, 3221

Professionally Posed
J.A., Paris (No Airbrushing)

Egyptian Woman
L. Scortzis & Co., 439

Afrique Occidentale
53, "Fille Soussou"

name of the particular tribe and whether the pictured semi-nude is a maiden (fille) or a woman (femme) is usually captioned on each card.

The publishers **L & L** produced a colorful numbered series of Arabians, Algerians, Tunisians, etc., that are also very collectible. Others, titled "Scenes et Types," "Egyptian Types," and a group of "Deutsch Sud West Africa" natives by **Albert Aust**, are also commanding good prices from collectors interested in this type material.

Black and white or sepia copies of many series were also produced. These are not as popular and prices are around 50% less than those produced in color. Real photo types, if original, are priced higher.

Afrique Occidentale		
Filles	12 - 15	15 - 20
Femmes	10 - 12	12 - 15
Others	8 - 10	10 - 12
L & L	10 - 12	12 - 15
Scenes et Types		
Egyptian Types		
P/Albert Aust	12 - 15	15 - 20
Other Nationalities	8 - 10	10 - 15

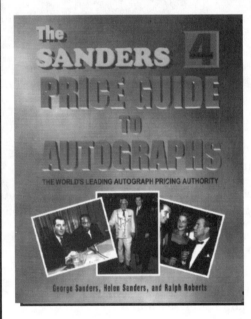

SOWERBY

Amy Millicent Sowerby was an English artist and illustrator of many wonderful children's books. Her most famous was Lewis Carroll's *"Alice in Wonderland,"* and afterward Robert Lewis Stevenson's *"A Child's Garden of Verse."* Wonderful illustrations of beautiful children, fairies, fairy tales and nursery rhymes also appeared on picture postcards that were intended for children, and they have become very desirable by all who collect these motifs.

Her cards all have precise detail, the colors are exceptionally bright, and the lithography is excellent. Most of Sowerby's cards were published in England by Henry Frowde and Hodder & Stoughton, Humphrey Milford, and by B. Dondorf in Germany. The American Post Card Co. and Reinthal & Newman, of New York, published several series for U.S. distribution.

SOWERBY, AMY MILLICENT (G.B.)

I. BEAUTIFUL CHILDREN

	VG	EX
B.D. (**B. Dondorf**, Frankfurt) (Art Deco)		
Series 130 (6)		
Little Girl with basket of apples	$20 - 25	$25 - 28
Others		
Series 154 Victorian Children (6)		
Little girls stand on stools		
Girl ties others shoes		
Others		
Series 168 (6)		
Girls having tea		
Others		
Series 169 (6)		

Misch & Co.
"Greenaway Girls" Series 833

B. Dondorf, Series 168
No Caption

B. Dondorf, Series 130
No Caption

C. W. Faulkner, Series 568
"It was a lover and his lass."

Henry Frowde and Hodder & Stoughton
"Playtime" Series -- "See-Saw"

Reinthal & Newman
(Chas. Hauff)
"Weather" Series, "Cold"

H. Frowde & Hodder & Stoughton
"Little Folk of Many Lands" Series
"Out of Reach"

Boy and girl take out washing	18 - 22	22 - 25
Mother-Daughter		
Series 170 (6)		
C. W. Faulkner & Co.		
Series 568 (6)		
"It was a lover and his lass"		
Others		
Henry Frowde and Hodder & Stoughton		
"Britain & Her Friends" (6)		
"Belgium," "England"	18 - 22	22 - 25
"France," "Portugal"		
"Russia," "U.S."		
"The Children's Day" Series (6)		
"Morning," "Mid-Morning"	15 - 18	18 - 22
"Noon," "Afternoon"		
"Evening," "Night"		
"Happy Little People" Series (6)		
"Union is Strength"	18 - 22	22 - 25
Others		
"Little Folk of Many Lands" Series (6)		
"England," "Holland," "Italy"	20 - 25	25 - 28
"Negro - North American"	25 - 30	30 - 35
"Russia," "Turkey"	20 - 25	25 - 28
"Little Jewels" Series (6)		
"Amethyst," "Emerald," "Pearl," "Ruby"	35 - 40	40 - 45

"Amethyst"   "Emerald"   "Pearl"

"Sapphire"   "Ruby"   "Turquoise"

THE BEAUTIFUL "LITTLE JEWELS" SERIES
PUBLISHED BY HENRY FROWDE AND HODDER & STOUGHTON

"Sapphire," "Turquoise"		
"Little Patriot" Series (6)		
"For the Soldiers"	20 - 22	22 - 25
"Playtime" Series (6)		
"Blind Man's Bluff," "A Three-Legged Race"	25 - 30	30 - 35
"A Tug of War," "Leap Frog"		
"See-Saw," "With Bat and Ball"		
"Pleasant Days" Series (6)		
"My Lady's Chair"	20 - 22	22 - 25
Humphrey Milford, London		
"Farmyard Pets" Series (6)	15 - 18	18 - 22
"I know you like some fruit"		
"Golden Days" Series (6)	15 - 18	18 - 22
"Guides and Brownies" Series (6) Scouts	20 - 25	25 - 28

"In Spring a gardening we go..."
"Happy Days" Series (6)
  "We've waited long to greet you"   15 - 18   18 - 22
  Others
"Happy as Kings" Series (6)
"Just" Series (6)
"Old Time Games" Series (6)
  "In Days of Old when John was King"   18 - 22   22 - 25
Meissner & Buch
  Series 1427 (6)
  Boy kisses girl's hand
Humphrey Milford, London (See Fairy Tales)
  Name of Series
  "Farmyard Pets" (6)
    "I know you like some fruit..."
  "Golden Days" (6)
  "Guides and Brownies" (6) Scouts
    "In Spring a gardening we go..."
  "Happy as Kings" (6)   12 - 15   15 - 18
  "Happy Days" (6)
    "We've waited long to greet you..."   15 - 18   18 - 22
  "Just" (6)
    "Just in time!"   10 - 12   12 - 15
    "Just-too-late!"
  "Old Time Games" (6)
    "In Days of Old, when John was King..."   15 - 18   18 - 22
Misch & Co.
  "Greenaway Girls"
  Series 833 (6)
  Girl with tea tray.   18 - 22   22 - 25
Reinthal & Newman, N.Y.
  Series 2001 (6)
    "Pamela," "Pat," "Peggy"   22 - 25   25 - 28
    "Phoebe," "Phyllis," "Priscilla"
  "Weather" Series (6) (Charles Hauff)
    "Cloudy," "Cold," "Dry"
    "Dull," "Fair," "Wet"

II. FAIRIES

Humphrey Milford, London
  "Bird Children" Series (6)
    "Good Gracious Me!..."   25 - 28   28 - 32
    "Hark, Mister Owl!..."
    "Kingfisher Green..."
    "When Robin Sings Above..."
    "When the First Star..."
    "When the First Swallows..."
  "Fairy Frolic" Series (6)
    "This Fay among the berries swings..."
    "The Summer Elves"
    "This Springtime Fairy Pipes..."
    "When Crocuses and Snowdrops Peep..."
    "When Winter Comes..."

Humphrey Milford
"Guides and Brownies" Series
"In Spring a Gardening We ..."

Frowde and Hodder & Stoughton
"Britain and Her Friends" Series
"Off to the War" (France)

"Flower Children" Series (6)
"Day-Lily," "Evening Primrose," "King-Cups"   25 - 28   28 - 32
"Love-in-a-Mist," "Pansies," "Snowdrop"
"Flower Fairies" Series (6)
"Says Jolly Red-cap in the Tree..."
"This Elf and Field-Mouse Play..."
"Flowers and Wings" Series (6)
"By Moonlight the Wood Fairies..."
"Daddy Longlegs, Flying Strong..."
"Grasshopper, Grasshopper..."
"Oh Bumble Bee..."
"Says Periwinkle Elf..."
"This Poor Little Elf..."
"Merry Elves" Series (6)
"At Dawn the Sun..."
"Hedgerow Elves in Roses..."
"This Baby Elf flew..."
"This Elf has found some Grapes..."
"Two Dicky Birds sat..."
"When the Mother Bird..."
"Peter Pan Postcards" Series (6)
"In the Lost Boys' Cozy Cave..."   22 - 25   25 - 28
"The Lost Boys..."
"Peter Pan is afloat on a nest..."
"To the Velvety Tree Tops..."
"Wendy and Joan and Michael..."

PETER PAN IS AFLOAT ON A NEST ~ ~ ~
YOU'LL SEE HE IS ONLY HALF DRESSED, ~
BUT THE NEVER-LAND BREEZE WILL NOT FAIL
WHEN HE HOLDS UP HIS COAT FOR A SAIL.

H. Milford, "Peter Pan Postcards"
"Peter Pan is afloat on a nest..."

DAY-LILY
I ONLY LIVE A SINGLE DAY, ~
AND NEVER SEE THE NIGHT; ~
BUT I AM ALWAYS GLAD AND GAY
MY FACE IS ALWAYS BRIGHT! ~

H. Milford, "Flower Children"
"Day-Lily"

'LARGE WHITE'
AND
CATERPILLAR

I'M THE FIRST BUTTERFLY OF SPRING,
WHEN HEDGES BUD AND THRUSHES SING
MY CATERPILLAR'S RATHER PALE ~ ~
HE'S FOND OF STANDING ON HIS TAIL.

H. Milford, "Pretty Wings"
"Large White" and Caterpillar

'ORANGE TIP'
AND
CATERPILLAR

IN ORANGE-TIPPED WINGS I AM DRESSED,
ON A KIND 'CATERPILLOW' I REST. ~ ~
HE AMIABLY CURLS ROUND HIS ENDS.
YOU SEE, WE ARE VERY OLD FRIENDS.

H. Milford, "Pretty Wings"
"Orange Tip" and Caterpillar

"Beauty & the Beast"

"Goldilocks"

"Cinderella"

"Little-Jack-Horner"

"Little-Bo-Peep"

"Little Boy Blue"

STORIES AND RHYMES FROM "FAVORITE NURSERY STORIES" AND "FAVORITE NURSERY RHYMES" -- PUBLISHED BY H. MILFORD

"When Peter Lost his Shadow..."		
"Pretty Wings" Series (6)		
"Brimstone" and Caterpillar	28 - 32	32 - 35
"Clifton Blue" and Caterpillar		
"Large White" and Caterpillar		
"Orange Tip" and Caterpillar		
"Peacock" and Caterpillar		
"Red Admiral" and Caterpillar		
"Sky Fairies" Series (6)		
"This Fairy got up in good time..."	25 - 28	28 - 32
"To See-Saw on a Sunbeam is..."		
"Two Sky Fairies are hiding..."		
"When Mr. Dustman scatters..."		
"Woodland Games" Series (6)		
"Listen Bun. We'll have some fun..."	20 - 25	25 - 28

Flower Children
"King-Cups"

Flowers and Wings
"Says Periwinkle
Elf ..."

"Shakespeare's
Heroines" -- "What's
Done is Done"

"Oh come and float on My..."
"The Rules of Fairy Leapfrog..."
"The Elf makes the Squirrels..."
"To swing over Poppies is Nice"
"Two Elves on the Wing..."
"Fairies Friends" Series (6)   22 - 25   25 - 30

III.   FAIRY TALES & NURSERY RHYMES

Humphrey Milford, London
   "Favourite Nursery Rhymes" (6)
   "Little-Bo-Peep,"   "Little-Jack-Horner"   25 - 30   30 - 35
   "Little-Miss-Muffet,"   "Mistress-Mary"
   "The-Piper's-Son,"   "Wee-Willie-Winkle"
   "Favourite Nursery Stories" (6)
   "The Babes in the Wood"
   "Beauty and the Beast"
   "Cinderella,"   "Goldilocks"
   "Jack and the Beanstalk,"   "Red Riding Hood"
   "Storyland Children" (6)
   "Little Boy Blue,"   "Little-Bo-Peep"
   "Little Miss Muffet,"   "Red Riding Hood"
   "Tom, the Piper's Son"

IV.   BEAUTIFUL LADIES

Humphrey Milford, London
   "Shakespeare's Heroines" (6)
   "A Maid so Tender, Fair and Happy"   25 - 30   30 - 35
   "And She is Fair..."
   "The Brightness of Her Cheek..."
   "From the East to Western..."
   "My Lady Disdain..."
   "What's Done is Done" *Macbeth*

6
SANTAS

Santa Claus is a mythical old man who visits at Christmas and brings toys and goodies to children who have been good. U.S. Santas are plump, jolly, wear red suits, with a twinkle to the eye. Depending on the country, European Santas are called Father Christmas, St. Nicholas, or Nicolo.

The German Father Christmas, or "Weihnachtensmanner," is thin, wears fur-trimmed robes of various colors, and sometimes has an angel to assist him on his many long journeys. He is sometimes seen carrying the Christ Child. However, most cards portray him as having a very stern countenance and he may be seen carrying switches to punish mean children. St. Nicholas and Nicolo have the impish devil Krampus as their helper.

Probably the most avidly collected cards of all time are Santas. In greatest demand are the early chromolithographs and embossed issues of German origin with robes of colors other than red. Robes of white, yellow, orange, black, and gray are the most desired. The outstanding works of A. Mailick, Hold-to-Light issues, and PFB and Winsch issues are also in great demand.

It is impossible to identify the countless number of great Santas because many are unsigned and do not have a publisher byline. Some have only a series number or "Printed in Germany" as the only means of identification. This is especially true of those not published for American distribution.

SANTAS, ST. NICHOLAS & KRAMPUS

ARTIST-SIGNED

	VG	EX
BOWLEY, A. L. (G.B.)		
Raphael Tuck		
Series 512 (6) (Unsigned)	$ 25 - 30	$ 30 - 35

Series C1758 , C2099		
Series 8437, 8449		
BRUNDAGE, FRANCES (U.S.)		
Raphael Tuck		
Series 4 (12)	20 - 25	25 - 28
Series 525, Santa Scroll Series (6)	12 - 15	15 - 20
Series 1822 (6)	30 - 35	35 - 40
Sam Gabriel		
Series 200, 300	15 - 20	20 - 25
BAUMGARTEN, FRITZ or F.B. (Germany)		
Comical Santas, various color robes	20 - 25	25 - 30
BEATY		
AH	8 - 10	10 - 12
CLAPSADDLE, ELLEN (U.S.)		
International Art		
Signed	18 - 22	22 - 25
Unsigned	15 - 18	18 - 22
Anonymous German		
Child Santa with Switches (Very Rare)	50 - 60	60 - 75
Other German unsigned issues	20 - 25	25 - 35
CHIOSTRI, SOFIA (Italy)		
Ballerini & Fratini		
Series 220 Black Robed Santa	50 - 60	60 - 75
Black Robed Father Time	40 - 50	50 - 60

R. Tuck, "Santa Claus" Series 512
"Wishing you a Merry Christmas"

John Winsch, © 1912
"A Joyful Christmas"

A. Mailick, W.W. 6670
Santa and Christ Child

Louis Wain, M. Ettlinger
Cat Santa Series, 5376

EBNER, PAULI (Austria)

B. Dondorf & M. Munk issues	25 - 30	30 - 35
FP Anonymous Publisher, Foreign Caption	175 - 200	200 - 225

GASSAWAY, KATHARINE (U.S.)

Raphael Tuck Series 501	20 - 25	25 - 40

HBG (H. B. GRIGGS) (U.S.)
   L & E
      Series 2224, 2264, 2275 (6)

Black Robe	30 - 35	35 - 40
Green or Brown Robe	25 - 30	30 - 35
Others	20 - 22	22 - 25

HARPER, R. FORD (U.S.)

Lady Santas (4)	30 - 35	35 - 45
HOGER, A. With Christ Child	30 - 35	35 - 40

HZONEY, CH. (Czech.)

Anonymous French Publisher (Black Santa)	110 - 120	120 - 130

KIRCHNER, RAPHAEL (Austria)

H & M Co. "Christmas" Series Santa	300 - 350	350 - 400
KÖHLER, MELA (WW) (Austria)	300 - 800	800 - 1000

MBH

R. Tuck Series 549 "Santa Claus" (6)	12 - 15	15 - 18

MEG

R. Tuck Series 535 "Santa Claus" (6)	10 - 12	12 - 15

MAILICK, A. (Germany)
   Hold-To-Light

Red Robe	150 - 250	250 - 350

D.R.G.M., Hold-to-Light Santa
Purple Robe

Robes of other Colors	250 - 300	300 - 400
Early Chromolithographs	25 - 50	50 - 100
W.W.		
Series 6308	65 - 75	75 - 85
Series 6670 (with Christ Child)	75 - 80	80 - 90
Red Robe	40 - 50	50 - 65
Robes of other Colors	65 - 75	75 - 100
St. Nicholas & Krampus Series	35 - 40	40 - 45
MAUFF, RICH. (Stengel Art Nouveau)	200 - 225	225 - 275
NYSTROM, JENNY (Sweden)		
Red Robes	15 - 18	18 - 22
Robes of other Colors	20 - 25	25 - 30
PHILLIPS, ART		
P. F. Volland & Co.	50 - 60	60 - 75
SANDFORD, H. D. (G.B.)		
Raphael Tuck Series 8247, 8248 (6)	18 - 22	22 - 25
SCHONIAN (Germany)		
T.S.N. Series 1090 Various Color Robes	30 - 35	35 - 40
SCHUBERT, H. (Austria) Various Color Robes	25 - 30	30 - 35
SHEPHEARD, E. (G.B.)		
Raphael Tuck Series 8415, 8421 (6)	15 - 18	18 - 22
WAIN, LOUIS (G.B.)		
M. Ettlinger		
Cat Santa Series 5226 (3)		
"Father Christmas disappointed"	300 - 350	350 - 400
"Father Christmas caught in snow"		
"Father Christmas finds his way blocked"		
Cat Santa Series 5376 (3) (Uns.)		
"A Jolly Christmas"	300 - 350	350 - 400
"A Merry Christmas"		

*HTL Uncle Sam Santa
Standing on Step*

*HTL Uncle Sam Santa
Trimming Tree*

"May Christmas Bring Good Luck"
Valentine & Sons
  "Santa Claus in Pussyland"   200 - 250   250 - 300
Wrench, Cat Santa Series
Anonymous (1)
  "With Best Wishes for a Happy Christmas"
GERMAN SANTAS (Anonymous)
  LARGE   FULL   FIGURES
    (Old World, thin figures)
      Black Robe   50 - 60   60 - 75
      Gray or White Robe   40 - 45   45 - 50
      Blue, Tan or Purple Robe   35 - 40   40 - 45
      Yellow or Orange Robe   45 - 50   50 - 60
      Brown or Wine Robe   30 - 35   35 - 40
      Striped, Two-color or Art Deco   45 - 50   50 - 60
      Red Robe   15 - 20   20 - 25
  HEADS, Upper Body or Small Image
    (Valued at 50%, or less, than Full Figures.)
HOLD-TO-LIGHT   (See Uncle Sam below)
  FULL FIGURES
    Red Robes   200 - 300   300 - 400
    Robes colored other than red   300 - 400   400 - 500
  HEADS, Upper Body or Small Image
    Red Robes   200 - 300   300 - 350
    Robes colored other than red   300 - 350   350 - 400
TRANSPARENCIES   75 - 100   100 - 125

Jmport, Series 2198
(Unsigned F. Baumgarten)

Jmport, 2508-1
Finnish Caption

Rich. Mauff, Stengel & Company (Chromolithograph)
Series 10, No. 23 (Brown Robe)

*J.E.P., Stecher Series 68-A
"Joy to You at Christmas Time"*

S.B., Series 135	*S.W.S.B., 8157 (Blue Robe)*	
Embossed, Brown Robe	*Varied Transportation*	

MECHANICALS

Honeycomb Folders	60 - 70	70 - 80
Pop-outs	35 - 40	40 - 45
Pull-tabs	250 - 300	300 - 400
Stand-ups	50 - 75	75 - 100
Wheel-type	200 - 250	250 - 300

SILK APPLIQUE

FULL FIGURES

Langsdorf	40 - 50	50 - 60
AMB	35 - 40	40 - 45
Others	25 - 30	30 - 35
SMALL FIGURES	15 - 20	20 - 25

UNCLE SAM SANTAS

(1) Flat-Printed (4)	600 - 650	650 - 750
(2) Embossed (4)	700 - 800	800 - 900
(3) Squeakers (4)	1600 - 1650	1650 - 1700
(4) Hold-to-Light (4)		
a. Santa Knocking on Door	2750 - 3200	3200 - 3800
b. Santa Trimming the Tree		
c. Santa Standing on Step		
d. Santa at Window (bag of toys)	3200 - 3500	3500 - 4200

PUBLISHERS

AA (Anglo American)

Series 705, 708, 709 (6)	12 - 15	15 - 20
AMB Silks	35 - 40	40 - 50

Jmport, 2780
"Herzliche Weihnachtsgrüsse"

Jmport, 2780
"Frohe Weihnachten"

AMP		
Modes of transportation	12 - 15	15 - 20
Others	8 - 10	10 - 12
ASB		
Series 87 Various color robes	30 - 35	35 - 40
Barton & Spooner	6 - 8	8 - 10
B.W., Germany		
Series 291, 296, 305, 324	15 - 18	18 - 20
Series 297	20 - 25	25 - 30
MAB		
Series 15850 Chromolithos	25 - 30	30 - 40
Julius Bien		
Series 500	10 - 12	12 - 15
Series 5000		
Cellaro (Scandinavian)		
Green Robed Santa (Drinking?)	25 - 30	30 - 35
R. L. Conwell	10 - 12	12 - 15
E.A.S.	20 - 25	25 - 30
Child Santas	30 - 35	35 - 40
Embossed German Santas		
Gibson Art	6 - 8	8 - 10
Sepia	5 - 6	6 - 7
International Art		
Signed Clapsaddle	18 - 22	22 - 25
Unsigned Clapsaddle	15 - 18	18 - 22
L&B		
Series 16284 (Blue-Gray Robe)	25 - 30	30 - 35

P.F.B., Series 6481
Brown Robe

S.W.S.B., 8650
Finnish Caption

Langsdorf
    Series 1320   20 - 22   22 - 28
    Silks   40 - 50   50 - 60
M.M.B.   15 - 18   18 - 22
J. Marks
    Series 538 (6)   5 - 8   8 - 10
Meissner & Buch
    S/F.B.   20 - 25   25 - 28
E. Nash
    Series 3 Heads, Smoking pipe   12 - 15   15 - 18
    Series 18
Nister, E.
    Series 2046 (6)   30 - 35   35 - 40
    Series 2409 (6) Small images   20 - 25   25 - 28
O.P.F.   40 - 50   50 - 65
P.F.B. **(Paul Finkenrath, Berlin)** (Emb.)
    Series 5431, 6227, 7933 (6)   40 - 45   45 - 50
    Series 7312, 6481 (6)   25 - 30   30 - 35
    Series 7930, 5434 (6)   20 - 22   22 - 25
    Series 6434, 9593 (6)   35 - 40   40 - 45
    Series 6439, 8935 St. Nicholas (6)   35 - 40   40 - 45
    Other St. Nicholas Series   30 - 35   35 - 40
    Other Santas   25 - 30   30 - 35
Robbins Bros.
    Series 1163 Old Style (6) (Emb.)   25 - 30   30 - 35
Rotograph Co.

E.A.S., Embossed, Green Robed
"Ein frohes Weihnachtsfest"

Cellaro, Scandinavian Green
Robed Santa, Taking a Drink?

R. Tuck, Series 598
Pine Cone Man Santa, "Joyeuse Noël"

H3025 Black Robe	60 - 70	70 - 80
SB Series 433, 7519 (6) Old Style	30 - 35	35 - 40
S&M		
Series 36 (6)	20 - 25	25 - 28
Series 149 "Big Sack" Series (6)		
Samson Bros.		
Series 31, 705 (6)	12 - 15	15 - 20
Series 3102	25 - 28	28 - 32
P. Sander		
Lady Santas (4) -- Signed Harper	30 - 35	35 - 40
Black Santa - No No. Full Figure	100 - 125	125 - 150
No No. Full Figure	15 - 18	18 - 22
Large Images	20 - 25	25 - 28
Silk Santas	30 - 40	40 - 50
Santway		
Large Images, various color robes	30 - 35	35 - 40
Series 1251 Small Images	10 - 12	12 - 15
Souvenir P.C. Co.		
Series 426 (6)	8 - 10	10 - 12
Stecher Litho. Co.		
Series 55, 1555 (6)	8 - 10	10 - 12
Series 61, 203, 314, 504, 732, 737 (6)	10 - 12	12 - 15
Series 68 (6) Uns. **James E. Pitts**	12 - 15	15 - 20
Series 213 (6)	12 - 15	15 - 18
Series 227 (6)	15 - 18	18 - 22
Reprints of 1930's, 40's	3 - 4	4 - 5
Stengel & Co.		
Rich. Mauff Series 10-23	200 - 225	225 - 275
S.W.S.B.		
Red Robes	20 - 22	22 - 25
Other Color Robes	30 - 35	35 - 40
Transportation	20 - 22	22 - 25
Raphael Tuck* **		
Series 1, 102, 8000, 8619	30 - 35	35 - 40
Series 5, "Kris Kringle"	10 - 12	12 - 15
Series 55, 1029, 1744	25 - 30	30 - 35
Series 1766 Chromolithos	40 - 45	45 - 50
Series 136, 501	10 - 12	12 - 15
Series 512, 535, 806	12 - 15	15 - 18
Series 598 (6) Pine Cone Man Santa	20 - 25	25 - 30
Series 505, "The Christmas Series"	25 - 30	30 - 35
White Robes	40 - 50	50 - 60
Series 576B	25 - 30	30 - 35
Colors other than red	30 - 35	35 - 40
Series 1803, 8267, 8320	15 - 18	18 - 22
Series 8263	25 - 30	30 - 35
Series 8620 Various Color Robes	25 - 30	30 - 35
No No. Series "Christmas Postcards"	10 - 12	12 - 15

* Most series contain cards of children.
* Most series contain 6 cards.

Ullman Co.		
National Santa Claus Series 2000	25 - 30	30 - 35
Valentine and Sons		
"Christmas in Coonland: We've come to..."	300 - 400	400 - 500

DRGM 88077
Purple Suit, with Angel

Art Phillips, P. F. Volland & Co.
"A Merry Christmas ..."

WB **Series 307**	10 - 12	12 - 15
George C. Whitney		
Full Santas	15 - 18	18 - 22
Small Figure Santas	8 - 10	10 - 12
John Winsch*		
Copyright 1912 - Vertical (4)		
Red Robe, yellow/gold background	25 - 30	30 - 35
"A Joyful Christmas"		
Red Robe, green background		
"A Merry Christmas"		
Santa on gold background		
"I Wish You a Merry Christmas"		
Orange Robe, blue background		
"May Your Christmas be Bright..."		
Copyright 1912 - Vertical (4)		
Children watch Santa in plane	18 - 22	22 - 26
"A Merry Christmas"		
Child watching Santa's shadow		
"A Joyful Christmas"		
Child watching Santa around chimney		
"Best Christmas Wishes" (Horizontal)		
Children see Santa coming from chimney		
"A Joyful Christmas"		
Copyright 1912 - Vertical (2)		
Red-Robed Santa with Teddy Bear and	35 - 40	40 - 45
Golliwogg at chimney		

Real Photo, P.R.H., 805
Brown-Tinted Robe

Real Photo
Anonymous, 150

"Best Christmas Wishes"
Santa in red jacket, blue-striped
    pants flying bi-plane
"A Happy Christmastide"
Copyright 1913 - Horizontal (4)
    Red Robe, Teddy Bear, Smokes pipe   40 - 50   50 - 60
    "Best Christmas Wishes"
    Red Robe, teddy bear, jack-in-box"
    "Christmas Greetings"
    Red Robe, with arm-load of dolls
    "Christmas Wishes"
    Red/Pink Robe carrying bag of fruit
    "Merry Christmas"
Copyright 1913 - Horizontal (4)
    Santa in airplane tosses toys to
        children on balcony   25 - 30   30 - 35
    "A Joyful Christmas"
    Santa in airplane tosses toys to
        children on ground
    "A Joyous Christmas"
    Children watch Santa in balloon basket
    "A Merry Christmas"
    Children on balcony watch Santa with
        toys in airplane
    "A Christmas Greeting"
Copyright 1913 - Vertical (2)
    Red Robe, driving car, big clock   25 - 30   30 - 35

Anonymous, 2018 (Red Robe)
St. Nicholas, German Caption

O.P.F., Comical St. Nicholas
Die Cut on Bark Background

  "Christmas Greetings"
  Santa driving motor bus
  "A Christmas Greeting"
  Red Robe, two Children...one on back
  "Best Christmas Wishes"
  Red Robe, kissing one of two children
  "A Joyful Christmas"
  Red Robe, one of two children whispers
  "A Merry Christmas"
 Copyright 1914 - Vertical
  Add-on, Santa and children on bell
 No Copyright Date
  Red & Gold Borders, Horizontal

Children greet Red Robe Santa at door	50 - 55	55 - 60

  "Christmas Wishes" -- No. 4164
  Children greeting Santa from bed
  "A Merry Christmas"
 * With Silk or Ribbon Inserts add $3-5.
REAL PHOTOS
 French & European

Black & White	10 - 15	15 - 18
Tinted	15 - 18	18 - 20
St. Nicholas	10 - 15	15 - 18
U.S. Real Photos	15 - 20	20 - 30
Tinted	20 - 25	25 - 35

OTHER SANTAS

Child Santas	20 - 25	25 - 35
Lady Santas	25 - 30	30 - 40

Santa W/Christ Child - Add $10.
Santa W/Switches - Add $5 - $10.
Santa W/Angels - Add $5.00.
Santa Switching Child - Add $5 - $10.
Santa W/Odd Transportation - Add $5 - $10.
    Airplanes - Add $5.
    Autos - Add $5.00
    Balloons - Add $5.00
    Boats, Canoes - Add $5.00
    Donkey - Add $6.00
    Motorcycle - Add $7.
    Parachute - Add $8.

Santas in Zeppelins	25 - 100	100 - 200

Santa W/Golliwogg - Add $10.
Santa W/Teddy Bear - Add $5.
Santa W/Krampus - Add $10 - $15.
Santa Smoking Pipe - Add $5.
Santa and Mrs. Claus - Add $10.

SAINT NICHOLAS, NICOLO

PFB Series 6439	25 - 30	30 - 35
Real Photo Types	10 - 12	12 - 15
Wearing Red/white Robe		
Full Figure	20 - 25	25 - 30
Small Figure, Head or Upper Body	10 - 12	12 - 15
Wearing Robes other than Red/White		
Full Figure	25 - 30	30 - 35
Small Figure, Head or Upper Body	15 - 18	18 - 22

KRAMPUS

Krampus was the impish devil with one cloven hoof who helped Saint Nicholas distribute toys, gifts, fruits, and nuts during the Christmas season, especially in Austria, Czechoslovakia and some other European countries. While traveling with Nicholas he played with and was good to the children who had been good. However, he always carried chains and a big bundle of switches, and made use of a large basket on his back to help in the storage and later punishment of children and adults who had been bad.

Those who knew they had been bad in any way quickly scurried away to escape his wrath. Krampus, however, chased and always caught them and put them in his basket. This terrified them, thinking they were going to be switched or thrown in the flames. The crying children or adults were later released after promising Krampus they would be on their best behavior during the coming year.

He was also painted as being very suave and debonair around the pretty ladies, and many cards imply that they welcomed his passionate advances toward them. However, it was not so with the older and ugly ladies. He usually made fun of them or threw them into burning flames.

The cards of Krampus, being part of the fantasy world, are highly desirable and very collectible. The early 1900's images, especially those signed by artists and without the red backgrounds, command very high prices. Cards by artists of the highly regarded Wiener Werkstaette and any containing Art Nouveau renderings are especially in demand, as are those with both Krampus and St. Nicholas together on the same card.

On early Krampus cards, collectors will find that many artists signed only their initials or did not sign them at all. Most of the red background cards are unsigned, making them less desirable. Krampus cards are a continuing tradition, much like our Santas, and are still being produced for each Christmas season. Therefore, collectors must be wary and be sure of the era of the cards they plan to buy. All listings below are pre-1930.

KRAMPUS

B.F.	12 - 15	15 - 18
BOURGET (Austria) Lady Krampus	30 - 35	35 - 40
BRAUN, W. H. (Austria)		
W.R.B. & Co. Series 22 (32)	25 - 30	30 - 35
C.B.		
Georg Wagrandl, Wien		
Russian Krampus teased by soldiers	30 - 35	35 - 40
CR		
A.R., Wien Girl Krampus	25 - 30	30 - 35
DIVEKY, JOSEF VON (Hungary)		
Wiener Werkstaette, 238	300 - 500	500 - 750
DOCKER, E. (Austria)		
Series 45 (6) K. & Nicholas Series	25 - 28	28 - 32
Series 83 Krampus & Nicholas Series (6)	20 - 25	25 - 30
DYLER **B.K.W.I.** **Krampus Series**	18 - 22	22 - 25
EBERLE, JOSEF (Austria)		
Deutschen Schulverein, 122	30 - 32	32 - 35
EBNER, PAULI (Austria)		
M. Munk Krampus and children (6)	25 - 30	30 - 35
ENDRODI (Austria)		
Lady Krampus plays Diabolo	22 - 25	25 - 30
F.G. K. jumps through fire	22 - 25	25 - 28
FASCHE, TH. (Germany) **M. Munk** Series 1086	20 - 22	22 - 25
G.L. Little Krampus looks down in basket		
GEL, H. (Austria)		
Mean Krampus with kids (6)	25 - 28	28 - 32
Silhouettes (6)	18 - 22	22 - 25
GELLARO	20 - 25	25 - 30
H. Series 234 (6)		
Krampus with old ladies	25 - 28	28 - 32
Krampus wrestles old lady	25 - 28	28 - 32
H.B. Krampus & Nicholas Series (6)	22 - 25	25 - 30
H.G. **H.H.i.W.**, Wien **Series 695**		

K.V. (The Krampus Family)
"Gruss vom Krampus!"

S.W.B., 1179/80
No Caption

P.R., FKG 3480-1
Foreign Caption

Unsigned, C.H.W. VIII, 2507-4
"Pozdrav od Krampusa!"

B.K.W.I., Series 2840/II
"Diebesten Grüsse vom Krampus"

K. hands lady to Devil in furnace	25 - 30	30 - 35
Others		
Series 568 Krampus with crying boy		
H.W.	15 - 18	18 - 22
FEIERTAG, KARL (Austria)		
Child Krampus Series (6)	15 - 18	18 - 22
HARTMANN, A. (Austria)		
C.H.W. VIII		
Series 2460 (6)		
K. whips lovers; kids in basket	25 - 30	30 - 35
K. and kids above hot flames		
K. and Nicholas. K. whips kids		
Kids play ring-around K. with adults in basket		
Series 2489, 2490 (6)	30 - 35	35 - 40
Series 2491 (6)		
K. watches lovers. Kids in chains, basket.		
HATZ, H. (Austria)		
Dachshund dressed as Krampus	25 - 28	28 - 32
Others		
HETZEL (Austria)		
B.K.W.I.		
Series 2013 (6) K. dressed as a dandy	25 - 28	28 - 32
K.V. The Krampus Family	30 - 35	35 - 40
KUDERNY, F. (Austria)		
B.K.W.I.		
Series 2601 (6)		

Toy Krampus	15 - 18	18 - 22
KUTZER, ERNST (Austria)		
B.K.W.I.		
Series 3236 (6)		
Krampus listens to angel	20 - 22	22 - 25
Girl on skis with small Krampus		
Krampus behind angel		
Deutschen Schulverein		
Kids fight Krampus and Nicholas	25 - 30	30 - 35
Small Krampus and Nicholas on skis		
Others		
M.S.H. Little Krampuses	15 - 18	18 - 22
MAILICK, A. (Germany)		
Krampus and St. Nicholas	25 - 30	30 - 35
Others		
MORAUS St. Nicholas and Krampus	22 - 25	25 - 28
O.W. Women as Krampus	25 - 28	28 - 32
OHLER, C. (Hungary)		
B.K.W.I. Series 2565 (6)	25 - 28	28 - 32
P.R. F.K.G. Series 3480/1	15 - 20	20 - 25
PAL Krampus and Nicholas in autos	15 - 18	18 - 22
PAYER, E. (Germany) Krampus and St. Nicholas	25 - 30	30 - 35
SASULSKI, K. (Poland)		
Pocztowski 269 Krampus and St. Nicholas	30 - 35	35 - 40
SCHEINER (Czech)		
K. leads rich man away from his money	25 - 28	28 - 32
SCHÖNPFLUG, FRITZ (Austria)		
B.K.W.I.		
Series 2586		
Thinly built Krampus - red striped shorts	30 - 35	35 - 38
Krampus carries officer on shoulders		
Krampus sits on stool, brushes hair		
Krampus tweaks chin of ugly old lady		
Krampus sits on mean bulldog's house		
Krampus hates tennis players		
Series 22 (6)	30 - 35	35 - 38
SINGER, SUZI (Austria)		
Wiener Werkstaette, 319, 320	750 - 900	900 - 1000
B.K.W.I. (6)	50 - 60	60 - 125
T.W.		
Girl Krampus and Nicholas	30 - 35	35 - 38
PUBLISHERS		
B.K.W.I.		
Series 2017, (6)	20 - 25	25 - 28
Series 2840/II (6) (Emb., Red B.G.)		
Suavely dressed Krampus Series	25 - 30	30 - 35
Series 3041 (6)	15 - 20	20 - 25
C.H.W.		
Series 2461 (6)		
Man-woman in basket, K. switches kids	28 - 32	32 - 35
Series 2502 (6) Red B.G.		
Kids give Krampus hard time	12 - 15	15 - 18
Series 2507 (6) Red B.G.		

Anon., C.H.W. VIII
2502-2, German Caption

A. Hartmann, C.H.W.
VIII/2, Series 2489

Unsigned Schönpflug
B.K.W.I. Series 2586-3

EAS

Krampus pulls girl's pony tail　(Emb.)	30 - 35	35 - 38
Others		
Erika		
Series 2　(6) K. and St. Nicholas	15 - 18	18 - 22
H.H.i.W.		
Series 1608, 1626, 1628　(6)	25 - 30	30 - 35
Krampus chases beautiful lady	30 - 35	35 - 38
LP		
Series 3977　Krampus with mean kids	35 - 38	38 - 42
LWKW,　Series 9000 Red B.G.　(10)	12 - 15	15 - 18
M. Munk, Wien		
Series 1043　(6)　K. & Nicholas Series	25 - 30	30 - 35
O.K.W.		
Series 1633　Krampus & Nicholas (6)	28 - 32	32 - 35
O.P.F.	60 - 75	75 - 125
SB　Series 3180		
Crying girl in basket	25 - 30	30 - 35
SBW　Series 1179		
"TEHO"		
Giant Krampus head eating kids	28 - 32	32 - 35
Anonymous Polish Krampus	28 - 32	32 - 35

MISCELLANEOUS

Pre-1920 Artist drawn	15 - 18	18 - 22
1920-1940　Artist drawn	12 - 15	15 - 18
Pre-1920 Black on red background	15 - 20	20 - 25
1940+ Black Krampus on red background	5 - 8	8 - 10
1940+ Artist drawn		

7 GREETINGS

Greeting cards are those sent to recognize a holiday, birthday, or just to say "Hello." These were, by far, the largest single type of early postcards printed; there are millions still available today.

Many were beautifully printed and very desirable, while others were poorly designed and bland, unwanted by collectors and destined today to postcard dealers' "25 cent" boxes. The majority of cards in huge accumulations or the remnants of a dealer's stock are represented in this group. Easter, Birthday, Thanksgiving, and common flowered greetings make up the greater proportion.

On the other hand, there are high quality Greeting cards by signed artists such as Ellen H. Clapsaddle, Rose O'Neill, Frances Brundage, S. L. Schmucker, H. B. Griggs, Dwig, Grace Drayton-Wiederseim and others. Outstanding cards were also produced by publishers such as John Winsch, Paul Finkenrath (PFB), Raphael Tuck, Nash, Santway, and Gabriel.

NEW YEAR

	VG	EX
Common	$0.50 - 1	$1 - 1.50
With Children, Father Time, unsigned	2 - 3	3 - 6
With Beautiful Ladies		
With Pigs	4 - 6	6 - 10
With Dressed Pigs	8 - 12	12 - 20
With Chimney Sweeps		
With Pigs/Chimney Sweeps	10 - 15	15 - 22
With Elves/Mushrooms/Gold, etc.	5 - 8	8 - 12
With Big Snowmen	8 - 12	12 - 20
With Year Date - See Year Dates		

Anonymous, EAS M-569
Hungarian New Year Greetings

S. Chiostri, Ballerini & Fratini
220, Black-Robed Father Time

With Dressed Mushrooms, Gnomes	8 - 12	12 - 18
Ballerini & Fratini S/Chiostri		
Series 220, Black-Robed Father Time	40 - 50	50 - 60
Sam Gabriel S/Brundage		
Series 300, 302, 316 (10)	12 - 15	15 - 20
International Art Pub. Co. S/Clapsaddle		
Common	5 - 8	8 - 10
With Children	8 - 12	12 - 18
L & E S/H.B.G.		
Series 2225, 2227, 2266, 2276 (6)	8 - 10	10 - 16
Series 2276 (6)		
P.F.B.		
Series 9501 Children/Auto (6)	8 - 10	10 - 15
Others	6 - 8	8 - 12
Raphael Tuck Various Series		
Simple	0.50 - 1	1 - 2
With Children	2 - 3	3 - 6
Series 601 (Unsigned Brundage)	8 - 12	12 - 16
Raphael Tuck (American)		
Unsigned S. L. Schmucker		
Series 618 "Joyous" (6)	40 - 45	45 - 55
Series 619 "Ye Olden Days" (6)	30 - 35	35 - 45
John Winsch, Copyright		
Unsigned S. L. Schmucker		
Copyright, 1910 - Vertical (4)		
Reprints of 1910 Christmas issue		

with New Year Captions, Vertical	20 - 25	25 - 35
Silks, with no copyright	25 - 30	30 - 40
Copyright, 1910 - Father Time, Vertical (4)		
With lady in purple	45 - 55	55 - 65
"Jan. 1st."		
With lady in gold		
"Jan. 1st.		
With lady in pink flowered dress		
"Jan. 1st."		
With lady in red		
"Jan 1st."		
Copyright, 1910 - 1911 Year - Vertical (4)		
1911 Baby New Year rides big bell	30 - 35	35 - 45
"To wish you a Happy New Year"		
Stork carrying Baby New Year		
"A Happy New year"		
Baby New Year/Father Time		
"Best New Year Wishes"		
Baby New Year sits on trunk		
"A Happy New Year to You"		
Copyright, 1911 - Vertical* (4)		
Girl in red hugs snowman	40 - 45	45 - 50
"A Happy New Year"		
Girl in Blue with dark red scarf		
"With Best New Year Wishes"		
Girl in green with yellow scarf		
"A Happy New Year to You"		
Girl with red mittens and snowballs		
"To Wish you a Happy New Year"		
* Reprints of 1911 Christmas Series as New Year		
George C. Whitney		
Unsigned Schmucker	50 - 60	60 - 75
Wolf Co. S/Clapsaddle, Uns./Clapsaddle		
Add $3-5 per card to **Int. Art Pub. Co.** prices.		
Anonymous		
Foreign Unsigned **Ellen Clapsaddle**	15 - 20	20 - 30

EASTER

Common	0.50 - 1	1 - 1.50
With Children, Unsigned	3 - 5	5 - 7
With Chicks, Lambs, Bunnies	2 - 3	3 - 6
With Dressed Chicks	8 - 10	10 - 15
With Dressed Bunnies	8 - 12	12 - 16
With Transportation	3 - 6	6 - 10
Easter Witches (Scandinavian) Normal	8 - 12	12 - 16
Easter Witches (Scandinavian) Small cards	10 - 14	14 - 18
(See Artist-Signed)		
International Art. Pub. Co. S/Clapsaddle		
Children	8 - 12	12 - 18
Series 5837, 8270, 8684 (6)	8 - 10	10 - 12
John Winsch		
Unsigned S. L. Schmucker		
Copyright, 1910 - Flower Faces, Vertical (6)		

Anon., Series S.520
"A Joyous Easter"

E. Clapsaddle, Inter.
Art Co., "Let Erin..."

E. Clapsaddle, Wolf &
Co., "It is a bit of..."

4 Ladies' faces in red and pink flowers "A Happy Easter"	30 - 35	35 - 45
5 Children's faces in pink flowers "Welcome Easter Morning"		
4 Ladies' faces in pansies "A Joyful Eastertide"		
5 Ladies' faces in tulips "Best Easter Wishes"		
5 Ladies' faces in daffodils "Glad Easter Greeting"		
5 Ladies' faces in Easter Lilies "Easter Greeting"		

Wolf & Co.   S/Clapsaddle, Uns./Clapsaddle
Add $2-5 per card to **Int. Art Pub. Co.** prices.
Anonymous

Foreign Unsigned E. Clapsaddle	20 - 25	25 - 30

PFINGSTEN (WHITSUN)

Common	3 - 5	5 - 8
With Children	6 - 8	8 - 12
With Miakafirs (May Bugs)	10 - 12	12 - 18
With Dressed Miakafirs	15 - 18	18 - 26
With Bugs, Insects	7 - 10	10 - 15
With Frogs	12 - 18	18 - 22
With Dressed Frogs	15 - 25	25 - 35

ST. PATRICK'S DAY

Common	1 - 1.50	1.50 - 2
With Children, Ladies	4 - 8	8 - 12
With Comics	2 - 3	3 - 6
With Uncle Sam or Ethnic Slurs	6 - 8	8 - 12
With Flags, Pipes	2 - 4	4 - 7

ASB
    Series 340 (6)   4 - 6   6 - 10
Anglo American (AA)
    Series 776, 815 (6)   4 - 6   6 - 10
Julius Bien
    Series 740 (6)   4 - 6   6 - 9
Sam Gabriel
    Series 140   Unsigned/**Brundage** (10)   10 - 12   12 - 16
    Series 141 (10)   3 - 5   5 - 7
Gottschalk, Dreyfuss & Davis
    Series 2040, 2092, 2190, 2410   4 - 6   6 - 9
International Art Pub. Co.   S/Clapsaddle
    Children   10 - 15   15 - 22
    Others   4 - 5   6 - 9
L & E   S/H.B.G   8 - 10   10 - 16
John Winsch, Copyright
    Unsigned S. L. Schmucker
    Copyright, 1911 - Vertical (4)
        Pretty lady sitting in shamrock wreath   28 - 32   32 - 38
        "Erin Go Bragh"
        Lady sitting atop map of Ireland
        "St. Patrick's Day Greetings"
        Lady sitting on Irish hat
        "The Scots man loves ..."
        Lady at window, Horizontal
        "St. Patrick's Day in the morning"
Copyright, 1912 - Transportation, Vertical (4)
        Man/woman riding shamrock sailboat   40 - 45   45 - 55
        "St. Patrick's Day Souvenir"
        Man/lady riding in shamrock cart   35 - 40   40 - 50
        Lady sitting atop map of Ireland
        "St. Patrick's Day Greetings"
        Man swinging lady on shamrock swing   35 - 40   40 - 45
        "Erin Go Bragh"
        Man/lady riding in shamrock airship   45 - 50   50 - 60
        "St. Patrick's Day Greeting"
Copyright, 1912 - Named Views, Horiz. (4)
        Lady playing harp   22 - 26   26 - 32
        "Erin Go Bragh"
        Lady wearing shamrock hat, with harp
        "St. Patrick's Day Greetings"
        Lady on map of Ireland   15 - 20   20 - 25
        "St. Patrick's Day Souvenir"
        Lady and man dancing   22 - 26   26 - 32
        "St. Patrick's Day Greetings"
Winsch Backs, No Copyright (9 known)
        Lady with pig, wreath behind   28 - 32   32 - 38
        "Erin Go Bragh"
        Lady standing in front of crossed pipes
        "St. Patrick's Day Souvenir"
        Lady sitting on bouquet of shamrocks
        "St. Patrick's Day"
        Lady with pig, wreath behind   22 - 26   26 - 32
        "Erin Go Bragh"

E. Clapsaddle, Inter.
Art Co., 2736

Anon. (Whitney Made)
"I'll pick you for my..."

Uns. Greiner, Tuck
185, "Of all sweet..."

Lady in shamrock dress, holds big pipe "St. Patrick's Day Greetings"		
Lady riding big white pipe "St. Patrick's Day Souvenir"	20 - 25	25 - 32
Lady sitting on big harp, mesh background "Erin Go Bragh"	28 - 32	32 - 36
Lady holds big pipe, mesh background "St. Patrick's Day Greetings"		
Lady at the window - Horizontal "The Top of the Mornin' to you..."		

Wolf & Co.   S/Clapsaddle, Uns./Clapsaddle
Add $2-3 per card to **Int. Art** prices.

VALENTINE'S DAY

Common	1 - 1.50	1.50 - 2
With Children, Ladies	5 - 7	7 - 12
With Comics	2 - 3	3 - 6
With Animals		
A.S.B.		
Series 227, 229, 267 (6)	2 - 3	3 - 7
B.B. London		
Series 1501 (6)	2 - 3	3 - 7
B.W. Many Series (6)		
S. Bergman Many Series (6)	1 - 2	2 - 3
Julius Bien		
Series 335 (6)	1 - 3	3 - 5
L. R. Conwell Ser. 329, 409 (6)		
Sam Gabriel		
S/J. Johnson, Series 407 (6)	4 - 5	5 - 8
Uns./Brundage Series 413 (6)	8 - 10	10 - 16
Others	1 - 2	2 - 4
International Art. Pub. Co. S/Clapsaddle		
Angels, Cherubs	6 - 8	8 - 12
Greetings	4 - 6	6 - 8

Children	10 - 15	15 - 22
E. Nash Many Series	1 - 2	2 - 5
P.F.B.		
Series 7185 Cupids	5 - 8	8 - 12
Samson Bros. Many Series	2 - 3	3 - 5
Raphael Tuck Signed/Brundage		
Series 11 (4) **Uns./Brundage**	10 - 12	12 - 15
Series 20, 26 Uns./Brundage	12 - 15	15 - 20
Series 102 (6)		
Blacks	22 - 25	25 - 30
Series 115 (4)	8 - 10	10 - 15
Blacks	22 - 25	25 - 30
Series 100, 101 (6) **Uns./Brundage**	12 - 15	15 - 20
Blacks	22 - 25	25 - 30
Leatherette, Series 114, 116 (6)	3 - 5	5 - 8
Series 107, 117 Uns./Brundage	10 - 12	12 - 15
Blacks	22 - 25	25 - 30
Series 1033 Blacks	20 - 22	22 - 25
Other Unsigned/Brundage	8 - 10	10 - 12
Blacks	20 - 22	22 - 25
Series 106, 111, 112 S/Outcault	8 - 10	10 - 15
Black Series 108 (6)	22 - 25	25 - 28
Raphael Tuck		
Series A, B, C, 5, 6 & 7	4 - 5	5 - 6
Series 231, "Poster Girls	25 - 30	30 - 35
Signed/Curtis (36)	4 - 6	6 - 10
H. Wessler	5 - 7	7 - 10
John Winsch, Copyright		
Unsigned S. L. Schmucker		
Copyright, 1910 - Vertical (6)		
Girl in purple w/2 red heart faces	50 - 55	55 - 60
"St. Valentine's Greeting"		
Side view of blonde, gold halo and hearts	35 - 40	40 - 45
"My Valentine, think of me"		
Red head, large green heart behind		
"I Greet Thee, Valentine"		
Red head wearing blue, green heart		
"To my Valentine"		
Lady wearing white chiffon hat		
"Be my Valentine"		
Blond wearing chiffon scarf		
"A Valentine Message"		
Copyright, 1910 - Green Heart, Vertical (4)		
Irish lady and Irish cupid	35 - 40	40 - 45
"Be my Valentine"		
Oriental lady and oriental cupid		
"To my Valentine"		
Indian maid and Indian cupid		
"A Valentine Message"		
Spanish Girl and Spanish cupid		
"St. Valentine's Greeting"		
Copyright, 1910 - Sports Cupid, Horiz. (4)		
Fishing Cupid	30 - 35	35 - 40
"To My Valentine"		

Football Cupid
"A Valentine Message"
Golfing Cupid
"To My Valentine"
Tennis Cupid
"To My Valentine"

Copyright, 1910 - Vertical (4)

Blonde holding large red heart	30 - 35	35 - 45
"My Valentine think of me"		
Blonde Sleeping - purple-pink flowers	40 - 45	45 - 55
"Valentine Greetings"		
Blonde lady wearing ermine hat		
"To my Valentine"		
Lady in red sitting on flower heart	30 - 35	35 - 45
"St. Valentine's Greeting"		

Copyright, 1911 - Gold Heart, Vertical (4)

Golf Girl	35 - 40	40 - 50
"Valentine Greeting"		
Fishing Girl		
"To my Valentine"		
Football Girl		
"My Valentine"		
Tennis Girl		
"Greeting to my Valentine"		
Girl in red sweater kicking football		
heart - Very Rare	80 - 90	90 - 95
"Valentine Greeting"		

Winsch-Back, Non-Copyright (6)

Nurse bandaging a broken heart	35 - 40	40 - 50
"A Valentine Message"		
Side view of blonde with hearts in hair		
"I greet thee Valentine"		
Spider web background, with/hearts entangled	45 - 50	50 - 60
"My Valentine, think of me" Signed SLS		
Dark-haired lady, spider web background	55 - 60	60 - 70
"Be my Valentine"		
Blonde lady holds red heart, spider web	40 - 45	45 - 55
"To my Valentine"		
Lady floating in water with hearts	40 - 45	45 - 55
"St. Valentine's Greeting"		

Copyright, 1911 - Vertical (4)

Lady in blue holding green umbrella	30 - 35	35 - 45
"A Prayer to Valentine"		
Blonde lady in pink carrying basket		
"Gathering Hearts"		
Lady in yellow catching butterfly hearts		
"Your Valentine"		
Lady in green playing heart guitar		
"Valentine Plea"		
Common	1 - 1.50	1.50 - 2
W/Children or Ladies	5 - 6	6 - 8
Booklet-types	6 - 7	7 - 10
Silk Inserts (Ladies)	10 - 15	15 - 18
Rose Co. Comic Series	2 - 3	3 - 5

Fritz Baumgarten, M. & B. 3052
"Happy Birthday"

Anon., Photo Production, Ltd.
"You're ONE To-day"

Illustrated P.C. Co. Comics		
S/**H. Horina** Series 5004	3 - 4	4 - 6
Aurochrome Co. Comics		
S/**Meyer**	3 - 4	4 - 5
Wolf & Co. S/Clapsaddle, Uns./Clapsaddle		
Add $3-5 per card to **Int. Art Pub. Co.** prices.		

BIRTHDAY

Common	0.50 - 1	1 - 1.50
With Children	2 - 3	3 - 6
BRC -- Unsigned LD	6 - 8	8 - 10
International Art S/Clapsaddle	8 - 12	12 - 16
Raphael Tuck (American)		
"Birthday Children" Series 102 (10)	2 - 3	3 - 5
Unsigned S. L. Schmucker		
Series 198 "Quaint Dutch" (6)	70 - 80	80 - 90
Winsch, Copyright	4 - 5	5 - 8
Wolf & Co. S/Clapsaddle, Uns./Clapsaddle		
Add $2-3 to **Int. Art Pub. Co.** prices.		

APRIL FOOL'S DAY

Henderson Litho Series 102	7 - 8	8 - 10
P.C.K. (Paul C. Kober)		
S/**A. Hutaf**	6 - 8	8 - 12

Ullman Mfg. Co. S/B. Wall		
Series 156 (6)	6 - 7	7 - 8
Winsch Backs Series 1	8 - 10	10 - 15
FRENCH 1st of Avril Fish	8 - 12	12 - 22
P.F.B.		
Series 553, 6505	10 - 12	12 - 16

LEAP YEAR

S/Brill, B&W and Red (12)	3 - 4	4 - 7
D.P. Crane S/Zim	7 - 9	9 - 12
Sam Gabriel Series 401 (12) S/Dwig	10 - 12	12 - 15
Grollman, 1908	6 - 8	8 - 12
H.T.M. 1060-1071 (12)		
Henderson Litho Series 102		
Illustrated P.C. Co. Series 217		
P.C. Koeber S/Hutaf	8 - 10	10 - 12
B.B. London Series E44, E81	8 - 9	9 - 10
E. Nash		
"Lemon" Series 1 (12)	8 - 10	10 - 15
"Diamond Ring" Series, 1912		
"Captured him in his lair"		
"Caught on the run"		
"Don't give up the ship"		
"Lay for him"		
"On the Trail"		
"Ring up the man you want"		
Rose Co. S/G. Brill (6)	6 - 8	8 - 10
P. Sanders, 1908	8 - 10	10 - 15

Anonymous, Leap Year Series 1065
"How to catch them -- in 1908."

A. M. Davis Co.	B.W., "Best wishes to you on
"Mother's Day"	George Washington's Birthday"

R. Tuck Series 7, S/Curtis (12)	8 - 9	9 - 11
S/L. Thackeray	8 - 10	10 - 12
Ullman Series 156	6 - 8	8 - 10
Anonymous Series 1065	8 - 10	10 - 12

GROUND HOG DAY (Also see Dressed Animals)

Henderson Litho Co., Series 101 (4)		
"Come out and make a shadow"		
"Don't get so chesty..."		
"May the Shadow of your Purse..."	160 - 180	180 - 210
Linens	12 - 15	15 - 20

MOTHER'S DAY

Metro Litho Co. Series 446 (6)	10 - 12	12 - 15
Anonymous		
Lady & Soldier, "Mother's Day"	8 - 10	10 - 15
Mother holds Baby, "Mother's Day"		
Mother holds baby at arm's length.	20 - 25	25 - 30
Silhouette Types	10 - 12	12 - 15

GEORGE WASHINGTON'S BIRTHDAY

Anglo American (AA)		
Open Book Series 725 (6)	15 - 20	20 - 22

Series **728** (6)

B.W.	8 - 10	10 - 12
Julius Bien Series **605** (6)	6 - 8	8 - 10
Series **760** (4)		
Gottschalk, Dreyfuss and Davis Series **216** (12)	8 - 10	10 - 12
International Art Co.		
Series **51646** (8)	8 - 10	10 - 12
S/Clapsaddle		
Series **16208, 16209** (4)	7 - 8	8 - 10
Uns./Clapsaddle Series **16250** (6)		
S/Clapsaddle Series **51896** (6)	8 - 10	10 - 12
S/Veenfliet Signed **51766** (6)	6 - 8	8 - 10
L & E,		
S/H.B.G. Series **2242** (8)	10 - 12	12 - 15
Lounsbury Series **2020** (4)		
Series **1, 2, 4** (6)	5 - 8	8 - 10
Series **W5, W6, W7** (4)	5 - 6	6 - 8
Series **W9, W11, 14, 15** (4)		
H.I. Robbins Series **329** (8)	6 - 8	8 - 10
P. Sander Series **414** (6)		
M.W. Taggart, NY Series **605** (6)		
Raphael Tuck Series **124, 156, 171, 178** (6)	6 - 8	8 - 10

DECORATION DAY/MEMORIAL DAY

A.S.B. Series **283** (6)	6 - 8	8 - 10
Conwell Series **376-381** (6)		
S. Gabriel Series **150** (6)	8 - 10	10 - 12
Illustrated P.C. Company Series **151** (8)	6 - 8	8 - 10
Int. Art Co.		
S/Chapman Series **6** (6)	8 - 10	10 - 12
S/Clapsaddle Series **6** (6)	10 - 12	12 - 16
S/Clapsaddle **973, 2444** (6)		
S/Clapsaddle **2935** (6)		
S/Clapsaddle **4397** (6)	8 - 10	10 - 12
Lounsbury, S/Bunnell Series **2083** (4)	10 - 12	12 - 16
E. Nash		
Series **1, 2, 3, D4** (6)	8 - 10	10 - 12
Series **6** (6)	10 - 12	12 - 16
Series **21** (6)	8 - 10	10 - 12
Santway Series **157** (6)		
Taggert Series **602 and 603** (6 each)		
Raphael Tuck		
Series **107, 158** (12)	8 - 10	10 - 14
Series **173, 179** (12)	12 - 15	15 - 20
Anonymous Series No. 1	5 - 6	6 - 8
Others	4 - 5	5 - 6

CONFEDERATE MEMORIAL DAY

R. Tuck's		
"Confederate" Series Divided Backs (12)		
"For though Conquered ..."	10 - 15	15 -20

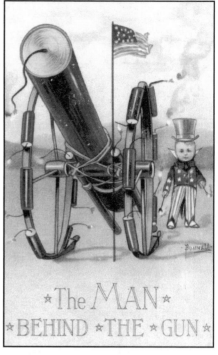

E. Clapsaddle, Inter. Art Co.
2935, "On Fame's eternal..."

Bunnell, P.F.B. Series 9507
"The Man behind the gun"

"Furl that Banner!"		
General Joseph E. Johnson	15 - 18	18 - 25
General Robert E. Lee	25 - 30	30 - 35
General Stonewall Jackson		
Headquarters, Army of N. Virginia	10 - 15	15 - 22
"In Memoriam ..." 2 flags		
"In Memoriam ..." 3 flags		
"The Hands that grasped ..." 4 flags		
"The Warriors Banner takes its Flight"		
"Twill live in Song and Story ..."		
"United Daughters Confederacy ..."		
R. Tuck		
"Heroes of the South" Series 2510	20 - 25	25 - 32
Souvenir P.C. Co. With "Bee Brand" (6)	10 - 15	15 - 18
Jamestown A & V Co.		
Jamestown Expo Cards (11) See Expositions		
Veteran Art Co. "National Souvenir" Set	8 - 10	10 - 15
Winsch-back, No Publisher	10 - 12	12 - 15
Two Southern Generals Card	12 - 15	15 - 22

ABRAHAM LINCOLN'S BIRTHDAY

Anglo American (AA)		
Open Book Series 726 (6)	20 - 25	25 - 30
Series 727 (6)		

Century Co.
    Sepia Series (6)   8 - 10   10 - 12
Int. Art Pub. Co. Series 51658 (6)
    "Lincoln and the Contrabands" (1)   12 - 15   15 - 18
Lounsbury Centennial (4)   8 - 10   10 - 12
Nash
    Series 1 (6)   7 - 8   8 - 10
    Gold or Silver 2 (6)
P.F.B. Series 9463 (6)   10 - 12   12 - 15
P. Sander Series 415 (6)   7 - 8   8 - 10
Sheehan, M.A. Series (18)
Raphael Tuck Series 155 (6)   10 - 12   12 - 14

FOURTH OF JULY

Common	2 - 3	3 - 5
With Children, Ladies	5 - 8	8 - 10
With Uncle Sam (See Uncle Sam below)		
Julius Bien Series 700 (6)	8 - 10	10 - 14
Conwell Series 380 (6)	6 - 8	8 - 12
S. Garre Series 51668 (6)		
S/Chapman	8 - 10	10 - 14
Gottschalk, Dreyfuss & Davis		
Series 2172, 2099 (6)		
Int. Art Pub Co. S/Clapsaddle		
Series 974, 2443, 2936, 4398 (6)	8 - 10	10 - 16
Series 51668 S/Chapman (6)	8 - 10	10 - 14
Fred C. Lounsbury S/Bunnell		
Series 2076 (6)	8 - 10	10 - 14
Uncle Sam Series (4)	15 - 18	18 - 22
Nash Comic Series 1 (6)	6 - 8	8 - 10
1 "How to prevent your boy..."		
2 "Ye Spit-Devil is a wily..."		
3 "The Giant Cracker..."		
4 "Photograph your boy..."		
5 "Where ignorance is bliss"		
6 "The Dog ..."		
Series 4, 5 (6)	7 - 8	8 - 10
Series J6 (6)	6 - 7	7 - 8
Series J8 (6)	8 - 10	10 - 12
With Uncle Sam, Lady Liberty	15 - 20	20 - 25
P.F.B.		
Series 8252 (6)	12 - 15	15 - 20
Series 9507 S/Bunnell (6)	15 - 18	18 - 22
Rotograph Co. S/Gene Carr		
Series 219 (6)	7 - 8	8 - 10
P. Sander Series 440 (6)	8 - 10	10 - 14
Steiner Series 129 (6)	6 - 8	8 - 10
Tower Series 106 (6)	5 - 6	6 - 8
R. Tuck Series 109, 159 (12)	6 - 8	8 - 10
Ullman Co. Series 124 (6)		
Wolf S/Clapsaddle, Uns./Clapsaddle		

    Add $2-3 per card to **Int. Art Pub. Co.** prices.

<table>
</table>

E. Nash Series J-8
"Hurrah for the Fourth of July"

E. Nash Series J-8
"Greetings from a Patriot"

Anonymous
    Series 312, 752   8 - 10   10 - 12

FLAG OF THE U.S.

Julius Bien	Series 710, 716	6 - 8	8 - 10
Ill. P.C. Co.	Series 207	5 - 6	6 - 8
Souvenir P.C. Co.		4 - 5	5 - 7

HALLOWEEN

AUBURN POSTCARD CO.		
S/H.W.A. Series 2500	8 - 10	10 - 12
S/E. Weaver Series 2339, 2399 (8)		
Unsigned	6 - 8	8 - 10
AA (Anglo American) Series 876 Witch Series (6)	12 - 15	15 - 18
AMP CO.	10 - 12	12 - 15
B.B., LONDON (Birn Bros.) Series E-59 (6)	12 - 15	15 - 18
BANKS, E. C. (Signed by) See Langsdorf & Co.		
BERGMAN CO. Many Series	8 - 10	10 - 12
S/E. Von. H. Series 6026, 6027	12 - 15	15 - 18
S/Bernhardt Wall Series 9101		
No No. Cat Series	15 - 18	18 - 22
No. No. Children Series	12 - 15	15 - 18
A. C. BOSSELMAN		
JULIUS BIEN & CO. Series 980 (6)	15 - 18	18 - 22
R. L. CONWELL CO.	10 - 12	12 - 15

A. M. DAVIS S/AEH Series 657 (12)	18 - 22	22 - 25
FAIRMAN CO. "Pink of Perfection"	10 - 12	12 - 15
S/Kathryn Elliott (B&W)	8 - 10	10 - 12
S/Bernhardt Wall (B&W		
SAM GABRIEL or GABRIEL & SONS		
Series 120, 121, 123 S/Brundage (10)	20 - 22	22 - 25
Series 124 S/M LaFa R (Mary Russell) (6)	10 - 12	12 - 15
Series 125 S/Brundage (6)	12 - 15	15 - 18
GIBSON ART		
Series 606 Children	12 - 15	15 - 18
S/Kathryn Elliott Sepia (12 or more)	8 - 10	10 - 12
S/Bernhardt Wall Sepia (12)		
Many other unnumbered series.	6 - 8	8 - 10
GOTTSCHALK, DREYFUSS & DAVIS		
Series 2010A, 2097, 2171	12 - 15	15 - 18
Series 2243, 2279		
Series 2339, 2401, 2402, 2470, 2471 (4)	15 - 18	18 - 22
Series 2504, 2516, 2525, 2526, 2662 (4)		
Series 2693, 2696 (4)		
Girl/Mailbox Symbol (possibly GD&S) issues	15 - 18	18 - 22
Some have B. Hoffman copyright, 1909.		
INTERNATIONAL ART MFG. CO.		
No No. S/Clapsaddle (12)	15 - 18	18 - 22
Series 501 S/Clapsaddle (4)	20 - 30	30 - 40
Series 978 S/Clapsaddle (6)	15 - 18	18 - 22
Series 1002 S/Aleinmuller (6)	12 - 15	15 - 18
Series 1236 S/Clapsaddle Mechanicals (4)		
White Children	200 - 250	250 - 275
Black Child	400 - 450	450 - 500
Series 1237, 1238 S/Clapsaddle (4)	15 - 18	18 - 22
Series 1301 S/Clapsaddle (12)	50 - 60	60 - 75
Series 1393 S/Clapsaddle (6)	15 - 18	18 - 22
Series 1667 S/Clapsaddle (12)	12 - 15	15 - 18
Series 1815 Uns./Clapsaddle (6)	10 - 12	12 - 15
Series 4439 S/Clapsaddle (6)	15 - 18	18 - 22
Series 1002 S/Heinmuller (6)	12 - 15	15 - 18
No No. S/Bernhardt Wall (12)		
S/M. L. JACKSON "Don't" Series	18 - 20	20 - 22
L & E		
H.B.G. (H.B. Griggs)		
Series 2214, 2215 (4)	12 - 15	15 - 18
Series 2216 (Uns.) (4)	20 - 22	22 - 25
Series E2231, 2262, 2272, 4010 (12)	12 - 15	15 - 18
S. LANGSDORF & CO.		
No No. Gel Finish (12)	10 - 12	12 - 15
S/E.C. Banks	15 - 18	18 - 22
S/R. H. LORD (Robert H. Lord)	10 - 12	12 - 15
FRED LOUNSBURY CO. Series 2052 (6)	15 - 18	18 - 20
J. MARKS		
Series 980 S/Dwig (12)	15 - 18	18 - 22
Series 981 Unsigned Dwig (6)	25 - 30	30 - 35
METROPOLITAN NEWS CO. (M in Bean Pot)	10 - 12	12 - 15

R. Tuck, "Hallowe'en" Ser. 150
"Hallowe'en"

E. Clapsaddle, Wolf & Co. 501
"Wishing you a Highly..."

Whitney Made Hallow'een
"I've heard of witches and ..."

E. NASH		
Series 1, 2, 3, 4, 5, 6 (6)	12 - 15	15 - 18
Series 6, H-6 through 28, H-28		
Series H-12, Series 29, H-29 through H-49		
NATIONAL ART CO. S/Archie Gunn	22 - 25	25 - 28
NATIONAL ART PUB. CO. Series 70 (4)	12 - 15	15 - 18
F. A. OWEN	6 - 8	8 - 10
S/OUTCAULT Buster Brown Calendar	40 - 50	50 - 60
P.F.B. (Paul Finkenrath, Berlin)		
Series 778 (6)	20 - 25	25 - 28
Series 9422 (6) Same as Series 778		
G. K. PRINCE Series 421 S/M.M.S.	10 - 12	12 - 15
H.I. ROBBINS		
Series 142 (12) **Series 363**	10 - 12	12 - 15
Series 383 (12?) Same as **Series 142**		
THE ROSE CO.	8 - 10	10 - 12
RUSTCRAFT SHOP	10 - 12	12 - 15
SAS CO.		
SB		
SAMSON BROS.		
P. SANDER		
SANFORD CARD CO. S/A.B.C. and S/A.M.C.	8 - 10	10 - 12
STECHER LITHO CO.		
S/M.E.P. (Margaret E. Price)		
Series 400, 419 (6)	15 - 18	18 - 22
Series 1239 Flat printed (4)	10 - 12	12 - 15

Uns. J.E.P. Series 57, 63 (6)	12 - 15	15 - 18
Many other series	10 - 12	12 - 15
T. P. & CO. (Taylor-Platt) Series 866	6 - 8	8 - 10
M. W. TAGGART		
Series 803, 804, 806 (8)	12 - 15	15 - 18
TAYLOR ART	15 - 18	18 - 20
TOWER CO. Series 103S (6)	6 - 8	8 - 10
R. TUCK & SONS, LTD. -- New York		
Series 100 (9 known)		
Uns. S.L. Schmucker		
Girl dressed in sheet, many JOL's	100 - 125	125 - 150
"Bats and owls and witch-y capers ..."		
Girl pixie dressed in black, 3 JOL's		
"Hallowe'en Greetings ..."		
Girl with cape and Japanese lanterns		
"Hallowe'en Wishes"		
Girl with mask, 5 big masks behind		
"This maid will mask on Hallowe'en"		
Boy with Japanese lanterns, big moon		
"Sing a Song of Hallowe'en"		
Girl wears checked dress and JOL man		
"This maiden here is dancing with ..."		
Girl wears JOL cloak, with JOL on stick		
"Were you this maid on Hallowe'en"		
Girl dressed as clown, JOL on a stick		
"Witches, Fay's and Sprites unseen ..."		
Boy with flute sits on big JOL		
"When you're away on Hallowe'en"		
Series 150, 183 (12)	10 - 12	12 - 15
Series 160 (12) 190 (10)	15 - 18	18 - 22
Series 174 Uns. Brundage (6)	20 - 25	25 - 28
Series 184 Uns. Brundage (12)	18 - 22	22 - 25
Series 181 S/C.B.T. (10)	12 - 15	15 - 18
Series 188 (10)	15 - 18	18 - 22
Series 803, 816	10 - 12	12 - 15
Series 830, 831 (3)		
Series 197 S/E.M.H.	20 - 22	22 - 25
Series 807 Uns/Wiederseim (4)	80 - 90	90 - 100
ULLMAN MFG. CO.		
No No. (B&W)	8 - 10	10 - 12
No No. (Color) (8)	10 - 12	12 - 15
Series 143, 182 (7)		
S/Bernhardt Wall	15 - 20	20 - 30
VALENTINE & SONS	10 - 12	12 - 15
(Signed & Uns. B. Wall)	12 - 15	15 - 18
P.F. VOLLAND & CO. (4041-4048)	15 - 18	18 - 22
S/E. WEAVER		
Series 2335, 2399 (8)	8 - 10	10 - 12
Series 556, Christmas (8)	30 - 35	35 - 40
"Long Ago Children"		
Series 619, New Year's (6)	30 - 35	35 - 45
"Ye Olden Days"		
Halloween Fold-Outs	100 - 125	125 - 150

E. Clapsaddle, Int. Art 1301
"A Joyful Halloween"

Unsigned Jason Freixas, Winsch
1914, "Hallowe'en Pumpkins..."

B. Wall, Valentine & Sons
"For a Jolly Halloween"

B. Wall, Valentine & Sons
"Halloween"

George C. Whitney
"A gay young witch I'd like to ..."

Anonymous, 552
"A pumpkin head I would like ..."

Real Photo
Children in Halloween Ghost Costumes

GEORGE C. WHITNEY	12 - 15	15 - 18
Unsigned S.L. Schmucker (6)		
Boy and girl with lantern, green imps	80 - 90	90 - 100
"Be brave and bold on Hallowe'en night ..."		
Three children w/pumpkins, JOL, imp/owl		
"Hallowe'en Greetings to You"		
Three children with clown on a stick		
"Just a wish for a Happy Hallowe'en"		
Dutch boy, girl in flowered dress, goblins		
"May you be Jolly and Gay ..."		
Two girls watch flying witch, big moon		
"On Hallowe'en watch and you may see ..."		
Boy and girl meet big vegetable man		
"Since I am here and you are there ..."		
Halloween Fold-Outs Uns./Schmucker	100 - 125	125 - 150

JOHN WINSCH, COPYRIGHT

Winsch combined the works of S.L. Schmucker and Jason Freixas on a number of variations and reduced designs. On these designs Freixas children are usually shown but Schmucker designs are on remainder of card. These now bring a premium above those of non-combined issues.

Copyright, 1911 - Vertical* (6)		
Head & shoulders of blonde, black hood	75 - 100	100 - 125
"A Happy Hallowe'en"		
Lady riding broom, moon behind		
"All Hallowe'en"		
Lady in long white hooded robe		
"On Hallowe'en"		
Lady in red dress, owl on head		
"Hallowe'en Greeting"		
Lady in black evening gown		
"Greetings at Hallowe'en"		
Lady asleep, 3 fairies		
"Hallowe'en Time"		
* 3 different sets of variations of 1911		
series show smaller same design images		
but with different captions	Range	60 - 150
Copyright, 1912 - Vertical* (6)		
Lady witch in front of big cauldron	75 - 100	100 - 125
"The Hallowe'en Cauldron"		
Lady in black, leering moon behind		
"The Hallowe'en Lantern"		
Lady in white-hooded cape, JOL's		
"The Magic Hallowe'en"		
Lady in red elfin costume		
"The Hallowe'en Witch's Wand"		
Lady in white clown suit, owls		
"A Hallowe'en Morning"		
Lady in green dress, JOL man		
"A Hallowe'en Wish"		

* 4 different sets of variations of 1912 series (one same size images and 3 smaller; 3 are copyrighted; 2 are vertical and 2 are horizontal)		75 - 150
Copyright, 1913 "Mask Series" - Horiz.* (4)		
Clown in red and Jack-in-the Box	75 - 100	100 - 125
"Hallowe'en Surprises"		
Witch and clown hold jump rope		
"Hallowe'en Gambols!"		
Woman in long white hooded robe		
"Hallowe'en Faces"		
Girl in white dress, huge masks		
"Hallowe'en Faces"		
* One other set of variation of 1913 series has embossed design, black/gold stars border, different captions and cards are not copyrighted (#4972 on reverse)	100 - 125	125 - 150
Copyright, 1913 -- Horizontal* (4)		
Girl in white dress with pink dress	75 - 100	100 - 125
"A Starry Hallowe'en"		
Girl in dotted dress sits on pumpkin		
"Hallowe'en Night"		
Boy surrounded by big JOL's		
"Hallowe'en Pumpkins"		
Girl in white between owl and vegetable		
"Hallowe'en Jollity"		
* 4 other sets of variations of 1913 series and all are copyrighted 1913.		
Other Winsch Issues		
1912 German, Unsigned (6)	60 - 75	75 - 90
German, smaller variations	90 - 100	100 - 140
1913 German, Unsigned	60 - 80	80 - 90
Smaller variations	60 - 70	70 - 80
1914, Copyright, Children, Uns./J. Freixas	70 - 80	80 - 90
Variations	70 - 80	80 - 90
1914, Copyright Unsigned Witches, owls	65 - 75	75 - 95
Variations	50 - 60	60 - 70
1915, Copyright, Children, Uns./Freixas and other artists	100 - 120	120 - 140
Black Checkered Border, no copyright Uns./Freixas	70 - 80	80 - 90
Orange Border, Children, no copyright	100 - 125	125 - 150
Series 4975, No copyright, cats, goblins (4)	50 - 60	60 - 70
WOLF & CO.		
S/Ellen Clapsaddle		
Series 1	15 - 18	18 - 22
Series 31 (18?)		
Series 501 (6) (Black & Orange Colored)	40 - 50	50 - 60
H.L. WOHLER	15 - 18	18 - 22
A.A. ZWIEBEL, Wilkes-Barre		
Children frolics (2 known)	80 - 90	90 - 100
ANONYMOUS PUBLISHERS		
Series B37, 38, 142, 160	12 - 15	15 - 18
Series 303, 304, 308, 363, 374		

Series 552 (6) (Emb.)	25 - 28	28 - 32
Series 0624, 876, 914, 1026, 1028	10 - 12	12 - 15
Series 1015, 1035	12 - 15	15 - 18
BLACKS ON HALLOWEEN		
Card No. 6505 "You would laugh too..."	30 - 35	35 - 50
Card No. 6508 "Strange sights are seen..."		
REAL PHOTOS		
Children in Costumes	Range	50 - 200
Adults in Costumes	Range	75 - 200
Halloween Parties	Range	40 - 150

THANKSGIVING

Common	0.50 - 1	1 - 1.50
W/Turkeys	1 - 1.50	1.50 - 2
W/Children, Ladies, etc.	2 - 3	3 - 6
A.S.B. Series 282, 290 (6)	0.50 - 1	1 - 3
AA (Anglo American) Series 875	0.50 - 1	1 - 3
B.B. London		
Series 2700, 2701 (6)	1 - 2	2 - 4
Conwell Series 637 (6)	0.50 - 1	1 - 2
Sam Gabriel S/Brundage		
Series 130, 132, 133 (10)	8 - 12	12 - 15
Series 135 (6)	8 - 10	10 - 12
Others	0.50 - 1	1 - 2
Ill. P.C. Co.	0.50 - 1	1 - 2
International Art. Pub. Co.		
S/Ellen H. Clapsaddle		
Series 1311, 1660, 1817	5 - 6	6 - 9
Series 2445, 4154, 4440, 51670	6 - 8	8 - 10
W/Children	5 - 6	6 - 9
W/Pilgrims, Turkeys, Corn	3 - 4	4 - 5
Others	1 - 2	2 - 3
L. & E. S/H.B.G.		
Series 2212, 2213, 2233	6 - 8	8 - 12
Series 2263, 2273 (6)		
P.F.B.		
Series 8429, 8857 (6)	6 - 7	7 - 8
Taggart Blacks (6)	10 - 15	15 - 20
Raphael Tuck (American)		
Series 101	2 - 3	3 - 5
Whitney	5 - 6	6 - 8
Winsch, Copyright		
Common	1 - 1.50	1.50 - 2
Indians	3 - 4	4 - 6
Ladies	5 - 7	7 - 10
Wolf & Co. S/Clapsaddle, Uns./Clapsaddle		
Add $2-3 per card to **Int. Art Pub. Co.** prices.		

LABOR DAY

Lounsbury Series 2046 (4)	250 - 275	275 - 325
"Our Latest Holiday"	325 - 375	375 - 425

Anon., Santway 100
"Thanks-Giving Greeting"

Anon., Illustrated Postal Card
Co., "A Merry Christmas"

Nash Labor Day Series 1	80 - 100	100 - 120
1 "Service Shall With Steeled ..."		
2 "Labor Conquers Everything"		

CHRISTMAS

Common	0.50 - 1	1 - 2
W/Children, Animals	2 - 3	3 - 4
W/Children, w/Toys	4 - 5	5 - 7
Small Santas, Red Suit	4 - 5	5 - 6
Large Santas, Red Suit	6 - 9	9 - 12
Lady Santa	10 - 20	20 - 40
Sam Gabriel S/Frances Brundage		
Series 200, 208, 219 (10)	10 - 12	12 - 15
International Art Pub. Co. S/Clapsaddle		
Children	7 - 9	9 - 12
Wolf & Co. S/Clapsaddle	10 - 12	12 - 15
P.F.B.		
Series 7143 Boy/Girl (6)	7 - 8	8 - 10
Series 7422 Children/Tree (6)	10 - 12	12 - 14
Raphael Tuck (American)		
"Playtime" Series 550 (10)		
"A Christmas Message" Series (10)		
"Holly Landscape" Series (10)		
"Glad Christmas" Series (10)		

Uns. E. Clapsaddle, Wolf & Co.
1948C, "Christmas promises..."

Uns. S. L. Schmucker, Tuck
556, "I like the Christmas..."

"Christmas Greetings" Series 555 (10) (Identical to New Year Series 620) "Long Ago Children" Series 556 (6)		
Unsigned **S. L. Schmucker**	30 - 35	35 - 40
"Joys of Youth" Series (10) "Christmas Poinsettia" Series 558 "Muff Kiddies" Series 559 "Christmas Symbols" Series 560 S/E. von H. (Evelyn Von Hartmann)		
Winsch, Copyright (Uns. S. L. Schmucker) **Copyright, 1910** - Vertical* (4)		
Lady in poinsettia dress and background "Christmas Wishes"	20 - 25	25 - 30
Lady in green dress, poinsettia coat "Christmas Greeting" Lady in yellow dress, holly background "A Merry Christmas" Lady in white dress and red jacket "A Joyful Christmas"		
* Smaller images reprinted in 1915 with different captions, Vertical	25 - 30	30 - 35
Copyright, 1911 - Vertical (4)		
Girl in red hugs big snowman "A Merry Christmas" Girl in blue with dark red scarf	45 - 50	50 - 60

Anonymous
"Fröhliches Neues Jahr" 1906

Illustrated Postal Card Co. 15148
Uncle Sam

M.S.i.B., 13548
"Glüchkliches Neujahr" 1908

"Christmas Greetings"
Girl in green with yellow scarf
"Merry Christmas"
Girl with red mittens and snowballs
"A Joyful Christmas"
Winsch Backs, No Copyright (4)

Glamour blonde with Santa mask	45 - 50	50 - 60
"A Joyful Christmas"		
Blonde lady with ermine fur		
"A Merry Christmas"		
Blond lady sleeps, Santa watches		
"A Merry Christmas"		
Lady in red sitting on gold bell		
"Christmas Greeting"		
Common	1 - 1.50	1.50 - 2
W/Children	4 - 5	5 - 7
W/Ladies	8 - 10	10 - 12
W/Silk Inserts, Common	3 - 5	5 - 7
W/Silk Ladies	12 - 15	15 - 20
Booklets, Common	3 - 5	5 - 7
Booklets W/Ladies	5 - 7	7 - 10
Copyright, 1913 (4) (Non-Schmucker)	18 - 22	22 - 25
Copyright, 1914 (4) (Non-Schmucker)		

SANTA CLAUS AND KRAMPUS (See Santas)

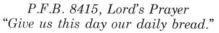

P.F.B. 8415, Lord's Prayer
"Give us this day our daily bread."

A.S.B. 264, Lord's Prayer
"Thy Will be done on Earth..."

UNCLE SAM

Common	6 - 7	7 - 9
Better Publishers	10 - 12	12 - 18
Franz Huld Installment Set	20 - 22	22 - 25
See Fourth of July		
Uncle Sam Santa (See Santas)		

YEAR DATES

1894-1895	75 - 85	85 - 100
1896	50 - 60	60 - 75
1897	40 - 50	50 - 65
1898	35 - 40	40 - 50
1899	30 - 35	35 - 45
1900 Common	20 - 25	25 - 30
W/Animals, People	25 - 30	30 - 35
Hold-To-Light	50 - 55	55 - 65
1901 Common	15 - 20	20 - 25
W/Animals, People	20 - 25	25 - 28
Hold-To-Light	50 - 55	55 - 65
1902 Common	10 - 12	12 - 15
W/Animals, People	15 - 18	18 - 22
Hold-To-Light	30 - 35	35 - 40
1903 Common	8 - 10	10 - 12

W/Animals, People	10 - 12	12 - 15
Hold-To-Light	25 - 30	30 - 35
1904 Common	7 - 9	9 - 12
W/Animals, People	9 - 12	12 - 14
Hold-To-Light	22 - 25	25 - 28
1905 Common	5 - 6	6 - 8
W/Animals, People	6 - 8	8 - 10
Hold-To-Light	20 - 22	22 - 25
1906-1911 Common	4 - 5	5 - 6
W/Animals, People	6 - 7	7 - 8
1912-1914 Common	8 - 10	10 - 12
W/Animals, People	12 - 14	14 - 16
1915-1918 Common	10 - 12	12 - 14
W/Animals, People	12 - 14	14 - 16
1919-1925	20 - 25	25 - 30
1926-1930	25 - 28	28 - 32

RELIGIOUS, VIRTUES, ETC.

CHILD'S PRAYER		
Cunningham (6)	8 - 10	10 - 12
Geo. F. Holbrook (4)	10 - 12	12 - 15
GUARDIAN ANGEL		
A.S.B. Series 250 (4)	8 - 10	10 - 12
Mark Emege Series 178 (4)		
Birn Bros. Series 2109 (4)	7 - 8	8 - 10
PFB		
Series 8618, 8621 (4)	10 - 12	12 - 15
THE HOLY SCRIPTURE		
S/Leinweber, Old Testament	4 - 5	5 - 6
LORD'S PRAYER		
A.S.B. Series 264, 350 (8)	5 - 7	7 - 8
DB Series 350 (8)	6 - 8	8 - 10
I. S. Co. Series (8)	6 - 7	7 - 8
PFB		
Series 7064-7070, Series 8415 (8)	10 - 12	12 - 15
Unknown Publisher		
Series N-700 G (8)	6 - 8	8 - 10
TEN COMMANDMENTS		
PFB		
Series 163, 8554 (10)	8 - 10	10 - 12
Taggart Series (10)		
Rose Series (10)	10 - 12	12 - 15
R. Tuck Series 163 (10)	8 - 10	10 - 12
VIRTUES - FAITH, HOPE, CHARITY		
A.S.B. Series 178 (6)	6 - 8	8 - 10
E.A.S. Series	7 - 8	8 - 12
G.B. Series (6)	8 - 10	10 - 12
Langsdorf Series	7 - 9	9 - 12
PFB		
Series 8797, 8798	10 - 12	12 - 14
Rotograph P.96	5 - 6	6 - 7

SETS & SERIES

Whether there were two, six or fifty, early publishers saw the great benefit of producing cards in sets or series. They commissioned artists and photographers to submit their works in series and packaged them to appeal to the customers. This method, as history has proven, turned out to be a good merchandising scheme, and greatly enhanced the interest and collectibility of postcards at that time, as well as today.

What a thrill it is to finally find the sixth and final card to complete the set! Collectors have been known to pay double or triple value for that last elusive card.

Because of the comprehensive listings in this price guide, this section lists only a small number of the more important sets and series. Over 1900 others are listed in other sections, either under artist or motif.

PUBLISHER SETS & SERIES

	VG	EX
A.L. Alphabet Series 1099 (26)	$ 3 - 4	$ 4 - 5
Acmegraph Co. "Lovelights" (20)	3 - 4	4 - 5
American Colortype, 1909		
"American Beauty" Series 12	6 - 8	8 - 10
American Historical Art Co.		
"Colonial Heroes" (40)	5 - 6	6 - 8
American Souvenir Co.		
"Patriographics" Views 15 sets of 12 each	12 - 15	15 - 18
Boston Series, Alaska Series	15 - 18	18 - 22
J.I. Austen		
"Famous Americans" Series (24) (A325-A348)		
A325 John Greenleaf Whittier	6 - 8	8 - 10
A326 John Phillip Sousa		

A327	Cyrus McCormick		
A328	Alexander Graham Bell		
A329	George Washington	8 - 10	10 - 12
A330	Thomas Jefferson		
A331	Cyrus West Field	6 - 8	8 - 10
A332	Ulyses S. Grant	8 - 10	10 - 12
A333	Robert Perry	6 - 8	8 - 10
A334	Henry Wadsworth Longfellow		
A335	Wright Brothers		
A336	Andrew Carnegie		
A337	George Dewey		
A338	Henry M. Stanley		
A339	Benjamin Franklin		
A340	Thomas Alva Edison		
A341	Luther Burbank		
A342	Roberd Edmund Lee	12 - 15	15 - 20
A343	Mark Twain	6 - 8	8 - 10
A344	Samuel F.B. Morse		
A345	Theodore Roosevelt	10 - 12	12 - 14
A346	Abraham Lincoln		
A347	James McNeil Whistler	6 - 8	8 - 10
A348	Robert Fulton		
A349	Mark Twain	6 - 8	8 - 10
Austin "Tours of the World" (100)		0.25 - 0.50	0.50 - 1
B.B., London Alphabet Series 3700 (26)		3 - 4	4 - 5

American Souvenir
"Patriographics" – "Alaska 6"

Donaldson's Heroes
Bamforth Co., "Oliver H. Perry"

American Souvenir
"Patriographics" – Philadelphia 12

"Playing Card Series" E47 (6)	4 - 5	5 - 6
Bamforth Co.		
Song Series 063 "America's Mighty Army"	4 - 6	6 - 8
A. Bauman "Homely Girl" Series (6)	5 - 6	6 - 8
Bergman "College Girls"	8 - 10	10 - 12
A. C. Bosselman State Capitals and Seals	6 - 8	8 - 10
Cromwell "Roosevelt in Africa" (16)	7 - 8	8 - 10
Cunningham College Girls	6 - 8	8 - 10
Davidson Bros.		
S/Tom Browne		
Series 2569 "Adv. of a very young policeman" (6)	8 - 10	10 - 12
Series 2580 "Three Men in a Boat" (6)		
Donaldson, H. M.		
"American Heroes" (13)		
David Farragut	10 - 12	12 - 15
Sam Houston		
Andrew Jackson		
John Paul Jones		
Gen. Robert E. Lee	15 - 20	20 - 25
Abraham Lincoln	15 - 18	18 - 22
William Penn	10 - 12	12 - 15
Oliver H. Perry		
Israel Putnam		
Paul Revere		
Winfield Scott		
Philip Sheridan	15 - 18	18 - 22
Capt. John Smith	10 - 12	12 - 15
George Washington	12 - 15	15 - 18
Douglas Postcard Co.		
"American Girl" (B&W)	3 - 4	4 - 5
Ferloni, L. "Ferloni Popes" 1903	5 - 6	6 - 8
P. Gordon, 1908 Ladies (10)		
Golf Girl, Tennis Girl	18 - 22	22 - 25
Others	6 - 8	8 - 10
W. R. Gordon, Phila.		
Presidential Series (25) Unnumbered (B&W)	4 - 5	5 - 6
Grollman, I.		
"Merry Widow Hat" Series (16)	4 - 5	5 - 6
E. Gross & Co.		
S/Hamilton King		
"Bathing Beauty" Series (12)	15 - 20	20 - 25
Hill University Girls, Series 8	6 - 8	8 - 10
Hillson, D., 1907		
American Beauty Series 4100 (Red) (23)	6 - 8	8 - 10
The Auto Girl		
The Broadway		
The College Widow		
The Debutante		
The Girl from Golden West		
Hello Girl		
Lady of the Lake		
Lady of the Wind		
The Matinee Girl		
My Coy Maiden		

Hamilton King, E. Gross
"Bar Harbor Girl"

St. John, National Art Company
National Ladies, "Sweden"

My Lady Fair
A Society Bud
My Southern Rose
Naughty
Queen of Sports
"Smile"
Stingy
Sweet Sixteen
The Yachting Girl
The Lady of My Heart
The Fair Graduate
Sympathy
Saucy Scamp
Vanity

College Girls, Ivy League	10 - 12	12 - 15
Illustrated Post Card Co. State Capitols (47)	5 - 6	6 - 8
Klein Alphabet Series (See **Topicals**)		
Kober, P.C. (PCK)		
"Advice to the Lovelorn" S/Hutaf	8 - 10	10 - 12
Butterflies with Views in Wings	15 - 18	18 - 20
"Diabolo" S/Hutaf	10 - 12	12 - 15
Pansies with Views in Petals	12 - 15	15 - 18
State Flags	8 - 10	10 - 12
Koehler, J.		
"Hold-To-Light" Series		
New York City (24)	35 - 40	40 - 45

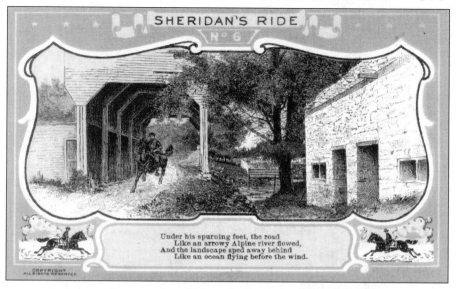

Anonymous, "Sheridan's Ride – No. 6"
"Under his spurning feet, the road..."

Coney Island (12)	35 - 40	40 - 50
"Fighting the Flames"	1500 - 1750	1750 - 2000
Washington, D.C. (12)	25 - 30	30 - 35
Hudson River (12)		
Philadelphia (12)	30 - 32	32 - 38
Boston (12)		
Chicago (12)	30 - 35	35 - 45
Atlantic City (6)		
Buffalo (6)	30 - 32	32 - 38
Niagara Falls (6)	22 - 25	25 - 35
K.V.i.B. National Flag Series		
Woman in Flag Dress Series 80 200+	6 - 8	8 - 10
Langsdorf, S. & Co.		
Alligator Borders (165)		
Blacks	80 - 90	90 - 100
Views	30 - 35	35 - 40
Shell Border Views	10 - 15	15 - 20
State Capitals (5)	8 - 10	10 - 12
State Girls (30)	12 - 15	15 - 20
Embossed	15 - 18	18 - 22
Puzzles	30 - 35	35 - 40
Silk Applique	30 - 35	35 - 38
Military Series	10 - 12	12 - 15
Hugh Leighton & Co.		
Bathing Beauties Series (12)	8 - 10	10 - 12
State Capitols	6 - 8	8 - 10
Unnamed Presidential Series		
Fred C. Lounsbury, 1908		
American Flags & Betsy Ross	8 - 10	10 - 12
National Girls (4)		
The American Girl	12 - 14	14 - 16

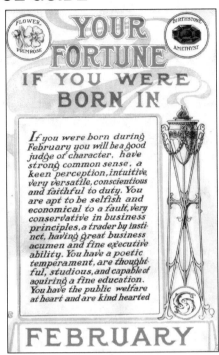

Platinachrome Co.
"State Girl Series — Idaho"

M. T. Sheahan
"Your Fortune — February"

Others	6 - 8	8 - 10
E.H. Mitchell **"Zodiac"** S/Aenz (12)	8 - 10	10 - 12
E. Nash		
Months of the Year, Series 37 (12)	6 - 8	8 - 10
National Art Co.		
National Girls S/St. John	8 - 10	10 - 12
State Girls (46)	6 - 7	7 - 8
National Colortype Co. State Capitols	6 - 7	7 - 8
P.F.B. (Paul Finkenrath, Berlin)		
Series 5563 Girl and Cat (6)	8 - 10	10 - 12
Series 5897 Mother-in-Law Series (6)	10 - 12	12 - 15
Series 6012 **"Punch and Judy"** (6)	12 - 15	15 - 20
Series 6307 Comic Lovers (6)	6 - 8	8 - 10
Series 9327 **"Diabolo"** 6)	12 - 15	15 - 18
Series 6538 **"Domestic Squabbles"** (6)	8 - 10	10 - 12
Series 6800 Children and Roosters (6)		
Series 6943 **"Children's Games ..."** (6)		
Series 6949 Bride & Groom (6)		
Series 7185 Cupids & Large Hearts (6)		
Series 7318 Children in Vehicles (6)	10 - 12	12 - 15
Series 7608 Comic Lovers (6)		
Series 8120 Nymph and Shell (6)	12 - 15	15 - 18
Series 8180 Two Mischievous Boys (6)	8 - 10	10 - 12
Series 8403 Dressed Rooster or Hen (6)	12 - 15	15 - 18
Platinachrome Co.		
National Girls (23)	10 - 12	12 - 15

State Girls (45)	7 - 8	8 - 10
Charles Rose, 1908		
Rose Song Cards (24)	6 - 8	8 - 10
"Maids" Series	5 - 6	6 - 8
"Ten Commandments" (10)	7 - 8	8 - 10
Rotograph Alphabet B-247 thru B-452 (26)	4 - 5	5 - 6
Rotograph College Girls Series FL100 (6)	10 - 12	12 - 15
Samson Brothers		
Series 86 "Vegetables" (12)	3 - 4	4 - 6
"Uneedn't" (12)	3 - 4	4 - 6
M. A. Sheehan (1940's)		
Serigraphs of Presidents by P. Dubosclard (32) 4 - 5		5 - 6
M. T. Sheehan "Your Fortune ...		
if you were born in..." (12)	5 - 6	6 - 8
Souvenir Post Card Co., 1905		
College Girl, Series 4 (6)	8 - 10	10 - 12
Raphael Tuck & Sons		
Advice to Scouts, Series 8745 (6)	12 - 15	15 - 20
Aeroplanes, Series 3101 (6)	15 - 18	18 - 22
Aeroplanes & Warships, Series 9857 (6)	10 - 12	12 - 15
Airships, Series 9495, 9998 (6)	10 - 15	15 - 18
All Sorts of Pets Series 5641, 8032 (6)	8 - 10	10 - 12
Allied Flags Series 872 (6)	10 - 12	12 - 15
Among The Bunnies, Series 9539 (6)	6 - 8	8 - 10
Animal Expressions, Series 9249 (6)		
Animal Life, Series 274, 1416, 1417, 1418, 1419	8 - 10	10 - 12
Animal Studies,		
Series 4453, 4454, 4455, 4461, 4462 (6)	8 - 10	10 - 12
Animal Studies		
S/H.J. Macguire		
Series 6713, 6714 (6)	10 - 12	12 - 15
"At the Carnival,"		
Series 117 (12)		
"A Gallant"	18 - 22	22 - 25
"Belle of the Ball"		
"The Cake Walk"		
"Confidants"		
"Grace and Beauty"		
"Harlequin and Columbine"		
"Jolly Comrades"		
"La Paloma"		
"Music Hath Charms"		
"Only Teasing"		
"The Queen"		
"Ticklish Situation"		
"Celebrated Painters" Series 9404 (6)	8 - 10	10 - 12
"Characters from Dickens" S/Kyd		
Series 540, 541, 856, 5441 (6)	10 - 12	12 - 15
College Girls "Football," Series 2344 (6)	12 - 15	15 - 18
"Diabolo," Series 102, Uns./Brundage (6)	18 - 22	22 - 25
"Greetings from the Seaside," Series 116 (12)	5 - 7	7 - 8
Heraldic Series, 3308-3331 (24)	15 - 18	18 - 22
Heraldic Series Boston #5010-5019 (Emb.)		
Hiawatha, Series 9011 (6)	10 - 12	12 - 15

Langsdorf & Company, Shell Borders S81
"Asbury Avenue looking West from Casino, Asbury Park, N.J."

"Ideal Heads" Series 9392 (6)	15 - 18	18 - 22
"Indian Chiefs" Series 3495 (6)	12 - 15	15 - 18
"Portraits of Presidents" Series 2328 (25)	10 - 12	12 - 15
"Presidents of the U.S." (26)	8 - 10	10 - 12
"Shakespeare" Series 472 (6)	8 - 10	10 - 12
"Shakespeare's Heroes & Heroines"		
Series 1277 (6)	12 - 15	15 - 20
"State Belles" Series 2669 (45)	10 - 12	12 - 15
"Zodiac" S/Dwig Series 128 (12)	12 - 15	15 - 18
Homes of U.S. Presidents, Series 2900 (25)	6 - 8	8 - 10
State Capitols & Seals, Series 2454 (45)	5 - 6	6 - 8
Kings & Queens of England		
Series 614 (12)	10 - 12	15 - 20
Series 615 (12)		
Series 616 (12)		
Series 617 (6) -- All of Edward VII	20 - 25	25 - 30
John Winsch Authors	6 - 7	7 - 8
WOMEN'S WORLD		
"Lover's Lane, St. Jo" Eugene Field (12)	2 - 3	3 - 4
ANONYMOUS		
"Adventures of Lovely Lilly" Series 2026	30 - 35	35 - 40
Flag & Eagle Presidents		
Millard Fillmore, U.S. Grant, Benjamin		
Harrison, Thomas Jefferson, James Madison,		
Wm. McKinley, James Monroe, James Polk,		
T. Roosevelt, Zachary Taylor, John Tyler,		
George Washington	10 - 12	12 - 15
"Sheridan's Ride" (10)	8 - 10	10 - 12
"Your Fortune" (12) Birthstone, Zodiac,		
Fortune, etc., (Emb.) Beautiful Series	10 - 12	12 - 15

9
ADVERTISING

The tiny advertising trade card was introduced in the early 1870's to increase business for manufacturers. Salesmen carried them to be distributed by local merchants who then gave them to customers as a means of advertising and glorifying products and services. This method worked wonders, and greatly enhanced the sales of many products.

The success of the trade card prompted the start of the letter, or cover, advertising, and millions were sent through the mail. The cost of three cents for mailing the letter was deemed rather high by businessmen, and thus came the advent of the now famous advertising postcard.

The postcard, as an advertising medium, began in 1893 when cards were printed for vendors at the Colombian Exposition in Chicago. Those visiting the Exposition purchased these cards and sent them back home to friends as proof of their attendance at the gala event. Most of the cards issued showed buildings of the Expo. However, there were many issues by the exhibitors showing their products and telling of their services.

This first special trial was extremely successful and prompted manufacturers and service oriented businesses throughout the U.S. to "jump on the bandwagon." The great acceptance by the public and the reduced postage rates for postcards made the difference.

Millions of advertising postcards, both color and black and white, were printed and mailed during the first year alone. Advertisers either mailed their own cards or gave them to customers to distribute.

High competition in all modes of product manufacturing and services prompted advertisers and merchants to publish high quality and beautiful sets and series by the artists of the day. As can be seen from the following listings, some of the companies are still in business and this alone makes them more collectible. The beauty and elusiveness of many of these cards have played a major role in making advertising postcards one of the favorites by many in the hobby.

ADVERTISING

	VG	EX
A.B.A. Travelers' Cheques	$ 10 - 12	$ 12 - 15
Absorbine Pain Killer	8 - 10	10 - 12
Acker's Swiss Chocolates		
Acroline Dandruff Remover		
Albert Hosiery Co. (12)		
Alexander, M.H. Co., Molasses		
Allentown Adpostals (7) Multiple ads	35 - 40	40 - 45
American Enamel Co., 1906	5 - 6	6 - 8
American Journal Examiner See Comics Section		
Comics, by many artists	8 - 10	10 - 15
American Fence Co.	5 - 6	6 - 8
American Lady Corsets	8 - 10	10 - 12
American Motor Co. (B&W)		
Motor Cycle Ad w/Miles per gallon	30 - 35	35 - 40
American Thermos Bottles (10)	5 - 6	6 -8
American Woolen Co.	8 - 10	10 - 12
Anheuser-Busch Brewing Co.(Western)	6 - 8	8 - 10
Anheuser-Busch Brewery Scenes	8 - 10	10 - 12
Anheuser-Busch Beer Wagon/Horses	10 - 12	12 - 15
Argand Stoves	6 - 8	8 - 10
Armour & Co.		
American Girl Series (12)		
The Karl Anderson Girl	12 - 15	15 - 20
The Walter A. Clark Girl		
The John C. Clay Girl		
The Howard C. Christy Girl	15 - 20	20 - 25
The Harrison Fisher Girl	45 - 50	50 - 55
The C. Allen Gilbert Girl	15 - 20	20 - 25
The Henry Hutt Girl		
The Hamilton King Girl		
The F. S. Manning Girl	10 - 12	12 - 15
The Thomas M. Pierce Girl		
The W. T. Smedley Girl		
The G. G. Wiederseim Girl	30 - 35	35 - 45
German Published - Add $5-10 per card.		
Armour Star - "The Ham What Am"	8 - 10	10 - 12
Arbuckle Coffee	5 - 6	7 - 8
Do-Wa-Jack Paintings, S/Souler	18 - 22	22 - 25
Asbestos Century Shingles	6 - 8	8 - 10
Asbestos Sad Irons		
Autopiano Player Pianos	8 - 10	10 - 12

5 A Horse Blankets	15 - 20	20 - 25

    "Athol"   "Bouncer"
    "Briar"   "Buster"
    "Essex"   "Fashion"
    "Myrtle"   "Paris Faun"
    "Stratton"   "Plush Robe"   1300
    "Plush Robe"   1652
    "Plush Robe"   1853

Promotional Cards		
"Great For Wear"	15 - 18	18 - 22
"They Make Philadelphia Famous"	15 - 18	18 - 22
Bacardi Rum	10 - 15	15 - 18
Bakers Chocolate	6 - 7	7 - 8
Ballard's Obelisk Flour	8 - 10	10 - 12
Bauer Sisters Candy Delicatessen, Coney Island	10 - 12	12 - 15
Bear Brand Hosiery		
Bell Telephone (12)	15 - 18	18 - 22

    R1 "Announces Unexpected Guests"
    R2 "The Convenience of Marketing"
    R3 "Keeps the Traveler in Touch"
    R4 "Into the Heart of Shopping District"
    R5 "When Servants Fail You"
    R6 "The Social Call"
    R7 "A Doctor Quick"
    R8 "Guards the Home"
    R9 "In Household Emergencies"
    R10 "Relieves Anxieties"
    R11 "Gives Instant Alarms"
    R12 "When the Elements are Against You"

Ben-Hur Book	5 - 6	6 - 8
Ben-Hur Flour	6 - 8	8 - 10
Ben-Hur (Sears-Roebuck)	10 - 12	12 - 15
Bensdorp's Royal Dutch Cocoa (Dutch Life)	5 - 6	6 - 8
Costumed Children Series	15 - 18	18 - 22
Benjamin Suits	10 - 12	12 - 15
Berry Brothers Varnishes (18)	12 - 15	15 - 18
Bester Dairy Appliances	10 - 12	12 - 15
Bissel Carpet Sweepers		
Toledo Frogs (8)		
Baseball Frog	50 - 60	60 - 70
Golf Frog		
Others	40 - 45	45 - 50
Bismark Beer	12 - 15	15 - 20
Black Beauty Axel Grease Black man on Donkey	40 - 50	50 - 60
Blair's Pencil Tablets	10 - 12	12 - 15
Blanke's Coffee		
Overprints on Louisiana Purchase Expo Views	18 - 22	22 - 25
Blatchford Calf Meal Co.	5 - 6	6 - 8
Blatz Beer		
Signed by **Grace Drayton**	80 - 90	90 - 100
Bloomingdale's S/Outcault	90 - 100	100 - 120
Borden's (Elsie Says)	6 - 8	8 - 10
Dairy views	5 - 6	6 - 8
Boston Rubber Shoe Co. (10) (Historic Boston)	3 - 4	4 - 6

Blair's Pencil Tablets

Buffalo Bill's Wild West Show
"W. F. Cody"

Boy's Newspaper	3 - 4	4 - 6
Brockton Shoe Industry	5 - 6	6 -8
Brodrick Buggies	10 - 12	12 - 15
Brown's Bronchial Trochs	3 - 4	4 - 5
Brown & Bigelow Calendars		
Women by Arthur & Stuart Travis	10 - 12	12 - 15
Women by Hamilton King	12 - 15	15 - 18
Couples by Will Grefe	10 - 12	12 - 15
Children by B. P. Gutmann (mis-spelled Gutman)	75 - 85	85 - 100
Brown Shoes		
Buster Brown Canendars, Signed by **Outcault** (12)	20 - 25	25 - 35
Buchan's Soap (6)		
White Bears and Children	18 - 22	22 - 25
Buckbee's Seeds (6)	3 - 4	4 - 6
Budweiser Barley Malt Syrup	12 - 15	15 - 20
Budweiser Beer (early)	12 - 15	15 - 20
Budweiser Yeast	8 - 10	10 - 12
Buffalo Bill's Wild West (Posters) (6)	25 - 30	30 - 35
Bull Durham, S/Outcault (33 Countries)	75 - 85	85 - 100
Bulte's Best Flour (6) Kids	8 - 10	10 - 12

    1. "Bulte's Best"
    2 "Homeward Bound ..."
    3 "Into the Oven ..."
    4 "Of All the Flour ..."
    5 "Out Piping Hot ..."
    6 "Patty Cake"

Grace Drayton-Wiederseim, "Campbells Soups, 10¢ a Can"
No. 3, "Add Zest to Appetite"

Burke's Medicine	6 - 8	8 - 10
Burke's Whiskey	10 - 12	12 - 15
Burlington Zephyr (Train Poster)	15 - 18	18 - 22
Burro Japs Patent Shoes	10 - 12	12 - 15
Busch Extra Dry Ginger Ale	20 - 25	25 - 30
Butter-Krust Bread	10 - 12	12 - 15
Butternut Bread S/Long Black boy with razor	30 - 35	35 - 38
Cadbury's Cocoa	6 - 8	8 - 10
Calox Oxygen Tooth Powder	8 - 10	10 - 12
Calumet Powder	4 - 5	5 - 6
Calumet Baking Powder, S/Outcault	20 - 25	25 - 30
Campbell Soup		
Campbell Soup Kids		
Grace Wiederseim/Grace Drayton (Uns.)		
Horiz. issues - (4) (with variations) (1909)	35 - 40	40 - 50
Vertical issues - (10 cents a can) - 24 * **		
Series 1-12 with **No Series No.** (1912)	125 - 150	150 - 175
Series 1 Numbered 1 thru 6 (1912)	120 - 140	140 - 160
Series 2 Numbered 7 thru 12 (1912)		
Card 7 with Suffragette jingles (2)	150 - 175	175 - 200
Series 3 Numbered 13 thru 18 (1913)	120 - 140	140 - 160
Series 4 Numbered 19 thru 24 (1913)		

* The 24 images have from 3 to 4 different
jingles on each card...meaning there could be
as many as 80 to 96 different total cards.

** Grace Wiederseim remarried in 1911 so
any of these cards with copyright after that
would be by Grace Drayton. Nos. 1 thru 24
were copyright 1912-1913.

Cardui Woman's Tonic	8 - 10	10 - 12

Clark Candy Bar
D. L. Clark Company

Cherry Smash
(John E. Fowler, Richmond, Va.)

Clark's Teaberry Quality Gum
D. L. Clark Company

Carnation Milk	6 - 8	8 - 10
Carnation Milk (A.Y.P. Expo)	12 - 15	15 - 18
Carswell Horse Shoe Nails	6 - 8	8 - 10
Canadian Club Whiskey	12 - 15	15 - 18
Candee Rubbers, by Goodyear Comics	12 - 15	15 - 18
Black Boy in water - "A Well Balanced Rubber"	100 - 125	125 - 150
Case Steam Engines	8 - 10	10 - 12
Case Ten-ton Roan Roller	20 - 25	25 - 30
Case Threshing Machines	10 - 12	12 - 15
Cauchois' Fulton Mills Coffee	6 - 8	8 - 10
Champion Spark Plugs (ad on auto)	15 - 20	20 - 25
A.B. Chase Co. Pianos	10 - 12	12 - 15
Chase & Sanborn Co.	8 - 10	10 - 12
Cherry Blossom Calendar Cards (blacks) **S/Remy**	20 - 25	25 - 30
Cherry Ripe Ice Cream Gum	10 - 12	12 - 15
Cherry Smash (On Lawn at Mt. Vernon)	70 - 75	75 - 85
Chesterfield Cigarettes		
Servicemen, **Uns./Leyendecker**	100 - 125	125 - 150
Chesterfield Cigarettes - Poster, Man Smoking	18 - 20	20 - 25
Chicago, Milwaukee, and St. Paul R.R.	8 - 10	10 - 12
Chi-Namel Varnish	10 - 12	12 - 15
Chocolate Lombart, Air Plane Series	15 - 18	18 - 22
Clark Candy Bar (D. L. Clark Company) - 40's	12 - 15	15 - 18
Clark's Teaberry Quality Gum		
Cleveland Six Automobile	15 - 18	18 - 22
Clyde Steamship Lines Posters Color	25 - 30	30 - 35

Hamilton King
"The Coca-Cola Girl"

Faultless Fashions Clothes
"In 1750 they wore clothes like..."

Black & white advertising Ships	10 - 15	15 - 18
Coca Cola (Girl Driving)	1000 - 1200	1200 - 1500
Coca Cola (Girl's Head) **S/H. King**	700 - 900	900 - 1000
Community Silver	3 - 4	4 - 5
Community Silver Plate		
S/Coles Phillips	40 - 45	45 - 55
Continental Pneumatic Tires	15 - 20	20 - 25
Continental Rubber Tires (Bike)		
Continental Rubber Tires (Tennis)	25 - 30	30 - 35
Corbin Coaster Brakes (Bicycles) Famous Rides	20 - 25	25 - 30
Cook Beer	5 - 6	6 - 7
Coon Chicken Inn, Curt Teich		
3 diff. views of the Restaurant	175 - 200	200 - 250
Cracker Jack Bears (16) By **B. E. Moreland**		
See Teddy Bear Chapter for individual values		
Creamlac, Bicycle Cleaner (1898)	40 - 45	45 - 50
Crescent Flour	5 - 6	6 - 8
Crocker & Best Flour	5 - 6	6 - 8
Crown Millinery Co., 1910	5 - 6	6 - 8
Crown Flour	5 - 6	6 - 8
Curtis Publishing Co.	4 - 5	5 - 6
Daniel Webster Cigars	10 - 12	12 - 15
Daniel Webster Flour	4 - 5	5 - 6
Dannemiller's Royal Coffee	10 - 12	12 - 15
Denver Zephyrs (Train)	15 - 20	20 - 25
Derby's Croup Mix (w/Children)	6 - 8	8 - 10

Continental Pneumatic Bicycle Tires

Devars Whiskey	12 - 15	15 - 18
De Laval Cream Separator	10 - 12	12 - 15
Diamont Rubber Co., Akron	4 - 5	5 - 7
Dinah Black Enamel, Mechanical	45 - 55	55 - 75
Disinfectine Soap (Whole Dam Family) - 1905	12 - 15	15 - 18
Domino Sugar	6 - 8	8 - 10
Do-Wah-Jack, w/Indians - Months of Year Ser.	15 - 18	18 - 22
Round Oak Baseburner Stoves		
Dutch Boy Paints	8 - 10	10 - 12
Dunlop Tires (Inventor/Elves)	30 - 40	40 - 45
DuPont Bird & Wild Game (12) **By Osthaus**	35 - 40	40 - 50

   "Blue Wing Teal"   "Mallards"
   "Canada Goose"   "Prairie Chicken"
   "Canvas Back"   "Quail"
   "Gray Squirrel"   "Ruffled Grouse"
   "Jack Rabbit"   "Wild Turkey"
   "Jack Snipe"   "Woodcock"

Wyeth Painting Card	30 - 35	35 - 40
DuPont Dogs (13) **By Osthaus**	95 - 105	105 - 140

   "Joe Cummings"   "Mohawk II"
   "Allmabagh"   "Monora"
   "Count Gladstone IV"   "Pioneer"
   "Count Whitestone"   "Prince-Whitestone"
   "Geneva"   "Sioux"
   "Lady's Count Gladstone"   "Tony's Gale"
   "Manitoba Rap"

Eastman Cameras	12 - 15	15 - 18
Eclipse Coaster Brakes (Bicycles) Cartoons	15 - 18	18 - 22
Champion Cyclists	20 - 25	25 - 30

Edison Phonograph (Famous Singers)	10 - 12	12 - 15
Egg Climax Incubator	6 - 8	8 - 10
Egg-O-See Cereals w/Children	8 - 10	10 - 12
Eiffel Hosiery	6 - 8	8 - 10
Eldredge Rotary Sewing Machines	10 - 12	12 - 15
Elgin Watch Co.	12 - 15	15 - 20
Emerson Foot-lift Plows	15 - 20	20 - 25
Erasmic Soap - Beautiful Girl	6 - 8	8 - 10
EMF Auto (Glidden Tour)	12 - 15	15 - 18
Eskay's Foods	4 - 5	5 - 7
Evinrude Motor Girl, Real Photo	40 - 50	50 - 60
Excelsior Pneumatic Tires	15 - 20	20 - 25
Excelsior Stove & Mfg. Co.	6 - 8	8 - 10
F. A. Whitney Carriage Co.		
Fall River Line		
Early Color Poster	25 - 30	30 - 35
B & W, with Ships	8 - 10	10 - 12
Falstaff Beer See Lemp Beer		
Farm Journal Magazine	8 - 10	10 - 12
Faun Butters	4 - 5	5 - 6
Federal Cord Tires (3 1/2" x 6")	7 - 8	8 - 10
Firestone Tires (Calendars 1915 and 1916)	18 - 22	22 - 25
Fisk Tires		
"Time to Re-Tire" Small Boy, various	20 - 25	25 - 28
Fisk Red Top Tires	18 - 22	22 - 25
Fisk Removable Rims	12 - 15	15 - 18
Fitz Overalls	8 - 10	10 - 12
Flanders "20" Fore-Door Touring Cars	18 - 22	22 - 26
Flanders "30" Glidden Pathfinder Autos	15 - 18	18 - 22
Fleischmann Co. Yeast	3 - 4	4 - 5
Flexible Flyer Sleds	12 - 15	15 - 20
Flexible Flyer Sleds (Government Postal)	12 - 15	15 - 20
Flood & Conklin & Co., Varnish		
P. Boileau Ladies	100 - 110	110 - 125
Flower City Stoves and Ranges	8 - 10	10 - 12
Ford Motor Co.		
Early Union News color issues	15 - 18	18 - 22
1935 Ford V-8	22 - 25	25 - 28
Formosa Oolong Tea	4 - 5	5 - 8
Foss Orange Extract	8 - 10	10 - 12
Foss Pure Extract	6 - 8	8 - 10
Fowler's Cherry Smash		
W/George Washington	200 - 250	250 - 275
Fox Head Lager Beer	5 - 8	8 - 10
Fralinger's Original Salt Water Taffy		
Beach Series	4 - 5	5 - 6
Series 18, Nursery Rhymes (24), S/Burd	30 - 40	40 - 50
Others, S/Burd	10 - 12	12 - 15
Fralingers Salt Water Taffy - others	5 - 7	7 - 9
Franklin Davis Nursery Co.	2 - 3	3 - 5
Free Sewing Machine Co.	8 - 10	10 - 12
Frog in the Throat Lozenge Co.		
(PMC, 12, oversized)		
1 "A Social Success"	45 - 50	50 - 60

2 "A Universal Favorite"		
3 "Don't Be Without It"		
4 "Favorite at all Times"		
5 "Fore Everybody" Golf	50 - 55	55 - 65
6 "For Singers"	45 - 50	50 - 55
7 "Innocent and Instantaneous"		
8 "My Old Friend Dr. Frog"		
9 "Needs No Introduction"		
10 "Nothing Better"		
11 "Pleasant to Take"		
12 "Popular Everywhere"		
"Frog in the Throat" Series (10) Oversized	40 - 45	45 - 50
Fry's Chocolates, S/Tom Browne	10 - 12	12 - 15
Fry's Cocoa	5 - 6	6 - 7
Fuller Brush Co.	3 - 4	4 - 5
Fuller Floor Wax	4 - 5	5 - 6
Gaar-Scott & Co. (Tractor)	12 - 15	15 - 20
Gales Chocolates (4" x 6")	4 - 6	6 - 8
Gates Tires	10 - 12	12 - 15
G.E. Refrigerator Drowned in Water (30's)	20 - 25	25 - 30
German-American Coffee	10 - 12	12 - 15
Gilles Coffee	3 - 4	4 - 5
Gillette Safety Razor Co. (Child Shaving)	12 - 15	15 - 18
Gladwell's Lawn Mowers	10 - 12	12 - 15
Glidden Tour Autos See auto listings		
Globe-Wernicke Bookcases	6 - 8	8 - 10
Gold Dust Twins Cleanser (4) Uns/E. B. Kemble	40 - 50	50 - 60
Gold Dust Fairbanks Cleanser		
Gold Dust Twins Dressed as Black Santas	100 - 110	110 - 120
Thanksgiving	50 - 60	60 - 70
Real Photos of Black-Face Children w/products		
and costumes	150 - 175	175 - 200
Gold Label Beer	8 - 10	10 - 12
Golden Tree Syrup	3 - 4	4 - 6
Gold Medal Flour	3 - 4	4 - 6
Good Luck Baking Powder (Jamestown Expo)	15 - 18	18 - 22
Goodrich Silvertown Tires	8 - 10	10 - 12
Gorham Silver Polish (1903)	8 - 10	10 - 12
Grande Ronde Meat Co., LaGrande, Oregon	6 - 8	8 - 10
Great Northern Railway	5 - 7	7 - 8
Interior Views		
Green River Whiskey		
Black Man and horse with whiskey keg	60 - 70	70 - 80
Greenfield's Chocolate Sponge	5 - 7	7 - 8
Grollman Hats, 1918	5 - 6	6 - 8
Gulf Refining Co. (Typical Filling Station)	12 - 15	15 - 20
Hackett Carbart & Co. Clothing	3 - 4	4 - 5
Happy Day Washers	5 - 7	7 - 8
Happy Thought Chewing Tobacco (12)	8 - 10	10 - 12
Hamm Brewing Co.	12 - 15	15 - 18
Hart Hats, S/Hoffman	5 - 6	6 - 8
Harley Davidson Motorcycles (6) - Govt. Postals	22 - 25	25 - 28
Hart-Parr Co. (Tractors)	10 - 12	12 - 15
Hartford Suspensions Shock Absorbers (Auto ads)	25 - 30	30 - 35

Hart Schaffner & Marx		
S/Ed. Penfield	22 - 25	25 - 30
Hathaway's Bread	4 - 6	6 - 8
Havana Club Rum	8 - 10	10 - 12
Heather Bloom Petticoats (E. Barrymore)	6 - 8	8 - 10
Heinz Foods, 57 Varieties (w/Product on Front)	12 - 15	15 - 20
Heinz Foods - others	3 - 4	4 - 5
Hendel Motorcycles	12 - 15	15 - 18
Herman Reel Co. (Indians)	8 - 10	10 - 12
Hershey's Cocoa & Chocolates	2 - 3	3 - 4
High Life Beer	10 - 12	12 - 15
Hinds Honey and Almond Cream	6 - 8	8 - 9
Hiram Walker & Sons Liquors	8 - 10	10 - 12
Hires Root Bear	8 - 10	10 - 12
H-O Co. See Korn-Kinks		
Holsum Bread (Cartoons)	8 - 10	10 - 12
Holsum Bread, w/Billy Baker	10 - 12	12 - 15
Hoods Sarsaparilla	6 - 8	8 - 10
Humpty-Dumpty Stockings (N. Rhymes)	10 - 12	12 - 15
Humphrey's Witch Hazel Oil	6 - 8	8 - 10
Hupmobile, 1911	20 - 25	25 - 28
Touring car	25 - 28	28 - 32
Huyler's Candy (w/Children)	8 - 10	10 - 12
S/Von Hartmann	12 - 15	15 - 18
I. X. L. Tamales	5 - 6	6 - 8
Imperial Auto (Pig cartoons) (4)	12 - 15	15 - 18
Imperial Diamond Needles	5 - 6	6 - 8
Independent Wall Paper Co.	3 - 4	4 - 5
India & Ceylon Tea	7 - 8	8 - 10
India Tea Growers	7 - 8	8 - 10
International Harvester, 1909 (12)	5 - 6	6 - 8
International Harvester, 1910 (12)	5 - 6	6 - 8
Inter-State Auto, Chilton		
Inter-State Forty Roadster, Model 32	20 - 25	25 - 30
Inter-State Bull Dog 40"		
Iowa Seed Co.	2 - 3	3 - 4
Jack Sprat Oleomargarine	6 - 8	8 -10
Jackson Auto, Chilton		
Model #35 - $1250	20 - 25	25 - 28
Japan Tea	6 - 8	8 - 10
Johnson's Corn Flower	8 - 10	10 - 12
Joplin Overalls (Girl)	6 - 8	8 - 10
Juniata Horse Shoes, w/Indian Girl	10 - 12	12 - 15
Kalodont Toothpaste & Mouthwash (German)	20 - 25	25 - 30
Kansas City Casket & Furniture Co.	5 - 6	6 - 8
Kaufman & Strauss F. G. Long Black Cartoons	25 - 30	30 - 35
Kelloggs Corn Flakes (Allentown Adpostal)	35 - 40	40 - 45
Kelloggs Corn Flakes, others	5 - 6	6 - 7
Kineto Clocks	15 - 18	18 - 22
King Bee Trimmed Hats	10 - 12	12 - 15
Kinsey Pure Rye Whiskey	6 - 8	8 - 10
Klumbacher Beer (German Beer)	18 - 22	22 - 26
Knapp Calendars (See Artist-Signed Section)		
Frank Desch, Lester Ralph		

Köhler Sewing Machine Wagon
(With Swastika Flag on Fender)

Archie Gunn, No. 5
"Lowney's Chocolates"

Lloyd Italiano Shipping Lines
"Mediterraneo-Buenos Aires"

Kodak Cameras	20 - 25	25 - 28
Köhler Sewing Machine (German)	20 - 25	25 - 30
Kohn Brothers Fine Clothing	10 - 12	12 - 15
Kolb's Bakery W. W. Denslow	50 - 60	60 - 75
Korn-Kinks, H.O. Company		
The Jocular Jinks of Kornelia Kinks		
Series A (6)		
1 "Said Momma to Me ..."	28 - 32	32 - 35
2 "Man, Whar's Your Politeness"		
3 "Gran'pa done say dat ..."		
4 "I'se a going to be ..."		
5 "It ain't a bit o'use ..."		
6 "Susie done 'through' ..."		
The Korn-Kinks Advertising cards (2)		
Souvenir Card Back	30 - 35	35 - 40
Jocular Jinks of Kornelia Kinks"	30 - 32	32 - 35
Rare Variation (Kite in air; no 5 cents on bldg.)	50 - 60	60 - 70
Korvin Ice Cream, Jersey Shore Creamery	6 - 8	8 - 9
Kulmbacher Export Beer, Gruss Aus	25 - 30	30 - 35
Kuppenheimer Suits, Uns./**Leyendecker**	15 - 18	18 - 22
Laco Lamps (Children/Bulbs)	12 - 15	15 - 18
Lady Like Shoes (Beautiful Girls' Heads)	15 - 20	20 - 25
Lash Bitters (Laxative) Drunks	15 - 18	18 - 22
Lehr Pianos	3 - 4	4 - 5
Lekko Hand Soap	8 - 10	10 - 12
Lemp Falstaff Beer Women Sportsmen Fadeways	15 - 20	20 - 25

Falstaff Bottled Beer	12 - 15	15 - 18
Lemp Beer, by Selige Co. (B&W)	6 - 8	`8 - 10
Leonard's Bulk Seed	2 - 3	3 - 4
Lindholm Piano Co.	5 - 6	6 - 8
Lindsay Gas Light Mantles	4 - 5	5 - 6
Lipton Tea (6)	5 - 6	6 - 7
Listerated Pepsin Gum (10), Bears	15 - 18	18 - 22
Lloyd Shipping Lines	20 - 25	25 - 28
Locomobile Auto, Chilton		
Model "3" Locomobile Roadster	20 - 25	25 - 30
Vanderbilt Cup Race, 1905 (7)	12 - 15	15 - 18
Vanderbilt Cup Race, 1908 (10)		
London & Northwestern R.R. Promotional Issues		
Promotional Issues, 28 sets of 6 each (1905)	6 - 7	7 - 8
01 Railways in the "Thirties"		
02 Old Locomotives		
03 Bridges		
04 Royal Saloons		
05 Royal Trains		
06 Express Trains		
07 Places of Interest		
08 Places of Interest		
09 Modern Locomotives		
10 Modern Steamships		
11 Famous Locomotives		
12 Exhibition Engines		
13 Carriages		
14 Miscellaneous		
15 Old London & Birmingham		
16 Tunnels		
17 Locomotives		
18 The London & Birmingham R.R. in 1837-8		
19 Signal Boxes, etc.		
20 Old & New Steamships		
21 Railway Cuttings		
22 Rolling Stock		
23 Goods & Passenger Trains		
24 Stations		
25 Miscellaneous		
26 Old Railway Views		
27 Road Vehicles		
28 Old Railway Prints		
Lowney's Chocolates (Indians)	10 - 12	12 - 15
Girl Golfers, S/Archie Gunn	22 - 25	25 - 28
Magic Curlers	3 - 4	4 - 5
Majestic Stove Ranges	10 - 12	12 - 15
Malt Breakfast Food	4 - 5	5 - 6
Malted Cereal Co.	4 - 5	5 - 6
Mansville & Sons Pianos	6 - 8	8 - 10
Mason & Hanson Woolens, w/Pretty Girls	6 - 8	8 - 10
Men in mode of dress by century	8 - 10	10 - 12
Mason Auto	15 - 18	18 - 22
Mauser's Best Flour	8 - 10	10 - 12
Maxwell Automobiles	30 - 35	35 - 45

"Drink Moxie"
The Moxie Company

Maxwell Exclusive Line Wall Paper	3 - 4	4 - 5
McCallum, D. & J. "Perfection" Scotch Whiskey	8 - 10	10 - 12
McPhail Pianos (Boston Views)	2 - 3	3 - 4
Mecca Cigarettes	18 - 22	22 - 25
Mecca Slippers Black man with guitar	18 - 22	22 - 26
Meier & Frank Dept. Store (set of flags)		
Portland, Oregon	10 - 12	12 - 15
Men-tho-la-tum Salve	6 - 8	8 - 10
Metz Motorcycles	18 - 22	22 - 25
Michelin Tires	15 - 18	18 - 22
Michelin Tire Man	80 - 90	90 - 100
Michelin Tires, s/Vincent	10 - 12	12 - 15
Middlebrook Razors	6 - 8	8 - 10
Miller High Life Beer - Kids in Auto	15 - 20	20 - 25
Minneapolis Knitting Works (Fairy Tales)	15 - 18	18 - 22
Mirroscope Postcard Projector	60 - 70	70 - 80
Mistletoe Margarine	12 - 15	15 - 18
Mogul Egyptian Cigarettes (La. Purch. Expo)	12 - 15	15 - 18
Monarch Typewriters	8 - 10	10 - 12
Moxie	40 - 50	50 - 60
20 Mule Team Borax	8 - 10	10 - 12
Mulford, H. K., Vaccine	5 - 6	6 - 7
Murad Cigarettes (Views)	6 - 8	8 - 10
National Girls	5 - 6	6 - 8
National Biscuit Co.	5 - 6	6 - 8
National Cash Register	4 - 5	5 - 6
National Cloak & Suit Co.	6 - 8	8 - 10
National Light Oil	5 - 6	6 - 8
National Lead Paint (Dutch Boy)	10 - 12	12 - 15
Others	4 - 5	5 - 6

Nestle's Baby Food	6 - 7	7 - 8
With Black child	18 - 22	22 - 25
Nestle's Chocolate	6 - 7	7 - 8
New Departure Brakes (Jack & Jill)	18 - 22	22 - 25
New Idea Manure Spreader	12 - 15	15 - 18
New Home Sewing Machine	8 - 10	10 - 12
Niagara Maid Silk Gloves	15 - 20	20 - 25
Northern Pacific R.R.	5 - 6	6 - 8
Northwestern Hide & Fur Co.	10 - 12	12 - 15
Nu-Life Cereal	5 - 6	6 - 8
Nuvida Springs, California (Indian Girl)	7 - 8	8 - 10
Nylo Chocolates	5 - 6	6 - 7
Oakland Auto, Chilton		
Model 35 - $1075	25 - 30	30 - 35
Model 42 - $1600		
Ocherade Drink	6 - 8	8 - 10
Oil Pull Tractors	12 - 15	15 - 20
Old Style Lager	6 - 8	8 - 10
Oliver Farm Machinery	6 - 8	8 - 10
Old Prentice Whiskey	8 - 10	10 - 12
Oldsmobile Auto, 1907		
With celeberities	35 - 40	40 - 45
Model B Standard Runabout		
Model S - Palace Touring Car		
Hold-to-Lights	75 - 85	85 - 100
Omega Watch (French Poster)	35 - 40	40 - 45
Osborne Calendar Co.		
(See Artist-Signed section - Arthur, Boileau, Underwood, Vernon)		
Outcault Calendars See R.F. Outcault in Comics section		
Overland Auto		
83B Touring Car	25 - 28	28 - 32
Pabst Breweries (Views)	6 - 7	7 - 8
Pacific Mail Steamship Co.		
Color - ships	12 - 15	15 - 20
B & W	5 - 6	6 - 8
Pacific Tank & Pipe Co.	6 - 8	8 - 10
Palmolive Soap (Govt. Postal)	8 - 10	10 - 12
Parisian Belle Perfume	7 - 8	8 - 10
Parker Guns	20 - 25	25 - 30
Parker Shot Guns	18 - 22	22 - 25
Pears Soap	6 - 7	7 - 8
Peerless Auto		
On Glidden Tour	12 - 15	15 - 18
Peroxident Tooth Paste (Uns. Maud Humphreys)		
Paintings of beautiful ladies	15 - 18	18 - 22
Peter's Weatherbird Shoes (Months of Year)	8 - 10	10 - 12
Seasons	8 - 10	10 - 12
Halloween	22 - 25	25 - 30
Philadelphia Lawn Mowers	8 - 10	10 - 12
Phillips Arga - Poster	20 - 25	25 - 30
Phillips Lamps, w/Dutch Girl	22 - 25	25 - 28
Pillsbury Flour	4 - 5	5 - 6
Pinkham, Lydia E., Medicine Co.	4 - 5	5 - 6

Round Oak Baseburner Stoves
"Do-Wah-Jack -- December"

Russian Ad for Singer
Sewing Machine

Sauermann's Kinder-Nährwurst
(German Advertising)

Piso's Cure for Colds	6 - 8	8 - 10
Polarine Oil	6 - 8	8 - 10
Post Toasties Cereal	7 - 8	8 - 10
Ponds Bitters	6 - 7	7 - 8
Post Toasties Corn Flakes	8 - 10	10 - 12
Postum Cereal	3 - 4	4 - 6
Powell's N.Y. Chocolates	3 - 4	4 - 6
Premier Bicycles	20 - 25	25 - 30
Prisco Lantern	6 - 8	8 - 10
Private Estate Coffee	6 - 7	7 - 9
Prudential Insurance Co.		
Battleships	8 - 10	10 - 12
Indians	10 - 12	12 - 15
Others	6 - 8	8 - 10
Purina Chick Chow	8 - 10	10 - 12
Puritan Blouses and Shirts	5 - 6	6 - 8
Purity Salt, PMC	15 - 18	18 - 20
Quaker Oats, w/B&W foreign views	8 - 10	10 - 12
Quaker Maid Brand		
Comic Strip Characters	12 - 15	15 - 18
Movie Stars		
Quick Meal Gas Stoves	12 - 15	15 - 18
R. B. Cigars	10 - 12	12 - 15
Ranier Beer, Seattle	12 - 15	15 - 20
RCA, Dog & Mule Calendars	5 - 6	6 - 8
Rat Bis-Kit (Dog/Cat)	6 - 8	8 - 10

Red Bird Coffee	10 - 12	12 - 15
Red Cross Cotton	6 - 8	8 - 10
Red Horse Tobacco	8 - 10	10 - 12
Red Pig Knives (Posters) See **Roberson Cutlery**		
Red Star Lines, S/Cassiers See Transportation		
Regal Shoe Co. (La. Purchase Expo)	12 - 15	15 - 18
Reliance Baking Powder	5 - 6	6 - 8
Remington Arms	8 - 10	10 - 12
Reynolds Tobacco Co.		
Pre-1920	10 - 12	12 - 15
Others	8 - 10	10 - 12
Richardson Skates	8 - 10	10 - 12
Ringling Bros. Animals	4 - 5	5 - 6
Ringling Bros. Circus Ads	12 - 15	15 - 20
Early Posters	35 - 40	40 - 45
Robeson Cutlery		
"Red Pig" Knives (12)	60 - 70	70 - 80
Rockford Watches - Calendars **S/Outcault**	25 - 30	30 - 35
Round Up Cigars	8 - 10	10 - 12
Rumford Baking Powder	5 - 6	6 - 8
Rumley Tractors	10 - 12	12 - 15
Samoset Chocolates (8) Indians **S/Elwell**	15 - 18	18 - 22
Sandeman Scotch Whiskey	10 - 12	12 - 15
San Felice Cigars	10 - 12	12 - 15
Sanitol Girl	8 - 10	10 - 12
Santa Fe R.R.	6 - 8	8 - 10
Sauermann's Kinder Nahrwurst	15 - 20	20 - 25
Savannah Line, Coast Steamers	10 - 12	12 - 15
Posters	20 - 25	25 - 30
Sawyer Crystal Blue Laundry Soap	5 - 6	6 - 8
Schlitz Beer	8 - 10	10 - 12
Schraffts Chocolate	5 - 6	6 - 8
Schulze's Butter-Nut Bread	6 - 8	8 - 10
Scull, William S. Co., Coffee	6 - 8	8 - 10
Seattle Ice Co.	6 - 8	8 - 10
Selz Liberty Bell Shoes	5 - 6	6 - 8
Sen Sen Gum	10 - 12	12- 15
Sharples Cream Separator		
1 Boy and Girl	12 - 15	15 - 20
2 Cow and Ladies		
3 Mother and Child		
4 Farm Pleasures		
5 Helping Gramma		
6 Teddy	15 - 20	20 - 25
7 Modern Way	12 - 15	15 - 20
8 Dairyman's Choice		
Shredded Wheat Cereal	8 - 10	10 - 12
Shredded Wheat (Factory)	3 - 5	5 - 6
Simple Simon Oleo	6 - 8	8 - 10
Simplex Cream Separators	15 - 18	18 - 22
Simplex Typewriters	6 - 8	8 - 10
Singer Sewing Machines	6 - 8	8 - 10
Russian (Showing Machine)	15 - 20	20 - 25
Sleepy Eye Milling Co. (9) Indians	60 - 70	70 - 80

"Sleepy Eye" Flour
"Indian Artist"

"Sleepy Eye" Flour
"Old Sleepy Eye"

"Sleepy Eye" Flour
"Indian Mode of Conveyance"

"A Mark of Quality"		
"Chief Sleepy Eye Welcomes Whites"	90 - 100	100 - 120
"Indian Artist"	60 - 70	70 - 80
"Indian Canoeing"		
"Indian Mode of Conveyance"		
"Pipe of Peace"		
"Sleepy Eye Mills"		
"Sleepy Eye Monument"		
"Sleepy Eye, The Meritorious Flour"		
Monument	30 - 35	35 - 40
Snow Drift Cotton Oil Co.	5 - 6	6 - 8
Snow Drift Hogless Lard (Bunny & Pail of Lard)	15 - 18	18 - 22
Socony Gasoline	5 - 7	7 -10
Le Soleil Foods (Italy)	15 - 18	18 - 22
Solis Cigar Co. Columbian Exposition, 1893	100 - 125	125 - 150
Sonora Phonographs	8 - 10	10 - 12
Solis Cigar Co. (Columbian Expo)	15 - 18	18 - 22
South Bend Lathes	5 - 6	6 - 8
Southern Cotton Oil Co. (Snowdrift)	5 - 6	6 - 8
Southern Pacific R.R	8 - 10	10 - 12
Interiors of trains	10 - 12	12 - 15
Southern Railway		
Pre 1907	15 - 18	18 - 22
1908-1915	10 - 12	12 - 15
Others	5 - 8	8 - 10
Sperry Flour Co. (sketch by Malloy, signed)	10 - 12	12 - 15

Italian "Le Soleil" Foods
"Malines"

Italian "Suanito" Writing Pen
"Pluma Fuente -- Swan"

Spillers Victorian Dog Food	8 - 10	10 - 12
Stacey-Adams (shoe) **Company**	6 - 8	8 - 10
Standard Brewing Co.	8 - 10	10 - 12
Stanley Belting Corp. (B&W)	4 - 5	5 - 6
Sterling Ranges	6 - 8	8 - 10
Stiletto Lawn Mowers	8 - 10	10 - 12
Strauss Brothers Overcoats	6 - 8	8 - 10
Delivery Cars	30 - 35	35 - 38
Studebaker Corp.		
Pre-1915	30 - 35	35 - 40
1916-1940	20 - 25	25 - 35
Studebaker Jr. Wagons	25 - 30	30 - 35
Stukenbrok's Teutonia-Pneumatic Bicycles		
W/Golliwogg, Gruss aus with und/back	35 - 40	45 - 50
Suanito Writing Pens (Italy)	15 - 18	18 - 22
Suchard Cacao, Color Product, w/B&W views	10 - 12	12 - 15
Summit Shirts	5 - 6	6 - 8
Sunny Jim Whiskey	8 - 10	10 - 12
Swift & Co., 6-Horse Team	8 - 10	10 - 12
Swift's Premium Butterine	6 - 8	8 - 10
Swift's Premium Nursery Rhymes		
"Jack Spratt"	18 - 22	22 - 25
"Little Jack Horner"		
"Little Tommy Turner"		
"Old King Cole"		
"Queen of Hearts"		

Underwood Typewriters
"The $100,000.00 Typewriter"

"Simple Simon"		
Swift's Premium Oleomargarine		
"Children of World"	6 - 8	8 - 10
Swift's Pride, S/Grace Wiederseim		
Sunday's Child, Monday's Child, etc. (7)	35 - 40	40 - 45
Swift's Pride Soap (6) Shadows on Wall	10 - 12	12 - 15
Taylor's Headache Cologne	6 - 8	8 - 10
Templin's "Idea" Seeds	4 - 6	6 - 8
Teutonia-Pneumatic Bicycles (w/Golliwogg)	35 - 40	40 - 50
Texaco Axle Grease	8 - 10	10 - 12
Pre 1940 Local Gas Stations	10 - 15	15 - 20
Texaco Motor Oils	6 - 8	8 - 10
Tip Top Baking Goods Tip Top Boy	10 - 12	12 - 15
Thomas Brau Beer	15 - 20	20 - 25
Toledo Metal Wheel Co.	7 - 8	8 - 10
Toledo Scales	6 - 8	8 - 10
Troy Detachable Collars	4 - 5	5 - 6
True Fruit Flavors	5 - 6	6 - 8
Tudor Lights - Foreign Poster Style	15 - 18	18 - 22
Uhlen Baby Carriages	6 - 8	8 - 10
Uncle John's Syrup (Poster)	20 - 25	25 - 30
Underwood Typewriters	5 - 6	6 - 8
Union Pacific R.R.	5 - 6	6 - 8
Interior Views	10 - 12	12 - 15
Universal Regulators	5 - 6	6 - 8
USM City Collections	10 - 12	12 - 15
Utopia Yarns (Dutch Children)	5 - 6	6 - 7
Valentine's Varnishes (Auto)	10 - 12	12 - 15
Velvet Candy (Kissing on Joy Ride)	40 - 45	45 - 50

Velvetlawn Seeders	6 - 8	8 - 10
Verbeck & Lucas Stoves	6 - 8	8 - 10
Vick's Quality Seeds, Rochester	4 - 5	5 - 6
Voss Brothers Washing Machine	8 - 10	10 - 12
Wales-Goodyear Bear Brand Rubbers	10 - 12	12 - 15
Walker House, Toronto	5 - 6	6 - 8
Walk-Over Shoes, Famous Men (24)	6 - 8	8 - 10
Walk-Over Shoes, Dutch Children	4 - 5	5 - 6
Walk-Over Shoes, Pilgrim Series	4 - 5	5 - 6
Walk-Over Shoes, Scenes from Shakespeare (8)		
"Beatrice" - *Romeo and Juliet*	8 - 10	10 - 12
"Miranda" - *The Tempest*		
"Ophelia" - *Hamlet*		
"Portia" - *Merchant of Venice*		
"Rosalind" - *As You Like It*		
"Titania" - *Midsummer Night's Dream*		
"Viola" - *Twelfth Night*		
Walk-Over Shoes, Topsy Hosiery Blacks (B&W)	15 - 18	18 - 22
Walk-Over Shoes, Western Series	4 - 6	6 - 8
Watkins, J. R. Medical	5 - 6	6 - 8
Watson-Plummer Shoe Co.	6 - 8	8 - 10
Weatherbird Shoes Unsigned	8 - 10	10 - 12
Westinghouse Cooper Hewitt Mercury Rectifier	8 - 10	10 - 12
Westinghouse Electric Iron	6 - 7	7 - 8
Weyerheuser Lumber Co.	5 - 6	6 - 8
White Brothers Bread	6 - 7	7 - 8
White House Coffee & Tea	6 - 8	8 - 10
Whitney, F.A. Carriage Co.	8 - 10	10 - 12
Wilbur Chocolates, S/Henkels (6)	10 - 12	12 - 14
Willys-Overland Autos		
Model 59T	22 - 25	25 - 30
Roadster		
Wilson & Co., Meat Packers	6 - 8	8 - 10
Winchester Arms & Ammo, Folding card, 1906	10 - 12	12 - 15
Wings American Cigarettes		
Blacks dancing	75 - 85	85 - 100
Witch Hazel Ointment	5 - 6	6 - 8
Woods Electric Autos	25 - 28	28 - 32
Woodstock Typewriters	6 - 7	7 - 9
Woonsocket Rubber Co. (10)		
Footwear of Nations	12 - 15	15 - 18
Wyandotte Cleaner & Cleanser	5 - 6	6 - 8
Youth's Companion Magazine	4 - 5	5 - 6
Zang's Beer	8 - 10	10 - 12
Zeiss Ikon Camera (20's)	15 - 18	18 - 20
Zeiss Ikon Film (20's)	15 - 18	18 - 20
Zenith Watches	5 - 8	8 - 10
Zeno Gum Co.	5 - 6	6 - 8

Although there are over 600 listings in our Advertising Postcards section, this by no means includes all that were issued. For a more comprehensive listing we suggest that you obtain a copy of Fred and Mary Megson's fine book, **American Advertising Postcards, Sets and Series, 1890-1920,**

Kippendorf Foot Rest Shoes   *1939 Plymouth Automobile*
"Style for Autumn Comfort"   *"So beautiful you won't believe..."*

Catalog and Price Guide. It may be obtained from the Postcard Lovers,
Box 482, Martinsville, NJ 08836 at $21.50 postpaid.

LINEN ADVERTISING

Alamito Golden Guernsey Milk	6 - 8	8 - 10
Bouquet Brand Rock Lobster	8 - 10	10 - 12
Buick Auto, 1939-41	10 - 12	12 - 15
Buster Brown Shoes, P/Curt Teich	10 - 12	12 - 15
Chevrolet Auto, 1938-41	10 - 12	12 - 15
Chicken in the Rough	6 - 8	8 - 10
Griswold Cast Ware	8 - 10	10 - 12
Habler Bros. Brush Paint Remover	10 - 12	12 - 15
Harvey Brothers Shirts & Ties	8 - 10	10 - 12
Himmel & Sons Furriers, P/Curt Teich	6 - 8	8 - 10
Hudson 1953 "Jet"	10 - 12	12 - 15
Johnson Candies (with Santa)	20 - 25	25 - 28
Kahn Tailors	6 - 8	8 - 10
Kippendorf Foot Rest Shoes	8 - 10	10 - 12
Love's Finer Candies, Rochester, NY	8 - 10	10 - 12
Marathon Auto 1950's Checkey	12 - 15	15 - 18
Maytag Kitchen Washers	8 - 10	10 - 12
Automatic Washers		
Meco Kiln and Man Koolers (fans), P/C. Teich	8 - 10	10 - 12
Mitchell Mortuary Stretcher	8 - 10	10 - 12
Oster "Stim-u-Lax" Massager	12 - 15	15 - 20
Ozark Pencil Company	6 - 8	8 - 10
Plymouth Auto, 1939-41	10 - 12	12 - 15
Pontiac, 1933 Pontiac 8, 2-door Sedan	20 - 25	25 - 28
1937 Pontiac 8		
Soapine Soap Powder	8 - 10	10 - 12
Swann "Pastel" Hats	8 - 10	10 - 12
Storiettes-Books	6 - 8	8 - 10
Trans World Airlines	12 - 15	15 - 20
Tredstep Shoes	8 - 10	10 - 12
Tropic Isle Restaurant, Embossed Breasts Nude	8 - 10	10 - 12
United Air Lines	10 - 12	12 - 15
Weather Shield for Autos - Wilson Company	6 - 8	8 - 10
Wellco House Slippers	6 - 8	8 -10

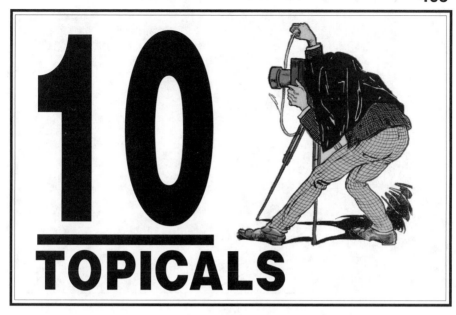

10 TOPICALS

Topical postcards, as the name implies, are those of a particular place, a particular subject, and are any type not listed in a specific section of this publication. They are very special to the collecting fraternity, and make up a large part of every collection.

There were thousands of topics or motifs printed on postcards, and many are sure to appeal to any collector's fancy. As a general rule, collectors "specialize" in a particular subject or theme and try to obtain every card available, old or modern, until the collection is complete. Usually, because of their profound interest, they will also research the subject and become very knowledgeable about it and its history. This, in part, is one of the things that makes the collecting of postcards so interesting, and provides the momentum for the hobby to continue to grow and prosper.

Unless definite cards or sets are listed, values are for a generalized selection in each particular topic. There may be cards in each topic that will command higher, or even lower, prices.

ACTORS, ACTRESSES & PERFORMERS

	VG	EX
Astaire, Fred	$ 6 - 8	$8 - 10
Baker, Josephine		
See Artist-Signed and Blacks		
Bogart, H.	8 - 10	10 - 15
Bergman, I.	5 - 6	6 - 8
Cagney, J.		
Chaplin, Charles	6 - 8	8 - 10
Crosby, Bing		
Davis, Bette		
Dean, James	10 - 12	12 - 18

Early Marilyn Monroe — "The Charmer"
Tichnor Bros., "Lusterchrome" L-40

Dietrich, Marlene	8 - 10	10 - 15
Fields, W. C.	4 - 6	6 - 8
Flynn, Errol	8 - 10	10 - 12
Gable, Clark		
Garbo, Greta	8 - 10	10 - 15
Garland, Judy	6 - 8	8 - 10
Harlow, Jean		
Laurel & Hardy	10 - 12	12 - 15
Lloyd, Harold	4 - 6	6 - 8
Marx Brothers	8 - 10	10 - 12
Mix, Tom		
Monroe, Marilyn		
Rogers, Ginger	3 - 4	4 - 6
Temple, Shirley	6 - 8	8 - 10
Valentino, R.	8 - 10	10 - 15
Wayne, John		
West, Mae	6 - 8	8 - 10
AESOP'S FABLES		
Raphael Tuck		
"Aesop's Fables Up to Date" (6)	20 - 25	25 - 30
AIRPLANES, Military	5 - 6	6 - 8
AIRPLANES (See Transportation)		
AIRPORTS (See Views)	4 - 5	5 - 6
ALLIGATORS, CROCODILES	2 - 3	3 - 4
ALLIGATOR BORDER CARDS, (5500-5664)		
S. Langsdorf & Co.		
Views	30 - 35	35 - 40
Blacks on views "Greetings from the Sunny South" (30) S631-S660	80 - 90	90 - 100
ALPHABET		
Simple	2 - 3	3 - 5

Luna Park, Surf Avenue by Night, Coney Island, N.Y.
Manhattan Post Card Company, 38102

W/Children, Ladies, Animals	4 - 5	5 - 8
Signed **C. Klein**, **Flower Series 148**	12 - 15	15 - 20
Letters U,V,W,X,Y,Z	22 - 25	25 - 28
Rotograph Co. Series B428	4 - 5	5 - 6
AMISH PEOPLE	2 - 3	3 - 6
AMUSEMENT PARKS, Views	6 - 7	7 - 8
Ferris Wheels	5 - 8	8 - 12
Rides, Shows	10 - 12	12 - 15
Coney Island, Etc.	8 - 10	10 - 12
Real Photos, Views	10 - 12	12 - 15
Real Photos, Rides, Shows	20 - 25	25 - 35
Real Photos, Merry-Go-Rounds	35 - 40	40 - 50
ANGELS	3 - 6	6 - 12
Signed by **Mailick**	10 - 15	15 - 20
Others	5 - 8	8 - 15
ANIMALS, Domestic Also See Artist-Signed.	1 - 2	2 - 3
P.F.B. "Cake Walk" **Series 3903** (6)	15 - 18	18 - 22
Raphael Tuck		
Series 6989 "Russian Greyhounds"	10 - 12	12 - 18
ANIMALS, Wild	2 - 3	3 - 6
Official New York Zoo	2 - 3	3 - 4
ANIMALS, Prehistoric	2 - 3	3 - 5
ANTI-CATHOLIC	5 - 8	8 - 10
APPLIQUE (Add-Ons) (See Novelties)		
ART MASTERPIECES (Reproductions)		
Stengel	1 - 2	2 - 3
Nudes	5 - 6	6 - 8
Sborgi	1 - 2	2 - 3
ASTROLOGY	3 - 5	5 - 8
ASYLUMS	5 - 7	7 - 10

P.F.B. Series 8174
Billiards

Christmas Angel
"Fröhliche Weihnachten"

Coins of Mexico, Embossed
Walter Erhard

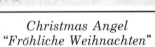

AUTHORS	3 - 4	4 - 5
John Winsch (Author Series)	6 - 7	7 - 8
Others	3 - 5	5 - 6
AUTO RACING, Early	15 - 20	20 - 25
AUTO SERVICE STATIONS See R. Photos, Views.		
BABIES (Multiple, or badies by the dozen)	3 - 5	5 - 10
BALLET DANCING (Also see artist-signed)	4 - 5	5 - 7
BALLOONS, Flying, Early	8 - 10	10 - 15
Real Photo	15 - 20	20 - 25
BANDS, Musical	6 - 8	8 - 10
Military	5 - 6	6 - 8
BANDSTANDS	3 - 4	4 - 6
BANKS (See Views and Real Photos)		
BASEBALL PARKS, STADIUMS (See Baseball, Etc.)		
BASEBALL PLAYERS (See Baseball, Etc.)		
BASKETBALL PLAYERS, Home Teams, Schools	8 - 10	10 - 15
Real Photo	12 - 15	15 - 25
BATHING BEAUTIES		
Illustrated P.C. Co. **Series 80**	6 - 8	8 - 10
Langsdorf & Co. (10)		
Leighton & Co. (10)		
J. Marks "Summer Girl" **Series 155**		
P.F.B. Series 6271 (6)	8 - 10	10 - 12
Souvenir Postcard Co. **Series 526** (6)	6 - 7	7 - 8
E. L. Theochrome **Series 1035**	5 - 6	6 - 7
W. M. Taggert **Series 25**	6 - 8	8 - 10

R. Tuck		
Ser. 116, 1363, 9414, E9466, 9494 (6)	8 - 9	9 - 10
Ullman Mfg. Co. "Seashore Girls" **Series 90**	7 - 8	8 - 10
Foreign Series 583 (6)	6 - 7	7 - 8
Foreign Series 1070 (6)		
Tinted Photos	10 - 12	12 - 15
Others	4 - 6	6 - 8
BATTLESHIPS (See Transportation)		
BEACH SCENES	1 - 2	2 - 4
W/Bathers	3 - 4	4 - 6
Real Photo	6 - 8	8 - 12
BEARS, Real (See Teddy Bear Section)	1 - 2	2 - 3
BICYCLES	3 - 4	4 - 6
Real Photo	8 - 10	10 - 15
Advertising	10 - 15	15 - 20
BILLIARDS	6 - 8	8 - 10
Artist-Signed	8 - 10	10 - 15
BIRDS	2 - 3	3 - 4
Signed C. Klein	5 - 6	6 - 10
Audubon Society	1 - 2	2 - 3
BIRTH ANNOUNCEMENTS	4 - 5	5 - 6
BIRTHSTONES		
E. Nash Series 1	6 - 8	8 - 10
E.P.C. Co. Series 100, 200	2 - 3	3 - 5
BLACKS, U.S. (See Artist-Signed, Uns. Blacks)	5 - 6	6 - 10
Foreign	4 - 5	5 - 6
BOATS, Large Image	2 - 3	3 - 4
Small	1 - 1.50	1 - 50 - 2
BOER WAR	8 - 10	10 - 20
BOOKS	1 - 1.50	1.50 - 2
BOWLING	3 - 4	4 - 6
BOXING (See Baseball, Etc.)		
BOY SCOUTS		
A. E. Marty, Hemostyl Adv. Scout Card	35 - 40	40 - 48
Colortype Co., Chicago Sepia	15 - 20	20 - 25
Gartner & Bender, Chicago	12 - 15	15 - 22
Henninger Co., N.Y.		
Scouts Law (12)	12 - 15	15 - 22
Scouts Gum Co. S/H. S. Edwards (12)	18 - 22	22 - 26
1 "Bugle Calls"		
2 "The Diving Board"		
3 "Fire Without Matches"		
4 "Blazing a Trail"		
5		
6 "Hiding a Trail"		
7 "Vaulting a Stream"		
8 "Loading a Canoe"		
9 "Toting"		
10 "First Aid"		
11 "Flag of Salute"		
12 "The Camp Fire"		
R. Tuck Boy Scout Series 9950 (6)	125 - 150	150 - 175
Series 8745 S/Shepheard		
"Advice to Scouts" (6)	15 - 20	20 - 25

BREWERIES - Exteriors	6 - 8	8 - 12
Interiors	10 - 12	12 - 15
BRIDGES	1 - 2	2 - 3
Covered Bridges	4 - 6	6 - 8
BROOKLYN EAGLE VIEWS	2 - 3	3 - 5
BULL FIGHTS	2 - 3	3 - 5
BUS DEPOTS	4 - 5	5 - 8
See Views and Real Photos.		
BUSES - 1900-1920	12 - 15	15 - 25
1920-1940	10 - 12	12 - 20
BUTTERFLIES	1 - 2	2 - 3
On Greetings	2 - 3	3 - 5
BUTTON FACES - BUTTON FAMILY		
George Jervis	18 - 20	20 - 25
Blacks	25 - 30	30 - 35
CACTUS	1 - 2	2 - 3
CAKE WALK	5 - 10	10 - 15
Blacks	10 - 15	15 - 25
CALCIUM LIGHTS		
J. Plant "Army-Navy Series"	3 - 4	4 - 5
CALENDARS, 1900	15 - 20	20 - 25
Pre-1904	8 - 10	10 - 12
1905-1910	4 - 6	6 - 8
1910-1915	3 - 5	5 - 7
1915-1940	2 - 3	3 - 4
CAMERAS		
Kodak Advertising	15 - 18	18 - 25
Artist-Signed	7 - 10	10 - 16
Comics	2 - 3	3 - 5
CANALS	1 - 2	2 - 3
Panama Canal Construction Views	5 - 7	7 - 10
CANOEING	1 - 2	2 - 3
CAPITALS See Sets & Series		
State Capitols & Seals.		
CARNIVAL		
Raphael Tuck "Carnival" Series 117 (12)	15 - 18	18 - 22
Oilette Series 6435 (6)	12 - 15	15 - 18
Oilette "Mardi Gras" Ser. 2551 (6)	7 - 8	8 - 10
T. Gessner "Mardi Gras" Series	6 - 7	7 - 8
Foreign Early Chromolithos	25 - 35	35 - 50
Real Carnivals		
Sideshows, Color	6 - 8	8 - 10
Sideshows, Real Photo	15 - 18	18 - 25
CAROUSELS Color	10 - 12	12 - 15
Real Photo	15 - 20	20 - 30
CARTS		
Goat, Pony	10 - 12	12 - 15
Horse, Oxen	8 - 10	10 - 12
See Real Photos		
CASTLES	1 - 2	2 - 3
Castles on the Rhine, etc.	3 - 5	5 - 7
CATHEDRALS	1 - 1.50	1.50 - 2
CATS See Artist-Signed Cats		
CATTLE	1 - 2	2 - 3

B. Dondorf, Series 285
Circus Clown

Louis Wain, R. Tuck Series 9563
"The Stick Trick"

CAVES and CAVERNS	1 - 2	2 - 3
CEMETERIES	1 - 1.50	1.50 - 2.00
CHESS/CHECKERS	5 - 7	7 - 12
CHICKENS	1 - 3	3 - 6
Dressed like people.	8 - 10	10 - 15
CHILDREN, Foreign	1 - 2	2 - 4
Playing	2 - 3	3 - 5
W/Dolls, Toys	8 - 10	10 - 16
W/Animals	6 - 7	7 - 10
See Real Photos		
CHINESE PEOPLE	2 - 3	3 - 5
CHRISTMAS TREES		
Raphael Tuck Series 529 (6)	7 - 8	8 - 10
Real Photos with toys, gifts	10 - 15	15 - 20
CHURCHES (See Views)		
CIGARETTES, CIGARS (Also see Advertising)	4 - 5	5 - 8
CIRCUS		
Barnum & Bailey - 1900-1920	25 - 30	30 - 35
Posters	30 - 40	40 - 50
1920-1940	15 - 20	20 - 25
Other Circus	10 - 15	15 - 20
CIVIL WAR		
Raphael Tuck Series 2510		
"Heroes of the South"	25 - 28	28 - 32
1. General Lee & Traveler		
2. General Robert E. Lee		

3. Lee in Confederate Uniform
4. Gen. Thomas J. "Stonewall" Jackson
5. Lee and Jackson
6. Prayer in "Stonewall" Jackson's Camp

Jamestown A&V Co., 1907
    Jamestown Expo Series #50-59 & 67
    Confederate Cards   See Expositions

Others	10 - 12	12 - 15
CLOCKS	1 - 2	2 - 3
CLOWNS - Barnum & Bailey	15 - 20	20 - 25
Barnum & Bailey early Posters with clowns	30 - 40	40 - 50
Early Chromolithographs	30 - 35	35 - 40
Others	10 - 12	12 - 14
COACHES, CARRIAGES	5 - 6	6 - 8
COAT-OF-ARMS	3 - 4	4 - 6
COCA COLA SIGNS		
Small	4 - 6	6 - 8
Large	8 - 10	10 - 15
COIN CARDS, Embossed		
Walter Erhard	8 - 10	10 - 12
Flat Printed	7 - 9	9 - 12
H. Guggenheim (Emb.)	10 - 12	12 - 15
H.S.M.		
COLISEUMS (See Views)		
COLLEGES (See Views)		
COMETS		
Halley's	10 - 12	12 - 20
COMIC STRIP CHARACTERS (See Comics)		
COMPOSERS	2 - 3	3 - 5
CONFEDERATE STATES		
See Expositions: Jamestown Exposition		
"Sheridan's Ride" (10)	8 - 10	10 - 12
CONVENTS	2 - 3	3 - 4
CONVICTS	10 - 12	12 - 15
Black Men	60 - 70	70 - 80
Real Photos		
Black Men	400 - 450	450 - 500
Black Women	450 - 500	500 - 550
CORPSE, In Casket	2 - 3	3 - 4
Real Photo	6 - 8	8 - 10
COSTUMES, Native & Foreign	1 - 2	2 - 3
COURT HOUSES (See Views)		
COVERED BRIDGES	5 - 6	6 - 8
COWBOYS	3 - 5	5 - 8
R. Tuck "Among the Cowboys" Ser. 2499	8 - 10	10 - 15
Real Photos	12 - 15	15 - 25
COWGIRLS	6 - 7	7 - 8
Real Photos	12 - 15	15 - 25
CRADLES	2 - 3	3 - 4
CROSSES	1 - 1.50	1.50 - 2.00
CUPIDS	2 - 3	3 - 5
DAIRIES & Creameries (See Views)		
DAMS	1 -1.50	1.50 - 2.00
DANCING	3 - 5	5 - 6

Artist-Signed See specific artists		
DAYS OF WEEK (Also see Teddy Bears, Sunbonnets)	2 - 3	3 - 6
DEATH (Also See Death Fantasy)	2 - 3	3 - 6
DEER	1 -1.50	1.50 - 2.00
DENTAL	12 - 15	15 - 18
Artist-Signed		
DEPARTMENT STORES	4 - 5	5 -8
Interiors	5 - 6	6 - 8
Interiors, Real Photos	8 - 10	10 - 15
DETROIT PUB. CO. VIEWS		
Early PMC Cards -- Better Views	15 - 20	20 - 25
Common	5 - 6	6 - 8
Others - Better Views	6 - 8	8 - 10
Common	1 - 2	2 - 3
DEVIL or Satan	5 - 8	8 - 10
DIABOLO		
Davidson Ser. 2627 S/Tom Browne	12 - 15	15 - 20
Langsdorf Ser. 711 S/Kinsella (6)		
R. Tuck Ser. N49 S/G. E. Shepherd		
LOUIS WAIN Ser. 9563, 9564 (6)	60 - 70	70 - 90
DICE	3 - 4	4 - 6
DIME STORES (Newberry's, Kress, etc.)	2 - 3	3 - 6
DINERS (See Views, R. Photos, Roadside America)		
DIONNE QUINTUPLETS	15 - 18	18 - 25
DIRIGIBLES, AIRSHIPS, ZEPPELINS	10 - 12	12 - 20
(Also see Transportation & Real Photos)		
DISASTERS		
Earthquakes (San Francisco & others)	2 - 3	3 - 8
Tornados & Hurricanes	5 - 8	8 - 15
Floods, Fire, etc.	6 - 8	8 - 12
(Also see Real Photos)		
DIVERS	2 - 3	3 - 5
DOG CARTS	6 - 8	8 - 12
Sleds	6 - 8	8 - 10
DOGS (Also see Artist-Signed Dogs)	2 - 3	3 - 5
A.S.B. Series 245	6 - 8	8 - 12
A. & M. B. Series 54		
B.B. London Series E32		
H.S.M. Series 719		
P.F.B. Series 8163 (6) Large Image	15 - 17	17 - 20
Raphael Tuck "Art" Series 855 (6)	10 - 12	12 - 15
"Connoisseur" Series 2546 (6)		
DOLLS (See Golliwoggs, Real Photos, Children)		
Gartner & Bender Rag Doll Series	6 - 8	8 - 10
"A Wise Guy" (6)		
"Amybility" (6)		
"Antie Quate" (6)		
"Dolly Dimple" (6)		
"Epi Gram" (6)		
"Gee Whiz" (6)		
"Gee Willikens" (6)		
"Heeza Korker" (6)		
"Jiminy" (6)		
"Optimistic Miss" (6)		

Real Photo Exaggeration
W. H. Martin, Pumpkins

R. Tuck, 9306 (Scaling Ladder)
"Fighting the Flames"

Real Photo, "Ruined by Fire —
Nov. 1908, Runersburg, Pa.

"Phil Osopher" (6)		
DONKEYS, MULES, BURROS	1 - 2	2 - 3
DOVES	0.50 - 1	1 - 1.50
DREAMING	2 - 3	3 - 6
DRINKING		
SCHMUCKER, S. L. (U.S.)		
"Drink" Series, Copyright 1907 (6)		
"Champagne"	150 - 200	200 - 250
"Claret"		
"Creme de Menthe"		
"Manhattan"		
"Martini"		
"Sherry"		
DRINKS Beer, Drunk Comics	2 - 3	3 - 5
DRUG STORES (See Views and Real Photos)		
DRUNKS	2 - 3	3 - 4
DRUGS, ADDICTS USING	8 - 10	10 - 12
DUCKS, GEESE (Also see Fantasy Dressed Animals)	1 - 2	2 - 3
DUTCH PEOPLE AND DUTCH CHILDREN	1 - 2	2 - 4
EARTHQUAKES	2 - 3	3 - 8
ELEPHANTS (Also see Fantasy Dressed Animals)	4 - 5	5 - 6
ELKS	2 - 3	3 - 4
Fraternal, Artist-Signed	6 - 7	7 - 10
ELVES, DWARFS (Also see Fantasy)	3 - 5	5 - 10
EVANGELISTS	2 - 4	4 - 7
EXAGGERATED		

Big Fish, Rabbits, Vegetables, Fruit, etc.	3 - 5	5 - 8
Big Grasshoppers	5 - 6	6 - 9
Add $8 -10 each to prices for Real Photos.		
EXECUTIONS	6 - 8	8 - 10
Chinese, Foreign	5 - 6	6 - 8
FAB PATCHWORK SILKS		
W.N. Sharpe		
Kings & Queens	25 - 30	30 - 35
Scenes	20 - 25	25 - 28
FACTORIES, PLANTS (See Views and Real Photos)		
FAIRY TALES (See Fairy Tales)		
FAIRS, FESTIVALS 5 - 6	6 - 10	
(See Views)		
FAMOUS PEOPLE'S HOMES		
Movie Stars	2 - 3	3 - 5
FANS	2 - 3	3 - 4
FARMING	2 - 3	3 - 5
FARMING EQUIPMENT		
Horse-Driven	6 - 8	8 - 10
Motor-Driven	8 - 10	10 - 12
(See Real Photos)		
FASHIONS	3 - 5	5 - 10
FAT PEOPLE, Real	6 - 8	8 - 10
Circus Side Shows (See Real Photos)	7 - 8	8 - 10
Comics	1 - 1.50	1.50 - 2.00
FELIX THE CAT	15 - 20	20 - 25
FENCING	3 - 4	4 - 6
FERRY BOATS (Also see Real Photos)	6 - 7	7 - 10
FIRE ENGINES, Horse	8 - 10	10 - 15
Motor driven (Also see Real Photos)	15 - 18	18 - 22
FIRE HOUSES and/or Equipment		
(Also see Real Photos)	10 - 12	12 - 15
R. Wilkenson, Providence, R.I. (38)	10 - 12	12 - 15
FIRES (Disasters)	6 - 8	8 - 12
Named (Also see Real Photos)	6 - 8	8 - 15
FIREWORKS	4 - 5	5 - 6
FISH, FISHING	3 - 4	4 - 8
FLAGS, U.S.	4 - 5	5 - 6
Jules Bien Series 710	6 - 8	8 - 10
Ill. Post Card Co. Series 207	6 - 8	8 - 10
National Art Co. "Hands Across the Sea"	7 - 8	8 - 9
Real Photo	8 - 10	10 - 12
Foreign	2 - 3	3 - 4
FLOODS (Disasters)	5 - 6	6 - 8
Named (See Real Photos)	8 - 10	10 - 12
FLOWERS	1 - 1.50	1.50 - 200
C. Klein	3 - 5	5 - 8
FLOWER FACES	6 - 7	8 - 12
FOOTBALL Players See Baseball, etc.)		
FORTS	1 - 2	2 - 3
FOREIGN VIEWS See Views	0.50 - 1	1 - 1.50
FORTUNE TELLING	3 - 4	4 - 6
FRATERNAL		
Ullman Mfg. Co. **Series 199**	7 - 8	8 - 10

Real Photo, KNG 2262-2
Young Golfer

Real Photo, Hoffmann 1197
Adolf Hitler

FREAKS, Animal	6 - 7	7 - 9
People	8 - 9	9 - 12
FROGS (Also see Dressed Animals)	1 - 2	2 - 3
FUNERAL HOMES (See Views)		
GAMBLING, Casinos, Dice, etc.	4 - 5	5 - 6
GEISHA GIRLS	3 - 5	5 - 6
GEYSERS	1 - 2	2 - 3
GHOSTS (Also see Fantasy)	2 - 3	3 - 5
GIANTS, MIDGETS	5 - 8	8 - 10
GIRL SCOUTS		
BALLINGER, E.		
Girl Scout Laws Series M572	10 - 12	12 - 15
GILLESPIE, JESSIE		
Silhouettes of Scout Activities (6)	12 - 14	14 - 18
PRICE, EDITH B.		
The Four Seasons (4)	10 - 12	12 - 15
PRICE, MARGARET EVANS		
Girl Scout Laws Series M-578	12 - 15	15 - 18
GOATS	1 - 2	2 - 3
Bergman Ser. 1052 Billy Goat Comics (6)	5 - 6	6 - 8
GOLF **Players in action**	3 - 4	4 - 5
Courses		
Golf Comics	10 - 15	15 - 25
Artist-Signed Beautiful Ladies	15 - 20	20 - 35
CHRISTY, F. EARL		
Knapp Co.		

"Always Winning"	18 - 22	22 - 28
"Goodbye Summer"		
R&N		
367 "The Day's Work"		
CORBELLA		
Series 316 (6)	15 - 20	20 - 25
GUTTANY		
E. Gross "A Tee Party"		
NANNI, G. Series 309 (6)	20 - 25	25 - 30
RELYEA		
W.C. 9, 10	15 - 18	18 - 22
UNDERWOOD, CLARENCE		
M. Munk "Lost"	15 - 18	18 - 22
Raphael Tuck		
Ser. 697 "Golf Hints" (6)	18 - 22	22 - 25
Ser. 9499 "Humorous Golf" (6)		
Ser. 3600 "Golf Humor" (6)		
S/Thackeray Ser. 9304, 9305 (6)		
Ser. 1627, 1628 (6)		
Ladies/Men Artist-Signed	12 - 14	14 - 18
Series 9427 Blacks, "More Coons" (1)	30 - 35	35 - 40
Valentine & Co. S/C. Crombie		
"Etiquette," "Local Rule," etc. (6)	15 - 18	18 - 22
Advertising, product	15 - 25	25 - 40
GOOD LUCK SYMBOLS		
Horseshoes, Four-leaf Clover	1 - 2	2 - 3
Swastikas	4 - 5	5 - 6
GRAND ARMY OF THE REPUBLIC	3 - 5	5 - 8
GRUSS AUS (See Foreign Views)		
GYMNASIUMS (See Views)		
GYMNASTICS	3 - 4	4 - 5
GYPSIES	5 - 6	6 - 8
HANDBALL	4 - 6	6 - 8
HANDS ACROSS THE SEA (See Silks)	4 - 6	6 - 8
HARBORS	2 - 3	3 - 4
W/Ships, Busy	4 - 5	5 - 7
HATS (Also see Artist-Signed)		
Ladies Big Hats	3 - 4	4 - 6
Real Photos	4 - 6	6 - 10
HERALDIC	4 - 5	5 - 10
Paul Kohl (84)	8 - 10	10 - 12
Raphael Tuck		
"Boston"	8 - 10	10 - 12
"Philadelphia"	8 - 10	10 - 12
"Washington, D.C." PMC's	10 - 12	12 - 14
HITLER		
Real Photos		
Postmarked	15 - 20	20 - 25
Unused	12 - 15	15 - 18
Color, Continental size, Common	15 - 18	18 - 25
Color, Continental size, Rarer issues	50 - 75	75 - 125
HOLD-TO-LIGHT		
Fairy Tales		
Transparencies	40 - 50	50 - 60

Maikäfirs (May Bugs)	40 - 50	50 - 60
Transparencies	30 - 35	35 - 40
New Year		
Snowmen		
Large	50 - 60	60 - 70
Small	40 - 50	50 - 60
Signed by Mailick	60 - 70	70 - 80
Year Dates	35 - 40	40 - 50
Figures made of children	40 - 50	50 - 60
Figures made of pigs	50 - 60	60 - 75
Figures made of snowmen	60 - 75	75 - 100
Unsigned Frances Brundage Children	50 - 60	60 - 75
Scenic types	25 - 30	30 - 35
Valentine's Day		
Children, Cupids	50 - 60	60 - 75
Easter		
Angels	30 - 40	40 - 50
Angels signed by Mailick	70 - 80	80 - 90
Bunnies, Bunnies & Children	60 - 70	70 - 80
Chicks	40 - 50	50 - 60
Children in Easter Eggs	50 - 60	60 - 70
Crosses, Churches, Scenic	25 - 30	30 - 35
Thanksgiving		
Turkeys	75 - 100	100 - 125
Children and Big Turkeys	150 - 175	175 - 200
Scenic, Vegetables, etc.	25 - 30	30 - 35
Christmas		
Angels	50 - 60	60 - 70
Angels with Christmas Trees	65 - 70	70 - 75
Signed by Mailick	70 - 80	80 - 100
Cherubs	40 - 50	50 - 60
Winter Scenes, Churches, etc.	25 - 30	30 - 35
Santas		
Santas in red robes	150 - 175	175 - 250
Large Santas, Robes other than red	250 - 300	300 - 400
Small Santas	150 - 200	200 - 250
Santas signed by Mailick (4) with		
variations by D.R.G.M.	200 - 250	250 - 400
Santa Transparencies	75 - 100	100 - 125
Uncle Sam Santas		
a. Santa knocking on door	2750 - 3200	3200 - 3800
b. Santa trimming tree		
c. Santa standing on step		
d. Santa at window with bag of toys	3200 - 3500	3500 - 4200
Children	40 - 50	50 - 60
Transparencies	25 - 30	30 - 35
Artist-Signed See Specific Artist		
Koehler (See Sets & Series)		
Other Publishers, Views	25 - 30	30 - 40
Statue of Liberty	30 - 35	35 - 40
Trains, Ships	30 - 35	35 - 40
Other Views, Bldgs., etc.	25 - 30	30 - 35
Comics	15 - 20	20 - 25
Foreign Gruss Aus City Views	20 - 25	25 - 30

Paris Exposition (12)	30 - 35	35 - 40
Foreign War Issues (Belgian)	12 - 15	15 - 20
Other See-Through Issues (Transparencies)		
Comics	15 - 20	20 - 25
Other Foreign		
HOROSCOPE		
Dietrich & Co.	6 - 8	8 - 10
Williamson-Haffner Ser. 985		
Others	5 - 6	6 - 7
HORSE & BUGGIES, Large Image, Color	8 - 10	10 - 12
Small Image	5 - 6	6 -8
See Real Photos.		
HORSES, Unsigned - Heads	5 - 7	7 - 10
Large Images		
Small Images	2 - 3	3 - 4
See Artist-Signed Horses.		
Dan Patch		
Wright, Barnett & Stilwell Co.	20 - 25	25 - 28
V.O. Hammond 155	18 - 22	22 - 25
T.P. & Co.	15 - 18	18 - 22
Real Photos	40 - 50	50 - 50
HOSPITALS (See Views, Real Photos)		
HOTELS (See Views, Real Photos)		
HOURS OF THE DAY		
Rose Co.	3 - 4	4 - 6
Warwick Co.		
HOUSEBOATS	4 - 5	5 - 6
HUNTING	1 - 2	2 - 4
ILLUMINATED WINDOWS	5 - 6	6 - 8
ILLUSTRATED SONGS		
Bamforth Many different.	2 - 3	3 - 5
E. Nash "National Song" Series (6)	6 - 8	8 - 10
E.L. Theochromes	2 - 3	3 - 4
Blacks	15 - 18	18 - 22
INCLINE RAILWAYS (See Transportation)		
INDIANS, Chiefs	8 - 10	10 - 15
Others	4 - 6	6 - 8
Real Photos	25 - 35	35 - 60
See Cowboys and Indians.		
INDUSTRY, Exteriors3 - 5	5 - 8	
Interior	5 - 6	6 - 10
See Views and Real Photos.		
INSECTS (Also see Fantasy, Artist-Signed)	.2 - 3	3 - 5
INSTALLMENT CARDS		
W.M. Beach		
Cow (4)	20 - 25	25 - 28
Others		
Huld		
1 Alligator (4)	32 - 35	35 - 38
2 Dachshund (4)		
3 Uncle Sam (4)	50 - 60	60 - 65
4 Fish (4)	25 - 30	30 - 35
5 Sea Serpent (4)		
6 Mosquito (4)		

Large Letter "Victoryville"
Army Flying School, California

Liepaja Zinagoga, Latvia   *German Mechanical Kaleidoscope*
(Jewish Synagogue), Real Photo   *DRGM, L.&B.-B*

7 Rip Van Winkle (4)		
8 New York City (4)		
9 Santa (4)	150 - 175	175 - 225
10 Christmas Tree (4)	35 - 40	40 - 45
11 Fisherwoman (4)	25 - 30	30 - 35
12 Fisherman (4)	25 - 30	30 - 35
14 Rabbit (4)		
15 Teddy Bear (4)	70 - 75	75 - 85
N.Y. Journal-American Comic Characters	6 - 8	8 - 10
H.M. Rose		
Wildwood Co.		
Wrench & Co.		
Ottmar Zieher	8 - 9	9 - 10
Standup Napoleon (10) Sepia	10 - 12	12 - 15
Albert of Belgium (10) B&W	8 - 10	10 - 12
Joan of Arc (10) B&W	10 - 12	12 - 15
JAILS	4 - 5	5 - 8
JAPANESE GIRLS P.C.K. Series	3 - 4	4 - 5
JAPANESE NAVY		
R. Tuck Oilette Series 9237 (6)	6 - 8	8 - 10
JERUSALEM		
R. Tuck Oilette Series 3355 (6)	6 - 8	8 - 10
JEWISH NEW YEAR		
Hebrew Pub. Co.	6 - 7	7 - 10
Others	4 - 5	5 - 7
JEWISH PEOPLE	3 - 5	5 - 8

Comics	10 - 15	15 - 25
JEWISH SYNAGOGUES	15 - 20	20 - 30
Foreign	20 - 25	25 - 35
KU KLUX KLAN		
Printed	50 - 75	75 - 100
Real Photo	200 - 250	250 - 500
LAKES, Named	0.50 - 1	1 - 1.50
LANGUAGE OF FLOWERS	1 - 2	2 - 3
LARGE LETTERS, Cities, States (Early)	2 - 3	3 - 6
Linens	1 - 2	2 - 3
Names Early	5 - 6	6 - 8
Letters of Alphabet	4 - 5	5 - 6
LEATHER (See Novelties)		
LESBIAN-RELATED	12 - 15	15 - 18
Real Photo Nudes	25 - 30	30 - 35
See specific Artists		
LIBRARIES (See Views)		
LIFE SAVING STATIONS	3 - 4	4 - 6
LIGHTHOUSES	2 - 4	4 - 6
Real Photos	5 - 8	8 - 12
LINENS (Postcards)		
Advertising, Product (See Advertising)		
Blacks (See Blacks)	3 - 4	4 - 10
Comics, Unsigned	.50 - 1	1 - 1.50
Comics, Signed	1 - 2	2 - 3
Comics, WW2	3 - 4	4 - 6
Hitler, Anti-	2 - 5	5 - 10
Indians	1 - 2	2 - 3
Large Letters	1 - 1.50	1.50 - 2
Army Bases	3 - 4	4 - 5
Pin-up Girls	2 - 3	3 - 6
Political, Presidential	2 - 3	3 - 7
Court House, Post Office, etc.	1 -1.50	1.50 - 2
Depots, small town	2 - 3	3 - 5
Street Scenes, Small Town	1 - 2	2 - 5
See **Roadside America** for others.		
LIONS	1 - 2	2 - 3
LIONS CLUB	3 - 5	5 - 8
LITERARY CHARACTERS	2 - 3	3 - 6
LOVERS	2 - 3	3 - 4
MACABRE	5 - 6	6 - 10
MAGICIANS	5 - 6	6 - 8
MAIN STREETS See Views and Real Photos.		
MAPS	1 - 2	2 - 5
MASONIC	3 - 4	4 - 6
National Art Co.		
Series 679	5 - 6	6 - 10
Series 1444		
MERRY WIDOW HATS		
Grollman	3 - 4	4 - 5
METAMORPHICS (Archiboldesque) Real Photos		
"Bléroit" Mermaids	50 - 60	60 - 75
"Francois Joseph"	40 - 50	50 - 60
"Graf Zeppelin"	65 - 70	70 - 80

Anon. Metamorphic   *Anon. Metamorphic*   *EDL Metamorphic, 33*
"Bacchus"   *"Mephisto"*   *"Francois Joseph"*

Skulls, "Diabolo"	25 - 30	30 - 35
"Theodore Roosevelt"	175 - 200	200 - 250
"Bismarck," "Napoleon the great conqueror,"	25 - 30	30 - 40
"A Sport," "Une Faune," "Rossini," "Bacchus"		
"Edouard VII," "Alphonse XII," "Satyr,"		
"Cherchez le viveur," "Un bon vivant," "Abdul		
Kamid," "Beethoven," "Goethe," "Liszt,"		
"Gourmand," "Horse with Frauen," "Mephisto,"		
"Napoleon I," "Napoleon II," Jockey and Race		
Horse, "Schiller," "J. Strauss," "Wagner,"		
"Groten van Noordwijk," "Xantippe"		
Many others	20 - 25	25 - 35
Black and White printed	10 - 15	15 - 25
MEXICAN REVOLUTION	5 - 6	6 - 8
Real Photos	10 - 15	15 - 22
Pancho Villa	22 - 25	25 - 28
W.H. Horne - Add $2-3 per card.		
MIDGETS, GIANTS	5 - 8	8 - 10
MILITARY		
Comics	3 - 4	4 - 5
Officers	3 - 5	5 - 8
Soldiers	2 - 3	3 - 4
Gale & Polden "Military Uniforms"	6 - 8	8 - 10
Langsdorf & Co. "Military Officers"	10 - 12	12 - 15
R. Tuck		
S/Harry Payne		
Write Away Series 18, 19, 20, 21, 22,		
23, 24, 25, 26 (6 in each series)	12 - 15	15 - 18
"Our Fighting Regiments"		
Series 3105 "Royal Artillery" (6)	8 - 10	10 - 12
Series 3163 "Ist Life Guards" (6)		
Series 3165 "First Dragoon Guards" (6)		
Military in London		
Series 3546 "Military in London" (6)	10 - 12	12 - 15
Series 6412 "Military in London" I (6)		

Series 9081 "Military in London" II (6)		
Series 9587 "Military in London" III (6)		
Series 3642 "Scots Pipers" (6)	8 - 10	10 - 12
Series 8637 "17th Lancers" (6)		
Series 8762 "The Red Cross" (6)		
Series 8807 "16th Lancers" (6)		
Series 9884 "The Golden Highlanders"		
Series 9885 "Seaforth Highlanders" (6)		
Series 9937 "Argyll & Southern Hilanders" (6)		
Series 9994 "The Black Watch" (6)		
Gale & Polden Issues	8 - 10	10 - 12
Valentine Co.	5 - 6	6 - 8
MILK CARTS	3 - 6	6 - 8
Real Photo	8 - 10	10 - 15
MILK WAGONS, TRUCKS See Real Photo		
MILLS, Industry	3 - 4	4 - 6
Real Photo Interior	10 - 15	15 - 20
Real Photo Exterior	8 - 10	10 - 15
MINING	5 - 6	6 - 8
Real Photo	8 - 10	10 - 15
Add $3 to $5 for Gold Mining		
MINING DISASTERS	10 - 15	15 - 20
MIRRORS	1 - 2	2 - 3
MONKEYS, APES (Also see Dressed Animals)	2 - 3	3 - 4
MONTHS OF YEAR	3 - 4	4 - 6
MONUMENTS	0.50 - 1	1 - 1.50
MOTHER & CHILD	4 - 5	5 - 8
MOTORCYCLES	6 - 8	8 - 10
Named	10 - 12	12 - 15
Others	6 - 8	8 - 10
See Real Photos.		
MOTTOES	0.50 - 1	1 - 2
MOVIE STARS (See Actors/Actresses)		
MUSHROOMS	1 - 2	2 - 3
MUSICAL INSTRUCTORS	2 - 3	3 - 5
MYTHOLOGY	5 - 6	6 -10
NAMES		
R. Tuck Series 131	5 - 6	6 - 8
Rotograph Co. Real Photos		
NATIONAL SOCIALISM	12 - 15	15 - 25
NATIVES	3 - 4	4 - 6
SEMI-NUDES	8 - 10	10 - 15
NAVY		
R. Tuck U.S. Navy Series 2326	8 - 10	10 - 12
Illustrated P.C. Co.		
NESBITT, EVELYN (Actress)	10 - 12	12 - 15
NEWSPAPER	3 - 4	4 - 6
NORTH POLE EXPEDITION	10 - 15	15 - 25
NOVELTIES		
APPLIQUED MATERIALS *		
Feathered Birds, Feathered Hats	4 - 5	5 - 6
Flowers, Beads, Shells, Ribbons	1 - 2	2 - 3

Jewelry, Real Photos, Celluloid	3 - 4	4 - 5
Metal Models, Good Luck Charms, Horse		
Shoes, Bells, Hearts, etc.	7 - 8	8 - 10
Real Hair (On Beautiful Ladies)	15 - 20	20 - 30
Glitter (Distracting on most cards)		
Love letters	2 - 3	3 - 4
Felt (pennants, etc.), Velvet	3 - 4	4 - 10
Silk (See Santas, Langsdorf Ladies, E. Christy)	4 - 8	8 - 15
Velvet, Silk, Felt	3 - 4	4 - 10
Miscellaneous	1 - 2	2 - 3

  * Motif may make value of card higher but can
make value lower, eg. - Glitter

NOVELTY PAPER CUT-OUTS

    Raphael Tuck

Series 3400 "Window Garden" (6)	50 - 75	75 - 100

    M.E. BANKS   Paper Dolls

Series 3381, (I) (6)	125 - 150	150 - 175

    Series 3382, (II) (6)
    "Baby Bunting"
    "Little Bo Beep"
    "Little Jack Horner"
    "The Knave of Hearts"
    "Mary, Mary Quite Contrary"
    "Little Miss Muffet"

Series 3383 (III) (6)	125 - 150	150 - 175

    Series 3384 (IV)   (6)

    LOUIS WAIN

Series 3385, (V) (6)	200 - 250	250 - 300

MECHANICALS *

    Special Types

Circle H Series 100	20 - 25	25 - 30
P.F.B. Series 9525 Day-Month-Date	40 - 45	45 - 50
Kaleidoscopes	20 - 30	30 - 50
Lever-pull	10 - 15	15 - 25
Rotating Wheels	20 - 25	25 - 30
Miscellaneous	8 - 10	10 - 15

    See Clapsaddle Halloween, others.

  * Prices relate to most common types. Other
specific and special types are valued to $200 ea.

TRANSPARENCIES (See Hold-To-Lights)

MISCELLANEOUS

Aluminum	4 - 6	6 - 10
Bas Relief	3 - 4	4 - 5
Royalty	10 - 15	15 - 25
Book Marks	2 - 5	5 - 10
Common	1 - 2	2 - 3
Artist-Signed	5 - 10	10 - 18
Celluloid	5 - 6	6 - 10
Glass Eyes	2 - 3	3 - 5
Hold-to-Light (See Hold-To-Lights)		
Jig Saw Puzzles	7 - 8	8 - 15
Leather		
Comics & Greetings	2 - 3	3 - 5

Blacks	10 - 12	12 - 15
Indians	8 - 10	10 - 12
Presidential or Political	15 - 20	20 - 30
Specials (Women, Golf, Bears, etc.)	6 - 10	10 - 20
Miniature Cards (Views, etc.)	4 - 5	5 - 8
Easter Witches of Scandinavia	12 - 15	15 - 20
Peat	6 - 8	8 - 12
Perfumed	3 - 4	4 - 5
Photo Inserts	1 - 2	2 - 3
Pull-outs (Views)	2 - 3	3 - 4
Records (Phonograph)	10 - 12	12 - 20
Satin Finish	4 - 5	5 - 6
Squeakers	2 - 3	3 - 4
Stamp Montage	6 - 7	7 - 10
Wire Tales	6 - 8	8 - 12
Wood, Bark	5 - 7	7 - 10
NUDES (See Nudes)		
NURSERY RHYMES (See Fantasy)		
NURSES (See specific artists)	5 - 6	6 - 8
OCEAN LINERS (See Transportation)		
OCCUPATIONS	6 - 8	8 - 12
R. Tuck -- A. Selige		
E. Curtis	8 - 10	10 - 12
"A cobbler sweetheart ..."		
"All a-tiptoe ..."		
"Be a baker ..."		
"Come let me whisper ..."		
"Cupid said you melted ..."		
"Dear little teacher, ..."		
"If I a sweetheart had ..."		
"If you can heal a wounded ..."		
"Just a line o'type ..."		
"Links of love ..."		
"My heart is nailed ..."		
"O, queen of cooks, ..."		
"O, would I were an artist ..."		
"Pray if you love me, ..."		
"Punch, punch, punch ..."		
"The lark with notes ..."		
"'Tis needless to try ..."		
"What a bargain ..."		
"When you're a grown-up ..."		
"You may add to ..."		
"You serve me kindly, ..."		
"You'd keep the peace, ..."		
"A little soldier ..."		
Others	3 - 5	5 - 6
OIL WELLS	3 - 4	4 - 6
OPERA SINGERS	4 - 6	6 - 10
OPIUM SMOKERS	4 - 6	6 - 10
ORANGES	1 - 2	2 - 3
ORCHESTRAS	5 - 6	6 - 8
ORGANS, MUSICAL	4 - 5	5 - 6
ORPHANAGES	4 - 5	5 - 8

Главлит № 29304. Тираж 50.000 экз.
Москва, 1924. 2-я фабр. „ГОЗНАК"

Lenin (Actual Name Vladimir Ilyich Ulyanov), 1924 (Russian Card)

OSTRICHES	2 - 3	3 - 4
OWLS (Artist drawn)	6 - 8	8 - 12
PALACES	2 - 3	3 - 4
PAPER DOLL CUT-OUTS (See Novelties)		
PARADES, Color	4 - 5	5 - 6
Real Photo	8 - 10	10 - 12
PASSION PLAY		
Conwell Red Borders	5 - 6	6 - 7
Others	4 - 5	5 - 6
PATRIOTIC (See Greetings)		
National Song Series (6)	4 - 6	6 - 8
PENITENTIARIES	4 - 5	5 - 6
PENNANTS	1 - 2	2 - 3
PERSONALITIES		
Buffalo Bill	10 - 12	12 - 15
Poster Types	25 - 30	30 - 40
Calamity Jane	6 - 8	8 - 10
Winston Churchill	8 - 10	10 - 12
Elvis	8 - 10	10 - 15
Wild Bill Hickock	6 - 8	8 - 10
Elbert Hubbard	5 - 6	6 - 8
Charles Lindbergh	10 - 15	15 - 25
Lenin	10 - 12	12 - 15
Benito Mussolini	10 - 15	15 - 20
Wally Post	6 - 8	8 - 10
Will Rogers	8 - 10	10 - 15
Billy Sunday	6 - 8	8 - 10
Joseph Stalin	12 - 15	15 - 20
PHONOGRAPHS	5 - 6	6 - 7
PHYSICIANS	5 - 6	6 - 8
Comics	6 - 8	8 - 10
PIANOS	3 - 4	4 - 5

PIGEONS	2 - 3	3 - 5
PIGS (Also See Dressed Animals)	3 - 4	4 - 5
PILGRIMS	2 - 3	3 - 4
PIN-UP GIRLS	3 - 4	4 - 8
PLAYING CARDS	4 - 6	6 - 8
POLICEMEN	4 - 5	5 - 8
POLITICAL (See		
"Billikens" (Bryan & Taft)	175 - 200	200 - 225
Others	8 - 10	10 - 12
AMP Co.		
Ethel DeWees		
"Billy Possum" Series (6)		
"Just a few lines..."	25 - 30	30 - 35
"It's a bad thing to ...		
"Yale's Favorite Son"		
"Arrived here just..."		
"I'm going to make..."		
"I'll make another..."		
Birn Brothers (B.B., London)		
Series E243 "We Love Billy Possum"	28 - 32	32 - 35
Frank J. Cohen & Son, Atlanta		
"Billy Possum"	200 - 250	250 - 300
Lester Book & Stationery, Atlanta		
Taft with Possum "Beat it Teddy Bear"	300 - 350	350 - 400
HSV CO.		
Crite		
"Billy Possum" Series (12)		
"Are You Dead - or Just Playing Possum?"	20 - 25	25 - 28
"Aw, don't play possum..."		
"The Boogie Man'll Get You..."		
"Dear Friends..."		
"Dear, Am unavoidably detained..."		
"Do it Now!"		
"Give my regards to Bill!"	25 - 30	30 - 35
"Good eating here"	30 - 35	35 - 40
"I'm having a high old time..."	20 - 25	25 - 28
"It's a Great Game..."	30 - 35	35 - 40
"Oo's 'ittle' possum is 'oo'?"	20 - 25	25 - 28
"Very Busy, Both Hands Full..."		
Lounsbury, Fred C.		
Billy Possum Series 2515, Emb., Sepia (4)		
1. "The only Possums that escaped"	20 - 25	25 - 28
2. "Billy Possum and Jimmie P. on links.."	28 - 32	32 - 35
3. "Moving day in Possum Town"	20 - 25	25 - 28
4. "Good bye Teddy"	28 - 32	32 - 35
Billy Possum Series 2517 (4)		
1. "Uncle Sam's new toy"	20 - 25	25 - 30
2. "Columbia's latest possum..."		
3. "Billy Possum to the front"		
4. "The Nation's Choice"		

W. M. Linn & Sons
"We Are All for Taft" (1908 Campaign)

F. A. Owen Co. (B&W)
   Billy Possum
   "Hurrah for Old Eli"   40 - 50   50 - 60
   Others
Fuller & Fuller Co.
Grollman Political Set
   Bryan and Taft, 1908 (16) with Uncle Sam
   Presidential Race, Baseball Game,
   Winners & Losers   50 - 60   60 - 65
Miscellaneous
1896 Campaign
   William McKinley-Hobart   50 - 55   55 - 60
   William J. Bryan   40 - 50   50 - 55
1900 Campaign
   Eugene V. Debs, Socialist Party   600 - 650   650 - 700
   Roosevelt-Fairbanks   35 - 40   40 - 45
   McKinley & Roosevelt Jugates, PMC   40 - 45   45 - 50
1904 Campaign
   Eugene V. Debs, Socialist Party   600 - 650   650 · 700
   Parker-Davis   100 - 150   150 - 200
   "Teddy Roosevelt, He's Good Enough
   for Me," P/Huld   20 - 25   25 - 30
   Roosevelt-Fairbanks
1908 Campaign
   Eugene V. Debs, Socialist Party   500 - 550   550 - 600
   Taft-Sherman Jugates   15 - 18   18 - 22
   William H. Taft

Political, "It's an Elephant's Job"
© 1932 C. L. Robinson

Political, "Glad Tidings"
(Teddy, Uncle Sam & Taft)

1964 Campaign
(Goldwater and LBJ)

1964 Campaign
(Goldwater and LBJ)

William Jennings Bryan	18 - 22	22 - 25
I. Grollman "Willie B. and Willie T. ..."		
1912 Campaign		
Eugene V. Debs, Socialist Party	500 - 550	550 - 600
Champ Clark	35 - 40	45 - 50
Woodrow Wilson-Marshall	15 - 18	18 - 22
Democratic Wire Tail Donkey-Wilson	30 - 35	35 - 40
Republican Wire Tail Donkey-Taft		
T. Roosevelt-Johnson (Progressive Party)	40 - 50	50 - 60
Taft-Roosevelt Mechanical	50 - 55	55 - 65
Prohibition Candidates		
Eugene Chafin/Aaron Watkins	80 - 90	90 - 100
1916 Campaign		
Eugene V. Debs, Socialist Party	300 - 350	350 - 400
Progressive party (Roosevelt)	35 - 40	40 - 50
Charles E. Hughes (Republican)	30 - 35	35 - 40
Wilson-Taft	18 - 20	20 - 22
Wire-tail Political (Roosevelt)	75 - 85	85 - 100
1920 Campaign		
Eugene V. Debs, Socialist Party	100 - 125	125 - 150
Harding-Coolidge	15 - 20	20 - 25
Cox-Roosevelt	20 - 25	25 - 28
1924 Campaign		

Anon. German R.P.   *E.D.L., 442*   *Lapina, Paris 3525*
"Präsident Roosevelt"   *Taft–Stamp Montage*   *"Le Président Wilson*

Coolidge-Dawes (w/borders), post election	20 - 25	25 - 30
John W. Davis		
LaFollette-Wheeler (Progressive)	50 - 60	60 - 75
1928 Campaign		
Hoover-Curtis	12 - 15	15 - 20
Al Smith	20 - 25	25 - 28
1932 Campaign		
Roosevelt-Garner	12 - 15	15 - 20
Herbert Hoover	15 - 20	20 - 25
1936 Campaign		
Landon-Knox	20 - 25	25 - 30
Roosevelt	15 - 18	18 - 22
1940 Campaign		
Wilkie-McNary	15 - 18	18 - 22
Roosevelt-Wallace		
"Franklin Roosevelt, Our Next President"	20 - 25	25 - 30
1944 Campaign		
Thomas Dewey, "Vote Republican Nov. 7"	15 - 18	18 - 22
Roosevelt-Truman	10 - 12	12 - 15
1948 Campaign		
Truman-Barkley	12 - 15	15 - 18
Thomas E. Dewey		
Wallace-Taylor (Progressive)	20 - 25	25 - 28
1952 Campaign		
Eisenhower-Nixon	12 - 15	15 - 18
Adlai Stevenson	10 - 12	12 - 15
1956 Campaign		
Eisenhower-Nixon	6 - 8	8 - 10
Stevenson	6 - 8	8 - 10
1960 Campaign		
Nixon-Lodge	6 - 8	8 - 10
Kennedy-Johnson	6 - 8	8 - 10

1964 Campaign		
Johnson-Humphrey	5 - 6	6 - 8
Barry Goldwater	4 - 5	5 - 6
1968 Campaign		
Nixon-Agnew-Humphrey	5 - 6	6 - 8
1972 Campaign		
McGovern-Eagleton	8 - 10	10 - 12
Nixon-Ford	4 - 5	5 - 6
1976 Campaign		
Jimmy Carter	6 - 8	8 - 10
1980 Campaign		
Carter-Mondale	4 - 5	5 - 6
Reagan	2 - 3	3 - 4
POSTCARD SHOPS	15 - 20	20 - 25
Advertising Postcards	12 - 15	15 - 20
POSTMEN	6 - 7	7 - 10
POULTRY	1 - 2	2 - 3
H.K. & Co., Series 356	4 - 5	5 - 7
T.S.N., Series 540	4 - 5	5 - 7
PRESIDENTS, also see SETS/SERIES		
Cromwell "Roosevelt in Africa" (16)	7 - 8	8 - 10
Hugh C. Leighton		
Unnamed Series		
Similar to **Tuck's** below. (25)	6 - 7	7 - 9
W. R. Gordon, Phila. Unnumbered (25) B&W	4 - 5	5 - 6
M. A. Sheehan (1940's) (32)		
Serigraphs by Paul Dubosclard (32)	4 - 5	5 - 6
R. Tuck Series 2328		
S/L. Spinner		
"Presidents of the United States" (24)	6 - 8	8 - 10
President Taft - Added Later	12 - 15	15 - 18
"President Theodore Roosevelt" Ser. 2333	15 - 18	18 - 22
Underwood & Underwood		
"Roosevelt's African Hunt" (40)	5 - 6	6 - 7
ANONYMOUS		
"Flag & Eagle" Presidents (Emb.)	6 - 8	8 - 10
PRISONS	5 - 6	6 - 7
PROPAGANDA	7 - 9	9 - 12
German	10 - 15	15 - 20
Russian	15 - 20	20 - 30
PUZZLES	3 - 4	4 - 5
QUEEN'S DOLL HOUSE		
R. Tuck		
Series 4500 Set 1 (8)	6 - 8	8 - 10
Series 4501 Set 2 (8)		
Series 4502 Set 3 (8)		
Series 4503 Set 3 (8)		
Series 4504 Set 4 (8)		
Series 4505 Set 5 (8)		

R. Tuck "Empire" Series 239
"Her Majesty Queen Alexandra" (Coronation Souvenir)

QUOTATIONS	1 - 2	2 - 3
RABBITS	1 - 2	2 - 3
Dressed (Also see Fantasy Dressed Animals)	5 - 8	8 - 20
RACING, Auto	8 - 10	10 - 12
Dog (Also see Dogs)	5 - 6	6 - 7
Horse (Also see Horses)	7 - 8	8 - 10
RADIO STARS, Early Years	6 - 7	7 - 8
RAINBOWS	3 - 4	4 - 6
REBUS CARDS	5 - 6	6 - 8
REGIMENTAL BADGES	4 - 6	6 - 8
REGIMENTAL AND MILITARY UNIFORMS		
RELIGIOUS (Also See Religious)	1 - 3	3 - 5
REPTILES (Also See Fantasy)	2 - 3	3 - 4
RESTAURANTS (See Views and Real Photos)		
RETIREMENT HOMES	2 - 3	3 - 4
RIVERS	0.50 - 1	1 - 1.50
RODEOS	3 - 4	4 - 5
Real Photos	6 - 8	8 - 10
ROWING	3 - 4	4 - 5

ROYALTY, EUROPEAN

GREAT BRITAIN

QUEEN VICTORIA
  1897 DIAMOND JUBILEE
Postally Used, 1897	200 - 220	220 - 235

H.M. King George V
George Pullman & Sons

Her Majesty Queen Elizabeth
Real Photo

Unused	100 - 110	110 - 125
Raphael Tuck & Sons		
Portraits	20 - 22	22 - 28
Family Groups	8 - 10	10 - 12
Foreign Issues	12 - 15	15 - 18
Mourning Issues	15 - 20	20 - 25
KING EDWARD VII		
1901 ROYAL TOUR		
Wrench "Links of Empire" (20)		
Postally Used from Tour Cities	30 - 35	35 - 40
Unused	20 - 25	25 - 30
1902 CORONATION SERIES		
Raphael Tuck & Sons		
Series 239 (Color/Embossed)	15 - 20	20 - 25
Series 655, B&W	10 - 12	12 - 15
Stewart & Woolf, Series 105 (10)	12 - 15	15 - 20
S/H. Cassiers, Views	8 - 10	10 - 14
Other Publishers	6 - 8	8 - 12
Views of Coronation Procession	3 - 6	4 - 6
Royal Visits to Foreign Countries	12 - 15	15 - 20
Royal Visits ot Great Britain	10 - 12	12 - 15
Mourning Cards	5 - 6	6 - 8
Portraits	5 - 6	6 - 8
Family Groups	4 - 5	5 - 6

Children	4 - 5	5 - 6
KING GEORGE V		
Souvenir Cards	10 - 12	12 - 15
Coronation Procession	2 - 3	3 - 5
Rotary Photo, Real Photos	8 - 10	10 - 12
Others	6 - 8	8 - 10
1935 SILVER JUBILEE		
Souvenir Cards	6 - 8	8 - 10
Portraits & Family Groups	2 - 3	3 - 5
Visits	10 - 12	12 - 15
Mourning & Funeral Cards	2 - 4	4 - 7
KING EDWARD VIII		
Wedding Souvenir	30 - 35	35 - 40
Coronation Souvenir	6 - 8	8 - 10
Portraits	3 - 5	5 - 7
King Edward w/Mrs. Simpson	30 - 35	35 - 40
Visits	10 - 12	12 - 18
KING GEORGE VI		
1937 Coronation Souvenir Card	4 - 5	5 - 7
Visits	8 - 10	10 - 15
Mourning Cards, 1952	5 - 6	6 - 8
Others	2 - 3	3 - 6
QUEEN ELIZABETH II		
Wedding, 1947 Souvenir Cards	5 - 6	6 - 8
Coronation Souvenir Cards	3 - 4	4 - 6
Raphael Tuck & Sons	5 - 6	6 - 8
Children	2 - 3	3 - 4
Portraits	2 - 3	3 - 4
Visits	7 - 8	8 - 10
MISCELLANEOUS BRITISH		
Raphael Tuck & Sons		
Kings & Queens of England		
Series 614, 615, 616 (12)	12 - 15	15 - 18
Series 617 (6)	15 - 18	18 - 22
Faulkner Series	8 - 10	10 - 12
RUSSIA		
Czar Nicholas & Family *		
Color Portraits	35 - 40	40 - 45
B&W Portraits	25 - 30	30 - 35
Family Groups	35 - 40	40 - 45
Children of the Czar	40 - 45	45 - 50
Alexandra	25 - 30	30 - 35
Rasputin	25 - 30	30 - 40
Comical/Propaganda	15 - 20	20 - 25
Czar Nicholas, 1896 Visit to France	40 - 45	45 - 50
* Russian published. Others around 20% lower.		
Others	8 - 10	10 - 12

R. Tuck, 8753 "War Notabilities"
"The Czar"

Real Photo, 1091
Alexandra and The Czarewitch

Rasputin and His Adoring Russian Followers
Real Photo

GERMANY		
Portraits	8 - 10	10 - 15
Family Groups	6 - 8	8 - 10
Comical/Propaganda	10 - 12	12 - 15
OTHER EUROPEAN	4 - 7	7 - 10
EASTERN EUROPE	5 - 8	8 - 10
P/AULT		
"RULERS OF THE WORLD" Series	8 - 10	10 - 12
Tsar Nicholas	30 - 35	35 - 40
OTHER RULERS	3 - 4	4 - 6
SAILORS	2 - 3	3 - 5
SAILBOATS	1 - 2	2 - 3
SALVATION ARMY	3 - 4	4 - 10
SAN FRANCISCO EARTHQUAKE	3 - 4	4 - 10
SANTA CLAUS (See Santas Chapter)		
SCHOOLS (See Views)		
23 SKIDDO	3 - 6	6 - 8
SCULPTURE	1 - 1.50	1.50 - 2
SCOUTS (See Boy Scouts)		
SEA SHELLS	1 - 2	2 - 3
SEPTEMBER MORN		
Various Cards	2 - 3	3 - 10
SHAKESPEARE	3 - 4	4 - 6
C. W. Faulkner Series	6 - 7	7 - 10
SHEEP	1 - 1.50	1.50 - 2
SHIP WRECKS (See specials, Titanic, etc.)	5 - 8	8 - 15
SHIP YARDS	3 - 4	4 - 6
SHOES	2 - 3	3 - 4
SHOPS, Industry Exteriors	4 - 6	6 - 7
Interiors Real Photo	8 - 10	10 - 15
SILKS (Also see Santas and Langsdorf Ladies)		
Beautiful Ladies, Children	15 - 18	18 - 25
Cats, other animals	10 - 12	12 - 15
Greetings	5 - 6	6 - 8
Woven Silks		
Glasgow Exhibition, 1911	45 - 50	50 - 55
"Hands Across the Sea" (19)	40 - 45	45 - 50
The Million Dollar Pier, Atlantic City	45 - 50	50 - 55
Presidential - Taft, Roosevelt, Wilson	150 - 175	175 - 200
St. Louis 1904 World's Fair (14)	300 - 325	325 - 350
Ships - RMS Arabic," "Baltic," "Ivernia,"		
"Mauretania," " Saxonia,"Others	60 - 70	70 - 80
See Transportation		
See **"P. Boileau"** for most expensive silk card.		
SINGERS	2 - 3	3 - 5
SKATING, Ice	3 - 6	6 - 8
Roller	4 - 6	6 - 10
SKELETONS, SKULLS (Also see Metamorphic)	4 - 6	6 - 10

SKIING	3 - 5	5 - 7
SLEDDING	3 - 4	4 - 5
SMOKING		
SCHMUCKER, S. L. (U.S.)		
"Smoke" Series, Copyright 1907 (6)		
Beautiful Girl's Head in Smoke	175 - 200	200 - 250
"Clarice" - Cigarette		
"Laughing Waters" - Indian Pipe		
"Lucinda" - Cigar		
"Maude Miller" - Corncob Pipe		
"Molly" - Clay Pipe		
"Virginia" - Brier Pipe		
SNAKES (See Fantasy)	3 - 4	4 - 6
SNOWMEN (See Fantasy)		
SONGS Charles Rose Series #11 (24)	6 - 8	8 - 10
Bamforth Song Series (Many)	2 - 3	3 - 5
Many Others		
SPOONS	3 - 4	4 - 5
STADIUMS, Football, Early	6 - 7	8 - 15
Others (See Baseball, Etc.)	3 - 4	4 - 8
STAGE		
Maude Adams	8 - 10	10 - 12
Lillian Russell	12 - 14	14 - 18
Others	4 - 5	5 - 8
SPANISH AMERICAN WAR	5 - 8	8 - 10
STAMP CARDS		
Kunzli Bros., Paris Series	12 - 15	15 - 20
Maduro, Jr., Panama Series	7 - 8	8 - 10
Menke-Huber Series	12 - 15	15 - 20
P/Piero, Luigi, Italy Series	7 - 8	8 - 10
P/Stengel Series (12)	8 - 9	9 - 10
P/VSM Series	7 - 8	8 - 10
Zieher, Ottmar (Add $2-3 if embossed)	10 - 12	12 - 15
S/Muller	12 - 15	15 - 18
Others	7 - 8	8 - 10
STAMP MONTAGE	5 - 6	6 - 10
STATE GIRLS (See Sets & Series)		
STATE CAPITALS & Seals (See Sets & Series)		
STATUE OF LIBERTY	2 - 4	4 - 8
Hold-To-Light	35 - 40	40 - 50
STATUES	1 - 1.50	1.50 - 2
STILL-LIFE PAINTINGS		
S/M. Billing	2 - 3	3 - 5
S/Mary Golay		
S/A. Gammis-Boecker		
S/C. Klein	3 - 5	5 - 8
See Alphabet		
STORKS	2 - 3	3 - 5

Ottmar Ziehar, Stamp Cards of Germany

Suffragettes, "Votes for Women"
Pub. by Mrs. F. J. Shuler

Dunston Wieler, Series 3
"Pantalette Suffragette"

STREET SCENES (See Views and Real Photos)

STRIKES, Labor	8 - 10	10 - 12
STUDENTS	2 - 3	3 - 4
STUNTMEN	4 - 5	5 - 8
SUBMARINES	4 - 6	6 - 10
SUBWAYS	3 - 5	5 - 10
SUFFRAGETTES		
AA Pub. Co.		
698/12 "Stumping For Votes"	12 - 15	15 - 20
Attwell, Mabel Lucie		
Little Girl, "Where's My Vote"	20 - 25	25 - 30
H.B.G. George Washington "Votes for Women"	70 - 75	75 - 85
LEVI, C.		
"Komical Koons" **Series 210, 3308**	20 - 22	22 - 25
Bergman Co.		
Series 6342, S/B. Wall	12 - 14	14 - 18
Cargill Co, Michigan		
Series 103-129	12 - 15	15 - 20
Campbell Art Co. S/Chamberlin (6)	15 - 18	18 - 22
Clapsaddle	60 - 70	70 - 80
Dunston-Weiler Litho Co.		
1 "Suffragette Madonna"	18 - 20	20 - 25
2 "Electioneering"		
3 "Pantalette Suffragette"		

1767   MOWING-TIME

Bernhardt Wall, Sunbonnets, "Hours-of-the-Day" Series 69
Ullman 1767, "10 A.M. – Mowing Time"

4	"Suffragette Vote-Getter"		
5	"Suffragette-Coppette"		
6	"Uncle Sam-Suffragette...Easiest Way"	25 - 30	30 - 35
7	"Election Day"	18 - 20	20 - 25
8	"I Don't Care"		
9	"Queen of the Poll"		
10	"Where, Oh Where is My ..."		
11	"I Want to Vote ..."		
12	"I Love My Husband, But Oh You Vote"		

Nash Suffragette Madonna
    "Crop of 1910"   12 - 16   16 - 22
ROSE O'NEILL
    Campbell Art Klever Card
    228 "Votes for Women-Do I get your...?"   150 - 175   175 - 200
    National Suffrage Pub. Co.
    "Votes for Women - Spirit of '76"   300 - 400   400 - 500
    "Votes for our Mothers" (not Kewpies   450 - 600   600 - 750
Roth & Langley, 1909 Issues   12 - 15   15 - 18
TWELVETREES, C., Unsigned
    Reinthal & Newman
    716 "I'll get that vote yet!!!"   20 - 25   25 - 30
WELLMAN, WALTER, Artist & Publisher
    The Suffragette Series   20 - 25   25 - 30
    "Bar"
    "Copess"
    "Every Year Will be Leap Year"

"For Speaker of the House"
"Generaless of the Army"
"I Can Heartily Recommend My Wife"
"Judgess"
"Just Politics"
"Letter Carrier"
"Morning Suffragette Bulletin"
"Our Choice, Miss Taffy"
"Secretaryess of Treasury"
"Should Women Mix in Politics"
"Studentess"
"To Whom It May Concern"

SUNBONNET BABIES

Bertha Corbett

Days of the Week 258-264 (7)	10 - 12	12 - 15
Series 119-124 (Uns.)		
Beckworth Series	12 - 15	15 - 18

Dorothy Dixon

Ullman Mfg. Co.

Sunbonnets Series 503-512 (10)	10 - 12	12 - 15
Sunbonnet Girls 1385-1390 (6)		

Bernhardt Wall

S. Bergman Issues	10 - 12	12 - 15
T.P. & Co. Issues		

Ullman

"Days-of-theWeek" 1408-1410,		
1491-1494 (Uns.) (7)	12 - 15	15 - 18
"Months of the Year" 1633-1644 (Uns.) (12)		
"Mottos" With 2 Girls **1645-1650** (6)	10 - 12	12 - 15
"Seasons" 1901-1904 (4)		
"The Sunbonnet Twins" 1645-1650 (6)		
1645 and 1649 are unsigned.		
"Nursery Rhymes" 1664-1669 (Uns.) (6)	15 - 18	18 - 22
"Mary and Her Lamb" 1759-1762 (4)		
1759 is Unsigned	15 - 18	18 - 22
"Hours of the Day" 1765-1770 (6)	10 - 12	12 - 15

Anonymous

Bergman Co.	8 - 10	10 - 12
H. I. Robbins Co. Series 897 (7)	12 - 15	15 - 18

Advertising

Majestic Range Series	18 - 22	22 - 25
SUPERLATIVES - Largest-Smallest	2 - 3	3 - 5
SWANS	1 - 2	2 - 3
SYNAGOGUES	20 - 25	25 - 35
TARTANS	3 - 4	4 - 5
TELEGRAMS	1 - 2	2 - 3
TELEPHONES	5 - 7	7 - 12
TEMPERANCE	4 - 6	6 - 10

SHIRLEY TEMPLE		
Real Photos	8 - 10	10 - 12
Black & White, Color	10 - 12	12 - 14
TENNIS, Courts	5 - 6	6 - 8
Matches in progress	6 - 7	7 - 8
Advertising Tennis Product	15 - 20	20 - 35
See Artist-Signed for Others.		
THEATRES (See Views and Real Photos)		
THEATRICAL		
Maude Adams	6 - 8	8 - 10
Sarah Bernhardt (See A. Mucha)	10 - 15	15 - 20
Enrico Caruso	8 - 10	10 - 12
Zena Dare	6 - 8	8 - 10
Evelyn Nesbitt	8 - 10	10 - 12
TIGERS	2 - 3	3 - 5
TOLL GATES	3 - 4	4 - 6
TORNADOES	6 - 8	8 - 12
TRAINS AND TROLLEYS		
(See Transportation and Real Photos)		
TRAMPS	2 - 3	3 - 4
TUNNELS		
TURKEYS	1 - 2	2 - 3
TYPEWRITERS	3 - 4	4 - 6
UMBRELLAS	2 - 3	3 - 4
UNCLE SAM (See Greetings)		
U.S. NAVY (See Transportation)		
R. Tuck Series 2326	5 - 6	6 - 10
Illustrated P.C. Co.	4 - 5	5 - 8
U.S. NAVY LIFE & MISCELLANEOUS		
Mitchell, Edw. H.		
No. 1316 - 1329 (Color)	2 - 3	3 - 6
No. 4314 - 4318 (Black & White)		
VIEWS (See Views and Real Photos)		
VOLCANOS	2 - 3	3 - 4
WANTED POSTERS	12 - 15	15 - 18
WAR BOND CAMPAIGNS POSTERS	12 - 15	15 - 20
Russian	30 - 35	35 - 45
WEDDINGS	3 - 5	5 - 6
Real Photos, Bride and Groom	8 - 10	10 - 12
Jewish	6 - 7	7 - 12
WHALES	10 - 12	12 - 15
Real Photos	15 - 20	20 - 25
WHOLE DAM FAMILY (Many)	4 - 5	5 - 10
WINDMILLS	2 - 4	4 - 6
WINERIES	3 - 5	5 - 8
WITCHES	6 - 8	8 - 10
Artist-Signed	10 - 15	15 - 30
Easter Witches, Scandinavian	12 - 15	15 - 25
Miniature cards	15 - 20	20 - 25

WORLD WAR I	3 - 5	5 - 10
Daily Mail Series I thru XX (100)	4 - 6	6 - 8
Kavanaugh War Postals	3 - 5	5 - 7
Comics, Common	3 - 4	4 - 6
Comics, Bamforth	6 - 8	8 - 12
Camp Scenes	3 - 4	4 - 8
U.S.O./Salvation Army	5 - 6	6 - 8
Red Cross 5 - 6	6 - 8	
War Scenes	4 - 5	5 - 6
W.C.A. Series 145-146	3 - 5	5 - 10
WORLD WAR II		
Comics, Linen	1 - 3	3 - 6
Hitler, Tojo, Mussolini Comics (Anti-)	3 - 5	5 - 12
Private Breger Comics	5 - 6	6 - 8
Camp Scenes	2 - 3	3 - 4
Army/Navy Air Force Bases	2 - 3	3 - 5
Third Reich Photos, with Swastika	12 - 15	15 - 25
Third Reich Black & White	8 - 10	10 - 15
(See Hitler)		
WRESTLING	5 - 7	7 - 10
YACHTING	2 - 3	3 - 5
YMCA	3 - 5	5 - 6
YWCA	4 - 5	6 - 8
ZODIAC		
S/Aenz	5 - 6	6 - 7
Julius Bien		
"Your Fortune" Series 37 (12)	8 - 10	10 - 12
P/Edw. H. Mitchell	12 - 15	15 - 19
P/R. Tuck,		
Series 128, s/DWIG	12 - 15	15 - 18
P/Paris Expo, 1900	100 - 125	125 - 150
P/Anon. 1970 Zodiac Series (12)	5 - 6	6 - 7
ZOOS	2 - 3	3 - 4

11
TRANSPORTATION

Collectors of most all transportation motifs are extremely fortunate that that material was highly collected in the late 70's and 80's. Although dormant since that time, that cycle has regained it's former momentum. This action has brought out many high quality collections and interest is currently very high, especially for better material.

Spiralling values of the ocean liner "Titanic" have fueled a surge in sales of Ocean Liners and other shippers and the big market in Railway and Trolley depots has also activated good movement in the rails and rail-related issues. There was some wonderful material, including great advertising, published in these fields, and collectors are now able to take advantage of the current low values.

RAIL TRANSPORTATION

ENGINES	VG	EX
Identified Close-up Images*		
Real Photos	$ 15 - 20	$ 20 - 25
Color	8 - 10	10 - 15
Black & White	6 - 8	8 - 12
Advertising	15 - 20	20 - 25
Linens	2 - 3	3 - 5
Chromes or Reproductions	.50 - 1	1 - 1.50
Foreign, pre-1930	2 - 3	3 - 5
*Unidentified - deduct 25-50%.		
Engines with Cars		
Identified Real Photos	12 - 15	15 - 20

*Real Photo, Train 7673 in
Kenilworth, Illinois Station*

*Real Photo, Santa Fe Depot
Eudora, Kansas*

*Real Photo, Train Wreck
Unidentified*

*Real Photo, Train Wreck, ca 1910
Near Atlantic City, New Jersey*

Color	6 - 8	8 - 12
Black & White	5 - 6	6 - 8
Advertising	10 - 12	12 - 20
Interiors, Advertising		
Linens	1 - 2	2 - 3
Chromes or Reproductions	.50 - 1	1 - 1.50
Foreign, pre-1930	1 - 2	2 - 3

*Unidentified - deduct 25-50%.
Small, faraway images have very little value.

Wrecks, Real Photo

Identified	10 - 15	15 - 25
Unidentified	5 - 8	8 - 12

Rail Yards, Repair Areas, etc.

Real Photo	8 - 10	10 - 15
Color	3 - 5	5 - 10
Black & White	2 - 3	3 - 5
Linens	1 - 2	2 - 3
Chromes	.50 - 1	1 - 1.50

TRAIN STATIONS, DEPOTS

Small Towns

Real Photos	10 - 15	15 - 30
Real Photos, Train in station	15 - 18	18 - 35
Color	5 - 8	8 - 12

Real Photo, Erie Railway Engine "Matt. H. Shay"
Built by the Baldwin Locomotive Works

Color, W/Train in Station	6 - 10	10 - 20
Linens	3 - 4	4 - 6
Chromes	1 - 2	2 - 3
Foreign, pre-1930	2 - 3	3 - 6
Large Cities		
Real Photo	4 - 5	5 - 10
Real Photo W/Train in Station	5 - 6	6 - 12
Color	1 - 2	2 - 3
Color, W/Train in Station	2 - 3	3 - 5
Linens	1 - 1.50	1.50 - 2
Chromes	.50 - .75	.75 - 1
Foreign, pre-1930	1 - 2	2 - 3

ELEVATED RAILWAYS

Large Cities (N.Y., Chicago, etc.)		
Close-up Images	2 - 3	3 - 5
Small Images	1 - 2	2 - 3
Linens	1 - 1.50	1.50 - 2
Chromes	.50 - 1	1 - 1.50
Smaller Cities		
Close-up Images	3 - 4	4 - 8
Small Images	2 - 3	3 - 4
Linens	1.50 - 2	2 - 2.50
Chromes	.75 - 1	1 - 1.50

INCLINE RAILWAYS

Identified Close-up Images*		
Mauch Chunk, Pikes Peak,		
Mt. Washington	2 - 3	3 - 5
Mt. Tom, Un-Ca-Noo-Nuc Mt., Lookout Mt.		

*Real Photo, Somerset Tracting Co.
Madison, Me. 23 (Electric Trolley)*

Angel's Flight, Mt. Penn, Mt. Beacon		
Other, lesser known	3 - 4	4 - 6
Identified Small Images*		
Most well known inclines	1 - 2	2 - 3
Other, lesser known	2 - 3	3 - 5
Real Photos, Identified - Add 50%		
*Unidentified - deduct 25-50%.		
SUBWAYS, IDENTIFIED *		
Large Car Images	6 - 8	8 - 10
Cars at Loading Platform	4 - 6	6 - 8
Linens	3 - 5	5 - 8
Chromes	1 - 2	3 - 4
* Unidentified - deduct 25-50%.		
ELECTRIC TROLLEYS		
Identified Close-up Images*		
Real Photo	15 - 20	20 - 35
Color	8 - 10	10 - 20
Black & White	6 - 8	8 - 12
Linens	3 - 4	4 - 6
Chromes and Reproductions	1 - 1.50	1.50 - 2
Foreign	3 - 4	4 - 6
* Unidentified - deduct 25-50%.		
Medium Size in Street Scenes		
Real Photos	8 - 10	10 - 20
Color	5 - 8	8 - 12
Black & White	2 - 4	4 - 6
Linens	2 - 3	3 - 4
Chromes and Reproductions	.50 - 1	1 - 1.50
Foreign	1 - 2	2 - 3

Wrecks, Real Photo

Identified	12 - 15	15 - 25
Unidentified	6 - 8	8 - 12

TROLLEY STATIONS
Small Towns

Real Photo	10 - 15	15 - 25
Real Photo W/Trolley in Station	15 - 20	20 - 30
Color	8 - 10	10 - 15
Color, W/Trolley in Station	10 - 12	12 - 18
Linens	3 - 4	4 - 6
Chromes	1 - 2	2 - 3
Foreign, pre-1930	3 - 4	4 - 6

Large Cities

Real Photo	4 - 6	6 - 10
Real Photo, W/Trolley in Station	6 - 8	8 - 12
Color	1 - 2	2 - 3
Color, W/Trolley in Station	2 - 3	3 - 5
Linens	.75 - 1	1 - 1.50
Chromes	.50 - .75	.75 - 1
Foreign, pre-1930	.50 - .75	.75 - 1

HORSE-DRAWN TROLLEYS

Real Photos	15 - 20	20 - 30
Color	10 - 12	12 - 15
Black & White	6 - 8	8 - 10
Linens, Chromes, Reproductions	1 - 2	2 - 3
Foreign, pre-1930	3 - 4	4 - 6
Unidentified - deduct 25-50%.		

AIR TRANSPORTATION

AIRPLANES

Pioneer, Named (1896-1910)	20 - 25	25 - 40
Early 1910-1914	12 - 25	25 - 35
Langley Plane (Real Photos)	30 - 40	40 - 60
Wright Flyers (Real Photos)	20 - 30	30 - 50
1910 Los Angeles Meet	20 - 25	25 - 35
Aeroplane Meet, Venice, CA		
"Hoxsey Death Flight, Dec. 31, 1910"	20 - 25	25 - 35
"Louis Paulman making record flight altitude"	15 - 20	20 - 25
"Graham-White starting engine, 1910"	12 - 15	15 - 25

MAX RIGOT, CHICAGO

1911 Chicago Aviation Meet	20 - 25	25 - 35
NC-4	30 - 40	40 - 60
"Spirit of St. Louis"	12 - 18	18 - 25
With Lindbergh	20 - 30	30 - 50
Air Meet, Compton, CA - 1910	20 - 25	25 - 35
Identified Accidents	30 - 40	40 - 50
Air Meet, Reims, France - 1909	20 - 25	25 - 30

MISCELLANEOUS
French Aviation Set

Glenn Curtis	30 - 35	35 - 45
De la Grange	25 - 30	30 - 35

*Rose, Paris, 36 - Locomotion
Aérienne, Hubert Latham*

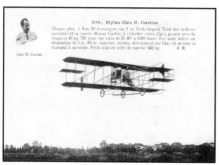

J. Hauser, 1156 *"Biplane Glen H. Curtiss"*		*Hans R. Schulze, No. 3* *"Reichs Marine Luftschiff"*
Henri Demanest		
Hubert Latham	30 - 35	35 - 45
Orville Wright		
Blériot	25 - 30	30 - 35
Voisin		
Roger Sommer		
Santo Dumont		
Robert E. Pelterie		
Anonymous Sepia Series 39424		
Glenn H. Curtis	20 - 25	25 - 35
Others	15 - 20	20 - 25
Raphael Tuck & Sons		
Aviation Series 9 (12)	12 - 15	15 - 25

"The Antoinette Monoplane"
"The Blériot Monoplane"
"The Farman Biplane"
"La Republic" Airship
"M. de Lesseps' Channel Flight"
"Nulli Secundus" Zeppelin type
"A.V. Roe Biplane"
"R.P.E. Monoplane"
"Spherical Balloons"
"The Voisin Biplane"
"Wright Brothers Biplane"
"Zeppelin"

Famous Aeroplanes Ser. 9943 (6)	18 - 20	20 - 25
Series 3101, 3103 (6)	12 - 15	15 - 20
Series 3144 (6)	15 - 18	18 - 25

DIRIGIBLES

Pioneer, Named	20 - 30	30 - 50
La France Airship	20 - 40	40 - 60
Early 1898-1924	15 - 25	25 - 40
"Akron"	10 - 15	15 - 25
"Hindenberg"	20 - 30	30 - 50
Los Angeles (Real Photos)	15 - 20	20 - 35
Macon	12 - 18	18 - 25
R-34	20 - 30	30 - 40
R101	20 - 30	30 - 40
"Shenandoah"	15 - 20	20 - 30
Goodyear (Early)	12 - 18	18 - 25
Goodyear (Linen)	6 - 10	10 - 15
"Astra Torres" P/John Drew Real Photo	15 - 20	20 - 30
"Baby" P/John Drew Black & White	15 - 18	18 - 25
"Beta II" and "Gamma II" P/Mays Real Photo		
"LeViolle de Paris, 1908" Real Photo	15 - 20	20 - 25

ZEPPELINS

Experimental Era 1898-1910	18 - 25	25 - 40
1910-1934	12 - 18	18 - 30
"Graf Zeppelin"	20 - 30	30 - 50

WAR PLANES

Pre-WWI	10 - 15	15 - 25
W.W. I	8 - 12	12 - 18
1918-1939	5 - 10	10 - 15
W.W. II	3 - 5	5 - 10
Post 1945 (Real Photos)	5 - 8	8 - 12

COMMERCIAL AIRLINES (Usually Advertising)

Identified, Pre-1930

Western Airlines (earliest - 1929)	15 - 20	20 - 25
Others	12 - 15	15 - 20

1930's-1940's Linens, Black & White

Penn Central	10 - 12	12 - 15
Central Airlines		
Midwest Airlines	8 - 10	10 - 12
Pan Am, Delta, Continental, TWA, United, Pacific Southwest, Braniff, Catalina, Eastern, Northwest, Mohawk, North American, National, Island Air, American Northwest Orient, Texas, International, Trans-Ocean, and Others	6 - 8	8 - 10
Real Photos - Add 25-50%.		
Chromes	1 - 2	2 - 5
Airfields, Linens	2 - 3	3 - 5

Alliance Series 115, Bas Relief Photo Card
Cunard Line -- "R.M.S. Mauretania"

Advertising, without plane image	3 - 5	5 - 8
Advertising Interiors	4 - 5	5 - 10

WATER TRANSPORTATION

OCEAN LINERS

During the 1890-1940 era immigrants from all over Europe, Asia, Scandinavia and the British Isles embarked for North and South America in search of a new life. These immigrants were the main cause of the tremendous growth of the ocean liner trade, and were the leading passengers on all ships on the Atlantic Routes.

The return trips to Europe were filled with prosperous Americans...the Rockefellers, Astors, and other millionaires of the times, for luxury vacations to the fashionable cities of their choice. To accommodate the elite upper class, owners of various lines commissioned shipbuilders to build the finest, most comfortable and most luxurious first class accommodations that money could buy.

Industrial advances in America and British Colony expansion buoyed the growth of British lines, while interests in East and Central Africa and commercial interests in South America led to great growth by the German shipping lines. America and other countries, viewing this great prosperity, began building ships so that they too could take advantage of the immigration to America. All tried to outdo the other by building bigger, faster, and more luxurious ships.

The British shipper, Cunard Lines, was the first and foremost in the industry. Their "Mauretania," became the fastest ship to cross the Atlantic

Hamburg Amerika Line
"Fürst Bismarck" - Engraving

Hamburg Amerika Line
M & J 988, "Cleveland"

and held the record for 22 years. The "Titanic," of the White Star Lines, was destined to be the world's most famous ship after hitting an iceberg and sinking on it's maiden voyage.

The advent of two World Wars was a great detriment to the growth of all the shipping and passenger lines. German submarines made the waters extremely treacherous. After the Cunard Liner "Lusitania" was sunk in 1914, shipping came to a standstill. Many of the liners became troop ships and were sunk on the open seas as well as in port. After the war new ships were built and business prospered as before.

The same was true at the start of World War II. When war was declared, shipping ceased and many of the great liners, such as "The Queen Mary" and "The Queen Elizabeth," became troops ships. As in the first war, the casualty rate was tremendous on the ocean liners of the world. Those that escaped were placed back in service, new ones were built, and the liner trade again prospered until the late 1950's when immigration to North America came to a standstill and the rich and famous began flying to the beautiful cities of Europe. The liners all began losing money and one by one they were scuttled and sold for scrap. Only a few now remain of the great number that once ruled the seas.

Postcard collectors have benefited throughout the Ocean Liner era as the lines advertised their services to the utmost. Beautiful advertising cards,

R. Tuck Celebrated Liners, 6229
Orient Pacific Line, "Ormuz"

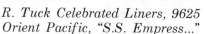

R. Tuck Celebrated Liners, 9625
Orient Pacific, "S.S. Empress..."

R. Tuck Celebrated Liners, 6229
Orient Pacific Line, "Ortona"

showing magnificent ships at the docks and on the open seas have have survived and there are reports of big advances in the auction values of most all "Titanic" cards and early Poster Advertising. These big gains are helping to elevate prices on all of the other beautiful Ocean Liner material.

AMERICAN EXPORT LINES (1950's-1960's)   2 - 3   3 - 6
AMERICAN LINE
"Haverford," "Kroonland," "Merian," "New York"
"Philadelphia," "St. Louis," "Westernland"

Color	10 - 15	15 - 18
Black & White	5 - 8	8 - 10
Interiors	10 - 15	15 - 20
Real Photos, Adverrtising	12 - 15	15 - 22

ANCHOR LINE*
"Athenia," "Bolivia," "Caledonia,"
"City of Rome," "Columbia," "Olympia,"
"Transylvania," "Tuscania"

Color	12 - 15	15 - 20
Black & White	6 - 8	8 - 10
Interiors	12 - 15	15 - 20
Real Photos	15 - 18	18 - 25
Artist-Signed by **W.T.N.**	12 - 15	15 - 25
Advertising	15 - 18	18 - 25

*Purchased by **CUNARD LINE** in 1912.

BERGEN LINE (Norway)	2 - 3	3 -6
CANADIAN PACIFIC		
Color	8 - 10	10 - 12
Black & White	4 - 5	5 - 8
Real Photos	12 - 15	15 - 18
"Empress of Ireland" - Disaster	12 - 15	15 - 25
Advertising	12 - 15	15 - 22

CUNARD LINES*

"Adriatic," "Alaunia" 1925, "Andavia,"
"Andonia," "Ansonia," "Antonia,"
"Aquiatania"1907, "Arabic," "Ascania,"
"Athenia" first ship torpedoed in WW2,
"Berengaria" 1918, "Britannic" 1934,
"Bothnia," "Campania" 1893, "Canopic,"
"Caronia" 1948 "Carpathia" 1903, "Catalonia,"
"Cedric," "Celtic," "Cephalonia," "Corinthia,"
"Coronia," "Cymbric," "Etruria," "Folia,"
"Franconia," "Gaelic," "Ivirnia," "Lancastria"
"Laurentic," "Luciana" 1893, "Lusitania"
1907, "Majestic," Mauretania" 1907, "Media"
1947, "Meganic," "Olympia," "Orduna,"
"Parthia" 1948, "Pavonia," "Persic,"
"Pittsburgh," "Republic," "Royal George,"
"Russia," "Saxonia," "Scythia," "Servia,"
"Teutonic," "Umbria," Others

*Artist-Signed cards by **James S. Mann,
C. E. Turner, O. Rosenvenge** and **Walter
Thomas** - add $3-5 per card.

Pre-1920 issues		
Color	10 - 12	12 - 18
Black & White	5 - 8	8 - 12
Real Photo	12 - 15	15 - 22
Interior Views	10 - 12	12 - 15
Poster Advertising	20 - 25	25 - 35
Sunk in WW I		
"Aurania," "Campania," "Franconia"		
Color	12 - 15	15 - 18
Black & White	5 - 6	6 - 10
Real Photo	15 - 18	18 - 25
Interiors	10 - 15	15 - 20
"Lusitania" Sunk by Germans		
Color	15 - 20	20 - 25
Black & White	8 - 10	10 - 12
Real Photos	15 - 20	20 - 30
Interiors	10 - 15	15 - 20
Interior Real Photos	15 - 20	20 - 25
Memorial Issues	**15 - 20**	**20 - 25**
Disaster Sketches	12 - 15	15 - 20
"Carpathia" 1903 Rescuer of Titanic		
Color, telling of rescue	12 - 15	15 - 20
Real Photo, telling of rescue	20 - 25	25 - 30

CUNARD-WHITE STAR LINE, 1934-1948
New "Mauretania"
"Queen Elizabeth" 1938, "Queen
Mary" 1936, "Georgic" 1934, Others

Color	5 - 8	8 - 10
Black & White	2 - 3	3 - 5
Interiors	6 - 8	8 - 10
Advertising	10 - 12	12 - 15

CUNARD LINE, AFTER 1948

"Caronia" 1948, "Queen E. II" 1969	2 - 3	3 - 5
DOMINION LINE　(Hands Across the Sea)	8 - 10	10 - 12

FRENCH LINE

Color	8 - 10	10 - 15
Black & White	5 - 7	8 - 10
Advertising	12 - 15	15 - 20
GDYNIA AMERICA LINE (Poland)	3 - 6	6 - 10

THE GRACE LINE

GREAT WESTERN　("Grand Trunk" R.R. Ferry)	4 - 5	5 - 8
GREEK LINE (1940-1970's)	2 - 3	3 - 5

HAMBURG-AMERICA LINE
"Alb. Ballin," "Amerika," "Belgravia,"
"Bismarck" 1914, "Blucher," "Caribia,"
"Cleveland," "Columbia" 1889,
"Cordillera," "Deutchland" 1898,
"Furst Bismarck," "Graf," "Hamburg,"
"Hansa," "Iberia," "Imperator" 1913,
"Kaiser Friedrich," "Kaiserin Auguste
Victoria" 1889, "Milwaukee" 1929,
"Moltke," "New York," "Oceana,"
"Orinco," "Palatia," "Patricia,"
"Phoenicia," "Pres. Grant," "Princess
Victoria Luise," "Reliance," "Pres. Lincoln,"
"Pennsylvania," "St. Louis" 1929,

"Vaterland" 1914, "Waldersee," Others	10 - 12	12 - 15

Early Chromolithos, S/W. Stower &

H. Buzrdt, P/Muhlmeister & Johler	20 - 25	25 - 30

Black & White Steel Engravings,

S/W. Stower, P/Kutzner & Berger	15 - 20	20 - 25
Color	15 - 18	18 - 22
Black & White	6 - 8	8 - 10
Real Photos	15 - 20	20 - 25
Early Menus w/postcard attached	20 - 25	25 - 30
Poster Advertising	20 - 25	25 - 30
HAMBURG-SOUTH AMERICA LINE	8 - 10	10 - 15

HOLLAND-AMERICA LINE
"Edam" 1921, "Maasdam" 1952, "Niew
Amsterdam" 1906,"Nieuw Amsterdam II"
1938, "Potsdam" 1900, "Rotterdam"
1908, "Rotterdam II" 1959,"Ryndam,"
"Statendam" 1914, "Statendam II" 1929 -
Bombed in 1940, "Statendam IV" 1957,

"Veendam" 1923, "Volendam" 1920,
"Werkendam," "Westdam" 1946,
"Zaandam" 1938 - Torpedoed in war; Others

Early Chromolithos by

S/C. Dixon and F. Parsing	12 - 15	15 - 20
Color	10 - 12	12 - 15
Black & White	5 - 8	8 - 10
Real Photos	12 - 15	15 - 20
Poster Advertising	15 - 20	20 - 30
After 1935	3 - 5	5 - 8
HOME LINES (1939-1970's)	2 - 3	3 - 5
ITALIAN LINE		
Color	10 - 12	12 - 20
Black & White	3 - 5	5 - 8
Poster Advertising	20 - 25	25 - 30
After 1935	2 - 3	3 - 5
MATSON LINE (1920-1930's)		
Color	8 - 10	10 - 12
Black & White	3 - 5	5 - 8
MOORE-McCORMICK LINES, INC.		
"Brazil" and "Argentina"	4 - 5	5 - 8

NORDDEUTSCHER LLOYD, Bremen
(North German Lloyd Lines)
"Amerika," 1903, "Alb. Ballin" 1923,
"Elbe," 1900, was sunk in collision,
"Imperator" 1913,
"Aller," "Barbarossa," "Berlin" 1955,
"Bremen" 1928, "Bulow," "Coblenz,"
"Columbus" 1922, "Dresden," "Eider,"
"Ems,'"Europa" 1929, "Eitel Friedrich,"
"Fried. der Grosse," "Fulda," "Gen.
v. Steuben," "George Washington,"
"Goeben," "Grosser Kurfurst," "Havel,"
"Kaiser Wilhelm II," "Kleist,"
"Konig Albert," "Kronprinz Wilhelm,"
"Kronprinze. Cecille" 1904, "Muenchen,"
"Orotava" "Prinzess Alice," "Prinzess
Irene," "Prinz Regent Luitpold,"
"Roon," "Saale," "Scharnhorst," "Spree,"
"Trave," "Werra," "Wilh. Gostloff" was
torpedoed in 1945 (6,096 died),
"York," Others

Early Chromoliths, S/T.v.E.	18 - 22	22 - 30
Black & White vignettes, S/T.v.E.	12 - 15	15 - 22
Black & White Engravings	15 - 18	18 - 25
Color	12 - 15	15 - 18
Black & White	6 - 8	8 - 10
Real Photos	15 - 18	18 - 25
Early Menus with postcard attached	20 - 25	25 - 35
Poster Advertising	20 - 25	25 - 35
St. Louis Exposition	15 - 20	20 - 30

BECAME HAPAG-LLOYD LINE IN 1932	6 - 10	10 - 12
And BREMEN-AMERICAN LINE IN 1954	2 - 3	3 - 5
N.Y.K. LINE		
Color	8 - 10	10 -15
Black & White	4 - 6	6 - 8
NORWEGIAN-AMERICAN LINE (1940-1980's)	2 - 3	3 - 6
O.S.K. LINE		
Color	8 - 10	10 - 15
Black & White	4 - 6	6 - 8
ORIENT LINE (Britain)	5 - 8	8 - 10
P & O LINE		
Color	6 - 8	8 - 10
Black & White	3 - 4	4 - 5
PANAMA-PACIFIC LINE	5 - 6	6 - 10
RED STAR LINE		
"Belgenland," "Finland," "Friesland,"		
"Kensington," "Kroonland," "Lapland,"		
"Marquette," "Noordland," "Pennland,"		
"Westernland," "Vaderland," "Zeeland"	8 - 12	12 - 18
P/American Litho Co. PMC's	15 - 18	18 - 22
Chromolitho Posters, S/H. Cassiers		
A Ser., B&W, of Ships & Dutch People	15 - 18	18 - 22
B Ser., Color, of Ships & Dutch People	20 - 25	25 - 30
C Ser., Color		
H Ser., Color, of Ships in Harbor		
L Ser., View and people of Antwerp	10 - 12	12 - 15
Others S/H. Cassiers		
Posters, S/V. Greten, K Series	12 - 15	15 - 18
Wood Engravings, S/Edw. Pellens		
Art Deco O & P Series, P/J. L. Goffart	30 - 35	35 - 40
Poster Advertising	20 - 25	25 - 35
ROYAL MAIL LINE Britain-South America	5 - 8	8 - 12
SUD-ATLANTIQUE LINE		
"L'Atlantique"		
Color	8 - 10	10 - 15
Black & White	5 - 6	6 - 8
The L'Atlantique disaster	12 - 15	15 - 20
Others	6 - 7	7 - 9
SVENSKA (SWEDISH) AMERICA LINE		
Color	6 - 8	8 - 10
Black & White	4 - 5	5 - 6
Advertising	10 - 12	12 - 15
UNITED STATES LINE		
"Geo. Washington," "Leviathan,"		
"Manhattan," "Pres. Harding,"		
"Pres.Roosevelt," "Republic, "United States"		
1952, "The America" 1940		
S/Willy Stover	10 - 12	12 - 15
Color	8 - 10	10 - 12
Black & White	4 - 6	6 - 8

Real Photo, S.S. "Leviathan"
"The World's Largest Liner"

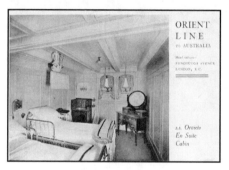

Orient Line
"S.S. Orvieto En Suite Cabin"

United States Lines
S.S. "America" (21144 Tons)

Real Photos10 - 14	14 - 18	
Advertising	10 - 12	12 - 15
UNITED FRUIT CO. (Great White Fleet)	1 - 2	2 - 3
WHITE STAR LINES*		

"Adriatic" 1902, "Albertic,"
"Baltic" 1902, "Britannic" 1914 lost
in WWI, "Britannic II" 1930,"Canopic,"
"Cedric" 1902, "Celtic" 1901, "Ceramic,"
"Cretic," "Doric" 1923, "Georgic,"
"Germanic," "Homeric," "Lapland,"
"Laurentic," "Majestic," "Megantic,"
"Oceanic" 1899, "Olympic" 1911,
"Republic" Rammed and sunk 1909,
"Runic," "Suevic," "Vedic," Others

Color	8 - 10	10 - 15
Black & White	5 - 7	7 - 10
Real Photos	10 - 15	15 - 20
S/Norman Wilkinsen or M. Black	10 - 15	15 - 20
Poster Advertising	20 - 30	30 - 40
Titanic - 1912		
Postally Used before 4/15/12	1250 - 1500	1500 - 2000
Woven Silk	1300 - 1600	1600 - 2200
Sea Trials - Belfast, Austrian R.P.	400 - 450	450 - 550
Pre-Sinking Real Photos	350 - 400	400 - 450
Real Photo Memorial Cards	100 - 125	125 - 150

Real Photo, White Star Line "Titanic"
Tells of Disaster and Loss of Lives

R. Tuck & Sons	65 - 75	75 - 100
"Among the Icebergs," Valentine Pub.	85 - 100	100 - 115
"Steamer Titanic," Tichnor Bros. Pub.	75 - 85	85 - 100
"Nearer My God to Thee," Bamforth (6)	40 - 50	50 - 75
Australian, French, Misc. Publishers	100 - 150	150 - 200
Titanic/Olympic	30 - 40	40 - 50
Olympic	15 - 20	20 - 35
AFTER 1934	3 - 5	5 - 8

*White Star and Cunard merged in 1934.

CELEBRATED LINERS SERIES
RAPHAEL TUCK (Oilette 6-Card sets)

Series 3378, 3379, 6228 "White Star Lines"	15 - 22	22 - 30
Series 3592	8 - 10	10 - 12
Series 6229 "Orient-Pacific Line"	15 - 20	20 - 25
Series 6230, 8960, 8961		
Series 9106 "The Cunard Line"	20 - 25	25 - 30
Series 9121, "Canadian-Pacific Line"	15 - 20	20 - 28
Series 9112, 9124, 9125	15 - 20	20 - 25
Series 9126 "Atlantic Transport Line"	15 - 20	20 - 25
Series 9133 "Union Castle Line"		
Series 914 "American Line"	20 - 25	25 - 28
Series 9151, 9155, 9213	15 - 20	20 - 25
Series 9215 "White Star Line"	20 - 25	25 - 30
Series 9268 "Cunard Line"		
"Mauretania" (Image 1)	15 - 20	20 - 25
"Lusitania" (Image 1)	25 - 30	30 - 35
"Carmania"	15 - 20	20 - 25
"Lusitania" (Image 2)	25 - 30	30 - 35

C. & B. Company, Steamer
"City of Buffalo," Lake Erie

Stevensgraph, Woven in Silk
"R.M.S. Lucania"

"Mauretania" (Image 2)	15 - 20	20 - 25
"Carpathia"	25 - 30	30 - 35
Series 9503 "White Star Line"	20 - 25	25 - 30
Series 9625 "Canadian Pacific," Series II	20 - 25	25 - 28
Series 9808 "White Star Line"		
"Titanic" (2)	75 - 100	100 - 125
Others	20 - 25	25 - 30
OTHER LINERS		
Pre - 1930		
Color	6 - 8	8 - 10
Black & White	4 - 5	5 - 7
Interiors, Real Photos	8 - 10	10 - 12
After 1930	2 - 3	3 - 5
OCEAN COAST LINERS		
CANADIAN PACIFIC RAILROAD		
"Princess Charlotte"	8 - 10	10 - 15
"Princess Charlene"		
"Princess Victoria"		
CLYDE STEAMSHIP LINE		
E. Coast, NY - Miami		
Early Vignettes, Black & White	12 - 15	15 - 20
Color	8 - 10	12 - 15
Real Photo	12 - 15	15 - 20
EASTERN STEAMSHIP LINES		
"Boston," "New York"		
Color	4 - 6	6 - 10
Black & White	3 - 4	4 - 5
Real Photo	8 - 10	10 - 15
FURNESS-BERMUDA LINE	2 - 3	3 - 5
MAINE STEAMSHIP CO.		
Color	4 - 6	6 - 10
Black & White	3 - 4	4 - 7
Real Photos	8 - 10	10 - 12
MATSON NAVIGATION CO. (San Francisco)	3 - 4	4 - 6
MERCHANTS & MINERS LINE (Atlantic Coast)		
Color	4 - 6	6 - 10

Real Photo, © By E. Muller 1904, B-478
"U.S.S. Newark" Battleship

Black & White	3 - 4	4 - 5
Real Photos 8 - 10	10 - 12	
Old Dominion Line	6 - 8	8 - 12
PACIFIC MAIL CO. LINE (Pacific Coast)		
Color	4 - 6	6 - 10
Black & White	3 - 4	4 - 5
Real Photo	8 - 10	10 - 12
PANAMA PACIFIC LINE		
"City of Baltimore," "Newport News,"		
"Norfolk," "L.A.," "S.F.," "Calif.," "Penna."		
"Virginia"		
Color	5 - 8	8 - 12
Black & White	3 - 5	5 - 7
Real Photos	8 - 10	10 - 15
SAVANNAH LINE (NY-Boston-Miami)		
"City of Birmingham," "City of Chattanooga,"		
"City of Savannah," Others		
Color	5 - 8	8 - 12
Black & White	3 - 5	5 - 8
Real Photos	6 - 8	8 - 10
WARDS LINE New York-Havana		
Color	6 - 8	8 - 10
Black & White	4 - 5	5 - 6
Real Photo of "Morro Castle" Wreck	10 - 12	12 - 15
WOVEN SILKS OF SHIPS		
Stevensgraphs		
"S. S. Haverford" and "R.M.S. Baltic"	70 - 80	80 - 90

"R.M.S. Mauretania," "Arabic," Baltic,	80 - 90	90 - 100
"Baltic," "Ivernia," "Lucania," "Saxonia,"	70 - 80	80 - 90
Hands Across the Sea/With Flags		
"R.M.S. Victorian," "Ivernia" "Romanic"	40 - 45	45 - 50

GREAT LAKES AND RIVER STEAMERS

HUDSON RIVER DAY LINE	4 - 6	6 - 8
"Robt. Fulton," "New York" "Hend. Hudson"		
Color	3 - 5	5 - 7
Black & White	2 - 3	3 - 4
Real Photos	8 - 10	10 - 12
D & C LINE		
"City of Cleveland," Others		
Color	5 - 6	6 - 8
Black & White	1 - 2	2 - 5

BATTLESHIPS/CRUISERS/NAVAL VESSELS

Arthur Livingston PMC's "Maine"	12 - 15	15 - 20
Others	8 - 10	10 - 12
H.A. Rost, Pioneers & PMC's	15 - 20	20 - 30
American News Co.	4 - 5	5 - 7
American Souvenir Card Co.		
The White Squadron (12) "Patriographic"	12 - 15	15 - 20
A.C. Bosselman	5 - 7	7 - 10
Boston P.C. Co. (Brown-tint)	4 - 5	5 - 8
Britton & Rey		
Brooklyn Eagle, Black & White	3 - 4	4 - 6
E.P. Charlton	5 - 7	7 - 10
Detroit Photographic Co.		
Allen Fanjoy	3 - 4	4 - 5
Henderson Litho S/Enrique Muller	5 - 7	7 - 10
Illustrated P.C. Co.		
L. Kaufmann & Sons	4 - 6	6 - 8
Hugh C. Leighton	5 - 7	7 - 10
Lowman & Hanford		
Metropolitan News Co.	4 - 6	6 - 8
Edward H. Mitchell	5 - 7	7 - 9
Enrique Muller, P/Rotograph Co.		
Real Photos, 1904, 1910	6 - 8	8 - 10
Prudential Insurance Co. (U.S. & Foreign)	4 - 6	6 - 8
Rotograph Co.		
Souvenir Postcard Co.	5 - 8	8 - 10
State of Washington, Puget Sound Ferries	5 - 7	7 - 9
Tichnor Bros. S/Enrique Muller	6 - 8	8 - 10
Raphael Tuck		
1076 "U.S. Navy"	7 - 8	8 - 12
1223 "U.S. Navy Cruisers"		
2324 "U.S. Navy-Battleships"		
4484 "U.S. Ironclads"		
Valentine Series C.E. Waterman, 1909	4 - 5	5 - 8

12

BASEBALL, ETC.

BASEBALL

Baseball enjoys the distinction of having two major collector groups, postcard and sports, who are vying for a great shortage of material. Therefore, any cards that surface are quickly purchased and, just as quickly, taken out of circulation again. Values vary widely, especially in some of the early 1900-1935 issues, and it is extremely difficult to value individual cards when so few are available.

Newer issues, especially those of Hall of Famers and those published by Perez Galleries, are enjoying much success because of the sports autograph craze. The cards are purchased by collectors and are signed by the players at sports card and autograph shows.

Values listed here are rather conservative and should be used only as a "ballpark" guide, as prices realized on some issues may be somewhat higher, especially on rare boxing and baseball real photos. Hopefully, more of these cards will surface so that an accurate listing can be made in future editions.

	VG	EX
A. C. DIETSCHE, 1907-09, B&W, Detroit Tigers		
Series I, 1907		
Tyrus Cobb	$150 - 175	$175 - 200
Hughie Jennings	90 - 100	100 - 110
Others	40 - 45	45 - 50
Series II, 1908-09		
Tyrus Cobb	150 - 175	175 - 200
Hughie Jennings	70 - 80	80 - 90
Team Picture	160 - 180	180 - 200

Others	40 - 45	45 - 50
A. C. DIETSCHE, 1907, B&W, Chicago Cubs		
Tinker, Evers, Chance, Brown	150 - 175	175 - 200
Others	40 - 50	50 - 60
AMERICAN LEAGUE PUB. CO., 1908, (7)		
Cleveland, B&W, Action + Oval Shots		
Ty Cobb, Honus Wagner	200 - 250	250 - 300
Nap Lajoie	100 - 150	150 - 200
H. H. BREGSTONE, 1909-11 (40) Unnumbered		
St. Louis Browns & Cardinals	90 - 100	100 - 125
BOSTON AMERICAN SERIES, 1912		
Cream color w/Sepia Photos, Red Sox		
Tris Speaker	90 - 100	100 - 125
BOSTON DAILY AMERICAN, 1912, B&W (3)	60 - 70	70 - 80
CINCINNATI REDS CHAMPIONS,		
1920, B&W, (24)		
Edd Roush	100 - 110	110 - 125
Others	50 - 60	60 - 70
EXHIBIT SUPPLY CO., Chicago, 1921-66		
Postcard Backs only, 50's (32?)		
Mantle, Mays	80 - 100	100 - 120
Musial, Campanella, Berra	30 - 40	40 - 50
Feller, Lemon, Kaline, Snider	20 - 30	30 - 40
Others	10 - 15	15 - 18
G. F. GRIGNON CO., 1907, Green Chicago Cubs		
Player Inset & Big Teddy Bear		
Tinker, Evers, Chance	150 - 175	175 - 200
Others	75 - 85	85 - 100

"The Pirates" -- *Pittsburgh's Great Baseball Team, 1908*
Masterpiece Jockey Club

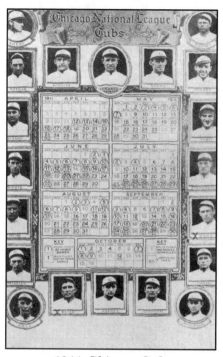

1911 Chicago Cubs
Players and Schedule

Bob Lemon, Cleveland Indians
Exhibit Supply Co., 1950s

GEORGE W. HALL, 1907, Black & White, (12)
  World Champs Chicago White Sox players
  in ovals on socks on clothesline   100 - 125   125 - 150
V. O. HAMMON
  Chicago Cubs Team   100 - 125   125 - 150
Masterpiece Jockey Club
  Pirates Team Players, Sepia (At Auction)   1000-1100   1100-1200
MORGAN STATIONERY CO., Cincinnati, 1907
  Unnumbered Issues   150 - 175   175 - 200
NOVELTY CUTLERY CO., 1910, Sepia, (25)
  Players enclosed in frame
    Wagner, Cobb, Johnson, Mathewson   175 - 200   200 - 225
    Cobb/Wagner   225 - 250   250 - 300
E. J. OFFERMAN, 1908, **Buffalo Players (20)**
  Action shot & photo inset   75 - 85   85 - 100
THE ROSE CO., 1909
  Players in Gold Frame above Diamond
  on yellow/green field (200+)
    Brown, Chicago, N.L.   150 - 175   175 - 200
    Other Hall of Famers
    Campbell, Cincinnati, N.L.   130 - 140   140 - 150
    Flaherty, Boston, N.L.
    Maloney, Brooklyn, N.L.
    Phillippi, Pittsburgh, N.L.
    Wiltse, New York, N.L.
  Scranton Players   60 - 70   70 - 80

THE ROTOGRAPH CO., 1905, B&W Photos

John McGraw, Clark Griffith	150 - 175	175 - 200
Others	100 - 120	120 - 140

SOUVENIR POSTCARD SHOP OF CLEVELAND (17+)

Cleveland Players, B&W Photos

Lajoie	150 - 175	175 - 200
Others	100 - 125	125 - 150

A. W. SPARGO, 1908, Black & White

Hartford Players (4?)	80 - 90	90 - 100

SPORTING NEWS, 1915, Color (6)

Ty Cobb	200 - 225	225 - 250
Walter Johnson	150 - 175	175 - 200
Others	75 - 100	100 - 125

MAX STEIN, P/U.S. PUB. HOUSE, 1909-16

35 Unnumbered, Sepia, "Noted People"

Cobb, Wagner	150 - 175	175 - 200
Mathewson	125 - 150	150 - 175
Speaker, Tinker, Evers, Chance	75 - 100	100 - 125
Others	40 - 50	50 - 60

H. M. TAYLOR, 1909-11, D. Tigers (7) B&W

Ty Cobb	200 - 225	225 - 150
Others	100 - 125	125 - 15

ANONYMOUS SEPIA SET, 1910 (25)

Wagner, Cobb, Johnson, Mathewson	150 - 175	175 - 200
Cobb/Wagner	175 - 200	200 - 225

Stan Musial, St. Louis Cardinals
Perez Steele, Hall of Fame Series

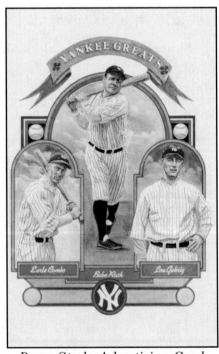

Perez Steele Advertising Card
"Yankee Greats" – Lithograph

Anonymous, "Youngest White Sox
Rooter in America," 1909

R. Tuck Ser. 6, Comic Valentine
"The ball player thinks he's..."

Acmegraph Company, 580
"National League, 'Cubs,' Ball Park, Chicago"

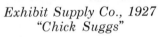

Exhibit Supply Co., 1927
"Chick Suggs"

Rotary Photo, A 517-5
"Kathleen Vincent"

Others	75 - 100	100 - 125
St. LOUIS CARDS "Dear Friends" Series		
Musial	10 - 15	15 - 20
Haddix, Hemus, Staley & others	8 - 10	10 - 12
TOPPING & CO., 1909, "Tiger Stars" (20)		
Black & yellow - Head in big star.		
Ty Cobb	150 - 175	175 - 200
Others	100 - 125	125 - 150
WOLVERINE NEWS CO., 1909, Tiger Players		
(2) Ty Cobb	150 - 175	175 - 200
"Shaefer & O'Leary work double play"	80 - 90	90 - 100
Others		
MISCELLANEOUS		
Boston Red Sox, **P/Furlong 1908**		
Mechanical, Cobb/Wagner	3000 - 3250	3250 - 3700
Boston Red Sox, 1915		
Team, Real Photo (including Babe Ruth)	6000 - 6250	6250 - 6750
Chicago Cubs, 1911 Schedule and Players	200 - 225	225 - 250
Art P.C. Company		
Fold-out Cards, 1907-1910	2000 - 2500	2500 - 3000
Team Issues		
Baltimore Orioles (1954-75) (B&W, Color)	8 - 12	12 - 20
Cincinnati Reds Yearly Issues (1954-66)		
Cleveland Indians (1948-75) (B&W)		
L.A. Dodgers (1959-73)		
St. Louis Cardinals (1950-74)		

Hall of Fame Issues
  Albertype Co.
  1936-1952 Inductees B&W, Plaques (62)

Ruth, Cobb, Gehrig	18 - 20	20 - 25
Others	5 - 10	10 - 12

  Artvue Co.
  1953-1963 Inductees

J. DiMaggio, J. Robinson	10 - 12	12 - 15
Others	3 - 5	5 - 8

  Curt Teich
    1964- (Yellow-Brown) 2 - 3 3 - 6
  Perez-Steele By Artist **George Perez**
  1981- Color Issued in Sets

Some of the Perez-Steele cards reached astronomical values in 1990-93 because of the sports autograph scenario. DiMaggio, Williams, Musial, and Mantle were sold at values of $150-200 each and many others in the $50-100 range. Collectors and dealers purchased them and the players autographed them by mail or at card shows. Early inductees (those deceased) are valued at $5-25. Living inductees images range from $20 to $150. Advertising issues are rare and are valued at $30-50.

Baseball Comics, Many Publishers (B&W & Color)	10 - 15	15 - 20
Baseball Stadiums, Major Leagues		
1900-1910 (Average)	40 - 60	60 - 80
1900-1920	30 - 40	40 - 60
1920-1940	15 - 20	20 - 30
Linens, 1940-1949	10 - 15	15 - 25
Chromes	2 - 4	4 - 8
Baseball Parks, Minor Leagues, 1900-1935	10 - 12	12 - 15
Others	5 - 8	8 - 10

BOXING

Early 1900-1930

Jim Jeffries	25 - 30	30 - 40
Jefferies-Johnson Fight	40 - 50	50 - 60
Jack Johnson, Heavyweight Champ, 1910	35 - 40	40 - 45
Real Photos *		
With U.S. Flag as Belt	125 - 150	150 - 250
"In front of his training quarters"	125 - 150	150 - 200
"Johnson-Cotton Sparring Match"	100 - 125	125 - 175
"Jack Johnson - Jo3" by Dana Studio		

  * Auctioneers of some quality Real Photos
    report one-time results as high as $500-800.

Dempsey-Carpentier Fight	30 - 35	35 - 40
Dempsey-Willard Fight		
I.F.S. from N. Moser Real Photos AZO backs		
"Willard & Dempsey-World Champ. Bout"	30 - 40	40 - 50
The Ring and surrounding Crowd	25 - 30	30 - 35
"Willard takes some heavy punishment"	40 - 45	45 - 55
"Willard Counted Out"		
Jack Dempsey, Real Photos	20 - 25	25 - 30
Sam Langford		
Boxing Series 613		
"American Colored Heavyweight"	25 - 30	30 - 35

Other Heavyweight Champions	10 - 20	20 - 30
Other Weight Champions	5 - 10	10 - 15
Exhibit Supply Company Issues	5 - 10	10 - 15
Georges Carpentier Real Photo	12 - 15	15 - 18
Aaron Brown, Frank Childs, George Dixon	15 - 20	20 - 25
Joe Gans, Denver Ed Martin, Sam McVey		

1930-1980

Joe Louis		
Real Photos	25 - 30	30 - 40
Color or Black & White	15 - 20	20 - 25
In Army Uniform	12 - 15	15 - 18
Billy Conn	10 - 12	12 - 15
Jersey Joe Walcott	12 - 15	15 - 18
Real Photos	15 - 20	20 - 25
"Sugar Ray" Robinson	10 - 12	12 - 15
Rocky Marciano	12 - 15	15 - 25
Cassius Clay	10 - 15	15 - 25
Muhammed Ali	8 - 10	10 - 20
Zora Foley, Real Photo		
"Top K.O. Contender, 1958"	20 - 25	25 - 30
Semi-Pro, High School	3 - 5	5 - 10

FOOTBALL

EXHIBIT SUPPLY CO. B&W, Tints (32)		
Postcard Backs only		
Baugh, Graham, Connerly, Waterfield	30 - 40	40 - 50
Hirsch, Matson, Layne, Ratterman,		
Fears, Motley, Matson, Trippi	20 - 25	25 - 30
Others	10 - 15	15 - 20
Red Grange	25 - 30	30 - 40
Jesse Owens	20 - 25	25 - 30
Real Photo	40 - 50	50 - 60
Jim Thorpe	30 - 40	40 - 50
Real Photo	50 - 70	70 - 90
Professional Stars, early	15 - 20	20 - 30
College Players, early	10 - 15	15 - 20
High School Players, early	8 - 10	10 - 12

GOLF

Pre-1930 Stars	40 - 50	50 - 60
1930-1960 Stars	30 - 35	35 - 45
Artist-Signed (See Artist-Signed Chapter)	15 - 20	20 - 35
Real Photos, Identified	12 - 15	15 - 25
Golf Advertising, Artist-Signed	35 - 45	45 - 75
Golf Courses with players in action	5 - 8	8 - 12

TENNIS

Artist-Signed	15 - 20	20 - 30
Tennis Advertising	25 - 35	35 - 50
Real Photos, Identified	10 - 15	15 - 20
Courts and players in action	4 - 6	6 - 10

13

VIEWS

U.S. VIEWS

From their beginning as the "Pioneers" in the 1890's through the "chromes" of today, view cards have been the dominant collectible type in the postcard hobby. Other types have always had periods of high interest only to level off and even lose popularity at times. Not so with view cards. The biggest majority of all postcard collectors begin their participation in the hobby by collecting views of their home town. They have this interest because of their familiarity with the city, town, or community as it is today...and the desire to know what it was like in the early growth years.

This desire prompts each collector-historian to search every possible avenue for these collectible gems of the early years. The more views they find of the court house, post office, etc., the more they wonder if there was one of the depot, a barber shop, a meat market, and others. As the search continues the interest expands to other views, possibly of a nearby town, a once visited memorable city, and finally for those from all over their state. The fever elevates until the home town collector has become a full-blown postcard collector who will travel hundreds of miles and spend countless hours to enhance his collection.

Although small town views are the most popular and, therefore, command the highest prices, they, plus large town and city views of busy main streets, trolleys, depots, banks, etc., are continually pursued by topical collectors who care not whether the town is large or small, whether in Missouri or North Carolina...it just doesn't really matter. This elevates the price of topicals and also makes the small town views much dearer.

On the negative side, however, views of large cities such as New York, Washington, Philadelphia, etc., and tourist attractions such as Niagara

Falls, Mount Vernon, Watkins Glen, Grand Canyon, Yellowstone Park and others, have very little value because of the millions produced for the people who visited. Only special views in these areas are of any value. Scenic views of mountains, rivers, etc., and unnamed views also are shunned by collectors.

THE VIEW PUBLISHER

There were many great and illustrious publishers of views in the early years. Among the great early Pioneer publishers were **The Albertype Co., American Souvenir Co., E.C. Kropp, Arthur Livingston, Ed. Lowey, H.A. Rost, Souvenir Postal Card Co.,** and **Walter Wirth**. Views by these, plus those by anonymous publishers pre-1900, are extremely scarce and are rarely found.

More familiar to today's view collector are names like **Albertype Co., A.C. Bosselman, Detroit Publishing Co., Illustrated Postcard Co., Kraemer Art, Hugh Leighton, Rotograph Co., Edw. H. Mitchell, Curt Teich, Raphael Tuck,** and **Valentine & Sons**. These names are among the most prolific of the era and most noted on cards that remain today. They usually sent representatives to all areas several times each year to take photos of the principal street scenes, statues, schools, and buildings. On the return trip, the representative would bring the photos and printing proofs and take orders from the drugstores and other postcard sellers. Each photo was retouched (power lines, obstructions, etc., removed) and colored to conform with the natural shade as nearly as possible. Resulting orders were returned to the merchant by mail. File copies of each card were retained by the merchant for future orders.

Basically, this is how the tremendous view card business was handled throughout the U.S. Thanks to these photographers, publishers and distributors, histories of small town America have been recorded for future generations and have made it possible for the postcard hobby to attain unbelievable heights.

VIEWS

View cards are classified as to Era for this listing.

> 1 = Postcard Era - 1900-1915
> 2 = White Border Era - 1915-1930
> 3 = Linen Era - 1930's-1940's

The values listed are for general views of the particular topic. Outstanding, or special subject matter, may be valued higher. On the other hand, a poorly printed image would lessen the value.

According to the majority of dealers and collectors, the actual selling prices of view cards have basically the same value structure in all states of the

U.S. It all depends on the particular view and how much the collector is willing to pay. For instance, a collector in North Carolina will pay much more for a North Carolina view than a collector from Florida would pay for the same view. See Real Photo Section for higher valued views.

	VG	EX
U.S. PIONEER VIEWS, 1893-1898		
Various Publishers	$10 - 15	$15 - 25
U.S. PRIVATE MAILING CARDS, 1898-1901		
Various Publishers	5 - 10	10 - 15
U.S. VIEWS		
Airports-1	5 - 8	8 - 10
Airports-2	4 - 5	5 - 8
Airports-3	1 - 2	2 - 3
Amusement Parks-1	8 - 12	12 - 18
Amusement Parks-2	6 - 8	8 - 12
Amusement Parks-3	2 - 3	3 - 4
Banks-1	2 - 3	3 - 6
Banks-2	1 - 2	2 - 3
Banks-3	0.50 - 1	1 - 1.50
Birds Eye View-1	3 - 4	4 - 8
Birds Eye View-2	2 - 3	3 - 4
Birds Eye View-3	1 - 1.50	1 .50 - 2
Bridges-1	1 - 2	2 - 3

Pioneer "Patriographic," Baltimore 12, American Souvenir-Card Co.

Anon. Pioneer "Souvenir of Philadelphia"

A. C. Bosselman, View of Dairy Building, Minnesota State Fair

Real Photo, First M.E. Church DeKalb, Ill.

Bridges-2	1.50 - 2	2 - 2.50
Bridges-3	0.50 - 1	1 - 1.50
Bus Stations-1	N/A	N/A
Bus Stations-2	4 - 5	5 - 10
Bus Stations-3	2 - 3	3 - 4
Cemetery-1	5 - 6	6 - 8
Cemetery-2	4 - 5	5 - 6
Cemetery-3	2 - 3	3 - 4
Churches-1	2 - 3	3 - 5
Churches-2	1 - 2	2 - 4
Churches-3	1 - 1.50	1.50 - 2
Colleges-1	2 - 3	3 - 6
Colleges-2	1 - 2	2 - 4
Colleges-3	1 - 1.50	1.50 - 2
County Fair-1	8 - 10	10 - 15
County Fair-2	5 - 6	6 - 8
County Fair-3	3 - 5	5 - 8
Court House-1	3 - 4	4 - 6
Court House-2	2 - 3	3 - 4
Court House-3	1 - 1.50	1.50 - 2
Depots-1	6 - 8	8 - 12
Depots-2	3 - 5	5 - 7
Depots-3	2 - 3	3 - 4
Diners-1	N/A	N/A
Diners-2	N/A	N/A
Diners-3	10 - 15	15 - 30

S. H. Knox Co.– Great Western
Cereal Company, Akron, Ohio

R.P., Tornado at N. 33rd St.
Omaha, Nebraska 1913

Portland P.C. Co., Nome, Alaska
"Over the House Tops"

PMC, Multi-View Souvenir
of New Orleans

Anonymous Real Photo
Store Front with Gas Pumps and Moxie Signs

Fire Department-1	8 - 10	10 - 15
Fire Department-2	5 - 6	6 - 10
Fire Department-3	3 - 4	4 - 5
Funeral Homes-1	7 - 8	8 - 12
Funeral Homes-2	6 - 8	9 - 10
Funeral Homes-3	4 - 5	5 - 6
Garages/Gas Stations-1	6 - 10	10 - 16
Garages/Gas Stations-2	5 - 6	6 - 10
Garages/Gas Stations-3	4 - 5	5 - 7
General Stores-1	5 - 6	6 - 10
General Stores-2	4 - 5	5 - 7
General Stores-3	2 - 3	3 - 4
Gymnasiums-1	4 - 5	5 - 7
Gymnasiums-2	3 - 4	4 - 5
Gymnasiums-3	1 - 2	2 - 3
Hospitals-1	3 - 4	4 - 6
Hospitals-2	2 - 3	3 - 4
Hospitals-3	1 - 1.50	1.50 - 2
Hotels-1	3 - 4	4 - 6
Hotels-2	2 - 3	3 - 4
Hotels-3	1 - 2	2 - 3
Library-1	3 - 4	4 - 5
Library-2	2 - 3	3 - 4
Library-3	1 - 2	2 - 3
Main Streets-1	5 - 6	6 - 10
Main Streets-2	4 - 5	5 - 7
Main Streets-3	1 - 2	2 - 3
Mills/Plants-1	4 - 5	5 - 10
Mills/Plants-2	3 - 4	4 - 6
Mills/Plants-3	1 - 2	2 - 4

Anonymous Real Photo of Rouse & Co. Signs Shop

Motels-1	N/A	N/A
Motels-2	4 - 5	5 - 7
Motels-3	1 - 2	2 - 4
Opera-1	5 - 7	7 - 12
Opera-2	4 - 5	5 - 7
Opera-3	2 - 3	3 - 5
Parks-1	1 - 2	2 - 3
Parks-2	1 - 1.50	1.50 - 2
Parks-3	0.50 - 1	1 - 1.50
Post Office-1	3 - 4	4 - 6
Post Office-2	2 - 3	3 - 4
Post Office-3	1 - 1.50	1.50 - 2
Restaurants-1	8 - 10	10 - 12
Restaurants-2	3 - 4	4 - 8
Restaurants-3	2 - 3	3 - 4
Rivers, Creeks-1	1 - 2	2 - 3
Rivers, Creeks-2	1 - 1.50	1.50 - 2
Rivers, Creeks-3	0.50 - 1	1 - 1.50
Roadside Stands-1	N/A	N/A
Roadside Stands-2	4 - 6	6 - 10
Roadside Stands-3	3 - 4	4 - 6
Schools-1	2 - 3	3 - 6
Schools-2	1 - 2	2 - 3
Schools-3	1 - 1.50	1.50 - 2
Statues-1	1 - 2	2 - 3
Statues-2	1.50 - 2	2 - 2.50
Statues-3	0.50 - 1	1 - 1.50
Street Scenes-1	4 - 8	8 - 12
Street Scenes-2	3 - 4	4 - 5
Street Scenes-3	1 - 2	2 - 4
W/Parades-1	8 - 10	10 - 15
W/Parades-2	5 - 5	6 - 8

W/Parades-3	2 - 3	3 - 5
Tennis Courts-1	6 - 10	10 - 15
Tennis Courts-2	6 - 7	7 - 10
Tennis Courts-3	3 - 4	4 - 5
Theatres-1	8 - 10	10 - 16
Theatres-2	7 - 8	8 - 10
Theatres-3	4 - 5	5 - 6

FOREIGN VIEWS

Just as the hobby in the U.S. grows yearly by leaps and bounds, postcard collecting is also thriving in the other countries of the world. Great Britain, France, Germany and Italy are the leaders in Europe, but others are not far behind. Called Topographicals by most foreigners, which simply are view cards showing all the various motifs of almost every description, these are the rage.

Much like the U.S. collector, foreigners also collect cards of their home towns and soon expand to views of other towns, cities, and countries searching for motifs of their choice. Therefore, the search for good material now includes most all countries, large and small, throughout the world. Collectors will do well to reevaluate the contents of those boxes and albums of old foreign cards they believed worthless. Of special interest are early pre-1905 Chromolithographic Gruss Aus and vignette views of all coun-

Gruss Aus Multi-Views
Chromolithos, "Gruss vom Rigi"

Gruss Aus Multi-Views
Chromolithos, "Szegzárdről"

"Gruss Aus München"
Carl Otto Hayd, 222B

"A Greeting from London"
Saddle Brothers

Art Nouveau Multiple View Fantasy Card
Russian, with Russian City Views

tries. These early chromolithographs, usually multi-views, were printed by a special process where the design was etched on soft stone and printed in the various colors. Large irregular dots can be seen, usually with a magnifying glass, throughout the image surface as opposed to dots all the same size in the regularly printed lithograph cards.

After the chromolithograph cards, the most desired are identified topographicals...of people doing things, occupations, events, happenings, disasters, store and business fronts, exceptional busy street scenes, etc. These types, of course, are also those most desired by like collectors in the U.S., and the values are comparable in most instances. Therefore, the value to a collector of a small town depot in England or Germany would have a relative value to an American collector of a depot in a small town in the U.S.

The rarest and most highly valued foreign views are those of the tiny and thinly populated countries, colony possessions, and islands. Rarer still, with even higher valuations, are "postally used in country of origin" views of these cards. The philatelic value can be many times that of the image or scene. An unused view of tiny Bhutan is valued at around $6 while the same card stamped and postmarked in Bhutan commands $40 or more.

Special events also make many cards much more valuable. For instance, the Royal Visit to Ascension brings $40-45 unused and up to $250 if postmarked in Ascension during the visit. As can be seen from these examples, a thorough examination of all those seemingly "worthless" foreign views could prove to be most rewarding. Many foreign dealers are now appearing at postcard shows in the U.S., and most will be happy to purchase worthwhile views.

Most views taken in larger cities, especially those generated for the tourist trade, have little value. The hordes of visitors to Paris, Rome, London, Brussels, Venice, Vienna, and other cities during the golden years of the postcard purchased tons of views of museums, churches, statues, buildings, landmarks, etc., so that many still exist today. Many of these were the poorly printed black and white or sepia tones. However, many were beautifully printed with radiant colors and can often be purchased for under $1.00 each by the patient collector.

The listings below should only be used as a guide to average values of views. It must be realized that views of various images could be valued much higher or lower, depending on the motif, the publisher, whether it is black and white, in color, a real photo, and other factors. Also, the demand by collectors in the city, town, or country of origin would determine whether the value is higher or lower.

EARLY CHROMOLITHOGRAPHS, Pre-1910
ALL COUNTRIES

Gruss Aus/Vignettes Single & Multi-views	5 - 7	7 - 10
Named Landscapes	4 - 5	5 - 6
Exhibitions	12 - 15	15 - 30
Festivals	15 - 18	18 - 35
Heraldic	8 - 10	10 - 15
Royalty Commeratives	12 - 15	15 - 30
Town/City Views, Color	6 - 8	8 - 10
Town/City Views, B&W or Sepia	3 - 4	4 - 5
Views in Shells, Fish, Leaves, etc.	5 - 7	7 - 9

PRINTED, Color, B&W and Real Photo, 1900-1920
EUROPEAN COUNTRIES

Costumes	1 - 2	2 - 3
Disasters	2 - 5	5 - 10
Industrial	2 - 4	4 - 8
Occupations	3 - 5	5 - 10
Small Town Street Scenes	3 - 4	4 - 6
Large City Views, Street Scenes	0.50 - 1	1 - 1.50
Synagogues	10 - 15	15 - 30

Exceptional views can be much higher.
French Occupational views valued higher.

AFRICAN NATIONS

Early Cards	2 - 4	4 - 8
Ethnic	1 - 2	2 - 5

AUSTRALIA

Early Cards	8 - 10	10 - 12
Aborigines	5 - 7	7 - 9
Animal Carts, Teams, Etc.	4 - 6	6 - 8
Gold Mining	4 - 6	6 - 10
Railway Stations, Works	6 - 8	8 - 10
Street Scenes	2 - 3	3 - 4

CANADA

Most values compare to those in U.S.
Central and South America, Cuba, Costa Rica,
Bahamas, Barbados, Bermuda, Puerto Rico,

Dominican Republic, etc.

Early Cards	5 - 6	6 - 8
Costumes	1 - 2	2 - 2.50
Cities	1 - 1.50	1.50 - 2
Small Towns, Street Scenes, etc.	2 - 3	3 - 5
Industrial	2 - 3	3 - 4
Occupations	2 - 4	4 - 6
Railways, Stations	4 - 5	5 - 7
Ethnic	3 - 5	5 - 7

Exceptional views can be much higher.

RUSSIA & EASTERN EUROPE

Early Cards, Gruss Aus, etc.	4 - 6	6 - 10
Costumes	2 - 3	3 - 4
Cities	1 - 2	2 - 3
Small Towns, Street Scenes, etc.	4 - 5	5 - 6
Industrial	3 - 5	5 - 7
Occupations	4 - 6	6 - 8
Railways & Other Transportation	4 - 5	5 - 10
Ethnic	3 - 4	4 - 6

Exceptional views can be much higher.

FAR EASTERN COUNTRIES	Range	1 - 10

ISLANDS AND COLONIES, ETC., Early Cards*
    Price Range Only is listed

Aldabra	10 - 15
Andaman	8 - 10
Canary	3 - 6
Caroline	8 - 10
Cayman	20 - 25
Christmas	25 - 30
Coscos Keeling	25 - 30
Cook	12 - 15
Eastern	12 - 15
Falkland	10 - 35
Fanning	15 - 20
Faroe	12 - 15
Gilbert Isle and Lord Howe Isle	12 - 15
Mafia	8 - 12
New Guinea	8 - 12
Norfolk	20 - 25
Ocean	10 - 15
Perim	8 - 12
Pitcairn	15 - 20
Solomon	10 - 15
Thursday	15 - 20
Turks	15 - 20
Virgin	15 - 20
Others	1 - 10

* Cards stamped & postmarked in country of origin
  can have much higher values.

BRITISH, FRENCH, GERMAN, ETC., COLONIES

Early Cards	Range	4 - 15

Real-Photo cards are still among the popular groups as they continue their long climb from obscurity to the top of the view and topical fields. As stated earlier, their authenticity and portrayal of life and living as it actually was, plus the fact that many are one-of-a-kind, are determining factors to collectors.

It is important in most instances that the image be identified. Clarity and sharpness in the photo image is extremely important so that all detail can be seen and the time era can be determined. This is equally important if the photo is not identified. Each card must be judged on its own qualities and, therefore, it is extremely hard to base values on the auction price of another card. For instance, an ice delivery wagon which is close-up, has sharp and clear features with legible name of the ice company and the city location could bring **(to a person who really wanted it)** up to $300. If another collector **"really wanted it"** the card could be bid up to $500. This euphoria, however, does not make all ice delivery wagons worth $500...the image, the location and the desire make the price.

Photo cards most sought after are those taken by amateur photographers of everyday life and "happenings" such as accidents, disasters, etc. However, there were those taken by professionals, signed by them, and distributed to the wholesale and retail trade that are also widely collected. Real-photo collectors seek cards by these photographers just as avidly as a "beautiful lady" collector would seek cards of Harrison Fisher or Philip Boileau.

Various papers and processes were used for producing real photo postcards. AZO and VELOX were the most dominant with EKC, KRUXO, KODAK, CYKO, DARKO, EKKP and DOPS following. The process is usually notated in the stamp box on the reverse side although not all real photos have these listings. Most European real photos have no process byline listed.

Collectors of real photos should be wary of reproductions. This is true mainly in the modes of transportation fields. Although these are usually very easily spotted by the seasoned collector, some are actually being sold as originals to those who cannot spot the difference.

For other transportation-related subjects, please refer to the chapter entitled "Transportation."

Automobiles	VG	EX
Identified -- Large Image	$ 18 - 20	$ 20 - 25
Small Image	5 - 10	10 - 15
Unidentified -- Large Image	12 - 15	15 - 18
Small Image	5 - 8	8 - 10
Gas Pumps -- Large Image	12 - 15	15 - 18
Small Image	8 - 10	10 - 12
Trucks		
Identified -- Large Image	20 - 25	25 - 35
Small Image	10 - 15	15 - 20
Unidentified -- Large Image	10 - 12	12 - 15
Small Image	6 - 8	8 - 10
Auto Stage	35 - 40	40 - 45
Delivery Trucks		
Large Image, with Advertising	40 - 50	50 - 65
Small Image, with Advertising	30 - 35	35 - 40

Auto Stage, "E. Dilatus H. Prop." -- Allentown, N.J. (by AZO)

1911 Ford Roadster, Berlin, New York (by AZO)

Ranger Bill Miller Carrying Last Pony Express
California-New York (by AZO)

Farm Trucks
Large Image	15 - 20	20 - 25
Small Image	10 - 12	12 - 15

Service Vehicles
Dump Trucks, etc., Large Image	25 - 30	30 - 40
Small Image	15 - 18	18 - 22

BMW Bicycle with Side Car (by AGFA)

Mail Trucks -- Large Image	15 - 20	20 - 30
Small Image	10 - 15	15 - 25
Fire Engines -- Large Image	35 - 40	40 - 45
Small Image	12 - 15	15 - 20
Paddy Wagons	20 - 25	25 - 35
Farm Tractors		
Identified -- Large Image	20 - 25	25 - 35
Small Image	10 - 12	12 - 20
Unidentified -- Large Image	12 - 16	16 - 20
Small Image	8 - 12	12 - 15
Race Cars		
Large Image	20 - 30	30 - 40
Small Image	10 - 15	15 - 20
With Driver Identified -- Large Image	30 - 35	35 - 50
Small Image	15 - 18	18 - 25
Motorcycles		
Identified -- Large Image	25 - 30	30 - 35
BMW with side car	30 - 35	35 - 40
Small Image	15 - 18	18 - 22
Unidentified -- Large Image	15 - 18	18 - 22
Small Image	8 - 10	10 - 12
Bicycles		
Identified -- Large Image	25 - 30	30 - 40
Small Image	15 - 18	18 - 25
Unidentified -- Large Image	15 - 18	18 - 20
Small Image	10 - 12	12 - 15
Horse-Drawn Delivery Wagons		
Ice -- Large Image	50 - 60	60 - 80
Small Image	20 - 25	25 - 40
Mail -- Large Image	50 - 60	60 - 80
Small Image	20 - 25	25 - 30

Photo by Mossholder, Shelby, Ohio
Delivery Wagon, "Hoffstadt's City Green Houses"

Coal -- Large Image	50 - 60	60 - 70
Small Image	20 - 25	25 - 30
Others -- Large Image	40 - 50	50 - 60
Small Image	20 - 25	25 - 30
Moving Vans/Freight Wagons -- Large Image	40 - 50	50 - 60
Small Image	20 - 25	25 - 30

Delivery Wagon, Adams Express Company

Photo by E. C. Eddy (His Photograph Studio in Background)
Southern Pines, N.C. ca 1915 (AZO)

Horse-Drawn Sales Wagons

Ice Cream -- Large Image	60 - 70	70 - 100
Small Image	35 - 40	40 - 60
Bakery -- Large Image	50 - 60	60 - 80
Small Image	30 - 35	35 - 45
Grocery -- Large	50 - 60	60 - 80
Small Image	30 - 35	35 - 40
Others -- Large Image	45 - 50	50 - 60
Small Image	25 - 30	30 - 40
Horse & Buggy -- Large Image	12 - 15	15 - 25
Small Image	8 - 10	10 - 15
Horse & Wagon, Carts -- Large Image	12 - 15	15 - 20
Small Image	8 - 10	10 - 12
Goat Carts, With Children -- Large Image	20 - 25	25 - 35
Oxen-Driven Wagons	12 - 15	15 - 25
Fire Engines		
Hose Trucks	20 - 25	25 - 30
Horse-Driven Fire Engines	25 - 30	30 - 40
Horse-Driven Equipment	20 - 25	25 - 35
Trains, With Engine		
Identified -- Large Image	15 - 20	20 - 25
Unidentified -- Large Image	10 - 12	12 - 15
Passenger Car Interiors	20 - 25	25 - 30
Repair Shop Interiors	18 - 20	20 - 25
Train Wrecks		
Identified -- Large Image	10 - 15	15 - 25
Small Image	8 - 10	10 - 15
Unidentified -- Large Image	10 - 12	12 - 15
Small Image	6 - 8	8 - 10
Train Depots		
Small Town, East	10 - 15	15 - 25

Store Front and Post Office -- Wyoming, Minnesota

With Train in Station	15 - 20	20 - 30
Large Town, East	5 - 8	8 - 12
Small Town, West	15 - 20	20 - 30
With Train in Station	20 - 25	25 - 35
Large Town, West	10 - 12	12 - 15
Trolley Cars		
Identified -- Large Image	20 - 25	25 - 30
Small Image	12 - 15	15 - 20
Unidentified -- Large Image	12 - 15	15 - 20
Small Image	8 - 10	10 - 12
Airplanes		
Identified -- Large Image (1896-1910)	20 - 30	30 - 40
Small Image	10 - 12	12 - 18
With Pilot	20 - 25	25 - 35
Balloons		
Identified Large Image	20 - 25	25 - 30
Small Image	15 - 20	20 - 25
Unidentified -- Large Image	15 - 20	20 - 25
Small Image	10 - 12	12 - 15
Dirigibles (See Zeppelins)		
Identified -- Large Image (1898-1924)	20 - 30	30 - 50
Small Image	15 - 20	20 - 30
Unidentified -- Large Image	15 - 20	20 - 25
Small Image	10 - 12	12 - 15
Ships, Interior Views	10 - 15	15 - 25
Small Business Buildings, Identified		
Bakeries -- Store Fronts	20 - 25	25 - 40
Interiors	20 - 25	25 - 35
Banks -- Exteriors	12 - 15	15 - 20
Interiors	15 - 18	18 - 20
Billiard Parlors -- Exteriors	20 - 25	25 - 35
Interiors	25 - 30	30 - 35

Street Scene, 7th - E. Centre Streets — Ashland, Pa.

Bowling Alleys -- Exteriors	12 - 15	15 - 20
Interiors	18 - 20	20 - 25
Cigar/Tobacco Stores -- Interiors	50 - 55	55 - 60
Dairies -- Exteriors	10 - 15	15 - 20
Drug Stores -- Store Front	12 - 15	15 - 25
Interiors	20 - 25	25 - 30
Fish/Meat Markets -- Store Front	20 - 25	25 - 35
Interiors	30 - 35	35 - 40
General Stores -- Store Front	15 - 20	20 - 30
Interiors	25 - 30	30 - 35
Grocery Stores -- Store Front	15 - 20	20 - 25
Interiors	25 - 30	30 - 35
Ice Cream Parlors --Store Front	35 - 40	40 - 50
Interiors	40 - 45	45 - 55
Post Office -- Exteriors	10 - 12	12 - 18
Restaurants -- Store Front	10 - 12	12 - 15
Interiors	15 - 18	18 - 22
Service Stations -- Exteriors	18 - 22	22 - 25
Soda Fountains	20 - 25	25 - 30
With Ice Cream or Coca Cola Signs	25 - 30	30 - 35
Taverns -- Store Front	12 - 15	15 - 20
Interiors	15 - 20	20 - 25
Theaters -- Showing marque	20 - 25	25 - 35
Toy Store -- Exteriors	20 - 25	25 - 35
Interiors, Showing Toys	35 - 40	40 - 50

Street Scenes

Main Streets -- Small Towns	8 - 15	15 - 25
Large Towns	6 - 10	10 - 20
Others -- Small Towns	6 - 12	12 - 18
Large Towns	5 - 8	8 - 12

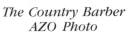

The Country Barber
AZO Photo

Hole-in-the-Wall
Wardrobe Laundry, AZO Photo

Bathing
Attractive Ladies	8 - 10	10 - 15
Groups	7 - 8	8 - 12

Blacks
Children	10 - 12	12 - 15
Men/Women	6 - 8	8 - 10
Blacks Working in Fields, etc.	10 - 12	12 - 15
Musical Groups	10 - 15	15 - 25
Black-Face Minstrels	40 - 50	50 - 60
Bands	20 - 25	25 - 35
Baseball Team	50 - 60	60 - 80

Children
Common	3 - 4	4 - 7
With Animals	7 - 8	8 - 12
With Dolls	15 - 18	18 - 25
With Dolls in Doll Carriage	20 - 25	25 - 30
With Toys	10 - 15	15 - 20
With Large Teddy Bears	25 - 30	30 - 40
With Small Teddy Bears	15 - 18	18 - 25
In Classroom/School	10 - 12	12 - 20
In Costumes	15 - 18	18 - 25
Halloween Costumes	40 - 50	50 - 75

Christmas Trees
	15 - 20	20 - 25
With Gifts Under Tree	20 - 25	25 - 30

Circus-Related
Trapeze Artist, Identified	15 - 20	20 - 25

Other Performers	10 - 15	15 - 20
Fat Ladies	15 - 20	20 - 25
Giants, Midgets, Strongmen, etc.	12 - 15	15 - 20
Advertising Circus	20 - 25	25 - 35
Animals -- Elephants, etc.	20 - 25	25 - 30
Add $5-8 for Barnum & Bailey Circus.		
Convicts or Chain Gang	20 - 25	25 - 35
Blacks	50 - 60	60 - 70
Black Women	150 - 200	200 - 250
Exaggerated		
Photos by W.H. Martin		
Big Fish	10 - 12	12 - 15
Grasshoppers, Onions, Watermelons	15 - 18	18 - 22
Farm Products, Farm Animals	12 - 15	15 - 18
Watermelons, with Blacks	22 - 25	25 - 28
Big Fruit		
Big Animals (Rabbits, etc.)	18 - 22	22 - 25
Buick Roadster chasing rabbit, other autos		
Photos by A.S. Johnson, Jr.	Range	30 - 100
Hangings/Lynchings	25 - 30	30 - 50
Blacks	500 - 600	600 - 1000
Adolf Hitler (By **Hoffman**)		
Used, With Postmark	15 - 18	18 - 25
Unused, No Postmark	12 - 15	15 - 18
Other Publishers		
Used, With Postmark	16 - 20	20 - 25
Unused, No Postmark	12 - 15	15 - 18
Indians		
Identified Chiefs	20 - 30	30 - 40
Others	12 - 15	15 - 25
Unidentified	8 - 10	10 - 20
Ku Klux Klan	75 - 100	100 - 150
Nudes (See "Real Photo Nudes")		
Plants, Mills		
Small Town -- Exteriors	20 - 25	25 - 35
Large Town -- Exteriors	10 - 15	15 - 20
Political		
Presidents	15 - 18	18 - 25
President and Running Mate	20 - 22	22 - 30
Losing Candidates	18 - 20	20 - 35
Governors	20 - 25	25 - 30
Pony Express	20 - 25	25 - 35
Last Ride	35 - 45	45 - 60
River Ferries	20 - 25	25 - 30
Shakers Group, Mt. Lebanon, etc.	50 - 75	75 - 100
Billy Sunday	10 - 12	12 - 15
U.S. Flag		
People Dressed or Wrapped in Flag	35 - 40	40 - 60
Uncle Sam in Flag	40 - 45	45 - 65
Rallies, Showing Flag	15 - 20	20 - 25
Orations or Debates, Showing Flag	20 - 25	25 - 35
Patriotic Children	20 - 25	25 - 35
Zeppelins	20 - 25	25 - 40

15
ROADSIDE AMERICA

The collecting of Roadside America material has continued to grow at a spectacular pace as collectors have become aware of the outstanding cards available. They like the possibility of getting into postcard groups where prices are still reasonable. Diners, gas stations, and drive-in restaurants are the most sought after, but they are becoming scarce.

Roadside America consists of cards that were published to advertise a place of business on or near a busy highway during the 30's, 40's, and 50's. The cards were usually given to travelers when they stopped by, or were mailed to prospective customers.

Most Roadside America cards were issued in the Linen and early Chrome Eras. There has, however, been some overlapping from the White Border Era, especially with cards of filling stations and restaurants. Real-photo views, and any views of diners, are always in great demand and command the highest prices.

Chromes, as many dealers attest, are also becoming popular. Those new to the hobby, usually 30-40 years of age, can identify with cards of the 50's and are seeking them for their collections. Chrome prices on many topics are not much below those of linens. In the final analysis, however, the particular view, its location, and the person buying it will determine the value.

Values are listed as follows:
  1   Linens
  2   Real Photos
  3   Chromes

Cooke Chevrolet Company, Evansville, Indiana
"New and Used Auto Sales"

	VG	EX
AUTOMOBILE DEALERSHIPS		
1	$ 6 - 8	$ 8 - 10
2	10 - 12	12 - 15
3	1 - 2	2 - 3
BAR & GRILL		

Snyder's Gateway Inn and Coffee Shop — Breezewood, Pa.
Curteich, "C.T. Art-Colortone"

1	5 - 6	6 - 8
2	6 - 8	8 - 10
3	1 - 2	2 - 3
CAFES		
1	6 - 8	8 - 10
2	8 - 10	10 - 15
3	1 - 2	2 - 3
COFFEE POT CAFE TYPES		
1	8 - 10	10 - 12
2	10 - 12	12 - 15
3	2 - 3	3 - 5
DINERS		
1	12 - 15	15 - 20
2	20 - 25	25 - 30
3	5 - 6	6 - 8
DRIVE-IN RESTAURANTS		
1	8 - 10	10 - 12
2	10 - 12	12 - 15
3	2 - 3	3 - 5
DRIVE-IN THEATERS		
1	8 - 10	10 - 12
2	12 - 15	15 - 20
3	6 - 8	8 - 10
EXAGGERATED BUILDINGS		
1	8 - 10	10 - 12
2	10 - 12	12 - 16
3	2 - 3	3 - 5
FILLING STATIONS/SERVICE STATIONS		
1	10 - 12	12 - 15
2	10 - 15	15 - 20

D. W. Caldwell's Grocery
Candler, North Carolina

Pines Camp Hotel Cottages, Vandosta, Georgia
L. L. Cook Co., Post Cards, Milwaukee — E-9513

3	3 - 4	4 - 6
FOOD MARKETS		
1	5 - 7	7 - 10
2	10 - 12	12 - 15
3	2 - 3	3 - 5
FRUIT, VEGETABLE STANDS		
1	5 - 10	10 - 12
2	8 - 10	10 - 15
3	2 - 3	3 - 5
GAS PUMPS		
1	5 - 8	8 - 10
2	10 - 12	12 - 15
3	2 - 3	3 - 5
HOTELS		
1	1 - 2	2 - 3
2	3 - 4	4 - 5
3	0.50 - 1	1 - 1.50
ICE CREAM SHOPS		
1	8 - 10	10 - 12
2	12 - 14	14 - 20
3	3 - 4	4 - 5
MINIATURE GOLF		
1	6 - 8	8 - 10
2	10 - 12	12 - 15
3	2 - 3	3 - 5
MOTELS, MOTOR COURTS, Single View		
1	1 - 2	2 - 3
2	4 - 5	5 - 6
3	0.50 - 1	1 - 1.50
MOTELS, MOTOR COURTS, Multiple Views		

High Locust Inn, Highway 31W and 41E near Nashville, Tennessee

Phil Blanco's Service Station, 6650 South Main, Houston, Texas

1	4 - 5	5 - 8
2	5 - 7	7 - 10
3	2 - 3	3 - 4
PECAN STANDS		
1	6 - 8	8 - 10
2	10 - 12	12 - 15

GRAND LAKE   KNAPKE LANDING

MODERN and CLEAN COTTAGES

Knapke Landing, Grand Lake "Modern and Clean Cottages"
© Hinkle Studio, Coldwater, Ohio

3	2 - 3	3 - 5
RESTAURANTS		
1	4 - 5	5 - 6
2	5 - 6	6 - 8
3	1 - 2	2 - 3
SANDWICH SHOPS		
1	6 - 8	8 - 10
2	8 - 10	10 - 15
3	2 - 3	3 - 5
SKATING RINKS		
1	4 - 5	5 - 8
2	8 - 10	10 - 15
3	1 - 2	2 - 4
SOUVENIR SHOPS, TRADING POSTS		
1	4 - 6	6 - 8
2	8 - 10	10 - 12
3	1 - 2	2 - 3
SWIMMING POOLS, COMMERCIAL (Not Motels)		
1	6 - 8	8 - 10
2	8 - 10	10 - 12
3	2 - 3	3 - 4
TAXI STANDS		
1	8 - 10	10 - 12
2	12 - 15	15 - 18
3	3 - 5	5 - 8
TRAILER PARKS, COMMERCIAL		
1	6 - 8	8 - 10
2	8 - 10	10 - 12
3	2 - 3	3 - 4

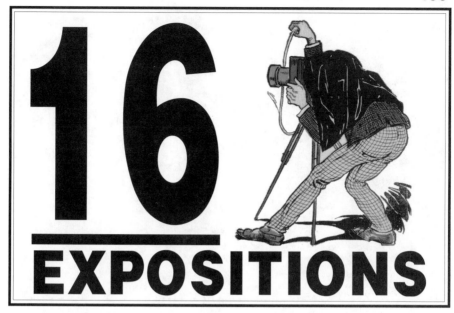

16 EXPOSITIONS

Exposition cards are starting to generate interest as some of the better quality material is beginning to appear in auctions and dealer stocks. They were heavily collected in the 1970-80 era but interest abated until recently. Continuing to lead the way are early hold-to-lights and woven silk issues. Interest should continue to grow as more of these fine collectibles re-appear.

	VG	EX
1893 COLUMBIAN EXPOSITION		
Goldsmith Pre-Official, no Seal	$100 - 130	$130 - 160
Officials, Series 1	15 - 20	20 - 30
J. Koehler B&W Issues	35 - 45	45 - 55
PMC or Post Card Backs	15 - 25	25 - 35
Puck Magazine Advertising Cards	135 - 140	140 - 150
Other Advertising Cards	100 - 120	120 - 150
Signed **R. SELINGER**	100 - 115	115 - 145
Anonymous Publishers	100 - 150	150 - 180
1894 CALIFORNIA MID-WINTER EXPO	200 - 250	250 - 300
1895 COTTON STATES & INT. EXPO	150 - 180	180 - 210
Negro Building	350 - 375	375 - 400
1897 TENNESSEE CENTENNIAL EXPO	160 - 170	170 - 200
1898 TRANS-MISSISSIPPI EXPO		
Trans-Mississippi Official Cards	50 - 60	60 - 70
Albertype Co. Views	90 - 100	100 - 120
1898 WORCESTER SEMI-CENTENNIAL	80 - 90	90 - 100
1900 PARIS EXPOSITION		
Scenes	10 - 12	12 - 15
Hold-To-Light	20 - 25	25 - 35
1901 PAN AMERICAN EXPOSITION		
Niagara Envelope Co. B&W	8 - 10	10 - 15
Color	10 - 15	15 - 20
Oversized	70 - 80	80 - 100

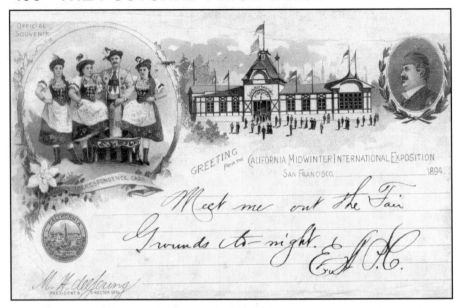

California Midwinter International Exposition, San Francisco, 1894

1902 SOUTH CAROLINA INTER-STATE

Albertype Co. Issues	125 - 150	150 - 175
Others	80 - 90	90 - 120

1903 20TH TRIENNIAL NAT. SANGERFEST

Franz Huld	15 - 20	20 - 30

1904 ST. LOUIS WORLD'S FAIR

Buxton & Skinner	8 - 10	10 - 15
Chisholm Bros.		
Samuel Cupples	8 - 12	12 - 15
Jumbo 6 x 9" H-T-L	200 - 225	225 - 250
Transparencies	8 - 10	10 - 15
Hold-To-Light	35 - 40	40 - 50
V.O. Hammon	6 - 8	8 - 10
The Inside Inn H-T-L	200 - 250	250 - 300
E.C. Kropp	5 - 10	10 - 12
Rotograph	10 - 12	12 - 15
Selige		
Raphael Tuck	5 - 10	10 - 15
Woven Silks (14)	250 - 400	400 - 500
Advertising Cards	10 - 12	12 - 15

1905 LEWIS & CLARK EXPOSITION

E.P. Charlton	6 - 8	8 - 10
Edw. H. Mitchell		
B.B. Rich (10)	8 - 10	10 - 15
A. Selige (10)	6 - 8	8 - 10
Advertising Cards		

1907 JAMESTOWN EXPOSITION

A.C. Bosselman	7 - 8	8 - 10
Illustrated Post Card Co.	25 - 30	35 - 40
Jamestown A&V	10 - 12	12 - 15

1893 Columbian Expo, Goldsmith
Administration Building

St. Louis World's Fair, 1904
Palace of Machinery

Portola Festival, 1909
Pacific Novelty Company

Confederate

50	Portrait of Jeff Davis	25 - 30	30 - 40
51	Beauvoir, Home of Jefferson Davis		
52	White House of the Confederacy		
53	Statue of Winnie Davis, Daughter of the Confederacy		
54	Portrait of General Robert E. Lee	40 - 45	45 - 55
55	General Robert E. Lee and Officers		
56	Last Meeting of Lee and Jackson		
57	Surrender of Lee		
58	"Arlington" Home of Gen. Lee..."	25 - 30	30 - 40
59	Statue of General Lee and Coat of Arms		
67	Leading Statesmen of the Confederacy		

Battleships	12 - 15	15 - 20
H.C. CHRISTY		
Army Girl	200 - 230	230 - 260
Navy Girl		
Raphael Tuck Oilettes	6 - 8	8 - 10
Silver Issues (10)	12 -15	15 - 20
1908 PHILADELPHIA FOUNDERS WEEK		
Illustrated Post Card Co. (10)	6 - 8	8 - 10
Fred Lounsbury (10)	8 - 10	10 - 12
1908 APPALACHIAN EXPO, Knoxville, TN	10 - 15	15 - 20
1909 ALASKA YUKON-PACIFIC EXPOSITION		
Edw. H. Mitchell	5 - 6	6 - 10
Portland Post Card Co.		

Lewis & Clark Expo, 1905
Portland, Or. (Agricultural Palace)

Jamestown Exposition, 1907
PCK Series, Captain John Smith

Panama-Pacific Int. Expo
San Francisco, 1915

Advertising Postcards	7 - 10	10 - 15
1909 HUDSON-FULTON CELEBRATION		
J. Koehler	4 - 6	6 - 8
Fred Lounsbury	7 - 8	8 - 10
Redfield Floats (72)	5 - 6	6 - 8
Raphael Tuck, Series 164 (6)	5 - 8	8 - 10
Valentine & Co., S/Wall (6)	6 - 8	8 - 12
1909 PORTOLA FESTIVAL		
Pacific Novelty	8 - 10	10 - 12
Others		
1910 APPALACHIAN EXPO, Knoxville	5 - 7	7 - 10
Advertising	7 - 8	8 - 12
1911-1912 GOLDEN POTLATCH-SEATTLE		
Edw. H. Mitchell (Sepia)	18 - 22	22 - 25
1915 PANAMA-PACIFIC EXPOSITION	3 - 4	5 - 6
Advertising Poster Cards	10 - 12	12 - 15
1915 PANAMA-CALIFORNIA EXPOSITION	3 - 4	5 - 7
Pre-Issues	5 - 6	6 - 8
Advertising Poster Cards	10 - 12	12 - 15
1933 CENTURY OF PROGRESS		
Exhibits	1 - 2	2 - 4
Advertising	2 - 3	3 - 5
Comics		
1936 TEXAS CENTENNIAL	2 - 3	3 - 5
1939 NEW YORK WORLD'S FAIR	1 - 3	3 - 6
1939 SAN FRANCISCO EXPOSITION	1 - 3	3 - 6

APPENDIX

POSTCARD PUBLISHERS & DISTRIBUTORS

Following are some of the major publishers of postcards world-wide. Minor publishers can be found under each particular listing throughout this book.

AMAG — Artist-Signed, Fantasy
A.M.B. — Meissner & Buch, Quality Greetings, Artist-Signed
A.S.B. — Greetings
Ackerman — Pioneer Views of New York City
Albertype Co. — Pioneer & Expo Views; Local Views
Am. Colortype Co. — Expositions
Am. News Co. — Local Views
Am. Post Card Co. — Comics
Am. Souvenir Co. — Pioneers
Anglo-Am. P.C. Co. (AA) — Greetings, Comics
Art Lithograph Co. — Local Views
Asheville P.C. Co. — Local Views, Comics
Auburn P.C. Mfg. Co. — Greetings, Comics
Austin, J. — Comics
Ballerini & Fratini, Italy — Chiostri, Art Deco
BKWI, German — Artist-Signed, Comics
Bamforth Co. — Comics, Song Cards
Barton and Spooner — Comics, Greetings
Bergman Co. — Comics, Artist-Signed Ladies, etc.
Julius Bien — Comics, Greetings, etc.
B.B. (Birn Brothers) — Greetings, Comics
Bosselman, A.C. — Local Views, Others
Britton & Rey — Expositions, Battleships, etc.
Brooklyn P.C. Co. — Views
Campbell Art Co. — Comics Rose O'Neill, etc.
Chapman Co. — Greetings, College Girls, etc.

Charlton, E.P. — Expositions, Local Views
Chisholm Bros. — Expositions, Local Views
Colonial Art Pub. Co. -- Scenics, Comics, Sepia Lovers
Conwell, L.R. — Greetings
Crocker, H.S. — Local Views
Davidson Bros. — Greetings, Artist-Signed
Dell Anna & Gasparini, Italy — Art Deco
Delta, Paris — French Fashion
Detroit Pub. Co. — Prolific Publisher, All Types
Faulkner, C.W., British — Artist-Signed, Greetings
Finkenrath, Paul, Berlin (PFB) — Greetings
Gabriel, Sam — Greetings
German-American Novelty Art — Greetings, Comics
Gibson Art Co. — Comics, Greetings
Gottschalk, Dreyfus & Davis — Greetings
Gross, Edward — Artist-Signed
Hammon, V.O. — Local Views
Henderson & Sons — Artist-Signed, Comics
Henderson Litho — Greetings, Comics, Local Views
S. Hildesheimer — Artist-Signed, Comics, Fantasy
Huld, Franz — Installment Sets, Expositions, etc.
Ill. Postal Card Co. — Greetings, Artist-Signed and Many Others
Int. Art Publishing Co. — Greetings by Clapsaddle, etc.
Knapp Co. — Artist-Signed
Koeber, Paul C. (P.C.K.) — Comics, Artist-Signed
Koehler, Joseph — H-T-L, Expositions, Local Views
Kropp, E.C. — Local Views, Battleships, etc.
Langsdorf, S. — Alligator and Shell Border Views, Local Views, Greetings
Lapina, Paris — Color Nudes and French Fashion
Leighton, Hugh — Local Views
Leubrie & Elkus (L.&E.) — Artist-Signed
Livingston, Arthur — Pioneers, Local Views
Lounsbury, Fred — Greetings, Local Views, etc.
Manhattan P.C. Co. — Local Views, Comics
Vivian Mansell & Co. — Artist-Signed
Marque L-E, Paris — French Fashion
Meissner & Buch, German — Artist-Signed, Greetings
Metropolitan News Co. — Local Views
Mitchell, Edward H. — Expositions, Battleships, Local Views
Munk, M., Vienna — Artist-Signed, Comics, etc.
Nash, E. — Greetings
National Art Co. — Artist-Signed, Greetings, etc.
Nister, E., British — Artist-Signed, Greetings
Novitas, Germany — Artist-Signed
Noyer, A., Paris — Nudes and French Fashion
O.P.F. — Quality German Artist-Signed
Oppel & Hess — Artist-Signed, Fantasy
Owen, F.A. — Greetings, Artist-Signed
Phillipp & Kramer, Vienna — Artist-Signed, Art Nouveau
Platinachrome — Artist-Signed, Earl Christy, etc.
Reichner Bros. — Local Views
Reinthal & Newman — Artist-Signed, Greetings
Rieder, M. — Local Views
Rose, Charles — Greetings, Song Cards, Artist-Signed, Comics

Rost, H.A. — Pioneer Views, Battleships
Roth & Langley — Greetings, Comics
Rotograph Co. — Local Views, Expostiions, Battleships, Artist-Signed, etc.
Sander, P. — Greetings, Comics, Artist-Signed
Santway — Greetings
Sborgi, E., Italy — Famous Art Reproductions
Selige, A. — Expositions, Western Views, People, etc.
Sheehan, M.T. — Local Views, Historical, Artist-Signed
Souvenir Post Card Co. — Local Views, Greetings, etc.
Stecher Litho Co. — Greetings, Artist-Signed
Stengel & Co., Germany — Famous Art Reproductions
Stewart & Woolf, British — Comics, Artist-Signed
Stokes, F.A. — Artist-Signed, Comics
Strauss, Arthur — Local Views, Historical, Expositions
Stroefer, Theo. (T.S.N.), Nürnburg — Artist-Signed, Animals, etc.
Taggart Co. — Greetings
Tammen, H.H. — Expositions, Historical, Local Views
Teich, Curt — Local Views, Artist-Signed, Comics
Tichnor Bros. — Later Local Views, Comics
Tuck, Raphael & Sons, British — Artist-Signed, Views, Comics, Greetings, etc.
Ullman Mfg. Co. — Greetings, Artist-Signed, Comics
Valentine & Sons, British — Artist-Signed, Comics, Views, etc.
Volland Co. — Artist-Signed, Greetings
Whitney & Co. — Greetings, Artist-Signed
Winsch, John — Greetings, Artist-Signed
Wirths, Walter — Pioneer Views

BIBLIOGRAPHY

The following publications, all related to the collection and study of postcards, are recommended for further reading.

All About Dwig, Bonnie P. Miller, Palm Bay, FL, 1976

American Advertising Postcards, Sets and Series, 1890-1920, Fred and Mary Megson, Martinsville, NJ, 1987

The American Postcard Guide to Tuck, Sally Carver, Brookline, MA, 1979

The American Postcard Journal, Roy and Marilyn Nuhn, New Haven, CT

The Artist-Signed Postcard Price Guide, J. L. Mashburn, Colonial House

Art Nouveau Post Cards, Alan Weill, Image Graphics, NY, 1977

Bessie Pease Gutmann, Published Work s Catalog, Victor J.W. Christie, Park Avenue Publishers, NJ, 1986

The Collector's Guide to Post Cards, Jane Wood, Gas City, IN

A Directory of Postcard Artists, Publishers & Trademarks, Barbara Andrews, 1975

Encyclopedia of Antique Postcards, Susan Nicholson, Wallace-Homestead, 1994

Larger Than Life: The American Tall-Tale Postcard 1905-1915. Exaggeration Real Photo Postcards, Morgan Williams and Cynthia Rubins

Guide to Artists' Signatures & Monograms on Postcards, Nouhad A. Saleh., 1993
Minerva Press, Boca Raton, FL 33429-0969, USA

Halloween Postcards Published by John Winsch, Hazel Leler, Houston, 1994

Neudin Cartes Postales de Collection, 1991, 35 rue G. St-Hilaire, 75005 Paris

Official Postcard Price Guide, Dianne Allmen, House of Collectibles, NY, 1990

Philip Boileau, Painter of Fair Women, D. Ryan, Gotham Book Mart, NY, 1981

Coles Phillips: A Collector's Guide, Norman Platnick, 50 Brentwood Rd., Bay Shore, New York 11706 ($16.00 plus $4.00 for Priority Mail)

The Postcard Catalogue, 1993, Venman, Smith, Mead, IPM, U.K.

Picture Postcards in the U.S., 1893-1918, Dorothy Ryan

Picture Postcards of the Golden Age, Tonie & Valmai Holt, U.K.

Prairie Fires & Paper Moons: The American Photographic Postcard, 1902-1920, Hal Morgan, Andreas Brown, Boston, 1981

Real Photo Postcards, Robert Ward, Bellevue, 1994

Fantasy Postcards With Price Guide, J. L. Mashburn, Colonial House, Enka, NC

Black Americana Postcard Price Guide, J. L. Mashburn, Colonial House, Enka, NC

The Postcards of Alphonse Mucha, Q. David Bowers, Mary Martin

Standard Postcard Catalog, 1982, James L. Lowe, PA

The Super Rare Postcards of Harrison Fisher, J. L. Mashburn, Colonial House

Vintage View of Christmas Past, Jim Morrison, York, PA, 1995

What Cheer News, Mrs. E.K. Austin, Editor, Rhode Island Postcard Club, RI

PERIODICALS

The Antique Trader Weekly, P.O. Box 1050, Dubuque, IA 52004

Antiques & Auction News, P.O. Box 500, Mt. Joy, PA 17552

Barr's Post Card News, 70 S. 6th St., Lansing, IA 52151

Collector News & Antique Reporter, P.O. Box 156, Grundy Center, IA 50638

New England Antiques Journal, 4 Church St., Ware, MA 01082

Paper Collectors Marketplace, P.O. Box 127, Scandinavia, WI 54977

Paper Pile Quarterly, P.O. Box 337, San Anselmo, CA 94979

Picture Post Card Monthly, 15 Debdale Ln, Keyworth, Nottingham NG12 5HT, U.K.

The Postcard Album, H. Luers, Anton-Gunther-Str. 12, W-2902, Rastede, Germany

Postcard Collector, P.O. Box 1050, Dubuque, IA 52004

MAJOR POSTCARD AUCTION HOUSES

Antique Paper Guild, P.O. Box 5742, Belleview, WA 98006 Real Photo Specialists

Bennett's, Pickering Road, Dover, NH 03820

Butterfield & Butterfield, 220 San Bruno Ave., San Francisco, CA 90046

The First National Postcard Auctions, P.O. Box 5398, Hamden, CT 06518

Swann Galleries, Inc., 104 East 25th St., New York, NY 10010

Index

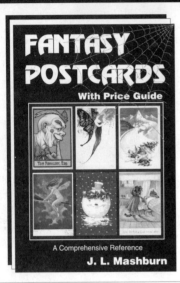
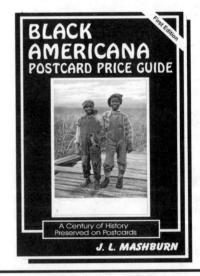